Antoine Gilly's
FEAST
OF
FRANCE

Photographs by Samuel Chamberlain – Line Drawings by William Teodecki

Antoine Gilly's
FEAST
OF
FRANCE

by Antoine Gilly and Jack Denton Scott

A cookbook of masterpieces in French cuisine

Galahad Books   New York City

Library of Congress Catalog Card Number: 73-92829
ISBN: 0-88365-210-2

Published by arrangement with Thomas Y. Crowell Company

Manufactured in the United States of America

Designed by Judith Woracek Barry

The authors want to express their gratitude
to Maria Luisa Scott, who is really the third author.
Without her knowledge of cooking, language, typing and
editing, there would be no FEAST OF FRANCE.

Foreword

In early summer a few years ago I was sitting on the terrace of the Hôtel de Paris in Monte Carlo with Antoine Gilly, playing that popular continental game which requires no greater financial investment than the price of a pot of coffee—celebrity watching. Suddenly I realized that I myself was sitting with a celebrity. People were stopping to talk to Antoine as if paying homage. Their respect was well deserved, for as one of the greatest living chefs, Antoine is indeed royalty.

In the years 1939 to 1961, epicures came from all over the world to dine at his internationally famed restaurants: La Crémaillère à la Campagne in Banksville, New York, and his original La Crémaillère in New York City. During the course of his memorable career, Antoine has cooked for the leading figures of Europe, including King George V of England and the Prince of Wales. He was head chef for the British Prime Minister, Lloyd George, at the Peace Conference following World War I, and he set up the kitchens and established the menus for the famed Blue Train running between Paris and the Riviera. He polished his art at the Hermitage in Monte Carlo, the Hôtel Regina and the Palais d'Orsay in Paris, and the Windsor Hotel in Brittany. Over the years his reputation became increasingly brilliant as he perfected his mastery of a most demanding profession.

Monsieur Gilly was not an overnight sensation. He loved to cook as a boy, having been initiated into his art by his grandmother when he was ten years old. Although he continued to benefit from her gifted and gentle tutoring over the years, he also learned the hard way in the commercial world—as a chef's apprentice.

In January 1916 he took his first real cooking job for fifteen francs a month, at the Hôtel du Palais d'Orsay, under Maître Chef Monsieur Etienne Adnot. One of a hundred apprentices, cooks, and chefs, he was selected to spend three months in each of nine departments, ranging from sauces to butchering. He was fortunate in working under some of France's greatest chefs, and had training which few living today can equal.

Given just two white jackets, which had to be immaculate when he began each day, he kept them that way by washing them at night, drying them at the steam tables in the kitchen and ironing them with a hot, heavy-bottomed saucepan. He had no money to spend on laundry. His room cost him the fifteen francs that he earned, and he considered himself lucky to have free food at the hotel.

He traveled a long way from those beginnings to the opening in New York City, in 1933, of his first restaurant: The Penthouse, on Central Park South, on the sixteenth floor, overlooking the park. Here the excellence of his cuisine rapidly attracted the most demanding of clients including Eleanor Roosevelt, Lily Pons, Eddie Rickenbacker, Charles Boyer, Sergei Rachmaninoff, Charles Laughton, Giovanni Martinelli, Fritz Kreisler, Wendell Willkie, Amelia Earhart, Billy Rose, Madeleine Carroll and Gene Tunney.

Antoine started The Penthouse in partnership with another chef, but after a while the partnership dissolved, and Antoine went on alone, moving in 1939 to Madison Avenue's upper sixties, establishing the first La Crémaillère, which was an immediate success. These words are easy to write: "immediate success," but the disappointments, the trials and errors, the fifteen-hour days, the patient teaching of kitchen staff and waiters, the difficulty in maintaining the perfection Antoine always demanded—they were what made that success.

Several years later, when it was decided that the building in which his restaurant was housed was to be razed and replaced with the Carlton House, Antoine went looking for a place in the country to open a new restaurant. He was advised against leaving New York City after having created such a following; even his best friends predicted failure.

That "failure" was a little white farmhouse, La Crémaillère à la Campagne, in Banksville, New York, which Frederick Wildman, a leading wine merchant and epicure, called the "best French country inn in the United States." This judgment was heartily seconded by experts and the public alike. Antoine's faith that beautiful surroundings and excellent food could not fail to attract appreciative customers was justified.

It requires an unusual blend of professional expertise and personal authority to run a truly great restaurant. Not only must each dish be superb, but many of the clients, often highly temperamental, must be firmly guided to an appreciation of the cuisine. At La Crémaillère Monsieur Gilly ruled, gently but surely. Indeed, only the foolhardy would consider challenging Antoine on his own ground, for even though he is modest and considerate, he has the ability to quietly but definitely deflate pomposity. This I observed one evening when a sleek young man minced into the restaurant, announced that the Duchess of Windsor was outside, and asked, "Is everything all right?" Antoine looked at the young man carefully, then at his customers at their tables. "Yes," he said slowly, without a smile, "I don't think the others will mind."

Many famous restaurant and hotel owners dined with Antoine Gilly. The late Henri Soulé, owner of New York City's Le Pavillon, liked to come to La Crémaillère. "For only here," he once said, in my hearing, "am I always certain to get the superb food to which I am accustomed." The late Gaston Lauryssen, a Belgian epicure of note, president of the New York Ritz Carlton, who was a passionate devotee of tripes à la mode de Caen, had this dish which he considered the world's best at "La Crème," as it was called, every other Sunday in Banksville. He was fond of publicly calling Antoine the "leading chef"—and Lauryssen knew personally the outstanding chefs of France. Louis Vaudable, owner of Maxim's of Paris, was so taken with Antoine's personality and knowledge that he asked Antoine to establish his Maxim's of Chicago.

Antoine and I have worked together in the kitchen and at the desk, and he is always amiable, always patient. He does, though, give anyone who thinks he has a knowledge of cooking an immediate and lasting inferiority complex. This is not intentional, of course; it is just that he is such a master. What a delight to watch him in the kitchen. He handles a cooking spoon or fork like a baton, and surgeons would envy his skill with a knife. He wastes not a motion, and in my opinion he makes the current crop of "chefs," male and female, publicized by television, radio, books and magazines, look like short order cooks at a roadside diner. However, Antoine himself does not feel that way. "These people," he says, "are doing a very good thing. They are educating the public. They are interesting Americans in fine food."

Antoine Gilly has been doing that for more than half a century. He is retired now, having leased his restaurant property to able friends, Robert Meyzen and Fred Decre, owners of Manhattan's excellent La

Caravelle and Le Poulailler. Antoine now lives in Nice, in what he calls a pied-à-terre, high above the city, where he often stands at dusk with a glass of dry white vermouth (gin floating on top; he does nothing the ordinary way) in hand and watches the Riviera lights come on "like blossoms." They remind him, he says, of the beautiful flower gardens and vineyards he left behind in Wilton, Connecticut.

He, however, has left in America something more valuable and lasting than the trees and grape vines he planted at his home in Wilton. The seeds of his inspirational talent were planted and nurtured in men who worked with him, giving them the desire, the ability, and the courage to create their own restaurants—living monuments to the master. These former employees, distinguished restaurateurs in their own right, still call him "Le Patron": *M. Albert Forgelle,* co-Propriétaire of La Potinière Restaurant, New York City, and La Potinière du Soir, New York City; *M. Camille Bermann,* founder and Propriétaire of Maxim's in Houston, Texas; *M. André Collin,* propriétaire of Restaurant Argenteuil, New York City; *M. Henri Diage,* founder of the Silver Spring Farm in Flanders, New Jersey; Propriétaire of Beaulieu Restaurant, Netcong, New Jersey; *M. Jean Fayat,* Propriétaire of Restaurant Lafayette, New York City; *M. Georges Moriaz,* Propriétaire of La Ruche Restaurant at Cold Spring, New York (M. Moriaz was M. Gilly's head chef for ten years); *M. Raymond Peron,* Propriétaire of Gay Pingouin Restaurant, White Plains, New York; *M. Gene La Salle* (Antoine Gilly is particularly proud of Gene La Salle, until lately Propriétaire of Restaurant Per Bacco, New York City; he proved to be one of the ablest restaurateurs in New York City, and may soon transfer his talents to Puerto Rico).

Having helped train these able professionals in the art of fine French cooking, Antoine Gilly now wants to guide the nonprofessional who appreciates fine food and would like to prepare it at home. This book was written for that purpose, and embodies the knowledge, skill, and integrity that have characterized his entire career. He offers no tricky shortcuts that appeal to efficiency rather than taste. On the other hand, Antoine equally rejects unnecessary frills that appeal to sensationalism and distract one from the food itself. Rather, he gives exact and clear instructions for the preparation of recipes (many original) refined over many years of experience.

Here he does what he has always tried to do: he offers his best.

—*Jack Denton Scott*

Acknowledgments

Thanks to two editors—Joanna Morris, whose fine hand weighed and measured everything, including words; and Margaret Miner, of Thomas Y. Crowell, for her eagle editorial eye.

CONTENTS

Notes and Terms

By "white flour" I mean all-purpose white flour, unless otherwise specified. When a recipe calls for bread crumbs, these should always be dry unless otherwise specified.

By "cooking oil" I mean corn oil, cottonseed, soy, poppy, sesame —take your choice. Olive oil is not used, except when specified.

Below is a brief glossary of terms you will encounter in the text and which may possibly be puzzling. They are collected here and defined for your convenience.

Anglaise/A mixture in which food to be rolled in bread crumbs and fried is first dipped. Our mixture (depending upon amount of food to be dipped) is 1 egg, ½ cup milk, 2 tablespoons vegetable oil, a dash salt and pepper, blended well.

Beurre manié/A thickening agent for a sauce that has turned out thin. Use equal amounts of flour and butter, say, half a tablespoon flour kneaded into half a tablespoon butter. Remove the sauce from the stove, and stir in the beurre manié in small lumps. Then place the sauce on the heat and simmer, stirring until it thickens.

Blanch/To plunge ingredients into boiling water, for the purpose of slightly cooking, as in the case of vegetables, or to remove excess flavors, such as smoke from bacon or salt from salt pork. The food is left in the water for only a few minutes, then drained.

Bouquet garni/A bouquet of herbs, used to add flavor. If you can't get fresh herbs, use dry ones and tie them in cheesecloth. The usual combination is parsley, bay leaf, thyme, celery, tied together. The bouquet garni is discarded after the dish is cooked.

Clarified butter/To clarify, melt butter over low heat. A clear oily substance will float to the top. A whitish residue settles to the bottom. Siphon off clear, oily substance into another container. Discard the white residue.

Croutons/These are cut from slices of white bread, browned in butter until crisp, drained on a paper towel, then used as a garnish or to accompany various dishes. If you want to arrange pieces of cooked chicken atop a crouton, obviously the crouton has to be large enough to hold the pieces of chicken. Croutons cut heart-shaped (or any shape or size you desire) enhance the presentation of dishes, and also are tasty. Small diced croutons are excellent with soup.

Épices Parisienne/A mixture of cloves, rosemary, marjoram, paprika, mace, nutmeg, cinnamon, bay leaf, sage. It can be obtained in fine food or herb shops. If you cannot get it, a mixture of equal parts of dry rosemary, marjoram, bay leaf and thyme will suffice. Use a small amount, depending on the recipe and your taste.

Flambé/To ignite brandy or some other alcoholic liquid, and allow to burn off. A specified amount of the liquid is poured over food, then set alight—as in preparing crêpes suzettes. It's embarrassing if the liquid fails to light. But if you use good brandy or other liquor, and warm it, then you can be sure of success.

Purée/To mash. Food to be puréed usually is cooked, then pushed through a sieve or food mill, or even worked into a purée in an electric blender.

Reduce/To boil down liquid, or "boil off" excess liquid to increase flavor.

Roux/This is butter and flour blended into a golden paste used as a thickening element. Proportions depend upon how much sauce you want. For example, to make 2 cups of white velouté, you would begin with 2 tablespoons butter and 3 tablespoons flour.

Truffle/A type of European fungus that grows underground—the most expensive and delicate of all seasonings. Pigs, dogs and even a species of fly will scent out truffle patches. In this book we use only the black truffle, which is French; Italian truffles are white. Fresh truffles are best, but almost unobtainable here; canned ones will do. If truffles are a major item in a recipe, and you don't have them, you had better prepare something else. There is no substitute for truffles.

Turtle herbs/A mixture of sweet basil, marjoram, rosemary, thyme leaves, bay leaves, coriander, sage, dry parsley, and dry mint—can be bought in fine food and herb shops.

1

HORS-D'OEUVRE

Hors-d'oeuvre reflect the imagination and taste of the host and hostess. They should spark conversation and appetite—not deaden them. It is disheartening when one is sipping one's evening cocktail to be handed a barely warm, tough frankfurter wrapped in a piece of soggy dough, fresh from the deepfreeze of the local supermarket: a foretaste of the doom of the dinner to come. The hostess is hardly evincing pleasure at seeing her guests when she trots out the typical offering of rubbery, stuffed hard-boiled eggs, overdone bullet-like shrimp, tasteless tinned-"meat" sandwiches, or bland cheese cubes and a sickly-sweet pickle speared on a toothpick.

The hors-d'oeuvre can be a slight offering, a tasty snack, before dinner (accent on tasty), unless, of course, you are giving a cocktail party with only hors-d'oeuvre; then the amount you serve depends upon appetites.

Hors-d'oeuvre, however, were originated by the French with more in mind than cocktail parties (an American invention) and are often served as part of luncheon or dinner. A rule of thumb is to serve cold hors-d'oeuvre at lunch, hot before soup at dinner. If guests are remaining for dinner, it is a mistake to serve too much. Some epicures who dined at my La Crémaillère à la Campagne in Banksville, New York, were content with just hot cheese rolls before dinner or a pâté of smoked salmon before lunch.

HORS-D'OEUVRE CHAUDS—Hot Hors-d'Oeuvre

FRUITS DE MER—SEAFOOD

Baked Clams Mexican Style FOR 8

> ½ cup chopped shallots
> ½ cup cooking oil
> 1 cup finely chopped green peppers
> 2 cloves garlic, finely chopped
> 1 teaspoon salt
> ½ teaspoon white pepper
> 1 teaspoon chopped tarragon
> 1 tablespoon chopped parsley
> ½ pound sweet butter
> ½ cup canned red pimentos
> ½ teaspoon tabasco sauce
> 4 dozen cherrystone clams
> 1 cup white bread crumbs

In a skillet, sauté shallots in the oil 2 minutes, add green peppers; simmer 10 minutes; do not brown. Add garlic, simmer 2 minutes, then salt, pepper, tarragon, parsley. In a bowl, mix butter with pimentos and force through a fine sieve. Add tabasco, season to taste. Remove clams from shells. Save half the shells. Put the clams with their liquid in a shallow saucepan; simmer 1 minute. Replace 1 clam in each shell, cover with green pepper mixture, then pimento mixture, sprinkle with bread crumbs. Place on round ovenproof fish dishes, each dish holding the desired number of clams per serving. Put in a preheated 450-degree oven 3 minutes. Then under broiler 2 minutes before serving.

Blinis of Clams Stony Brook FOR 4 OR 6

> 1 cup prepared pancake flour
> 1 cup sour cream
> 1 cup white bread crumbs
> 2 tablespoons finely diced white celery
> 2 tablespoons chopped chives
> 1 egg
> 1½ teaspoons salt
> ½ teaspoon white pepper
> 1 cup chopped kernels of soft shell clams (cooked)
> 1 cup cooking oil

Mix flour with cream, bread crumbs, celery, chives, egg, salt, pepper. When well mixed, blend in clams. Heat a small amount of oil in a frying pan. When hot, drop in a tablespoon of batter. Blinis should be 2½ inches in diameter. Flip just as you would a pancake. Add more oil as you need it. Serve hot and crisp.

Escargots à la Bourguignonne

[SNAILS STUFFED WITH SNAIL BUTTER] FOR 8

> *4 dozen canned snails (a bag of clean shells will be attached)*
> *1 cup dry white wine*
> *1 pound sweet butter*
> *¼ cup chopped garlic*
> *½ cup finely chopped shallots*
> *2 tablespoons chopped parsley*
> *½ teaspoon salt*
> *½ teaspoon white pepper*
> *1 cup grated Swiss cheese*

Remove snails from can, drain off liquid and place snails in a deep saucepan. Add wine, simmer 10 minutes. Cool. Mix butter, garlic, shallots, parsley, salt and pepper thoroughly. Half fill the shells with butter mixture, place one snail in each and finish filling the shells with the butter mixture. Dip shells into grated cheese before placing them on escargot plates, which will hold 6 snails (some 12). The plates plus special tongs and forks are available at many fine-food stores. Just before serving the escargots, place the plates in a preheated 450-degree oven 6 minutes. Serve with soft croutons to soak in the snail butter.

Escargots des Ducs d'Anjou

[CURRIED SNAILS AND MUSHROOMS] FOR 4

> *¼ pound sweet butter*
> *a dozen mushrooms, stems removed*
> *2 dozen canned snails*
> *¾ cup dry French vermouth*
> *1½ teaspoons curry powder*
> *1 cup Sauce Mornay (page 73)*
> *½ cup grated Parmesan cheese*
> *1 teaspoon salt*
> *½ teaspoon white pepper*

Melt 4 tablespoons of butter in a skillet, add mushrooms and cook 3 minutes. Remove the mushrooms and save the juice in the skillet. Melt 4 tablespoons of butter in a saucepan; sauté snails 2 minutes. Stir in the dry vermouth and the mushroom juice, then remove snails, reserving juice, and place one on each mushroom cap and arrange on a buttered baking dish. Blend curry powder into the reserved juice; simmer 3 minutes and stir in mornay sauce. Season with salt and pepper to taste. Bring to a boil, pour over the mushrooms and snails. Just before serving, sprinkle with Parmesan cheese and place in a preheated 450-degree oven 5 minutes.

Brochettes de Moules Provençale

[FRIED MUSSELS ON SKEWERS]   FOR 6 SKEWERS

    2½ quarts mussels, well scrubbed
    ½ cup dry white wine
    ½ cup milk
    ½ cup oil
     2 eggs
    ½ tablespoon salt
    ½ teaspoon white pepper
     1 cup white flour
     2 cups white bread crumbs
     2 tablespoons chives
     2 tablespoons parsley
       Oil for deep frying

Put the mussels into a skillet with wine. Bring to boil 2 minutes. Toss them several times so they will open up evenly. Cool. When cool enough to handle, remove mussels from shells and let them dry. Mix the milk, oil, eggs, salt and pepper. Roll the mussels in flour. Dip mussels in the milk-oil-egg mixture one by one, then roll in bread crumbs. Mix in chives and parsley with the bread crumbs left after the mussels have been rolled. Thread mussels on skewers (there should be at least 8 on each), then roll the whole skewer in the remaining bread crumb mixture just before you deep-fry them in hot oil. The deep fat should be 400 degrees; to get well browned and crisp the mussels should take 2 minutes. Serve with the sauce for crab meat (page 85) on the side.

Huîtres au Four St. Amour

[BAKED OYSTERS WITH CREAMED SPINACH
AND FENNEL]   FOR 6

24 *Blue Point oysters*
¼ *pound sweet butter*
½ *cup chopped fennel*
½ *cup chopped cooked spinach*
1 *cup cream*
1½ *teaspoons salt*
½ *teaspoon white pepper*
2 *beaten egg yolks*
1 *pinch nutmeg*
1 *cup grated Swiss cheese*

Shuck the oysters. Save the deep shell halves. In a shallow pan, over low
fire, simmer oysters in their liquor 1 minute. Put aside. Melt butter in another saucepan and sauté fennel 10 minutes. Blend in spinach and cream,
simmer 5 minutes. Sprinkle with salt and pepper, then add egg yolks and
nutmeg and simmer until thick, stirring constantly to avoid lumping.
Place a spoonful of this in each oyster shell, then an oyster, then more
sauce. Sprinkle with grated cheese and place under the broiler 2 minutes.

Pâtés of Smoked Salmon Nova Scotia   FOR 8

1 *cup chopped onions*
⅓ *cup cooking oil*
1 *cup chopped mushrooms*
½ *pound diced Nova Scotia smoked salmon*
3 *coarsely chopped hard boiled eggs*
⅓ *cup sorrel (if jarred), or 1 cup fresh sorrel, chopped*
    Pinch cayenne pepper
    Salt to taste, if salmon is not salted
1 *tablespoon white flour*
2 *tablespoons chopped parsley*
2 *tablespoons chopped chervil*
¼ *cup vodka*
1 *pound Puff Paste (page 284). May be obtained*
    frozen in some supermarkets.
1 *beaten egg*

Simmer onions in skillet with oil 5 minutes. Add mushrooms, simmer 5
minutes. Add smoked salmon, cook 2 minutes. Stir in eggs, sorrel, pepper,

salt, if needed, and flour; cook 3 minutes. Add parsley, chervil and vodka. Mix well. Set aside to cool, then refrigerate 2 hours. Roll the puff paste ¼-inch thick. With a fluted pastry cutter, cut into rounds 5 inches in diameter. Place the rounds on a moistened pastry sheet. Divide salmon mixture in even parts and place on rounds of pastry. Wet edges with pastry brush, fold into a half moon and seal edges. Brush tops with beaten egg, place in refrigerator until ready to bake. Before baking, make two incisions in top of pastry with pointed knife. Bake in a preheated 400-degree oven 20 minutes.

Croustades de Crevettes Cape Cod

[SHRIMPS IN TOAST SHELLS]   FOR 6

Step One: Croustades
6 soft, round rolls and melted butter

From the top, remove soft inside of each roll with a sharp knife, leaving just the shell. With a pastry brush, paint the inside and outside of the rolls with the melted butter. Put into a preheated 450-degree oven until brown and crisp.

Step Two: Filling
6 ounces sweet butter (1½ sticks)
2 tablespoons chopped onions
6 medium mushrooms, sliced
½ cup diced celery
6 ounces bay scallops
12 oysters, shucked
½ cup chopped green pepper
1 teaspoon salt
½ teaspoon white pepper
1 cup heavy cream
1 pound shrimps, in shells and washed
2 tablespoons chopped parsley
2 egg yolks, beaten

Melt the butter in a skillet, simmer onions 5 minutes. Add the mushrooms, cook 2 minutes. Stir in celery, scallops, oysters and green pepper and sprinkle with salt, pepper. Simmer 2 minutes more. Taste for seasoning. Remove scallops and oysters. Keep warm. Add cream and shrimps to the skillet, simmer 5 minutes. Remove the shrimps, shell and clean them, cut in small pieces and reserve with oysters and scallops. Add parsley to skillet, and reduce liquid to half. Blend in egg yolks to thicken and add shrimps, oysters and scallops. Mix well, fill croustades. Place in preheated 450-degree oven 5 minutes.

LÉGUMES—VEGETABLES

Artichauts Farcis Riviera

[ARTICHOKES STUFFED WITH MEAT,
MUSHROOMS AND GREEN OLIVES] FOR 6

6 large artichokes
6 very thin slices bacon
½ cup cooking oil
4 tablespoons sweet butter
½ cup chopped onions
½ tablespoon chopped garlic
1 cup chopped mushrooms
½ pound chopped, uncooked veal (lean veal from leg)
2 ounces tomato purée
¼ pound chopped boiled ham
1 teaspoon salt
1 teaspoon ground white pepper
1 tablespoon chopped sweet basil
½ cup white bread crumbs
½ cup chopped parsley
1 cup chopped green olives
1 egg, beaten
1 quart White Stock (page 61)

Trim, cook and dechoke artichokes following instructions on page 286. Line the center of each with a bacon slice. Prepare stuffing as follows: Heat oil and butter in saucepan, add the onions, simmer 10 minutes. Add garlic, simmer 2 minutes. Add mushrooms, simmer 2 minutes. Stir in veal, tomato purée, ham, salt and pepper. Blend well, simmer 5 minutes. Mix in thoroughly basil, bread crumbs, parsley, chopped olives and egg. Check seasoning. Stuff the center of the artichokes with this. Some of the stuffing may be placed between the leaves. Place artichokes in saucepan wedged together. Pour in white stock and bring to a boil on top of stove. Cover with aluminum foil and place in preheated 400-degree oven 45 minutes or until leaves pull out easily.

Chou Farci Charcutière

[CABBAGE STUFFED WITH
SAUSAGE MEAT]   FOR 12 CABBAGE BALLS

1 two-pound Savoy cabbage
½ cup cooking oil
½ cup chopped onions
1 teaspoon chopped garlic
1 pound sausage meat
1 egg, beaten
1 tablespoon salt
½ teaspoon white pepper
¼ teaspoon nutmeg
2 tablespoons chopped parsley
1 teaspoon chopped thyme leaves
1 cup cooked white rice
12 thin slices larding pork
½ cup dry sherry
2 cups Chicken Broth (page 62)

Separate 12 cabbage leaves without breaking. Place in a skillet of simmering water 3 minutes, then into cold water to cool. Spread on paper towel to dry. Heat oil in a saucepan, sauté onions 5 minutes; do not brown. Add garlic, sauté 2 minutes. Mix sausage meat and egg well, sauté with onion and garlic 2 minutes. Blend in salt, pepper, nutmeg, parsley, thyme, rice. Spread out the cabbage leaves, squeezing any moisture from them. Lay 1 slice of the larding pork on each. Divide meat mixture into 12 balls, putting 1 on each cabbage leaf. Wrap securely; place in an ovenproof shallow dish. Pour in sherry and chicken broth and bring to a boil on top of the stove. Cover and set in a preheated 400-degree oven 40 minutes. These should be served warm, but not hot.

Aubergines Niçoise

[EGGPLANT BROILED WITH TOMATO AND
CHEESE TOPPING]   FOR 6

6 one-inch slices eggplant with skin
1 tablespoon salt
1 teaspoon ground white pepper
½ cup cooking oil
4 tablespoons sweet butter
1 cup chopped onions
2 cloves garlic, chopped
4 tomatoes, peeled, seeded, chopped
1 teaspoon chopped thyme leaves
1 teaspoon powdered bay leaf
1 tablespoon chopped parsley
½ cup white bread crumbs
1 cup grated Swiss cheese

Lay eggplant slices in a shallow, oiled, ovenproof dish. Sprinkle with half
the salt and pepper and pour over the oil. Broil 8 minutes. Place butter in
a saucepan, add chopped onions and simmer 5 minutes; add garlic, stir in
tomatoes and simmer 7 minutes. Add the thyme, powdered bay leaf, parsley, remaining salt and pepper, and simmer 2 minutes. Add bread crumbs;
mix well. Place this tomato mixture evenly over the slices of eggplant.
Sprinkle with grated cheese and place under the broiler 2 minutes to
brown. Serve on a warm plate. This can be refrigerated and served cold or
warmed when needed.

Champignons en Croustade

[MUSHROOMS IN TOAST SHELLS]   FOR 6

    6 tablespoons sweet butter
    2 tablespoons chopped shallots
    1 tablespoon chopped garlic
    ½ pound mushrooms, finely sliced
    1 teaspoon salt
    ¼ teaspoon cayenne pepper
      Juice 1 lemon
    1 cup heavy cream
    ½ cup finely diced smoked beef tongue
    2 egg yolks
    1 teaspoon Lea & Perrins sauce
    6 Croustades (page 10)

Melt the butter in a saucepan. Add the shallots, simmer 5 minutes; do not
brown. Add garlic and mushrooms, cover pan and simmer 3 minutes.
Stir in salt, pepper, lemon juice, cream and beef tongue. Simmer 2 minutes.
Beat a little of this sauce into the egg yolks, so yolks will not curdle. Then
blend egg yolk mixture into the beef tongue and sauce. Add the Lea &
Perrins sauce. Check seasoning. Mix well. Spoon into the croustades; bake
5 minutes in a preheated 450-degree oven.

Champignons à l'Escargot (I)

[MUSHROOMS STUFFED WITH SNAIL BUTTER
AND WALNUTS]   FOR 4

    16 medium mushrooms
    ½ pound sweet butter
    2 tablespoons chopped walnuts
    4 shallots, finely chopped
    2 cloves garlic, finely chopped
    5 tablespoons chopped parsley
      Salt and pepper to taste
    ¼ cup dry white wine

Remove the stems from the mushrooms. Wash and dry the caps and lay
upside down in a well-buttered baking dish. Mix the butter, walnuts, shallots, garlic, parsley, salt and pepper thoroughly. Fill the mushroom caps
with this mixture (called snail butter, beurre d'escargot). Five minutes
before serving, place mushrooms under the broiler. Sprinkle the white
wine over the mushrooms as you take them from the broiler.

Champignons à l'Escargot (II)

[MUSHROOMS STUFFED WITH SNAIL BUTTER
AND HAM]   FOR 8

3 dozen medium mushrooms
1 pound sweet butter
½ cup chopped shallots
¼ pound lean ham, diced
⅓ cup chopped garlic
1 tablespoon salt
½ teaspoon white pepper
2 tablespoons chopped parsley
1 cup white bread crumbs

Remove the stems from the mushrooms. Wash and dry the caps and lay
upside down in a well-buttered baking dish. Melt 4 tablespoons of the
butter in a saucepan. Add shallots, simmer 5 minutes. Do not brown. Add
the ham and garlic; simmer 2 minutes. Cool. Add remaining butter, salt,
pepper, parsley; blend. Check seasoning. Fill the mushroom caps with this
mixture. Sprinkle with bread crumbs lightly and place in a preheated 400-
degree oven 5 minutes. Before serving place under broiler 2 minutes.

Oignons Farcis à la Turque

[ONIONS STUFFED WITH LAMB
AND MUSHROOMS]   FOR 12 STUFFED ONIONS

12 whole onions, 3 inches in diameter
½ cup cooking oil
½ cup finely chopped onions
2 cloves garlic, chopped
1 cup finely chopped mushrooms
1 cup ground cooked lamb
1 beaten egg
2 ounces tomato purée
½ cup white wine
1 tablespoon salt
½ teaspoon white pepper
   Pinch nutmeg
½ cup white bread crumbs
2 cups Brown Stock (page 63)
1 cup grated Parmesan cheese
1 bay leaf

Boil the whole onions in a skillet in salted water 10 minutes. Meanwhile, blend lamb with egg. Then remove onions from water; cool. With a spoon, scoop out a depression, making a hollow to be filled. Set aside onions. Heat the oil in a saucepan, add chopped onions, simmer 10 minutes; do not brown. Add garlic, simmer 2 minutes. Add mushrooms, simmer another 4 minutes. Stir in the lamb and egg mixture, tomato purée, wine, salt, pepper and nutmeg. Mix well, stirring in the bread crumbs. Stuff the onions with this mixture and place in an ovenproof baking dish with the bay leaf and brown stock. Bring to a boil on top of the stove, cover with aluminum foil and place in a preheated 400-degree oven 20 minutes or until onions are tender. Remove, sprinkle with cheese and place under broiler 2 minutes before serving. These can also be served cold.

PÂTISSERIE ET FROMAGE—PASTRY AND CHEESE

Pissaladière Niçoise

[ONION TART WITH TOMATOES, ANCHOVIES AND BLACK OLIVES]

FOR 6

Step One
Prepare 1 pound Pie Dough (page 185). Set aside.

Step Two
  1 pound thinly sliced yellow onions
  ½ cup cooking oil
  ½ tablespoon salt
  ¼ tablespoon pepper
  2 small whole tomatoes, peeled, seeded, quartered,
    cooked 5 minutes in 1 tablespoon oil

8 flat anchovy filets
16 small black pitted olives

Sauté onions slowly in oil 30 minutes; they should become very limp. Add salt and pepper while cooking. Line a 9½-inch pyrex pie plate with pastry rolled ⅛-inch thick. Cut edge and flute, prick bottom with a fork. Cover bottom evenly with onions. Distribute tomatoes over onions evenly. Line the anchovies from the center to the edge of the dish. Split olives and arrange between anchovies. Bake in a preheated 400-degree oven 35 minutes.

Pâté Chaud aux Truffes

[HOT PÂTÉ WITH TRUFFLES IN PUFF PASTRY]   FOR 6

Step One
Prepare 1 pound Puff Paste (page 284). Refrigerate. This may be obtained frozen in some supermarkets.

Step Two
  ½ cup chopped shallots
  4 tablespoons sweet butter
  ½ pound sausage meat
  2 tablespoons cognac
  2 tablespoons port
  ½ teaspoon salt
  ½ teaspoon ground black pepper
    Pinch nutmeg
  4 ounces coarsely chopped black truffles
  2 tablespoons chopped parsley
  1 egg, beaten

Melt the butter in skillet and sauté shallots 3 minutes; do not brown. Add sausage meat, cognac, port, salt, pepper, nutmeg. Stir well over a low fire, mixing well, 3 minutes. Add truffles and parsley. Check seasoning. Put aside to cool. Can be done the day before. Roll the puff paste ⅓-inch thick. With a fluted pastry cutter, cut twelve a½-inch rounds of pastry. Place 6 on a flat pastry sheet; using a pastry brush, moisten with water. Put sausage mixture in center of each round of dough, dividing evenly. With the pastry brush, moisten edges of the dough with water; place the other rounds of pastry on top, sealing edges carefully. With a pointed knife make a couple of incisions in the tops, brush with beaten egg. Place sheet in refrigerator for 1 hour before baking. Brush again with beaten egg, then bake in a preheated 400-degree oven for 20 minutes, or until nicely browned.

Flamiche Lorraine

[LEEK TART]   FOR 6

> ¼ pound butter
> ½ pound white leeks, chopped
> 1 nine-inch pastry shell
> 6 ounces salt pork, boiled 10 minutes, cut into small dice
> 2 cups heavy cream
> 4 eggs
> ½ tablespoon salt
> ¼ tablespoon white pepper
> Pinch nutmeg

Melt the butter in a skillet; sauté leeks 15 minutes until soft; do not brown. Spread leeks evenly on the bottom of the pastry shell. Sprinkle the pork over this. With a whisk, mix the cream gently, but thoroughly, with the eggs, salt, pepper and nutmeg. Pour over the leeks and salt pork; brush with beaten egg. Place in the refrigerator for at least 1 hour before baking. Brush again with beaten egg, then put in a preheated 400-degree oven 20 minutes or until nicely browned.

Fried Hot Cheese Rolls
Crémaillère   FOR 48 CHEESE ROLLS

This simple invention of mine was a favorite of John Olin and of the Duchess of Windsor. We had the cheese rolls hot at their respective tables almost before they sat down. The rolls kept coming until they reluctantly told us to stop.

> ¼ pound sweet butter
> 1 cup white flour
> 2 cups milk
> 2 cups grated Parmesan cheese
> 4 egg yolks, beaten
> 1 teaspoon salt
> ⅓ teaspoon cayenne pepper
> ¼ teaspoon nutmeg
> 1 loaf unsliced bread

Melt the butter in a saucepan. Add the flour a bit at a time and cook slowly 10 minutes, stirring constantly; do not brown. Cool. Heat milk to boiling point, then add hot milk to roux, mixing vigorously with a whisk. Simmer

10 minutes, stirring continuously. Add cheese, stirring until melted. Blend in the egg yolks, salt, cayenne and nutmeg. Simmer 2 minutes until mixture becomes a very thick paste. Cool. (This can be made the day before.) Take a loaf of sandwich bread or any *very soft* unsliced white bread; remove the crusts and cut 48 *very* thin slices. Bread must be extremely fresh and soft or it will break up when rolling. Spread cheese paste evenly over each slice of bread; roll tightly into a cigarette shape. When ready to serve, place the rolls, 12 at a time, in a wire basket and into very hot oil (370 degrees) until they brown, which will be almost immediately. Remove. Drain on paper towels to absorb the grease.

Quiche Lorraine

[BACON TART]   FOR 6 OR 8

Step One: Dough
   1 ⅓ cups white flour
      4 tablespoons sweet butter
      4 tablespoons lard
      1 teaspoon salt
      3 tablespoons cold water

Mix flour and fats with your fingertips. Blend in the salt and water but do not knead the dough after it is well mixed. Dough should be made 12 hours ahead and refrigerated, covered with cheesecloth.

Step Two: Filling
      Dough (already prepared)
    ¼ pound bacon, cut in 1-inch squares and lightly fried
    2 cups heavy cream
    3 eggs
    3 egg yolks
   1 ½ teaspoons salt
    ¼ teaspoon cayenne pepper
    ⅓ cup chopped chives

Roll the dough ¼-inch thick and line a 10-inch pie plate. Prick the bottom with a fork so it will not blister, and squeeze the edge with a pastry pincher. Spread the pieces of bacon on the bottom of the pastry shell. Beat the cream with the whole eggs and egg yolks, salt and cayenne. Pour this over the bacon to fill the pastry shell. Sprinkle the chives over and place in a preheated 400-degree oven 20 minutes or until the quiche rises and the top browns. Serve warm.

Quiche à la Vaudoise

This dish is prepared in the same way as quiche Lorraine except that small slices of Swiss cheese placed on top of the quiche are substituted for the chopped chives.

Gougère Bourguignonne

[CHEESE PUFFS]   FOR 6 OR 8

> 2 cups milk
> ¼ pound sweet butter
> 1½ teaspoons salt
>   Pinch nutmeg
> 1¾ cups white flour
> 5 eggs
> 1 cup grated Swiss cheese
> ⅛ teaspoon cayenne pepper

Bring the milk to a boil in a saucepan; add butter, salt and nutmeg. Remove from fire and stir in the flour, mixing quickly with a wooden spatula. Return the mixture to the fire 1 minute, stirring vigorously until it does not stick to the spatula or sides of pan. Remove from fire again before adding eggs. Add eggs, one at a time, mixing well after each addition. Blend in half of the grated cheese and the cayenne pepper. Place dough-like mass into a pastry bag with a large plain tip; squeeze out dollops about the size of large walnuts onto a buttered baking sheet. Place closely together. The finished dish looks like a tart. Sprinkle with the remaining cheese. Bake in a preheated 400-degree oven 15 minutes, or until golden, firm and crusty.

Soufflés au Fromage

[INDIVIDUAL CHEESE SOUFFLÉS]   FOR 4

> 4 tablespoons sweet butter
> 4 tablespoons white flour
> 1½ cups milk
> 1½ teaspoons salt
>   Pinch cayenne pepper
>   Pinch nutmeg
> 3 eggs, separated
> ¾ cup grated Swiss cheese
> 4 soufflé molds, 4 inches in
>   diameter by 2 inches deep

Melt the butter in a saucepan, add flour and simmer 5 minutes; do not brown. Remove from stove. Boil milk and blend smoothly into the roux; bring to a boil. Add the salt, pepper and nutmeg. Lower flame, simmer 10 minutes. Stir in the 3 egg yolks and the grated cheese; blend thoroughly. Cool. Beat the whites stiff, add to the cheese paste slowly, stirring with an upward motion. Butter soufflé molds and fill almost to edge with soufflé mixture; place on a hot pastry sheet which allows the soufflés to start cooking from the bottom, permitting them to rise easily. Place in a preheated 400-degree oven 10 minutes.

Pâte à Crêpes

[PANCAKE BATTER FOR MEAT,
FISH, OR CHICKEN]   FOR ABOUT 16 CRÊPES

> *2 cups sifted white flour*
> *4 eggs*
> *2 cups milk*
> *1 cup heavy cream*
> *1 teaspoon salt*
> *¼ pound melted sweet butter*

In a large bowl, add eggs to flour, one by one, mixing vigorously with wooden spatula to avoid lumping. Add milk, stirring in gradually, then blend in cream and salt. Batter should be made 12 hours before using. Refrigerate. When ready to use, add the melted butter and stir well so the butter will be completely mixed into the batter. Pancakes should be made very thin in a crêpe pan not more than 5 inches in diameter.

Crêpes à la Royale Soubise

[SAUCED PANCAKES STUFFED WITH
ONION PURÉE AND CHICKEN]   FOR 4

Step One: Prepare onion purée
    1 pound chopped white onions
    4 tablespoons sweet butter
    2 egg yolks
  1½ teaspoons salt
    ½ teaspoon white pepper

Melt butter in saucepan; sauté onions 15 minutes; do not brown. Force onions through fine sieve to obtain a thick purée, then mix well with egg yolks, salt and pepper. Cook over medium flame 2 minutes. Check seasoning. Reserve until ready to use. Keep warm.

Step Two
    ½ cup chopped shallots
    ¼ pound sweet butter
    1 cup chopped mushrooms
    ½ pound breast of cooked chicken, finely chopped
  1½ teaspoons salt
    ½ teaspoon white pepper
    1 tablespoon chopped parsley
    1 cup Sauce Béchamel (page 71)
    1 cup Sauce Hollandaise (page 81)
    ½ recipe Pâte à Crêpes (page 21)
    1 cup unsweetened whipped cream

Melt the butter in a saucepan; sauté shallots 3 minutes; do not brown. Add mushrooms, simmer 5 minutes. Add chicken, mix well, add salt, pepper, parsley, half of the béchamel and half of the hollandaise. Mix thoroughly; heat but do not boil. Check seasoning. Prepare 8 crêpes. Spread crêpes evenly with the reserved onion purée, topping with chicken mixture. Roll tightly and place in a shallow, buttered baking dish. With a spoon mix gently the remaining béchamel and hollandaise and whipped cream; pour over the crêpes. When ready to serve, place them in a preheated 450-degree oven 5 minutes. If not well browned, place under the broiler 1 minute before serving.

Crêpes Farcies Florida

[PANCAKES STUFFED WITH AVOCADO
AND CRAB MEAT]   FOR 6

> *2 avocados*
> *¼ pound sweet butter*
> *½ pound fresh crab meat lumps*
> *¼ cup cognac*
> *½ cup dry sherry*
> *1 cup cream*
> *1 teaspoon salt*
> *Pinch cayenne pepper*
> *1 cup Sauce Hollandaise (page 81)*
> *1½ teaspoons Dijon mustard*
> *1 recipe Pâte à Crêpes (page 21)*
> *1 cup white bread crumbs*

Cut avocados in half; spread half of the butter over them; place in pre-heated 400-degree oven 5 minutes. Scoop out the flesh and purée. Mix in pinch of salt, pinch of pepper. Set aside. Place crab meat in a shallow saucepan, then in a preheated 450-degree oven 3 minutes. Remove the "bones." Add cognac and flambé. Add dry sherry, cream, salt and pepper. Bring to a boil. Remove from fire, mix the hollandaise in gently, as crab should be kept in lumps; then the mustard. Check seasoning for salt. Preparc 12 crêpes. Spread crêpes evenly with the avocado purée, topping with crab meat. Roll tightly and place in a shallow baking dish. Sprinkle with bread crumbs, dot with remaining butter. When ready to serve, place in a preheated 400-degree oven 10 minutes, then under broiler for about 1 minute to brown.

HORS-D'OEUVRE FROIDS—Cold Hors-d'Oeuvre

FRUITS DE MER—SEAFOOD

Clams Crémaillère   FOR 12 CLAMS

> 12 cherrystone clams
> ½ cup dry white wine
> 1 cup finely chopped onions
> 1 celery stalk
> 1 parsley branch
> 1 bay leaf
> 1½ teaspoons chopped garlic
> ½ cup chopped parsley
> 1 teaspoon white pepper
> 1 tablespoon Dijon mustard
> 1 cup Mayonnaise (page 84)

Scrub clams. Put into a skillet with the wine, half of the onions, celery, parsley and bay leaf. Bring them to a boil and cook 3 minutes, shaking pan to open evenly. (If they do not open, discard them—they are dead.) Take the clams from the shells, and reserve half the shells. Remove hinge-muscles. (Clams have rubbery, tough fibrous hinge-muscles that open and close the shell.) Chop clams finely; blend with the rest of the onions, garlic, chopped parsley, pepper, mustard and half the mayonnaise. Check seasoning. Fill the clam shells, dividing the mixture evenly. Color half of the remaining mayonnaise green, using finely chopped watercress. Color the other half red with catsup. Spoon these sauces on clams, alternating colors. Serve on an oyster platter on a bed of shaved ice, garnished with decorated half lemons. To make this even more attractive, put half a green olive on each clam and sprinkle the sieved yolks of hard boiled eggs around the edges of the shells.

Poisson

Poisson en Coquille

[FISH IN SCALLOP SHELLS]   FOR 6

 1½ cups Mayonnaise (page 84)
  1 tablespoon chopped white celery
  1 tablespoon chopped shallots
  1 tablespoon chopped sour gherkins
  1 tablespoon chopped capers
  1 tablespoon Dijon mustard
  1 teaspoon Lea & Perrins sauce
 1½ teaspoons salt
  1 teaspoon white pepper
  1 tablespoon chopped tarragon (fresh or in vinegar)
  2 tablespoons chopped parsley
  6 Boston lettuce leaves
 ½ pound boneless, cooked, leftover fish, cubed
  2 hard boiled eggs (chop whites and yolks separately and finely)
  6 coquille shells

Mix the mayonnaise with all ingredients, except half of the parsley, lettuce leaves, fish and eggs. Place the lettuce leaves on the shells and spoon 1 tablespoon of the sauce on each leaf. Arrange fish on this and pour the remaining sauce evenly over the fish. Decorate with chopped egg yolks and whites. Sprinkle remaining chopped parsley around the edge of the shells. Serve very cold on a bed of shaved ice.

Moules Tartare

[MUSSELS IN MAYONNAISE SAUCE]   FOR 6

  2 quarts mussels, bearded and scrubbed
  6 tablespoons dry white wine
  1 teaspoon black pepper
  2 tablespoons chopped parsley
  1 cup Mayonnaise (page 84)
  1 teaspoon chopped garlic
  1 tablespoon chopped shallots
  1 tablespoon Dijon mustard
  1 teaspoon Lea & Perrins sauce
   Boston lettuce leaves
  1 finely chopped hard boiled egg yolk

Put the mussels in a skillet with the wine, pepper and half the parsley. Cook 3 minutes, shaking the mussels upward so all will open (discard unopened mussels). Remove mussel meat from shells and place in bowl. Mix mayonnaise, garlic, shallots, mustard, Lea & Perrins sauce. Check seasoning, adding salt only if needed. Pour over mussels, mix gently. Serve on a layer of lettuce leaves. Decorate with chopped hard boiled egg yolk and the remaining parsley.

"Route Nationale"

LÉGUMES—VEGETABLES

Fonds d'Artichauts à la Grecque

[MARINATED ARTICHOKE BOTTOMS]　　　　　　　FOR 4 OR 6

> *4 large artichokes*
> *2 cups water*
> *½ cup lemon juice*
> *1 tablespoon coriander seeds*
> *Bouquet garni*
> *1 tablespoon salt*
> *1 teaspoon ground white pepper*
> *1 cup olive oil*
> *1 cup dry white wine*

Cut the artichokes lengthwise into quarters. Remove the outer leaves and cut off tops within 1 inch of the bottoms. Remove the inside hairy choke with a spoon. Place artichokes in deep saucepan with water, lemon juice, coriander seeds, bouquet garni, salt, pepper, olive oil and wine. Cook for one half hour or until tender. Remove the artichokes, reserving liquid, and place in an earthenware terrine or glass dish. Reduce liquid to one-third its volume; pour through a strainer over artichokes. When cool, place in the refrigerator. Serve cold. This should marinate at least 24 hours before serving.

Fonds d'Artichauts à la Smyrne

[ARTICHOKE BOTTOMS WITH ONIONS,
TOMATOES AND RAISINS]   FOR 4 OR 6

> 4 large artichokes
> 18 small white onions
> 4 medium tomatoes, peeled, seeded, quartered
> 1 tablespoon chopped garlic
> 1 stick cinnamon
> 1 tablespoon honey
> 2 peeled garlic cloves and 2 unpeeled garlic cloves
>   Bouquet garni
> 1 teaspoon white pepper
> 1 tablespoon salt
>   Pinch nutmeg
> 1 cup water
> 1 cup dry white wine
> ¼ cup vodka
> 6 tablespoons lemon juice
> 1 cup olive oil
> ¾ cup dry raisins, soaked in water 2 hours before using

Cut the artichokes lengthwise into quarters. Remove the outer leaves and cut off tops within 1 inch of the bottoms. Remove the inside hairy choke with a spoon. Excepting the raisins, place all ingredients into a skillet. Simmer 35 minutes or until the artichoke bottoms are tender. Add the raisins, simmer 5 minutes more. Remove the bouquet garni, cinnamon and whole garlic cloves. Place artichokes in an earthenware terrine. When cool, place in the refrigerator. Serve very cold. This should marinate at least 24 hours before serving.

Céleri-Rave Sauce Gribiche

[CELERIAC IN A VINAIGRETTE SAUCE]   FOR 4

This vegetable is known variously as celery knob, celery root and celeriac.

> 2 celery knobs
> 1 quart water
> ½ cup fresh lemon juice
> 1 teaspoon salt
> ½ teaspoon white pepper
>   Sauce Gribiche (page 327)
>   Chopped parsley

Peel and cut celery knobs in half. Simmer in water, lemon juice, salt and pepper 40 minutes or until tender. Cool to lukewarm; cut into ⅛-inch slices. Arrange on a flat dish and top with gribiche sauce and parsley.

Céleri-Rave Rémoulade

[CELERIAC WITH A MUSTARD MAYONNAISE]   FOR 4

> 2 celery knobs (should weigh 8 ounces each)
> ¼ cup lemon juice
> 1 ounce Dijon mustard
> 1 cup Mayonnaise (page 84)
> 1 teaspoon salt
> ½ teaspoon white pepper
> 1 tablespoon finely chopped parsley
> Boston lettuce leaves

Peel celery knobs; slice lengthwise thinly, then cut lengthwise in julienne strips. Place in cold water in a saucepan, bring to a boil and cook 4 minutes. Drain, sprinkle with lemon juice. Mix this well so the celery will stay white. When cold, add mustard, mayonnaise, pepper and salt. Check seasoning. Spread lettuce leaves on a long hors-d'oeuvre dish; arrange celery on top and sprinkle with parsley.

Concombres à la Crème

[CUCUMBERS IN SOUR CREAM]   FOR 4

> 2 large peeled cucumbers
> 1 tablespoon salt
> 1 cup sour cream
> 1 teaspoon white pepper
> 1 tablespoon chopped parsley
> 1 tablespoon chopped chives
>   Boston lettuce leaves

Cut the cucumbers lengthwise and scrape out seeds with a spoon. Slice very thin. Add salt, mix well and chill 1 hour in the refrigerator. Place cucumbers in a cheesecloth and squeeze out moisture until very dry. Blend in sour cream, white pepper, parsley, chives. Serve on a bed of crisp lettuce leaves.

Ratatouille Niçoise (I)

[EGGPLANT WITH ZUCCHINI, TOMATOES
AND BLACK OLIVES]   FOR 6

> 4 cups peeled eggplant, cut into 1-inch cubes
> 4 cups unpeeled zucchini, cut in 1-inch cubes
> 1½ cups olive oil
> 1 tablespoon chopped garlic
> 1 cup finely chopped onions
> 4 tomatoes, peeled, seeded, quartered
> 1 tablespoon salt
> 1 teaspoon black pepper
>   Pinch dry thyme
> 1 bay leaf
> 1 tablespoon chopped sweet basil (1 teaspoon dry)
> ½ cup dry white wine
> ½ cup wine vinegar
> ½ cup small, pitted black olives
> 1 tablespoon chopped parsley

Sauté eggplant and zucchini together in oil 5 minutes. Add garlic and onions; simmer 3 minutes. Blend in tomatoes, salt, pepper, thyme, bay leaf, basil, wine, vinegar; simmer 3 minutes. Add olives and continue simmering 2 minutes. Check seasoning. Remove to serving casserole. Refrigerate. Sprinkle with parsley before serving very cold. (Ratatouille may be prepared and served in many ways. There is another recipe on page 303.)

Aubergine Méridionale

[EGGPLANT WITH ONIONS, TOMATOES
AND GREEN OLIVES]   FOR 6

10 ¼-inch-thick slices unpeeled eggplant (use small eggplants)
10 ¼-inch-thick slices onions
2 cups cooking oil
10 ¼-inch-thick slices peeled tomatoes
1 tablespoon salt
1 teaspoon pepper
⅓ cup chopped garlic
1 teaspoon dry thyme leaves
1 teaspoon crushed bay leaves
½ cup chopped green olives
Salt and pepper
½ cup dry white wine
1 tablespoon chopped parsley

Sauté eggplant in oil (add oil as needed) until brown. Sauté onions in oil until soft. In a shallow ovenproof dish, alternate slices of eggplant, onions and tomatoes. Sprinkle with salt and pepper. In a small amount of oil, sauté garlic 2 minutes; add thyme, bay leaves, green olives, salt, pepper and wine; blend. Pour evenly over the slices. Place in a preheated 400-degree oven 20 minutes. Remove, cool, sprinkle with parsley and serve cold.

Champignons aux Citrons

[MUSHROOMS WITH LEMONS]   FOR 6

1 pound button mushrooms
¾ cup dry white wine
¼ cup lemon juice
1 teaspoon salt
1 teaspoon white pepper
Pinch dry thyme leaves
1 bay leaf
2 cloves garlic, peeled
1½ teaspoons coriander seeds
3 whole lemons (separate the sections, being careful
to remove all of the white part, which is bitter)
½ cup oil

Place the mushrooms in a deep saucepan. Add wine, lemon juice, salt, pepper, thyme, bay leaf, garlic, coriander seeds; simmer 3 minutes. Add lemon sections and simmer 2 minutes. Check seasoning. Pour in oil and place in an earthenware terrine or crock. Refrigerate. Remove the thyme, bay leaf and cloves of garlic just before serving. Serve very cold.

Piments Doux en Gelée

[ASPIC OF RED PIMENTOS]   FOR 6

1 four-ounce can red pimentos
2 cups Chicken Broth (page 62)
1 tablespoon gelatin
1 tablespoon salt
  Pinch cayenne pepper
1 teaspoon tabasco sauce
1 tablespoon chopped sour gherkins
1 tablespoon chopped white celery
6 Boston lettuce leaves

Drain pimentos; dry on cheesecloth or paper towels. Cut in ½-inch squares. Soften gelatin in ¼ cup cold broth. Bring remainder to boil, remove from flame and add gelatin, stirring to dissolve, and salt, pepper, and tabasco. Mix pimentos with gherkins and celery. Pour the broth over, blend thoroughly. Check seasoning. Pour mixture in 6 small, round ramekins; place in refrigerator 2 hours to set. When ready to serve, dip ramekins in hot water for a few seconds to unmold aspic, and invert each ramekin on top of a lettuce leaf.

Légumes Assortis à la Grecque

[ASSORTED FRESH VEGETABLES À LA GRECQUE]   FOR 6

4 cups carrots, trimmed to size and shape of jumbo olives
12 small onions
1 cup green peppers, cut in 1-inch squares
1 cup dry white wine
1 cup water
½ cup cider vinegar
1 cup olive oil
1 tablespoon salt
1 teaspoon white pepper
2 cups celery stalks, cut in 1½-inch pieces
1½ teaspoons coriander seeds
Bouquet garni
2 cloves garlic
1 dozen small mushrooms
2 cups white turnips, trimmed to size and shape of jumbo olives
2 cups peeled, seeded cucumbers, trimmed to size and shape of jumbo olives
½ cup fresh green peas
1 cup green string beans, cut in 1-inch pieces
Chopped parsley

Simmer the carrots, onions and green peppers in the wine, water, vinegar, oil, salt and pepper 10 minutes. Add the celery, coriander seeds, bouquet garni and garlic. Simmer 5 minutes. Add the mushrooms and turnips; simmer 2 minutes. Stir in the cucumbers, peas and string beans; simmer 10 minutes. Check seasoning. Remove bouquet garni and transfer vegetables to a serving casserole. Refrigerate. Sprinkle some chopped parsley over the dish before serving. If you use very fresh vegetables (which you should), they will cook more quickly.

OEUFS ET MOUSSES—EGGS AND MOUSSES

Oeufs Durs Portugaise

[HARD BOILED EGGS WITH TOMATOES
AND ANCHOVIES]   FOR 4

> 5 hard boiled eggs
> 8 Boston lettuce leaves
> 8 slices peeled tomatoes
> 1 cup Mayonnaise (page 84)
> 16 flat anchovy filets
> 2 tablespoons capers
> 1 tablespoon chopped parsley
> 8 strips pimento

When eggs are cold, shell and cut 4 of them in half lengthwise. Arrange lettuce leaves on an oblong hors-d'oeuvre dish and place 1 slice of to-mato on each lettuce leaf. Top with an egg half. Spoon mayonnaise over these. Place anchovy filets in triangles on mayonnaise and spoon capers into the triangles. Push the yolk of the remaining egg through a sieve and sprinkle it and the parsley over the eggs. Place 1 pimento strip on each egg half.

Mousse d'Oeufs à l'Alsacienne

[MOUSSE OF EGGS AND FOIE GRAS]   FOR 6

> 6 hard boiled egg yolks, rubbed through a sieve
> ¼ pound foie gras
> 4 tablespoons sweet butter
> 1 tablespoon salt
> 1 teaspoon white pepper
>   Pinch cayenne pepper
> 2 tablespoons Madeira
> 2 tablespoons port
> 2 tablespoons cognac
> ¼ cup Chicken Broth (page 62)
> 1½ teaspoons gelatin
> 6 tablespoons heavy cream, whipped

Mix the egg yolks, foie gras and butter. Add the salt, pepper, cayenne, wines and cognac. Soften gelatin in ¼ cup water. Bring the broth to a boil. Remove from flame and add gelatin, stirring to dissolve thoroughly. Blend aspic with egg mixture. Mix well on top of cracked ice with wooden spatula until mixture thickens. Blend in whipped cream. Check seasoning. Keep the mousse in a deep soufflé dish in the refrigerator. Use for canapés or small pastry tarts.

Mousse de Foies de Volaille

[MOUSSE OF POULTRY LIVER]   FOR 6

½ pound livers (chicken, duck, turkey, goose
   or other bird) cut in small pieces
¼ cup cooking oil
½ cup chopped onions
 1 teaspoon chopped garlic
 1 tablespoon salt
 1 teaspoon white pepper
   Pinch nutmeg
 1 bay leaf
   Pinch dry thyme leaves
¼ pound sweet butter
 1 cup heavy cream
¼ cup cognac or good brandy
 1 tablespoon gelatin

Sauté livers in oil over a hot fire 4 minutes. Stir in the onions, garlic, salt, pepper, nutmeg, bay leaf and thyme. Cook 3 minutes. Drain; push through a fine sieve. Add butter and stir vigorously. Blend in heavy cream. Check seasoning. Soften gelatin in ¼ cup water in a metal container. Dissolve by placing container in hot water. Add cognac and dissolved gelatin to liver mixture. Mix well. Pack the mousse in small earthenware molds. Refrigerate. Serve with toast or on canapés.

Mousse de Jambon

[HAM MOUSSE]   FOR 6

½ pound boiled ham
¼ pound sweet butter
 1 cup heavy cream
 1 tablespoon salt
 1 teaspoon white pepper
   Pinch nutmeg
2½ tablespoons gelatin
 1 cup Chicken Broth (page 62)
½ cup Madeira
¼ cup cognac

Put ham through the meat grinder, using finest blade. Combine the ham and butter in a bowl, mixing well. Blend in the cream, stir vigorously, add salt, pepper and nutmeg. Soften the gelatin in the Madeira. Bring broth to a boil. Remove from flame and add gelatin, stirring to dissolve. Cool. Add to the ham. Check seasoning. Mix well with cognac and pack in 6 soufflé molds (3 ounces each), or in 1 large soufflé dish. Refrigerate. Use on canapés or to fill small croustades and pastry shells.

Mousse de Saumon Fumé Halifax

[MOUSSE OF SMOKED SALMON]   FOR 6

    6 ounces smoked salmon
    6 tablespoons sweet butter
    1 tablespoon salt (if salmon is unsalted)
      Pinch cayenne pepper
      Pinch nutmeg
  1½ teaspoons gelatin
    ½ cup Chicken Broth (page 62)
    2 tablespoons lemon juice
    ¼ cup cognac
    6 tablespoons heavy cream, whipped
    2 drops red vegetable coloring

Put salmon through meat chopper, using finest blade. Blend with butter thoroughly. Add the salt (if salmon is unsalted), cayenne and nutmeg. Mix gelatin with broth to dissolve, cool, then gradually add it to the salmon in a bowl on top of shaved ice to keep the mixture very cold. Stir in lemon juice and cognac. Stir the whipped cream in gradually. Check seasoning. Mix in coloring. Put mousse into small molds, or 1 large mold from which you can take small amounts when wanted. Refrigerate. Use to spread on toast or to fill small pastry tarts.

2

POTAGES—Soups

This morning's the day to "make the pot smile," as my grand-mother used to say when slowly simmering soup. Outside our windows the fields lay shining, a world of silver. Winter had come, the frost was here. Steam rose like flowering tendrils from the cows as my brother drove them out of the barns. The rooster was halfhearted this morning as he made his sore-throated crow to get his harem into action and bring the sun up over the mountain. We had no central heating; the floors were cold and the house was creaking its old bones in protest. But from the kitchen came an aroma that brought us all alive, eager to face the day. Grandmother had been up early preparing a soup—Mitonnée, chicken stock mixed with our rich, clotted cream and stale bread crumbs. What a way to start the day! I'll never forget it.

Soup has this way of stirring you into life. Napoleon said, "Soup makes the soldier," and always made certain that the soup kitchens were as close to the front as his men were.

For me, also, soup is a herald. If the soup is good, it is more than likely that the meal to follow will also be good. If the soup is bad, beware.

I remember Monsieur Étienne, Maître Chef at the Palais d'Orsay in Paris, patiently explaining to us young hopefuls his philosophy of food: "It is simply two processes," he said. "You seal in the natural juices in what you are roasting, frying, braising, grilling. Or you take those juices out so that they add their flavors to the contents of the pot. That is the basis of good soup."

Farm, Brittany

POTAGES CLAIRS—Clear Soups

Basically there are two kinds of soup: the clear (consommé and broth) and the thick (cream, velouté and strained vegetable). A tasty potage, either clear or thick, needs a solid stock, one made with the best of fresh meat, poultry or vegetables. Fish soups, especially, need stock with authority, made with substantial fish bones, such as the head and spine, or, even better, the whole fish (see Fumet, page 62).

For me, the most important and versatile stock is beef, often in France taken from the leftover pot au feu, which was a must on our table every Sunday, as it was with most other rural French families. This savory broth, containing beef and vegetables, is used to make other soups requiring a base of beef stock (see Pot-au-Feu, page 351).

Consommé de Boeuf

[BEEF CONSOMMÉ]   FOR 6

> *1 pound lean chopped beef*
> *1 cup thinly sliced celery*
> *1 cup thinly sliced leeks*
> *1 cup thinly sliced carrots*
> *½ cup thinly sliced white turnips*
> *2 cups whole canned tomatoes*
> *2 egg whites*
> *1 teaspoon thyme leaves*
> *½ bay leaf*
> *Sprig parsley*
> *1 quart cold water*
> *1 quart cold Beef Bouillon (page 64)*
> *Salt, if necessary*
> *White pepper to taste*

In a deep skillet, mix the beef thoroughly with the sliced vegetables, tomatoes, egg whites, thyme leaves, bay leaf and parsley. Add the water and stock. Simmer on a low flame. Stir with a wooden spatula every 2 minutes to prevent sticking. A skin will form. Do not stir anymore. Cover the pot and simmer gently 1 hour. Check seasoning, adding salt, if necessary, and pepper, if you like your consommé sharp. Strain through a fine cheesecloth. It should be crystal clear.

Consommé Madrilène

Follow previous recipe for Consommé de Boeuf, adding at the beginning:

    1 additional cup tomatoes
    2 green peppers, sliced
    1 small red pimento, sliced
    8 peppercorns
    ¼ cup sherry

Consommé de Volaille

[CHICKEN CONSOMMÉ]

For a plain consommé follow recipe for Clarifying Stock, page 64.

Consommé de Volaille aux Gombos

[CHICKEN CONSOMMÉ WITH OKRA]   FOR 6

    1 pound lean chopped beef
    2 green peppers, sliced
    1 cup sliced celery
    1 cup sliced leeks, green portion
    ¾ cup canned tomatoes
    2 sprigs parsley
    2 egg whites
    8 black peppercorns
    ½ tablespoon salt
    1 tablespoon coriander
    2 cloves
    2 quarts Chicken Broth (page 62)
    1 quart water
    ½ pound okra, cut in 1-inch-long pieces
    2 tomatoes, diced
    Few drops tabasco sauce
    1 cup boiled white rice

In a deep pot, blend the beef with the peppers, celery, leeks, canned tomatoes and parsley; then mix the egg whites in well. Add the peppercorns, salt, coriander, cloves, chicken broth and water. Bring to a boil, lower flame and simmer, stirring every 2 minutes so bottom will not stick and burn. Let simmer, uncovered, 1 hour. Strain through a fine cheesecloth, add okra and fresh tomatoes. Simmer 15 minutes. Check seasoning.

Add tabasco (this consommé should be a little sharp). Just before serving, stir in the rice.

Potage Tortue

[CLEAR TURTLE SOUP]   FOR 6

½ pound chopped lean beef
1 cup sliced celery
1 cup sliced white leeks
2 egg whites
1 quart Beef Bouillon (page 64)
1 quart Chicken Broth (page 62)
¼ pound Turtle Herbs (page 3)
½ pound turtle meat (cut half of turtle meat into ¼-inch
    squares and macerate in ½ cup Madeira;
    cut other half in larger pieces and do not macerate)
1 tablespoon crushed black peppercorns
    Salt to taste
1 tablespoon arrowroot mixed with ¼ cup Madeira

In a deep pot, mix the beef thoroughly with the celery, leeks and egg whites. Slowly stir in the beef and chicken stocks, turtle herbs, turtle meat cut in large pieces, pepper and salt. Bring to a slow boil, stirring often, so the meat does not stick to the bottom of the pot. Simmer, uncovered, 1½ hours. Strain through fine cheesecloth; bring to a boil again, add the arrowroot-Madeira mixture, simmer 20 minutes. Add the small squares of turtle meat that have been macerating in the Madeira. Cook 3 minutes; serve. To increase the fragrance of the soup, infuse 1 tablespoon turtle herbs with ½ cup Madeira and strain through a fine cheesecloth into the soup terrine before serving.

NOTE: Turtle meat may be obtained in cans.

POTAGES LIÉS—Thick Soups

Potage Queue de Boeuf

[OXTAIL SOUP]   FOR 6

Step One
> 3 pounds beef knuckles
> 3 pounds oxtail, cut in 4-inch pieces
> ½ pound carrots, sliced
> 1 cup sliced onions
> 1 cup sliced celery
> 1 clove garlic
>   Beef Bouillon (page 64) to cover bones
>   Large bouquet garni
> 1 tablespoon salt
> 1 tablespoon crushed black peppercorns

Place the knuckles and oxtail in a roasting pan in a preheated 500-degree oven; turn frequently so they brown evenly. Add vegetables for 10 minutes. Transfer to deep skillet and fill with beef broth to cover. Add the bouquet garni, salt and peppercorns. Simmer, uncovered, 2 hours or until oxtail is tender. Remove oxtail, dice meat to add before serving. Strain broth.

Step Two
> ¾ cup Madeira
> ½ cup finely diced cooked carrots
> ½ cup finely diced cooked celery
> ½ cup finely diced cooked turnips
>   Oxtail meat (enough to balance the vegetables)

To the above strained broth add the Madeira; bring to a boil. Add the carrots, celery, turnips and meat. Serve when vegetables and meat are hot.

Petite Marmite à la Moelle

[PETITE MARMITE WITH MARROW]   FOR 6

> 6 two-inch beef cubes, from the shoulder
> 1 two-pound chicken, cut in 8 pieces
>   Water to cover the above
> 1 quart water and 2 quarts Beef Bouillon (page 64),
>   to be used after first water is discarded
> 1 cup carrots, 1-inch long, trimmed into olive shapes
> 1 cup white turnips, trimmed like the carrots
> 1 cup celery, cut in 1-inch lengths
> 1 cup white leeks, cut in 1-inch lengths
> 1 cup green cabbage, cut in 2-inch squares
> 1 tablespoon salt
> ½ teaspoon black pepper
> 1 teaspoon thyme leaves
> 2 sprigs parsley
> 1 bay leaf
> 6 one-inch-thick beef marrow bones
> 1 tablespoon coarsely chopped chervil
>   Grated Parmesan cheese

Place the beef and chicken in a deep pot, cover with 1 quart cold water, bring to a boil and blanch 2 minutes. Remove the meat, rinse under cold water and discard the original water. Put the beef back in the pot with the quart of fresh water and beef stock; simmer, uncovered, 1 hour. Add the chicken and vegetables, salt, pepper, thyme, parsley and bay leaf; simmer 1 hour or until all are tender. Skim fat from top. Check seasoning. Cook marrow bones ½ hour in 2 cups of this broth. Using large soup plates, place 1 marrow bone in the bottom of each; add broth, 1 piece of beef, 1 of chicken and some vegetables. Sprinkle chervil over the soup. Serve with Parmesan and French bread on the side.

Soupe à l'Oignon au Gratin

[ONION SOUP WITH GRATED CHEESE]   FOR 6

¼ pound sweet butter
4 cups thinly sliced Bermuda onions
1 clove garlic, finely chopped
2 tablespoons white flour
1 cup dry white wine
2 quarts Beef Bouillon (page 64)
1 teaspoon salt
½ teaspoon black pepper
¼ cup dry sherry
12 small slices dry French bread
1 cup grated Parmesan cheese

Melt the butter in a deep saucepan, add the onions and cook 10 minutes over a high flame so they brown. Lower heat and add the garlic, cook 1 minute. Stirring, sprinkle in flour, mix well, cook 3 minutes or until flour is slightly brown. Add wine, stock, salt and pepper; simmer ½ hour. Let liquid reduce in volume to 6 large soup cups. Stir in sherry. Check seasoning. Pour into ovenproof soup cups. Sprinkle the bread with Parmesan and place 2 slices in each cup. Put under the broiler to brown.

Soupe de Poisson Marseillaise

[FISH SOUP OF MARSEILLE]   FOR 6

½ pound onions, sliced
1 cup cooking oil
1 cup sliced white leeks
6 cloves garlic, chopped
4 tomatoes, skinned, seeded, chopped
1 cup sliced celery
2 ounces tomato paste
2 cups dry white wine
2 quarts Fumet (page 62)
    Bouquet garni (3 sprigs parsley, 1 bay leaf, 1 branch thyme)
1 cup sliced fennel
1 ounce saffron
1 tablespoon salt
1 teaspoon white pepper
4 leaves sweet basil chopped (or good pinch of dry)
    Cooked vermicelli or boiled rice (optional)

Simmer the onions in oil in a deep saucepan 5 minutes; do not brown. Add the leeks and garlic, cook 5 minutes. Add the tomatoes, celery, tomato paste, wine and fumet, bouquet garni, fennel, saffron, salt and pepper. Simmer uncovered 1½ hours. Stir in the basil. Strain through a fine sieve, forcing the vegetables through. Check seasoning. Boil 5 minutes before serving. Add vermicelli or rice, if desired. Float sliced French bread croutons rubbed with garlic. This soup should be well seasoned.

Potage Parmentier

[LEEK AND POTATO SOUP]   FOR 6

¼ pound sweet butter
2 cups sliced white leeks
1 cup sliced onions
1 pound potatoes, sliced coarsely
1 quart Chicken Broth (page 62)
1 quart water
1 tablespoon salt
½ teaspoon white pepper
1 cup milk
¾ cup heavy cream

Melt the butter in a deep saucepan and add the leeks and onions. Cook over a low flame, stirring constantly 10 minutes; do not brown. Add the potatoes, chicken broth, water, salt and pepper; simmer 1 hour. Blend in milk; simmer 5 minutes and strain through a fine sieve, forcing vegetables through. Check seasoning. Blend in cream and heat 5 minutes before serving. Serve with Diced Croutons (recipe follows) on the side.

Diced Croutons

Cut 3 slices white bread (no crusts) into ¾-inch dice (about 1½ cups for 6). Melt a tablespoon or so of butter in a skillet; brown cubes on all sides. Drain on paper towels.

Potage St. Germain

[PEA SOUP]   FOR 6

1 pound dry green split peas
1 quart Chicken Broth (page 62)

1 *quart water*
1 *tablespoon salt*
½ *teaspoon white pepper*
½ *cup cooking oil*
1 *cup diced carrots*
1 *cup diced onions*
1 *cup diced celery*
¼ *teaspoon dry thyme leaves*
1 *bay leaf*
2 *sprigs parsley*
1 *ham knuckle or 1 pound side bacon*
¾ *cup heavy cream*
4 *tablespoons sweet butter*

Soak the peas overnight in a crock filled with cold water. Drain, place in a deep saucepan, add chicken broth and water, and bring to a boil. Skim off any scum, add salt and pepper. In a skillet, sauté the carrots and onions in cooking oil 10 minutes, until they take on a slight brown color; add to the pot with the peas. Add celery, thyme, bay leaf, parsley and ham knuckle. Bring to a boil, cover and place in a preheated 350-degree oven 2 hours. After removing the ham knuckle, press the vegetables through a fine sieve. Check seasoning. Bring to a boil and stir in the heavy cream. Add butter at the last minute, stirring gently so it will be incorporated without seeming oily. Serve hot, with Diced Croutons (recipe precedes) on the side.

Potage Germiny

[SORREL SOUP]   FOR 6

1 *quart Chicken Broth (page 62)*
1 *cup heavy cream*
1 *cup cooked sorrel (fresh if available)*
1 *tablespoon salt*
½ *teaspoon white pepper*
  Pinch nutmeg
4 *egg yolks*
4 *tablespoons soft, sweet butter*
⅓ *cup Madeira*
1 *teaspoon chopped fresh chervil*

Bring the broth to a boil in a deep saucepan; add the cream and sorrel, salt, pepper and nutmeg. In a 1-quart bowl, mix the egg yolks thoroughly with the butter; slowly add 1 cup hot broth to this, mixing with a whisk.

Add another cup, then another, so egg-and-butter mixture will be warm before pouring into the boiling broth. (This procedure prevents curdling.) Stir in the Madeira. Check seasoning. Sprinkle chervil over each serving.

Consommé Parfait   FOR 6

> 1 quart Consommé de Boeuf (page 38)
> 2 cups heavy cream
> 1 tablespoon salt
> ½ teaspoon white pepper
> 4 egg yolks
> 6 tablespoons sweet butter
> 6 tablespoons dry sherry
> 3 ounces black truffles, cut in julienne
> 3 ounces tapioca

Bring the consommé to a boil in a saucepan; add the cream, salt and pepper. Lower the heat and simmer. In a large bowl, blend well the egg yolks, butter and sherry; add truffles and set aside. Stir the tapioca into the consommé, simmer 5 minutes. Then, slowly, add 1 cup hot consommé to the egg mixture, then another cup, stirring constantly so it will not curdle. Then add the rest of the consommé. Check seasoning, bring almost to a boil before serving. The consommé should be thick and creamy.

Boston Black Bean Soup   FOR 8

> 1 pound dry black beans
> 2 quarts Chicken Broth (page 62)
> 1 quart water
> 1 pound potatoes, diced
> ½ pound side bacon, diced
> 1 onion stuck with 2 cloves
> 1 stick celery
> 2 sprigs parsley
> 1 bay leaf
> ½ teaspoon dry thyme leaves
> 1 tablespoon salt
> ½ teaspoon black pepper
> 2 cloves garlic
> ½ cup heavy cream
> 4 tablespoons sweet butter
> ¾ cup dry sherry

Soak the black beans, covered with water, overnight in a crock. Drain. Place in deep saucepan with chicken stock and water. Add all the ingredients through the garlic. Simmer, covered, 3 hours. If liquid diminishes add hot water to replace. Strain through a fine sieve. Return to saucepan, bring to a boil and stir in the cream, butter and sherry. Check seasoning. Serve with Diced Croutons (page 44) on the side.

Bisque de Homard

[LOBSTER BISQUE]   FOR 6

   1 cup cooking oil
   1 three-pound lobster, cut in 8 pieces (page 143)
½ cup cognac
   1 cup finely chopped onions
   4 cloves garlic, chopped
½ cup white flour
   1 cup dry white wine
   2 quarts Fumet (page 62)
   1 tablespoon salt
½ teaspoon ground white pepper
   4 tomatoes, peeled, seeded, diced
   2 ounces tomato paste
    Bouquet garni
⅓ teaspoon cayenne pepper
   1 cup heavy cream
¼ pound sweet butter

Heat the oil in a thick-bottomed deep saucepan. When very hot add the lobster, sauté quickly over a high flame 10 minutes, turning pieces so they take on a nice red color. Add cognac and flambé. Add onions, simmer over a low flame 5 minutes; add garlic, simmer 2 minutes. Sprinkle in flour, stirring constantly, simmer 5 minutes. Stir in all the ingredients through the bouquet garni. Mix well, bring to a boil; lower flame and simmer 1 hour, covered. Remove the lobster and strain the liquid, forcing the vegetables through a fine sieve. Cook 20 minutes, uncovered, to reduce liquid to 1½ quarts. Blend in cayenne and cream. Add the butter gradually in dots, stirring it in. Check seasoning. (The lobster meat can be served with Riz Pilaf, page 275.)

Bisque d'Écrevisses

[CRAYFISH BISQUE]   FOR 6

Use the same recipe as for Lobster Bisque (preceding) substituting 2 pounds crayfish for the lobster. However, do not cut up the crayfish, and simmer them ½ hour instead of 1 hour. Also add ½ cup finely diced truffles (macerated ½ hour in Madeira) to the soup terrine just before serving.

Potage au Pistou

[SOUP FROM PROVENCE, SOUTHEAST FRANCE]   FOR 8

Step One: Pistou
  6 cloves garlic
  4 sweet basil leaves
  ¾ cup grated Parmesan cheese
  ½ cup olive oil

Crush the ingredients into a paste in a mortar or wooden salad bowl, working in the oil. Set aside.

Step Two
  2 pounds white navy beans
  5 quarts cold water
  ½ pound potatoes, cut in small dice
  ½ pound carrots, cut in small dice
  2 cups white leeks, cut in small dice
  4 tomatoes, peeled, seeded, cut in small dice
  ½ pound green string beans, cut in small dice
  ½ pound zucchini squash, cut in large dice
  1 teaspoon salt
  1 teaspoon white pepper
  2 sage leaves
  6 ounces vermicelli

Soak the beans in cold water 12 hours. Drain, place in soup pot with the 5 quarts of water and bring to a boil; simmer 1 hour. Add the rest of the ingredients except the vermicelli; simmer, covered, 1 hour or until vegetables are tender. Add vermicelli, simmer 15 minutes. Mix the pistou well, then add to the soup just before serving, mixing slowly but thoroughly. Check seasoning. Do not let soup boil as you add the pistou, but keep it hot.

Boula Boula

FOR 6

    1 small can turtle meat
    ¾ cup Madeira
    3 cups Potage St. Germain (page 44)
    3 cups green turtle soup (canned)
    ¾ cup dry sherry
    ¾ cup cream, whipped, salted and white-peppered to taste

Warm the turtle meat and Madeira together. Heat the potage St. Germain and the turtle soup separately. Add the sherry to the turtle soup, mix well. In ovenproof soup bowls, divide the turtle and Madeira mixture equally. Then pour over this equal amounts of potage St. Germain. Pour the turtle soup over the St. Germain without mixing. Spread the whipped cream over the top of the turtle soup and place under the broiler to brown. Serve immediately for each guest to mix the soups together. Serve with cheese sticks.

Potage Mitonnée

[BREAD SOUP]

FOR 6

    1 quart Chicken Broth (page 62)
    1 quart milk
    4 cups toasted bread crumbs or crushed stale bread crumbs
    ¼ pound sweet butter
      Salt and white pepper to taste
    1 cup heavy cream

Blend all ingredients, except cream. Simmer, covered, 1 hour. Blend in cream. Serve very hot.

Potage Minestrone

Step One
> ½ cup cooking oil
> ½ cup diced onions
> 4 cloves garlic, chopped
> 1 cup diced carrots
> ½ cup diced white turnips
> 1 green pepper, diced
> ½ cup diced celery stems, white part only
> ½ cup diced leeks, white part only
> 4 tomatoes, skinned, seeded, chopped
> 1 cup diced green string beans
> ½ teaspoon dry thyme leaves
> ½ bay leaf
> ½ teaspoon dry oregano
> ½ teaspoon rosemary
> Sprig parsley
> 1½ quarts Chicken Broth (page 62)
> 2 cups water
> Salt and ground white pepper to taste
> ½ cup elbow macaroni
> 4-ounce can chick peas

Simmer onions in the oil in a deep saucepan or soup pot for 3 minutes; do not brown. Add garlic, cook 2 minutes; then add all other ingredients except the macaroni and chick peas. Simmer, covered, 1 hour; add elbow macaroni, cook 20 minutes; add chick peas, cook 5 minutes. Add more water if too much evaporates during cooking.

Step Two: While the above is cooking, prepare:
> ¼ pound larding pork, well chopped
> 1 tablespoon finely chopped fresh sweet basil

Work the larding pork and basil into a paste. When ready to serve soup, incorporate this into it in small lumps, keeping the soup hot but not boiling. This should give the soup thickness plus the full perfume of sweet basil. Serve grated Parmesan cheese on the side.

Yankee Pepper Pot   FOR 8

Step One

    ½ cup cooking oil
    1 cup diced onions
    1 cup diced leeks, white part only
    4 cloves garlic, chopped
    ½ cup diced celery stems, white part only
    ½ cup diced potatoes
    1 cup diced green peppers
      Bouquet garni
    1 quart Chicken Broth (page 62)
    2 cups water
      Salt and ground white pepper to taste
    ½ pound honeycomb tripe, cut in ½-inch squares,
      rinsed in several waters, cooked until tender

Heat the oil in a deep saucepan, add onions and leeks, simmer 20 minutes. Add garlic, cook 2 minutes; add the rest of the ingredients. Simmer, covered, 1 hour. Check seasoning.

Step Two: While the above is cooking, prepare:

    ½ cup white flour
    ½ teaspoon salt
    ½ teaspoon ground white pepper
    ½ teaspoon dry thyme leaves
      Pinch sage powder
    1 egg
    1 tablespoon heavy cream
    ½ teaspoon baking powder
    1 tablespoon Lea & Perrins sauce

Blend ingredients, except the Lea & Perrins sauce, thoroughly. Push through a large-holed colander over boiling soup. It will form lumps the size of popcorn. Stir in Lea & Perrins sauce; cook 5 minutes and serve.

Clammy-Leeky

FOR 4

24 soft shell clams (steamers)
2 quarts mussels
¾ cup dry white wine
2 cups finely diced leeks (white part only)
1 cup chopped fresh parsley
2 tablespoons crushed white peppercorns
4 tablespoons sweet butter
½ teaspoon dry thyme
½ bay leaf
2 egg yolks
2 cups heavy cream
½ cup chopped chives
    Paprika

Rinse the soft shell clams; scrub the mussels. Place in a deep saucepan with the wine, leeks, parsley, pepper and butter, thyme and bay leaf. Bring to a boil and simmer 5 minutes (discard any clams or mussels that do not open—they are dead). Drain the liquid; reserve. Mix the egg yolks and cream. Off fire, add this mixture slowly to the liquid from the clams and mussels so eggs do not curdle. Heat again almost to boiling; add chives. Check seasoning and add salt if necessary (shell fish are themselves salty). Ladle out into soup plates and sprinkle with a little paprika for color.

Cold Gillyssoise

FOR 8

6 ounces sweet butter (1½ sticks)
½ pound leeks (white part only), chopped
1 cup sliced onions
½ pound fresh sorrel or 1 cup dried sorrel
1 clove garlic, chopped
1 quart Chicken Broth (page 62)
2 cups water
½ pound potatoes, chopped
    Sprig fresh thyme or ½ teaspoon dried
    Sprig parsley
    Salt and ground white pepper to taste
2 cups heavy cream
½ cup chopped chives

Melt the butter in a deep saucepan. Add the leeks and onions, simmer 20 minutes; add sorrel and garlic, simmer 10 minutes. Add the chicken broth, water, potatoes, thyme, parsley, salt and pepper; simmer, covered, 1 hour or until the vegetables are tender. Strain through a fine sieve, forcing the vegetables through; simmer 10 minutes. Stir in the cream and bring to a boil. Strain again through a fine sieve. Cool. Check seasoning. Sprinkle chives over each serving. The soup should be very cold and smooth, served in cups kept in the refrigerator until ready.

Potage Crème de Volaille à l'Indienne

[CREAM OF CHICKEN SOUP WITH CURRY] FOR 6

¼ pound sweet butter
1 cup chopped onions
2 cloves garlic, chopped
1 cup peeled, cored and chopped apples
½ pound mushrooms, chopped
1 cup chopped celery
½ cup white flour
1½ tablespoons curry powder
1 quart Chicken Broth (page 62)
2 cups water
2 ounces tomato paste
½ teaspoon dry thyme
½ teaspoon white pepper
1 teaspoon salt
½ cup boiled rice
1 cup heavy cream

Melt the butter in a deep saucepan. Add the onions, garlic and apples and simmer 10 minutes. Add the mushrooms and celery; sprinkle with flour and curry powder and cook 10 minutes. Add the chicken broth, water, tomato paste, thyme, pepper and salt and simmer, covered, ½ hour. Strain through a fine sieve. Check seasoning. Stir in rice and cream just before serving.

Potage Tahitienne

[CHICKEN SOUP WITH AVOCADO AND COCONUT] FOR 6

6 tablespoons sweet butter
½ cup diced onions
½ cup diced celery
1 avocado, peeled, cut in quarters
½ cup sorrel (jarred)
⅓ cup white flour
1 quart Chicken Broth (page 62)
2 cups water
1 teaspoon salt
1 teaspoon white pepper
Bouquet garni
1 cup shredded fresh coconut
¼ pound smoked fish roe (tinned), minced
1 cup heavy cream

Melt the butter in a deep saucepan. Add the onions, and simmer 10 minutes; add the celery, avocado and sorrel; sprinkle with white flour and cook 5 minutes. Add the chicken broth, water, bouquet garni, salt and pepper; simmer, covered, 30 minutes. Mix the coconut with the fish eggs, making a paste, and gradually add to the soup. Simmer 5 minutes. Strain through a fine sieve. Bring to a boil and take off fire. Check seasoning. Add the cream, stirring clockwise; keep warm but do not boil. Serve with croutons.

3

SAUCES

Sauces, in my opinion, are as essential to cookery as tracks to a train, or tires to an automobile. The old masters with whom I worked and learned my profession looked with scorn upon any meat, fowl, fish or vegetable dish that wasn't served with the appropriate sauce. It is the sauce, properly prepared and served, that separates the men from the boys, the chefs from the short-order cooks. Unfortunately, many modern cooks, even some professional chefs, treat this fact too lightly, sometimes ignore it. As a result, their cooking suffers. Don't let yours. In the section that follows I present, without complex variations, the fundamental stocks and sauces necessary to prepare the recipes in this book.

Simply, sauces fall in two categories: whites and browns.

White sauces are made with milk, cream, or white stock, be it bouillon, chicken broth, fish broth, veal, lamb or mutton stock.

Brown sauces are prepared from the bones of veal, beef, chicken, and game that have been browned in the oven.

Most sauces take time. But remember, if you do not have sauce for the gander, he may come to the table dry and uninteresting. I am aware that there may be periods when you may not be able to invest time and effort in a sauce. But I cannot honestly say that this is the moment to use the products that grocery stores sell as easy sauces. I do not like them.

There are, however, a few exceptions and some steps you can take to save time. But I also point out that time spent in the kitchen is more wisely invested, and ultimately more rewarding, than time spent watching the television set. The "quick" sauces given here are for emergencies, and will not be as satisfying as the classic ones.

City of Angers, Anjou

You can make an emergency demi-glace, using prepared items: canned College Inn Beef Broth (and Chicken Broth) are acceptable. So is Valentine's Beef Flavor Base, found in glass jars. And glace de viande is more than acceptable; it is an excellent dark, rich meat jelly, also in a glass jar, that will give your "emergency" sauce personality. Bottled Escoffier Sauce Robert (for tomato flavor) and Sauce Diable (for bite) are quite good.

Quick Demi-Glace   FOR ABOUT 1 CUP

> ½ can College Inn Beef Broth
> 1 teaspoon cornstarch
> ½ teaspoon Valentine's Beef Flavor Base
> 1 teaspoon glace de viande, chopped (so it will melt quickly)

Pour the beef broth in a saucepan. Over medium heat, stir in the cornstarch, beef base and glace de viande. Simmer, stirring until the sauce is thickened and blended.

Quick Sauce for Chicken, Pork or
Veal Chops   FOR ABOUT ¾ CUP

> 3 tablespoons sweet butter
> 3 tablespoons minced shallots
>   Pinch dry thyme
> 2 tablespoons chopped Italian parsley
> 1 cup dry white wine
> 1 teaspoon Escoffier Sauce Robert
> 1 teaspoon Escoffier Sauce Diable
> 1½ teaspoons glace de viande, chopped

Melt the butter in a saucepan and sauté the shallots until soft. Stir in the thyme, parsley, wine, the two sauces and the glace de viande. Blend well over a medium flame until the sauce simmers. Simmer 3 minutes. Pass at the table.

Quick Sauce for Steak   FOR ABOUT ¾ CUP

Sauté the steak (boned shell or filet) in a saucepan with two tablespoons of butter and ½ tablespoon olive·oil to keep the butter from burning.

Turning often, brown both sides of the steak over a medium flame. When the steak is cooked to the degree desired, put aside on a warm plate in the stove warmer. Pour off the grease from the pan in which you cooked the steak, saving the browned particles in the bottom of the pan. Make the sauce in this pan.

> 1 tablespoon sweet butter
> 8 medium shallots, minced
> 2 tablespoons minced Italian parsley
> 4 medium mushrooms, thinly sliced
> 1½ tablespoons flour
> 1 cup dry white wine (should be warm)
> 1½ teaspoons glace de viande, chopped

Melt the butter. Stir in the shallots. Simmer until the shallots are soft. Add the parsley and mushrooms. Mix, stir in the flour and blend. Stir in the heated wine, a spoonful at a time; simmer 3 minutes. Blend well and add the glace de viande, stirring it in well. Keep the sauce at a simmer. Spoon over steak that you have kept warm. This sauce can be made for any roast.

Quick Hollandaise Sauce   FOR ABOUT ½ CUP

> 2 egg yolks
> Juice one lemon
> Hearty dash cayenne
> ¼ pound sweet butter, melted

Place the egg yolks, lemon juice and cayenne in the blender. Turn the blender on highest speed. Then turn off. Now turn blender on "mix," and pour in the melted butter; when well blended, turn off.

Quick Chicken or Beef Velouté   FOR ABOUT 1½ CUPS

> 2½ tablespoons sweet butter
> 3½ tablespoons flour
> 1 can College Inn Chicken Broth or Beef Broth (hot)
> Salt and pepper to taste

In a saucepan, melt the butter over low heat. Using a wooden spoon, adding a little at a time so it will not lump, stir in the flour, blending it with the butter, making a roux.

Remove from heat and stir in the chicken broth. There are two schools of thought about this: One adds the hot broth all at once, then uses a wire whisk to beat it into a smooth sauce; the other adds hot liquid a little at a time, stirring that into the roux smoothly before adding more. Both schools claim their method prevents lumping. Experience will tell you which you will prefer. When the sauce is smooth and blended, place it on the heat and simmer, stirring until the desired consistency is achieved. Season. This recipe can be used, substituting canned Beef Broth, for a fast brown sauce.

The veloutés and béchamel are basic sauces to which you can add other ingredients for richness and variance in flavor. Keys to success: The sauce can be kept warm over water simmering in a pan, large enough so that your sauce pan sets on top. To keep the sauce from "skinning," or forming a crust, spoon melted butter over the surface. Use a wire whisk to blend sauce ingredients into a smooth mixture. If sauce is too thick, add more hot stock, a spoonful at a time, blending well. If it is too thin, cook over medium heat, uncovered, stirring constantly until it has thickened, or add a tablespoon of butter which has had a teaspoon of flour kneaded into it. Many sauces will become smoother and finer if you stir in a tablespoon of soft sweet butter just before serving. Do not offer too much sauce. A tablespoon over the serving is enough to enhance the appearance and flavor.

Now that I have inspired confidence by demonstrating that sauces can be simple, please do not be distressed by the steps that follow. They, too, are uncomplicated. But these sauces are the classic ones that everyone sincerely interested in cooking should master. "Solve the sauce," an old chef teacher told me many years ago, "and you conquer the stove."

For you who strive to conquer, keep in mind that sauces can be made in large batches, frozen and defrosted easily when you need them. One morning or an hour or whatever time you want to spend on sauces is a sound culinary investment. To sauce or not to sauce? is an old question. No one, however, can argue the fact that a tasty sauce makes the meal sing. A piece of boiled beef without the special authority of a simple horse-radish sauce is a pretty plebeian thing. I could tick off half a hundred items, from breast of capon to loin of venison, that suffer without the proper saucing.

You will find that the basic sauces aren't difficult to prepare. And despite their simplicity, the mystique will still be there. When, for example, you bring that fresh bluefish to the table served with a tarragon sauce, your guests will comment on the sauce, not the fish. They know about fish: Fish swim; they are also good to eat. But most people do not know much about sauces, except that they taste delicious and enhance a meal.

I am not of the school that advocates drowning fish, veal, chicken or beef in *any* kind of sauce. Sauces should be selected and served judiciously to bring out the best in the food they accompany. But they should be served!

FONDS DE CUISINE—Stocks

White Stock

FOR ABOUT 2 QUARTS

> 5 pounds veal knuckle bones, cracked
>   (preferably from hind legs)
> 5 quarts water
> 4 medium carrots
> 1 large onion, stuck with 2 cloves
> 2 cloves garlic
>   Bouquet garni (celery, parsley, thyme,
>   bay leaf, 2 leeks tied together)
> 6 peppercorns
> 1 tablespoon salt

Place all ingredients into a stock pot; simmer, uncovered, 3 hours. Strain through cheesecloth.

Chicken Broth

FOR ABOUT 3 QUARTS

1 six-pound fowl with neck and gizzard
3 quarts water
2 stalks white celery, coarsely sliced
1 pound carrots, coarsely sliced
2 white leeks, coarsely sliced
1 onion stuck with 2 cloves
4 sprigs parsley
1 bay leaf
1 teaspoon thyme leaves
6 whole white peppercorns
2 tablespoons salt

Put the fowl in a deep pot with the cold water, bring to a boil and skim off the scum that will form. Add the vegetables and seasonings and simmer uncovered 3 hours, adding more water as liquid evaporates. Skim fat off frequently. Strain through a fine cloth. The fowl can be used for chicken pies, à la king, croquettes, sandwiches, chicken salad or chicken hash. Store broth for future use. It freezes well.

Fumet

[WHITE FISH STOCK]

FOR ABOUT 2 QUARTS

1 tablespoon cooking oil
1 large yellow or white onion, coarsely sliced
1 clove garlic, unpeeled
1 teaspoon salt
6 peppercorns
3 pounds fish bones and heads
¾ cup dry white wine
3 quarts water
Large bouquet garni
½ cup mushroom trimmings (such as stems, skins)

Heat the oil in a skillet. Simmer the sliced onions 15 minutes. Add garlic, salt, peppercorns, fish bones and heads and wine; simmer 3 minutes. Add the water, bouquet garni and mushroom trimmings and simmer 1 hour, uncovered. Strain through fine cheesecloth. Can be stored in the refrigerator for several days or frozen.

Court Bouillon   FOR ABOUT 2 QUARTS

This is a simple stock used mostly for poaching fish. Its purpose is to enhance the original flavor of whatever is poached in it.

> 1½ quarts water
> 2 cups white wine
> 1½ cups wine vinegar
>   Juice 1 lemon
> 2 white onions, sliced
> 1 bay leaf
> 2 carrots, sliced
> 2 celery stalks, chopped with tops
> 1 sprig thyme
> 10 peppercorns
> 3 sprigs parsley
> 1 tablespoon salt

Bring to a rolling boil, then simmer 20 minutes. Strain and store in refrigerator.

Brown Stock   FOR ABOUT 2 QUARTS

> 5 pounds cracked veal bones
> 1 cup Crisco or cooking oil
> 1 cup onions, cut in pieces 1-inch thick
> 1 cup carrots, cut in 1-inch cubes
> 1 cup celery stalks, cut in small pieces
> 1 clove garlic, crushed
> 4 tomatoes, peeled, seeded, chopped
> 4 sprigs parsley
> 1 bay leaf
>   Pinch chopped thyme leaves
> 1 cup mushroom trimmings (skins or stems), cut up
> 6 crushed peppercorns
> 3 ounces tomato paste
> 4 quarts water

Brown the bones in a 500-degree oven, turning often to color evenly. Melt the Crisco or oil in a skillet. Add the onions and carrots and brown. Place the browned bones in a stock pot. Add all the other ingredients, pouring in enough water to cover completely. Simmer, uncovered, 3 hours. If necessary, add more water. Strain through a fine strainer. No salt is used, since this stock will be reduced and salt added then. Beef or chicken bones can be used, but I prefer veal bones, which give a more gelatinous substance. For venison, use deer or moose bones.

Beef Bouillon or Stock   FOR ABOUT 2½ QUARTS

To make a good stock, it is necessary to have plenty of stock to begin with, i.e., beef and beef bones. They give the flavor.

4 pounds beef, shank or shin
5 quarts water
2 large beef bones (butcher will usually give these to you)
3 beef marrow bones
1 tablespoon salt
8 peppercorns (4 crushed)
6 white onions (peeled), studded, one clove to each
2 large leeks, each cut in three pieces
2 stalks celery, each cut in three pieces, with leaves
3 carrots, peeled, each cut in three pieces
4 sprigs parsley
2 small bay leaves

Place beef and bones in a very large kettle. Add the 5 quarts cold water (cold water gathers the flavors). Bring to a boil. Reduce heat until water simmers. Skim foam from surface. Stir in all the remaining ingredients. Simmer, uncovered, stirring frequently, and skimming the foam until it stops floating to the surface. Cooking time will be about 5 hours. Stock will reduce by at least 1 quart. Some of the meat can be cut up and frozen with the stock to be used for soup. It can be used for hash, or eaten with the broth the day you make the beef stock as a tasty supper. I then refrigerate the beef stock, for two reasons: When left overnight, a crust of fat will form on top. Remove this and discard. Also, to clarify the beef stock, it should be cold.

Clarifying Stock

8 cups of cold stock
4 egg whites (beaten until they peak, froth)
4 egg shells (broken in pieces)

Bring stock to a boil; then stir in frothy egg whites and egg shells. This will reduce the boil. Bring it to boil again, stirring as it boils, for 2 minutes. Remove from stove. Soak a finely-woven towel in cold water, wring water from it. Line a large strainer with the towel, and pour the stock through. Refrigerate. The egg whites and shells absorb the clouding particles from the stock, clearing it; the straining completes the clarification.

This method can be used with beef or chicken stock to make a consommé. For another recipe for Consommé de Boeuf see page 38.

SAUCES BLANCHES—White Sauces

VELOUTÉS

Sauce Velouté   FOR 1 QUART

> 4 tablespoons sweet butter
> 4 tablespoons Crisco
> 8 tablespoons flour
> 4 cups White Stock (page 61)

Melt the butter and Crisco in a saucepan. Add the flour slowly, mixing well, and simmer 30 minutes; do not brown. Cool. Add the white stock and simmer, stirring occasionally with a wire whisk to prevent lumping, on top of the stove 1 hour. Strain through a fine cheesecloth. Cool. Brush the top with melted butter so it will not crown, or form a skin. Store in refrigerator. This is used as a base; other recipes will call for it.

Chicken Velouté

Use the same procedure as in Sauce Velouté, preceding, substituting Chicken Broth (page 62) for white stock. This is used as a base; other recipes will call for it.

Fish Velouté   FOR 1 QUART

> 2 tablespoons sweet butter
> 2 tablespoons cooking oil
> ½ cup white flour
> 1 quart Fumet (page 62), boiling
>   Small bouquet garni
> ¼ cup dry white wine

Melt the butter in a skillet and add oil. When hot, stir in the flour and mix well. Keep stirring 10 minutes at a low temperature, to avoid browning and for a smooth mixture. Pour in the boiling fumet gradually, mixing vigorously with a wire whisk. Add the bouquet garni and the wine. Simmer, uncovered, 30 minutes. Strain through a fine cheesecloth into a bowl, moisten the top with melted butter so it will not crown (get a skin). Store in the refrigerator until ready to use. Note that no salt or pepper has been used. The fumet will provide sufficient seasoning.

Sauce Brillat-Savarin

FOR 3 CUPS

¼ cup chopped shallots
½ cup small diced carrots
½ cup cooking oil
1 teaspoon chopped garlic
12 crayfish
¼ cup cognac or good brandy
2 cups dry white wine
2 ounces tomato sauce
1 tablespoon salt
1 teaspoon cayenne pepper
  Bouquet garni
1 cup Fish Velouté (page 66)
¼ cup extra heavy cream
1 tablespoon chopped tarragon leaves
½ ounce black truffles, finely diced
4 tablespoons sweet butter

Simmer the shallots and carrots in the oil 10 minutes. Add garlic, cook 2 minutes. Turn up heat and add the crayfish; sauté 2 minutes, turning so they get a nice red color. Pour in the brandy and flambé; add the wine, tomato sauce, salt, pepper and bouquet garni. Simmer 15 minutes. Force through a fine sieve and add the velouté and the cream; reduce until of a fine consistency. Strain through a fine cheesecloth. Add the tarragon and truffles, simmer 2 minutes. Before serving, add 4 tablespoons sweet butter, mixing with a wire whisk slowly until the butter is well incorporated. The sauce should be well seasoned, so check the salt and pepper at all times. This sauce is served with Mousse de Saumon Brillat-Savarin (page 119) and other fish such as turbot or pompano, poached, broiled, or baked.

Sauce Câpre

[CAPER SAUCE]   FOR 5 CUPS

This is usually served with boiled mutton in Scotland; sometimes a variation of this sauce is used with cod, skate or halibut. If
used with fish, substitute Fumet (page 62) for mutton stock and omit
sugar.

> ¼ pound sweet butter
> 12 tablespoons flour
> 6 cups mutton stock
> 1 tablespoon salt
> 1 teaspoon peppercorns
> 2 egg yolks, beaten with small amount stock
> 1 teaspoon sugar
> ½ cup cider vinegar
> 1 cup capers

Melt the butter in a deep saucepan. Blend in the flour, simmer 10 minutes;
do not brown. Stir in the mutton broth, salt and peppercorns; simmer 15
minutes. While simmering, add the egg-yolk-and-stock mixture, stirring
well to prevent lumping. Strain through a fine cheesecloth. Boil the sugar
and vinegar until the sugar is dissolved. Add to the sauce. Stir in the
capers.

Hot Horse-Radish Sauce   FOR 6 CUPS

> 1 cup grated horse-radish (fresh,
>   if available; if not, jarred)
> 2 cups White Stock (page 61)
> ½ cup white cider vinegar
> ½ cup heavy cream
> 1 teaspoon salt
> 1 teaspoon ground white pepper
> 1 egg yolk, beaten
> 1 cup white bread crumbs
> 1 teaspoon Dijon mustard

Simmer the horse-radish with the stock and vinegar in a saucepan 10
minutes. Add the cream, salt and pepper; then the egg yolk and bread
crumbs; simmer 2 minutes. Stir in the mustard. Add more salt if necessary. Keep warm. This sauce is perfect with boiled beef, roast beef or
mutton.

Sauce Nantua

FOR 2 CUPS

½ cup cooking oil
12 crayfish
½ cup finely chopped onions
1 tablespoon finely diced carrots
1 teaspoon chopped garlic
2 tablespoons cognac
2 tomatoes, peeled, seeded and finely diced
1 teaspoon tomato paste
1 cup dry white wine
1 cup Fumet (page 62)
1 teaspoon salt
Pinch red cayenne pepper
Small bouquet garni
1 tablespoon heavy cream
1 tablespoon sweet butter
1 tablespoon truffle juice (from jar or can)

Heat the oil in a saucepan and sauté the crayfish over a brisk fire 3 minutes. Add the onions and carrots, simmer 3 minutes. Add the garlic, cook 1 minute. Pour in the cognac and flambé. Add the tomatoes, both fresh and paste, wine, fumet, salt, cayenne and bouquet garni. Bring to a boil, then cover the saucepan and place in a 400-degree oven 20 minutes. Remove the crayfish. Push the liquid through a fine strainer. Add the cream, simmer 2 minutes. Add the butter and truffle juice. This sauce should be fairly thick. It goes well with fish.

Sauce Poulette

FOR ABOUT 4 CUPS

¼ pound sweet butter
½ pound white mushrooms, chopped
½ cup chopped shallots
8 tablespoons white flour
2 cups White Stock (page 61)
1 cup dry white wine
2 egg yolks, mixed with 1 cup heavy cream
1 teaspoon chopped chives
1 teaspoon chopped parsley
1 tablespoon salt
1 teaspoon ground white pepper

Melt the butter in a deep saucepan. Add the mushrooms and shallots and simmer 10 minutes. Add the flour slowly, mixing well, and simmer 5 minutes; do not brown. Cool. Slowly add the white stock and wine. Stir well; simmer 15 minutes, stirring constantly. Strain through a fine cheesecloth. Slowly add the yolk-and-cream mixture, stirring well to prevent lumping. Heat to just below the boiling point, remove from heat; add the chives, parsley, salt and pepper. If the sauce is too thick, add more white stock and the juice of 1 lemon. This sauce is used with frog's legs, mussels and cod.

Sauce Soubise

[ONION SAUCE]   FOR 5 CUPS

> *1 cup sweet butter*
> *½ pound sliced Bermuda onions*
> *1 cup white rice*
> *2 cups White Stock (page 61)*
> *2 cups milk*
> *1 teaspoon salt*
>   *Bouquet garni*
>   *Pinch cayenne pepper*

Melt the butter in an ovenproof pot. Add the onions and simmer slowly ½ hour; do not brown. Add the rice, simmer 2 minutes. Add the white stock, milk, salt and bouquet garni. Bring to a boil, then place place in 375-degree oven 45 minutes. Strain through a sieve, forcing the rice and onions through. Bring to a boil in a deep saucepan. Add the cayenne. Check seasoning. If too thick, which depends on the kind of rice you use, add some boiling milk and stock. This sauce can be stored in the refrigerator. It is to be used with veal, steaks, egg dishes and chicken.

Sauce Béchamel

FOR 3 CUPS

It was not, as some believe, the Marquis de Béchamel, alias Marquis Louis de Nointel, who invented this. Béchamel is a chef's classic, an important sauce, used often in professional kitchens.

> 2 tablespoons sweet butter
> 2 tablespoons lard, margarine or Crisco
> 8 tablespoons white flour
> 4 cups boiling milk
> 1 large onion stuck with 3 cloves
> 1 stalk white celery
>   Salt to taste

Melt the butter and fat in a skillet. Stir in the flour slowly, making a paste or roux. Blend well, simmer 30 minutes, and continue stirring, so it remains a smooth paste. Cool. Add the milk, stirring fast with a wire whisk to prevent lumping. Bring to a boil, add onion, celery and salt and simmer 30 minutes. Stir often, preventing sticking to the bottom of the pan. Strain through a fine cheesecloth. To store leftover sauce in the refrigerator, cool and spread melted butter on top of it.

Bread Sauce

FOR 3 CUPS

> 2 cups milk
> 1 small onion, stuck with 2 cloves
>   Special bouquet garni (1 sprig celery, 1 sprig parsley,
>   1 white leek tied together with 1 bay leaf)
> 1 cup fine white bread crumbs
> 1 cup heavy cream
> 1 tablespoon salt
> ½ teaspoon cayenne pepper

Bring the milk to a boil. Add the onion and bouquet garni; simmer 10 minutes. Add the bread crumbs, simmer 5 minutes. Remove the onion and bouquet garni. Blend in the cream, salt and pepper. Used for poultry and game birds.

Sauce Cari

[CURRY SAUCE]   FOR ABOUT 1 QUART

1 cup cooking oil
1 cup chopped onions
1 cup chopped celery
1 tablespoon chopped garlic
4 tablespoons flour
½ cup curry powder
4 cups White Stock (page 61)
¾ cup dry white wine
¾ cup coconut milk
½ cup Sauce Tomate (page 83)
    Bouquet garni
1 cup peeled, chopped apples
1 tablespoon salt
    Pepper only if needed, after tasting
    Heavy cream

Heat the oil in a saucepan. Add the onions and celery; simmer 10 minutes. Add the garlic, flour and curry powder and blend. Place in a preheated 400-degree oven 10 minutes, stirring so it will not get too dark. Put back on the stove over a low heat; slowly stir in the white stock (which has been heated), the wine, coconut milk and tomato sauce. Add the bouquet garni, apples and salt. Simmer 1½ hours. Strain through a fine strainer, forcing ingredients through, or put in an electric blender. Put back in saucepan, bring to a boil, correct the seasoning with salt and pepper. Add ½ cup heavy cream for every 2 cups curry sauce and simmer for one half hour. Skim the fat off the top before serving. For shrimps, lobster, chicken, scallops, crab meat and mussels.

Egg Sauce

FOR 3 CUPS

2 cups Sauce Béchamel (page 71)
1 cup heavy cream
¼ cup Madeira
½ cup pot cheese
    Salt
    Ground white pepper to taste
4 hard boiled eggs, chopped coarsely
1 tablespoon chopped parsley

Simmer the béchamel with cream 5 minutes. Add the Madeira and pot cheese. Blend. Stir in well the salt, pepper, chopped hard boiled eggs and chopped parsley. Excellent with halibut, haddock, codfish.

Sauce Mornay

FOR 5 CUPS

2 cups Sauce Béchamel (page 71)
3 egg yolks
1 cup grated Parmesan cheese
1 cup whipped cream
½ teaspoon cayenne pepper
   Salt to taste

Heat the béchamel and add the yolks, stirring rapidly with a wire whisk to prevent curdling or scrambling. Add the grated cheese. Keep hot so that the cheese will melt in the sauce. Add the whipped cream, pepper and salt, if necessary. The whipped cream should be gently incorporated. Do not use a wire whisk, but a spatula or wooden spoon, turning over and over, mill fashion. This sauce should be used immediately or it will separate. If the sauce separates, whip it back with half a cup of warm water, mixing it slowly in a bowl. Used mostly for gratin dishes.

Sauce Moutarde

[MUSTARD SAUCE]

FOR ABOUT 2½ CUPS

This is easy. Make just before serving.

1 tablespoon French or English mustard
2 cups Sauce Béchamel (page 71)
6 tablespoons sweet butter

Combine the mustard, béchamel and butter and heat; do not boil, as it will become bitter. Boiling also causes the butter to detract from the sharpness of the mustard and makes the surface of the sauce shiny. Good with fish, boiled or broiled, and eggs.

Sauce Smitane

FOR 2 CUPS

½ cup finely chopped shallots
1 cup dry white wine
½ cup white cider vinegar
2 cups sour cream
½ cup Sauce Béchamel (page 71)
6 tablespoons Madeira
   Salt and pepper
1 teaspoon lemon juice

Combine the shallots, wine and vinegar in a saucepan, simmer 10 minutes. Add the sour cream, béchamel and Madeira. Salt and pepper to taste; simmer 5 minutes. Strain through a fine cheesecloth; blend in the lemon juice. This is a sour-sweet sauce, excellent with veal, chicken, guinea hen and light game such as hare and rabbit.

SAUCES BRUNES—Brown Sauces

Demi-Glace

[BROWN SAUCE]   FOR ABOUT 2 QUARTS

Demi-Glace replaces an old sauce, espagnole, which is too complicated for anyone but professionals.

> *Brown Stock (page 63)*
> *2 sprigs parsley*
> *1 stalk celery*
> *Fresh tomato trimmings (from tomatoes*
> *you may have used for salads)*
> *Branch fresh tarragon*
> *Mushroom trimmings (optional)*
> *1 cup arrowroot*
> *1 cup Madeira or sherry*
> *1 teaspoon salt*

To the previous recipe for brown stock, add parsley, celery, tomato trimmings, tarragon and mushroom trimmings. Cook, uncovered, 1 hour until reduced to 2 quarts. Then, in a separate bowl, blend in the cornstarch or arrowroot with the Madeira or sherry. Now remove pot from stove. When it stops boiling, slowly pour in the starch-wine mixture, stirring constantly to prevent lumping. Simmer one half hour. Add salt and strain through a fine cheesecloth. Check seasoning and add more salt if necessary. Cool. Brush butter on top so no crust will form. This is used as a base in some recipes, and can be stored in the refrigerator or frozen.

Sauce Bercy   FOR 1 QUART

½ cup finely chopped shallots
2 cups dry white wine
1 quart Demi-Glace (preceding)
1 tablespoon salt
Pinch ground white pepper
¼ pound sweet butter
12 slices beef marrow (put in hot water 3 minutes
so that marrow is warm but not melted)
Finely chopped parsley for garnish

Simmer the shallots with the wine 5 minutes. Blend in the demi-glace, salt and pepper. Add the butter just before serving, stirring in slowly with a spoon. Stir in the marrow and sprinkle with parsley. For steaks, filets of beef or veal.

Sauce Bourguignonne   FOR ABOUT 1 QUART

1 pound lean beef trimmings
1 cup chopped onions
1 cup mushroom trimmings (peels or stems)
1 cup diced carrots
1 cup diced pork skin
1 teaspoon chopped garlic
6 tablespoons marc or brandy
1 quart red Burgundy wine
2 cups Demi-Glace (page 74)
Bouquet garni
1 tablespoon salt
1 teaspoon crushed black peppercorns
¼ pound sweet butter

Brown the beef with the onions, mushroom trimmings, carrots and pork skin. Add garlic; simmer 2 minutes. Add the marc and flambé. Stir in the wine and demi-glace, bouquet garni, salt and peppercorns; simmer, uncovered, 1 hour, until thick (should reduce to 3 cups of sauce). Strain through a fine cheesecloth. Cool. If not used immediately store in refrigerator. When ready to use, add the butter, in lumps, to the warming sauce, stirring clockwise. For meat, fish, egg dishes.

Sauce Bordelaise

Follow the preceding recipe for Sauce Bourguignonne, but use Claret or Bordeaux instead of Burgundy. Rather than the butter used in bourguignonne, add ¼ pound beef marrow mashed into a soft paste, slowly stirred into each pint of sauce in very small lumps. As with bourguignonne this goes well with meat, fish and egg dishes.

Sauce Diable   FOR 1 CUP

1 tablespoon finely chopped shallots
¼ cup dry white wine
1 cup Demi-Glace (page 74)
2 tablespoons brandy
1 teaspoon Lea & Perrins sauce
2 tablespoons sweet butter
  Pinch cayenne pepper
  Salt

Cook the shallots with the wine in a saucepan until the liquid evaporates. Stir in the demi-glace; simmer 5 minutes. Strain through a cheesecloth and add the brandy and Lea & Perrins, simmer 2 minutes. Add the butter, moving the pan clockwise until the butter has been incorporated into the sauce. Stir in cayenne pepper, check the salt. For poultry.

Sauce Diane

FOR ABOUT 1 CUP

  2 tablespoons cooking oil
  1 tablespoon chopped shallots
  ½ teaspoon chopped garlic
  2 tablespoons cognac
    Pinch dry thyme leaves
  ½ tablespoon salt
  ½ teaspoon ground black pepper
  1 tablespoon catsup
  1 teaspoon Lea & Perrins sauce
  1 tablespoon Escoffier Sauce Robert
  1 teaspoon chili sauce
  ½ teaspoon Dijon mustard
  2 tablespoons Demi-Glace (page 74)
  2 tablespoons sweet butter
  1 tablespoon chopped parsley
  1 teaspoon chopped fresh tarragon

This sauce is to be used for steaks or beef, *not for game*. It can be prepared in the same saucepan in which you have sautéed your steaks or
filets, but drain off all the grease first. Remove the steaks; keep them warm.
Prepare Sauce Diane. Heat the oil and simmer shallots 1 minute or until
soft; do not brown. Add the garlic, simmer ½ minute, stir in the cognac
and flambé. Then add the rest of the ingredients except the butter,
parsley and tarragon. Stir well, bring to a boil. Just before serving over the
steaks or beef, stir in butter in small lumps, moving the saucepan clockwise as you add the butter. Check seasoning. Then stir in the parsley and
tarragon. If you do the sauce in a chafing dish the warm steaks can be
placed right in the sauce and served from the chafing dish.

Sauce à la Moelle

[MARROW SAUCE]

FOR 1 CUP

  1 tablespoon cooking oil
  1 tablespoon chopped shallots
  ¼ cup dry white wine
  1 tablespoon white wine vinegar
  1 cup Demi-Glace (page 74)
    Salt and white pepper to taste
  1 tablespoon beef marrow kneaded
    with 2 tablespoons butter
  1 teaspoon chopped tarragon
  1 teaspoon chopped parsley

Heat the oil in a saucepan. Add the shallots and cook 2 minutes until soft; do not brown. Add the white wine, vinegar and demi-glace; simmer 3 minutes. Season with the salt and pepper. You have the marrow and butter kneaded into a paste. Without boiling, mix this paste slowly into the sauce in a clockwise movement until wholly absorbed. Stir in the chopped tarragon and parsley before serving. Until ready to use, keep the sauce warm so it will not curdle.

Sauce Périgourdine

[TRUFFLE SAUCE]   FOR 1 CUP

> 1 large black truffle (remove skin, save trimmings)
> 2 tablespoons brandy
> ¼ cup Madeira
> 1 cup Demi-Glace (page 74)
> 2 tablespoons sweet butter
> Salt and pepper to taste

Dice the trimmed truffle. Soak in brandy 1 hour before using. Place truffle trimmings in a saucepan with the Madeira and demi-glace. Simmer 5 minutes or until the sauce reduces to 1 cup. Strain through fine sieve or cheesecloth. Return to the stove, simmer 3 minutes. Add the diced truffles and brandy. Blend in the butter, moving the pan slowly clockwise. Remove from heat. Check seasoning.

Sauce Poivrade

[PEPPER SAUCE]   FOR 3 CUPS

> 2 cups cider vinegar
> ½ cup crushed black peppercorns
> 1 cup sliced shallots
> 2 cups Demi-Glace (page 74)
> 6 tablespoons Armagnac
> ¼ pound sweet butter
> Salt

Simmer the vinegar, peppercorns and shallots in a saucepan until reduced almost to dryness. Add the demi-glace; simmer, uncovered, 15 minutes. Strain through cheesecloth, bring to a boil again; stir in the brandy. Add the butter, stirring gently into sauce. Salt to taste. Excellent with steaks, filets and venison. If you like a sweet sauce, add 1 teaspoon currant jelly instead of butter.

Sauce à la Portugaise
FOR 1 QUART

>   Peel of ½ lemon
>   Peel of ½ orange
>   2 tablespoons sugar
>   ¼ cup white cider vinegar
>   ¼ cup port
>   1 clove
>   1 cup Beef Bouillon (page 64)
>   1 tablespoon coriander seeds
>   2 cups Demi-Glace (page 74)
>   1 sprig tarragon
>   1 tablespoon salt
>   1 teaspoon cayenne pepper
>   ¼ pound sweet butter

Place the lemon and orange peels in a saucepan; add the sugar, cider vinegar, port, clove, broth and coriander seeds. Simmer 5 minutes. Add demi-glace, tarragon, salt and cayenne. Simmer 5 minutes. Strain through fine cheesecloth. Add the butter in small dots, stirring with a wooden spatula over a *low* fire; blend well, but do not let sauce boil. For beef, ham and calf's brains.

Sauce à l'Estragon

[TARRAGON SAUCE]
FOR 4 CUPS

>   1 cup dry white wine
>   1 cup cider vinegar
>   1 cup coarsely chopped tarragon stems and leaves (save 1
>   or 2 tablespoons chopped leaves to garnish sauce)
>   1 teaspoon crushed black peppercorns
>   ½ cup chopped shallots
>   4 cups Demi-Glace (page 74)

Put the wine, vinegar, tarragon stems, pepper and shallots into a shallow saucepan and simmer. When reduced, almost dry, add demi-glace. Simmer 10 minutes; strain through a cheesecloth. Sprinkle chopped tarragon leaves on top of the sauce before serving. Excellent with eggs, fish, lamb, meat and poultry.

Sauce Tortue

[TURTLE SAUCE]   FOR 4 CUPS

>   1 cup Madeira
>   ½ cup sliced shallots
>   1 cup sherry
>   ½ cup Turtle Herbs (page 3)
>   12 large pitted green olives
>   ¾ cup diced smoked beef tongue
>   2 cups Demi-Glace (page 74)
>   Salt

Put the Madeira into a saucepan with the shallots; simmer 5 minutes. Add the sherry, turtle herbs, olives and tongue; simmer 5 minutes; add demi-glace; simmer 10 minutes. Season to taste. Strain through a fine cheese-cloth. Used on calf's head, turtle steaks and smoked beef tongue.

Sauce Grand Veneur   FOR ABOUT 2 CUPS

>   2 cups Demi-Glace (page 74), using deer or
>   moose bones in original stock
>   1 teaspoon crushed, cooked juniper berries
>   1 tablespoon currant jelly
>   ¼ cup Cognac or Armagnac

Before serving heated demi-glace, add to each 2 cups sauce the juniper berries, currant jelly, Cognac or Armagnac. Serve with venison, wild boar, or bear meat. Also excellent with breast of pheasant or grouse.

Sauce Bigarade   FOR ABOUT 3 CUPS

Step One
>   3 pounds veal bones; wing tips, neck, gizzards,
>   hearts of the ducks you will serve for main course
>   6 oranges
>   3 quarts water

Make a Brown Stock (page 63), using 3 pounds veal bones (instead of 5 pounds) and the duck wing tips, necks, gizzards and hearts. Rather than 4 quarts water, use 3, and the juice of the oranges. Also, add the orange rinds (do not use the white part; it will give the stock a bitter taste).

Simmer, uncovered, 2 hours, reducing to 1 quart, then strain through a fine strainer.

Step Two
>   *1 cup sugar*
>   *2 cups cider vinegar*
>   *The above stock*
>   *1 cup corn starch or arrowroot*
>   *¾ cup Grand Marnier or other orange liqueur*
>   *Salt to taste*
>   *1 tablespoon orange marmalade*
>   *Blanched strips of orange cut in julienne*

Cook the sugar and vinegar until they caramelize. Add stock, simmer 10 minutes. Blend corn starch, or arrowroot, with the Grand Marnier. Add this blend to the stock slowly, stirring to avoid lumping. Stir in salt, simmer one half hour. Add the marmalade. Strain through a fine cheesecloth. Add blanched strips of orange. This sauce is for duck bigarade primarily, but may be used with pheasant or partridge, substituting the wing tips, necks, hearts, and other trimmings.

SAUCES HOLLANDAISE—Hollandaise Sauces

Sauce Hollandaise   FOR 1 CUP

>   *1⅓ sticks sweet butter*
>   *2 egg yolks beaten with 2 tablespoons water*
>   *1 teaspoon lemon juice*
>   *Pinch cayenne pepper*
>   *⅛ teaspoon ground white pepper*
>   *Salt to taste*

Melt the butter. Set aside. In a double boiler, beat eggs over not too hot water (if too hot, the eggs may curdle). When well beaten, slowly, drop by drop from a tablespoon, add butter, beating constantly with a whisk. If the sauce starts to get too thick, add 1 tablespoon warm water. Continue beating until all the butter has been added (do not add the watery substance at the bottom of the saucepan that the butter has been melted in). Add the lemon juice, cayenne, pepper and salt to taste. If the sauce should start to curdle, dribble a tablespoon of hot water down the side of the pan and whisk. Or start in a new pot (off fire) with 2 tablespoons of water and slowly add the sauce, beating with a whisk. Used on vegetables, such as asparagus and artichokes, fish and eggs. Also used for mixing with cream sauce, velouté, béchamel and mornay.

Sauce Bâtarde

Blend equal portions Sauce Hollandaise (page 81) with Sauce Béchamel (page 71), *mixed when hot*. Used for fish, eggs and vegetables.

Sauce Mousseline   FOR 4 CUPS

> *3 cups Sauce Hollandaise (page 81)*
> *1 cup unsweetened whipped cream*

Blend the hollandaise and whipped cream just before serving. Used on fish and vegetables.

SAUCES BÉARNAISE—BÉARNAISE SAUCES

Sauce Béarnaise   FOR 2 CUPS

> *½ cup finely sliced shallots*
> *1 cup cider vinegar*
> *1 tablespoon crushed white peppercorns*
> *½ cup chopped tarragon (save some of the finely*
> *   chopped leaves to add to the sauce when completed)*
> *3 egg yolks beaten with 1 tablespoon cold water*
> *½ pound melted sweet butter*
> *   Salt to taste*
> *   Pinch cayenne pepper (optional)*

Combine the shallots, vinegar, white pepper and tarragon in a shallow saucepan. Place over a medium flame and simmer until almost all liquid is evaporated. Cool on top of shaved ice. Blend in the egg-yolk-and-water mixture with a wire whisk, simmering over a low flame or in a double boiler, stirring rapidly and constantly until it thickens. Add the melted butter and salt in small amounts. If the sauce becomes too thick, add a spoonful of warm water. (For a sharper sauce, add the cayenne.) Put through a cheesecloth, add the saved chopped tarragon leaves and keep in a lukewarm place until ready to serve. Use for meat, fish and eggs.

Sauce Choron

[TOMATO-FLAVORED BÉARNAISE]   FOR 2 CUPS

Make a Sauce Béarnaise (preceding), blending in 1 teaspoonful tomato paste while cooking the vinegar, shallots, tarragon and pepper.

Sauce Foyon

[BÉARNAISE WITH MEAT GLAZE]

Make a Sauce Béarnaise (page 82); blend in 2 tablespoons melted glace de viande.

SAUCE TOMATE—Tomato Sauce

Sauce Tomate

[TOMATO SAUCE]   FOR 1 QUART

>   *1 cup cooking oil*
>   *1 cup diced carrots*
>   *1 cup chopped onions*
>   *1 teaspoon chopped garlic*
>   *½ cup flour*
>   *2 cups White Stock (page 61)*
>   *2 cups tomato purée*
>   *6 ounces tomato paste*
>   *4 tomatoes, chopped*
>   *1 tablespoon granulated sugar*
>   *2 teaspoons salt*
>   *1 teaspoon ground white pepper*
>   *Ham knuckle*
>   *Bouquet garni*

Place the oil, carrots and onions in an ovenproof skillet over a low flame; brown. Add the garlic, simmer 1 minute. Blend in the flour slowly, mixing well; simmer 15 minutes, stirring constantly; do not brown. Add the white stock slowly and continue stirring. Blend in the tomato purée, tomato paste, freshly cut tomatoes, sugar, salt and pepper. Bring to a boil and add the knuckle and bouquet garni. Place in a preheated 350-degree oven; simmer 1 hour covered. Strain through a fine sieve, bring again to a boil and simmer 15 minutes on top of the stove. Correct seasoning and consistency. If too thick, add white stock or bouillon. Can be refrigerated or frozen. Used in general cooking with other recipes.

SAUCES FROIDES—Cold Sauces

Mayonnaise   FOR ABOUT 2¼ CUPS

> 2 large egg yolks
> ½ teaspoon dry mustard (Colman's English)
> ½ teaspoon salt
>   Hearty pinch cayenne pepper
> 2 cups light olive oil or corn oil (or use 1 cup each)
>   Juice ½ lemon (or to taste)

All ingredients should be at room temperature. I use a bowl and a wire whisk, but you can use the hand-held type of electric beater. Combine all ingredients, up to the oil. Beat together well. Now drop in the oil, and I mean "drop." At first, while you are whisking in the oil, do it drop by drop. When your sauce starts to thicken, increase the amounts of oil you are adding to a teaspoon, then a tablespoon, whisking it in well until it is completely incorporated. Adding a small amount at a time, now beat in the lemon juice. Taste. If you like the sauce a bit more tart, increase the amount of lemon juice. Continue beating the sauce until it has the desired consistency. Chill. (If the sauce curdles, you are pouring in too much oil too fast or it is not at room temperature. If this happens, beat up another egg yolk in a bowl, add a very little oil, mix well, then beat the curdled sauce into this.)

Mayonnaise à la Moutarde

[MUSTARD MAYONNAISE]   FOR 2 CUPS

> 2 cups Mayonnaise (page 84)
> 3 tablespoons Dijon mustard

Blend well.

Mayonnaise Verte

[GREEN MAYONNAISE]   FOR 2½ CUPS

> 2 cups Mayonnaise (page 84)
> 4 tablespoons minced parsley
> 4 tablespoons minced chives
> 4 tablespoons minced watercress
> 4 tablespoons minced tarragon

First, all herbs should be fresh. Blend the herbs thoroughly with the mayonnaise.

Sauce for Crab Meat and Shrimps   FOR 5 CUPS

> 1 tablespoon horse-radish (fresh grated, if available)
> 1 tablespoon each chopped shallots, finely chopped green peppers,
>   chopped red pimentos, chopped celery, chopped capers, chopped
>   sour gherkins, chopped parsley, Dijon mustard and salt
> 1 teaspoon each chopped garlic, chopped chives,
>   chopped tarragon, ground black pepper
> 1 tablespoon each catchup, chili sauce
> 1 teaspoon tabasco sauce
> 1 teaspoon A1 sauce
> 1 tablespoon Lea & Perrins sauce
> 3 cups Mayonnaise (page 84)

In a bowl, mix all ingredients up to the catchup. Add the chili sauce and catchup. Blend. Stir in the tabasco, A1 and Lea & Perrins. Then the mayonnaise. Keep cool, but do not refrigerate; if too cold, it will curdle, the oily substance separating from the eggs in the mayonnaise.

Sauce Romanoff

FOR 2 CUPS

1 cup Mayonnaise (page 84)
1 tablespoon lemon juice
1 tablespoon horse-radish (fresh grated, if available)
½ cup sour cream
1 teaspoon salt
1 teaspoon cayenne pepper
½ cup fresh caviar

Mix all the ingredients except the caviar. Just before serving, gently stir in the caviar, avoid breaking. Add more salt if necessary. Used for crab meat or shrimp.

Sauce Tartare

[TARTAR SAUCE]   FOR 3 CUPS

 1 tablespoon each chopped onions, chopped sour pickles, chopped
   capers, chopped fresh parsley, chopped chervil, Dijon mustard
 1 chopped hard boiled egg yolk
 1 teaspoon each ground white pepper, tabasco sauce
 2 cups Mayonnaise (page 84)
 ¼ cup boiling cider vinegar
   Salt to taste

Mix all the ingredients well, except the mayonnaise and vinegar. Blend
in the mayonnaise, then the vinegar. Add salt if necessary. Used with fish.

Sauce Vincent   FOR 4 CUPS

 1 cup cider vinegar or white wine vinegar
 1 tablespoon crushed white peppercorns
 ½ cup chopped onions
 ½ cup chopped spinach
 ½ cup chopped sorrel
 ½ cup chopped watercress
 1 tablespoon chopped tarragon
 1 tablespoon chopped chervil
 1 tablespoon chopped parsley
 2 cups Mayonnaise (page 84)
 1 tablespoon lemon juice
 1 teaspoon tabasco sauce

Boil the vinegar with the peppercorns and onions 2 minutes. Add the
spinach, sorrel, watercress, tarragon, chervil and parsley. Simmer until
almost dry. Force through a cheesecloth or fine sieve. The mixture should
be very thick. Add the mayonnaise. Check seasoning. Blend in the lemon
juice and tabasco sauce. Used for salmon, shad or crab meat.

Cold Horse-Radish Sauce
for Smoked Fish

FOR 1½ CUPS

> 2 mushrooms, cut in small strips
> 1 tablespoon lemon juice
> 1 cup sour cream
> ½ cup horse-radish (fresh grated, if available)
> 1 tablespoon salt
> 1 teaspoon cayenne pepper

Pour the lemon juice over the raw mushrooms to keep them white. Blend the sour cream, horse-radish, salt and pepper; add the mushrooms and mix.

Sauce Mignonette for Oysters
or Clams

FOR 2 CUPS

> ½ cup coarsely ground black pepper
> ½ cup chopped shallots
> 1 cup wine vinegar
> 1 tablespoon salt
> 1 tablespoon oil
> 1 teaspoon chopped chervil
> 1 teaspoon chopped parsley

Blend all the ingredients well; spread the sauce over the shellfish.

BEURRES COMPOSÉS—Butter Sauces

Beurre Maître d'Hôtel

[MAÎTRE D'HÔTEL BUTTER]

FOR 4

This mixed butter is used mostly over grilled meat or fish and should be put on top of whatever is cooked just before serving: Mix thoroughly 4 tablespoons sweet butter with 1 tablespoon fresh chopped parsley, 1 teaspoon salt, 1 pinch white pepper and 1 tablespoon lemon juice. Knead well and keep in a cool place, on chopped ice, for example, before using.

Beurre d'Anchois

[ANCHOVY BUTTER] FOR 4

This mixed butter is used mostly on fish, grilled or sautéed dry, or sometimes on grilled steaks. Mix, kneading 4 tablespoons sweet butter with 1 teaspoon anchovy paste. Blend in 1 pinch red cayenne pepper and 1 teaspoon lemon juice.

Sauce Fleurette

FOR 1 CUP

This recipe was created by my friend Monsieur Alexandre Dumaine, famed chef-restaurateur from Saulieu, France.

½ cup finely chopped watercress leaves (do not use stems)
1 tablespoon finely chopped parsley
¼ pound sweet butter, softened
1 tablespoon lemon juice
1½ teaspoons salt
½ teaspoon white pepper
1 tablespoon extra heavy cream

Mix all the above ingredients together in a bowl with a whisk. Check seasoning. The sauce should be very smooth and light.

4

OEUFS—Eggs

For too many of us eggs are a common, taken-for-granted food to be fried with bacon for a quick breakfast, poached or soft boiled when we want something light, or scrambled or whipped into an omelette for supper or a late snack. Good, yes, but they are much more than this: They are an excellent, versatile food—one to hold in great respect. I often treat them classically and serve them as a luncheon entrée, or a first course for dinner, or even lunch, depending upon mood and appetite.

It is important that eggs be fresh. An egg that has been around too long will ruin any dish. Eggs should not be more than two days old. I test an egg for freshness by weight. It should be heavy. When you break a fresh egg the white should drip in long drops. After you hard boil an egg, hold it under cold running water, then peel. If it peels easily it is fresh. We used a simple test for freshness in France: sprinkle a large spoonful of salt in a medium pitcher of cold water. Then gently put in an egg. If it is very fresh, it will immediately sink; if several days old, it will float submerged in the water; if inedible, it will float on top.

OEUFS MOLLETS—Soft Boiled Eggs

Oeufs Mollets Duc d'Alba

[SOFT BOILED EGGS WITH SORREL AND AVOCADO]   FOR 6

> 6 ounces sorrel
> 6 ounces avocado
> 4 tablespoons sweet butter
> 6 eggs, boiled 5 minutes, shelled
> 2 cups Sauce Mornay (page 73)
> ¾ cup chopped almonds

Prepare a purée of sorrel and avocado by mincing the sorrel and peeling and cutting up the avocado; sautée both in the butter 15 minutes or until the moisture evaporates, then push through a fine sieve. Place this purée in a shallow, buttered baking dish and arrange the eggs on top. Cover with the mornay sauce and sprinkle with chopped almonds. Place in a pre-headed 400-degree oven 5 minutes, then under the broiler 2 minutes before serving.

Oeufs Mollets Horizon

[SOFT BOILED EGGS WITH GOOSE LIVERS
AND CHICKEN]   FOR 6

> ½ pound cooked chicken breast, cut in small dice
> ¼ pound goose livers, cut in small dice
> 1 ounce truffles, coarsely chopped
> 1 cup Sauce Béchamel (page 71)
> ¼ cup Madeira
>   Salt to taste
>   Pinch cayenne pepper
>   Pinch nutmeg
> 6 eggs, boiled 5 minutes, shelled
> ½ cup Sauce Hollandaise (page 81)
> 2 tablespoons salted whipped cream

Blend the chicken, goose livers, truffles, half of the béchamel, Madeira, salt, cayenne and nutmeg well and bring to a boil. Put this mixture in a shallow, buttered baking dish and place the eggs evenly on top. Heat the remaining béchamel and mix in the hollandaise and whipped cream. Pour the sauce over the eggs and place under a broiler until well browned.

Oeufs Mollets Impérial

[SOFT BOILED EGGS ON ARTICHOKE BOTTOMS]   FOR 6

> 6 cooked artichoke bottoms (fresh or canned)
> 6 slices foie gras
> 6 eggs, boiled 5 minutes, shelled
> 2 cups Sauce Périgourdine (page 78)
> 6 slices beef marrow
> 6 thin slices truffles

Place the artichoke bottoms in a shallow, buttered baking dish and arrange a slice of foie gras on each. Put in a preheated 350-degree oven 5 minutes. Place an egg on each artichoke bottom and cover with périgourdine sauce. Return the dish to the 350-degree oven 3 minutes. Boil the slices of marrow in a little water 1 minute, then drain. Put one slice on each egg and top with a slice of truffle. Surround the dish with heart-shaped croutons before serving.

Oeufs Mollets Soubise

[SOFT BOILED EGGS WITH ONIONS]   FOR 6

Step One: Prepare Purée Soubise
> *4 tablespoons sweet butter*
> *½ pound white onions, sliced*
> *1 cup rice*
> *2 cups Chicken Broth (page 62) or White Stock (page 61)*
> *Salt and white pepper to taste*
> *½ cup heavy cream*

Melt the butter in an ovenproof saucepan and add onions. Simmer slowly 10 minutes without letting the onions take on color. Add the rice, chicken broth, and salt and pepper; bring to a boil. Cover with aluminum foil *and* a lid and place in a preheated 350-degree oven one half hour or until the rice is cooked. Rub through a sieve and stir in the cream. Line a shallow, lightly-buttered baking dish with this purée.

Step Two
>   *6 eggs, boiled 5 minutes, shelled*
>   *2 cups Sauce Béchamel (page 71)*
>   *½ cup heavy cream*
>   *1 teaspoon celery salt*
>   *2 egg yolks, slightly mixed*

Lay the eggs evenly on the rice purée. Mix the béchamel with the cream and bring to a boil; add the celery salt. Remove from the fire and mix in the egg yolks. Pour the sauce over the eggs and place, uncovered, in a preheated 400-degree oven 4 minutes before serving.

OEUFS DURS—Hard Boiled Eggs

Oeufs Durs à la Tripe

[CREAMED EGGS ON TOAST]   FOR 6

I am particular about hard boiled eggs. They should be placed in a pot, covered with cold water, brought to a boil and boiled *exactly* ten minutes. They should be removed instantly and plunged into cold water. This way the white is not rubbery and the yolk is perfect, not too crumbly.

>   *4 tablespoons sweet butter*
>   *½ pound onions, sliced*
>   *2 cups Sauce Béchamel (page 71)*
>   *6 hard boiled eggs*
>   *1 cup heavy cream*
>   *1 teaspoon celery salt*
>   *½ teaspoon cayenne pepper*

Melt the butter in a saucepan, add the onions. Simmer slowly 10 minutes, stirring; do not brown. Blend in the béchamel and simmer 10 minutes. Strain through a fine sieve. Cut the eggs in medium-thick slices into this sauce and simmer 2 minutes, adding the cream and seasoning. Check seasoning. Serve on medium-thick slices of toast.

Oeufs au Gratin Chimay

[EGGS WITH MUSHROOMS AU GRATIN] FOR 6

        4 tablespoons sweet butter
        ½ pound mushrooms, chopped
        ½ cup chopped shallots
        1 tablespoon salt
        1 teaspoon white pepper
        6 hard boiled eggs
        1 cup Sauce Béchamel (page 71)
        ½ cup heavy cream
        ½ cup Sauce Hollandaise (page 81)
            Pinch nutmeg
        ½ cup chopped parsley
        ½ cup grated Swiss cheese

Melt the butter in a saucepan and add the mushrooms, shallots, salt and half of the pepper. Simmer 5 minutes. Cut the eggs in half, lengthwise, keeping the whites intact. Remove the yolks and push through a sieve, adding them to the saucepan. Mix thoroughly and add 2 tablespoons of the béchamel to make a smooth paste. Spread a thin coat of béchamel on the bottom of a shallow baking dish. Lay the egg whites on this. Bring the remaining béchamel and the cream to a simmer and stir in the hollandaise, the remaining pepper and the nutmeg. Strain through cheesecloth. Add the parsley to the thick egg-yolk paste and push the mixture through a fluted pastry tube into the egg whites, dividing evenly. Pour the sauce over and sprinkle with cheese. Place in a preheated 400-degree oven 4 minutes before serving.

Oeufs Durs Bombay

[HARD BOILED EGGS IN CURRY SAUCE]   FOR 6

The former world's heavyweight-boxing champion Gene Tunney was a frequent visitor to La Crémaillère. This dish was a favorite of his.

> 6 tablespoons sweet butter
> 1 cup chopped onions
> 1 clove garlic, chopped
> 2 tablespoons curry powder
> 1 tablespoon white flour
> ½ cup tomatoes, peeled, seeded, chopped
> 1 cup Chicken Broth (page 62) or White Stock (page 61)
> 1 tablespoon salt
>   Pinch cayenne pepper
> ½ cup chopped white celery
> 2 tablespoons applesauce
> 1 cup heavy cream
> 6 hard boiled eggs

Melt the butter in a saucepan and add the onions. Simmer 10 minutes. Add the garlic and sprinkle on the curry powder and flour; simmer 5 minutes; do not brown. Stir in the tomatoes, broth, salt, pepper, celery, applesauce and cream. Simmer 5 minutes or until the sauce thickens. Strain, forcing the ingredients through a sieve. Slice the eggs into a saucepan and cover with the strained curry sauce. Simmer 3 minutes before serving.

Oeufs Froids Farcis Dijonnaise

[COLD STUFFED DEVILED EGGS]   FOR 6

> 6 hard boiled eggs
>   Boston lettuce
> 2 tablespoons Dijon mustard
> 1 teaspoon salt
> ½ teaspoon white pepper
> ½ cup whipped cream
> ½ cup chopped chives
> 1 cup Mayonnaise (page 84) mixed
>   with 1 tablespoon Dijon mustard

Cut the eggs in half, lengthwise, keeping the whites intact. Remove the yolks. Arrange the whites on a bed of Boston lettuce. Push the yolks through a sieve into a bowl and add the mustard, salt and pepper; mix well with wooden spatula. Blend in whipped cream, mixing slowly, then the chives. Using a fluted pastry tube, fill the egg whites with the egg-yolk mixture, making a spiral design. Cover with the mayonnaise-mustard mixture. Decorate, if you wish, with sliced red pimentos or halved green olives.

OEUFS POCHÉS—Poached Eggs

Oeufs Pochés Bourguignonne

[EGGS POACHED IN RED WINE]   FOR 6

One of my favorite sports is to return to the region of my birth—Burgundy—to eat. Making the rounds there one day, I went to a small village where an uncle has an inn. My aunt was a Cordon Bleu and, I'm telling you, was some cook! They don't know what cocktails are in rural Burgundy, but serve a white wine, not too dry, that builds a roaring appetite. My aunt started the meal with some home-cured ham, sliced very thin, and some salami. The salami was made with young donkey, very fancy, wrapped in silver paper and with a very good taste. After that she had this wonderful recipe for eggs poached in a red wine sauce, which I coaxed from her. She followed the eggs with her pride, duckling with prunes (included in the poultry chapter). But that was a special meal for a nephew who liked good food as well as she. Under ordinary circumstances the egg dish should be the entrée.

> 6 slices French bread, ¼-inch thick, rubbed with clove
>   of garlic, fried in butter
> 6 medium mushrooms, peeled, stems removed (reserve
>   peelings and stems)
> ¼ cup lemon juice
>   Salt
> 1 quart red Burgundy
> 2 cups Chicken Broth (page 62) or White Stock (page 61)
>   Salt and pepper to taste
> 1 stalk celery, white part only
> 1 sprig thyme or ½ teaspoon dry thyme leaves
> 1 bay leaf
> 1 lump sugar
> 4 shallots, sliced
> 6 eggs
> 6 tablespoons sweet butter kneaded with 1 tablespoon white flour
> 4 tablespoons sweet butter to add at last moment to sauce
> 24 small white onions, cooked in butter, nicely browned
> 2 tablespoons chopped parsley

Prepare the bread and set aside. Simmer the mushrooms, lemon juice and salt 2 minutes, then set aside. Pour the wine into a deep saucepan and add the liquid that the mushrooms cooked in, the chicken broth, mushroom peelings and stems, salt, pepper, celery, thyme, bay leaf and sugar; simmer 3 minutes. Add the shallots and simmer 10 minutes. Strain this liquid through a cheesecloth and return to the saucepan. Bring to a boil. One by one, carefully drop the eggs in and poach for 2 minutes or until well set. Remove the eggs and keep them warm. Stir the kneaded butter into the wine sauce and, slowly, bring the sauce to a boil, stirring until thickened. On a serving platter, arrange the slices of bread with a mushroom-topped egg on each. Stir the 4 tablespoons of sweet butter into the sauce until melted. Check seasoning. Pour the sauce over the eggs and mushrooms and surround them with the browned onions. Sprinkle with parsley and serve very warm.

NOTE: Adding butter at the last minute will soften any acid taste which the wine might give. And if you cannot get French bread for the croutons, use sandwich bread, fried in butter, making sure it becomes crisp.

Oeufs Pochés Encore

[POACHED EGGS WITH CHICKEN HASH]   FOR 4

Step One: Bread Croustades
    4 slices sandwich bread, 4-inches square, 3-inches thick
    ¼ pound sweet butter, melted

With a small, sharp paring knife, hollow out a pit in the center of each slice of bread 1½-inches deep without breaking the bread. With a pastry brush, paint all surfaces of the bread with the melted butter. Put under the broiler, turning to brown all sides. Keep warm.

Step Two: Cooking
    ¼ pound sweet butter
    1 cup chopped mushrooms
    ½ cup heavy cream
    2 cups Volaille Hachée Blind Brook (page 168)
    2 ounces boiled ham, chopped
       Salt and white pepper to taste
    ½ cup Sauce Béchamel (page 71)
    1 cup Sauce Hollandaise (page 81)
    4 eggs, poached 3 minutes

Melt the butter in a saucepan and add the mushrooms. Cook 2 minutes. Add the cream and bring to a boil; lower fire and stir in the chicken hash, ham, salt and pepper; simmer 3 minutes. Add one half of the béchamel and mix well. Arrange the croustades in a shallow baking dish and spoon equal amounts of the sauce into the pit of each. Place an egg on top of each. Mix the remaining béchamel with the hollandaise. Check seasoning. Pour the sauce over the eggs. Place the croustades in a preheated 400-degree oven 3 minutes or until nicely browned before serving.

Oeufs Pochés Otero

[POACHED EGGS IN BAKED POTATOES]   FOR 4

> 4 large *Idaho potatoes*
> ¼ *pound sweet butter*
>   Salt for potatoes
> 1 *cup diced shrimps*
> 1 *cup chopped mushrooms*
> 1 *cup heavy cream*
> 2 *tablespoons cognac*
> ¼ *cup dry sherry*
> ½ *cup Sauce Béchamel (page 71)*
> 1 *cup Sauce Hollandaise (page 81)*
>   Salt and cayenne pepper to taste
> 4 *eggs, poached*

Bake the potatoes and slice tops; reserve. Remove the pulp, mashing it with butter and salt. Place a layer back into the shell, leaving room for the sauce and eggs to be added later. Simmer the shrimps in a saucepan with the mushrooms and cream 4 minutes. Add the cognac, sherry and béchamel and simmer 2 minutes, or until the sauce thickens. Add the hollandaise, salt and cayenne and mix well. Place the potatoes in a shallow baking dish and spoon half the sauce into the potatoes. Slip one egg into each potato and cover with the rest of the sauce. Place in a preheated 400-degree oven 5 minutes before serving. Cover each with the reserved potato tops and decorate the platter with sprigs of parsley or watercress.

Oeufs Pochés St. Patrick

[POACHED EGGS ST. PATRICK]   FOR 4

Step One: Prepare Codfish
> 6 *ounces salted codfish*
> 1 *cup heavy cream*
> ½ *cup Sauce Hollandaise (page 81)*

Soak codfish 10 hours. Drain, add fresh water and bring to a boil. Lower the flame and simmer 5 minutes. Separate the codfish into lumps and simmer with the cream in a saucepan 5 minutes or until tender. Mix the hollandaise in gently. Set aside in a pan of lukewarm water so that the hollandaise will not curdle.

Step Two: Prepare Potato Nests
> 1 *recipe Pommes de Terre Duchesse (page 314)*

While the potatoes are still warm, push them through a fluted pastry tube, building up four round nests, 4 inches in diameter and 3 inches high on the sides. Place the nests in a preheated 400-degree oven 5 minutes to become crisp and brown.

Step Three: Prepare Sauce Florentine
>   *1 cup spinach purée*
>   *1 cup Sauce Béchamel (page 71)*
>   *Salt and white pepper to taste*
>   *4 tablespoons sweet butter*

Put the spinach purée in a saucepan and simmer 2 minutes. Add the béchamel, salt and pepper. Simmer together 5 minutes. Add the butter in small nuggets, stirring slowly in order not to disturb the smoothness of the sauce. Strain through a fine sieve.

Step Four: Final assembly
>   *Creamed codfish, which you have prepared*
>   *4 potato nests, which you have prepared*
>   *4 poached eggs*
>   *Florentine sauce, which you have prepared*

Divide the codfish between the potato nests. Arrange one egg on top of the codfish in each nest and cover with florentine sauce. Place in a preheated 400-degree oven 3 minutes.

Oeufs Pochés Martiniquaise

[POACHED EGGS WITH SQUASH AND BANANAS]   FOR 4

>   *2 summer squash, cut in half lengthwise*
>   *¼ pound sweet butter*
>   *2 cups sliced white onions*
>   *1 cup diced celery*
>   *1 cup Chicken Broth (page 62)*
>   *1 cup heavy cream*
>   *Salt and white pepper to taste*
>   *Pinch nutmeg*
>   *1 cup banana purée (raw bananas pushed through sieve)*
>   *4 eggs, poached*
>   *2 cups Sauce Mornay (page 73)*
>   *1 tablespoon chopped almonds*
>   *1 tablespoon white bread crumbs*

With a sharp, pointed knife, make incisions in the pulp part of the squash, avoiding piercing the shell. Dot lumps of butter on each half, using one half the butter. Put in a preheated 400-degree oven 10 minutes. Remove the pulp and reserve, leaving the shells intact. Sauté the onions and celery in a skillet in the remaining butter until soft. Add the chicken broth and cream; simmer 30 minutes or until a purée has been obtained. Add the pepper and nutmeg. Stir in the squash pulp and banana purée, blending over a mild fire. Place the squash shells in a shallow baking dish and fill them with this smooth purée. Place one egg on top of each shell and cover with the mornay. Sprinkle with almonds and bread crumbs and put the squash in a preheated 400-degree oven 3 minutes. Brown under the broiler 1 minute and serve.

OEUFS BROUILLÉS—Scrambled Eggs

Oeufs Brouillés

[SCRAMBLED EGGS]   FOR 4

> *6 eggs*
> *¼ cup heavy cream*
> *Salt and white pepper to taste*
> *6 tablespoons sweet butter*

Beat the eggs well with a fork, lifting upward to get air into the mixture. Add the cream, salt and pepper. Melt the butter in a shallow saucepan over medium heat. Add the well-beaten eggs and stir with a wooden spatula until the eggs are fluffy. Avoid large lumps. Scrambled eggs take kindly to many garnishes, among them:

Chicken livers, sautéed
Lamb and veal kidneys, sautéed
Purée of tomato, warmed and stirred in
Mushrooms, sautéed
Cheese: Swiss or Parmesan, grated and stirred in
Truffles, thinly sliced and stirred in
Smoked salmon, diced, warmed and stirred in
Chicken hash
Fried croutons
Ham or tongue, diced and stirred in

OMELETTES

I recommend that when learning to make an omelette, you invest in four dozen eggs and practice. Nothing else will make you an expert—not words from the skilled, not observation (although it does help to watch an expert at work), only breaking eggs and going at it. You cannot, however, make an omelette in a pan that sticks, and you are defeated before you even begin if you try to proceed with a pan that has been used for other cookery. The first prerequisite in omelette cookery demands that the beaten eggs slide around easily in the pan. I (and all who cook omelettes) have one pan that is used for nothing else; it is never washed, but wiped clean with a cloth or paper towel and hung on its hook, reserved *only* for omelettes.

There are several types of omelette pans: Enameled iron, plain iron, stainless steel or plain or specially treated aluminum. They are all good, but I like the simple French style, plain iron, about one-eighth of an inch thick with two-inch sloping sides and an extra-long handle. The bottom should have a diameter of at least seven inches, which is just right for the usual two- or three-egg omelette. Directions on how to treat the pan before using should come with it.

The perfect omelette takes 30 seconds (the two- or three-egg omelette, best and easiest to handle). It should be creamy-soft inside, golden outside: The good omelette is *always* soft (baveuse)—slightly crusty, but soft. The hard omelette means that you have overcooked it or beaten the eggs too much. A good rule of thumb is to give each egg no more than twelve upward strokes in the mixing bowl—upward strokes to get air into them. In other words, if you are beating three eggs, make no more than 36 strokes.

I also recommend that you do a two-egg omelette for each person, rather than attempting a larger one. This small omelette is easier to handle, more elegant to serve individually.

Two-Egg Omelette   FOR 1

> *2 eggs*
> *2 tablespoons heavy cream*
> *4 tablespoons sweet butter (do not use salted butter*
> *or margarine, they cause too rapid browning)*
> *Salt and white pepper to taste*

Break the eggs in a mixing bowl and add the cream and about half the butter, cut in small pieces. Sprinkle in the salt and pepper. Beat the eggs with a kitchen fork, lifting up with each stroke to aerate, no more than 12 strokes for each egg. Do not overdo this beating. If you do, the eggs will be thin and tough in cooking.

Place the omelette pan on high heat. Put a piece of butter on a fork and hold it against the pan. If it instantly sizzles, add a generous piece of butter to the pan until it foams and turns white. Tilt the pan around so the butter covers its entire surface, sides included. Do all this fast. The eggs should go in when the butter reaches its peak heat—before burning. It should not be brown or it will color the omelette.

If the butter is at the right heat, the eggs will sizzle sharply as you pour them in. Almost instantly, they will begin to solidify, forming a foamy edge around the pan. Immediately stir eggs in a circular motion with the flat bottom of the fork, spreading the eggs about the pan. Holding the handle with the left hand, agitate the pan, moving the quickly-forming omelette back and forth. Stirring speeds the coagulation, and the agitation of the pan prevents sticking. Now stop stirring. Shake pan with both hands, raising it slightly above heat. At this point, I hit the handle of the pan sharply with the heel of my hand, which causes the far edge of the omelette to fold. If this doesn't work for you, lift the pan so that the liquid egg runs to end of pan where it will solidify. At the same time, slip your fork under the side of omelette near you and lift the edge, "helping" it to make the correct fold. When the liquid is nearly solid, flip the near edge over with the fork, continue to shake the pan so the eggs won't stick. Then prepare to tilt the omelette out of the pan.

Hold a warm serving plate in your left hand and, grasping the handle of the pan so that it is to your right, rest edge of pan on the plate, off center enough so the omelette will land in the middle of the plate. Now, simultaneously tilt pan and plate about 45 degrees against one another. In a fast motion, flip the pan upside down over the plate and the folded omelette will drop properly in place.

Keep the serving plates warm. Omelettes cool and harden quickly. I also rub soft butter over the omelette just before I serve it. Important! Serve immediately! If you dawdle over serving, your skillful egg-envelopes will taste not unlike those in which you mail a letter.

The varieties of fillings and ways to serve omelettes are limited only by your own imagination. Fillings are sprinkled in just after you begin the

Making an Omelette

(1) **Melt butter over high heat, tilting pan so that butter coats bottom and sides of pan. (2) Before butter browns, as it stops foaming, pour in beaten eggs. Move pan back and forth with left hand, and at the same time stir eggs with flat of fork, using a circular motion. Action is fast. As eggs thicken, spread evenly. Three seconds will do it. (3) Lift handle of pan, sending eggs to far side. Move pan back and forth to prevent sticking. All movements are fast. (4A) Strike lower handle of pan sharply four times with heel of right hand. This loosens eggs, causing them to flip over double to form omelette. (4B) If help is needed at this stage, slip edge of fork under eggs to encourage eggs to fold. Do not allow eggs to stick. (5) Hold warm serving plate with left hand, pan handle with right. Bring edge of pan to touch plate, almost in the middle. (6) Very quickly flip pan bottoms-up over plate, depositing folded omelette in center.**

stirring in the cooking pan. Livers, kidneys, mushrooms, vegetables and such fillings are lightly precooked first, but not in the omelette pan! To cook the fillings in the pan and then pour in the eggs can cause ruinous sticking. Grated cheese and minced fresh herbs need no precooking. Sprinkle them in, then fold over into the classic omelette fold. I also like to serve a plain omelette with a sauce—any sauce, tomato, mushroom, mornay. Simply pour the hot sauce over the omelette and serve.

Omelette Espagnole

[SPANISH OMELETTE]   FOR 4

    6 tablespoons sweet butter
    ½ cup sliced onions
    ½ cup red pimentos, chopped
    1 tablespoon chopped garlic
    6 eggs
        Salt and white pepper to taste
    ½ cup potato chips (crumbled)
    6 tablespoons olive oil

Melt the butter in a skillet and add the onions. Simmer slowly 10 minutes. Add the pimentos and garlic. Beat the eggs with upward strokes. Add the salt, pepper and potato chips and beat again to mix. Heat the oil in the omelette pan and stir in the onions, pimentos and garlic. Cook 2 minutes. Add the eggs, stirring constantly until you feel them coagulating. Do not roll as you do other omelettes, but let brown on the bottom like a pancake. Put a serving platter over the pan and turn out upside down on the platter.

Omelette aux Aromates

[HERB OMELETTE]   FOR 6

    6 ounces sweet butter (1½ sticks)
    ½ cup chopped shallots
    1 tablespoon chopped garlic
    1 cup chopped sorrel
    1 cup chopped fresh spinach
    ½ cup chopped parsley
    1 tablespoon chopped fresh sweet basil
    1 tablespoon chopped fresh marjoram
    1 tablespoon chopped fresh tarragon
    1 tablespoon chopped fresh chervil
    1 tablespoon chopped fresh chives

Pinch dry thyme leaves
Pinch dry rosemary leaves
½ cup sliced blanched almonds
Salt and white pepper to taste
Pinch nutmeg
8 eggs
6 tablespoons heavy cream

Melt ¼ pound of the butter over medium heat in a deep saucepan. Add the shallots and simmer 5 minutes; add the garlic, simmer 2 minutes; then the sorrel and spinach, 5 minutes. Stir in the herbs, almonds, salt, pepper and nutmeg and simmer 4 minutes. Beat the eggs with a kitchen fork. Add the cream, more salt and pepper, if desired, and then blend all ingredients together, mixing thoroughly. Melt the remaining 4 tablespoons of butter in the omelette pan. When foaming, pour in the egg mixture and cook over a quick fire, stirring constantly until the omelette is firm and the liquid gone. Place in a preheated 400-degree oven 3 minutes. Put a round serving platter over the omelette pan; turn upside down so the bottom of the omelette will be upward. It should be about 1½-inches thick. Any leftover omelette can be served as hors-d'oeuvre.

NOTE: Use only fresh herbs where indicated.

Omelette Soufflée au Fromage

[SOUFFLÉ OMELETTE WITH CHEESE]   FOR 6

12 eggs, separated
Salt and white pepper to taste
Pinch nutmeg
6 tablespoons heavy cream
1 cup grated Swiss cheese
2 tablespoons kirschwasser
¼ pound sweet butter

Beat the egg yolks thoroughly with a wire whisk. Add the salt, pepper and nutmeg and beat 2 minutes. Add the cream and continue beating 1 minute. Beat the egg whites until stiff. Fold gently with yolks and add grated cheese and kirschwasser. Melt the butter in an omelette pan. When foaming, pour in the egg mixture. Stir well 1 minute, then place in a preheated 400-degree oven 10 minutes or until the omelette puffs and its bottom is golden. To serve, place a round platter over the pan and turn upside down so the bottom will be upward.

NOTE: This omelette can be made with ¼-inch dice of larding pork instead of butter. Fry the larding pork 3 minutes, add the solid parts to the eggs and use the remaining fat instead of butter to cook the omelette in.

OEUFS ASSORTIS—Assorted Eggs

Croquettes d'Oeufs Périgourdine

[EGG CROQUETTES]   FOR 6

> ¼ pound sweet butter
> 1 cup chopped fresh mushrooms
> ½ cup chopped shallots
> 1 cup Sauce Béchamel (page 71)
> 2 egg yolks
> ½ cup diced boiled ham
> 1 tablespoon chopped tarragon
> 1 tablespoon chopped chives
>   Salt and white pepper to taste
>   Pinch nutmeg
>   Pinch cayenne pepper
> 6 hard boiled eggs, cut in small dice
> 1 cup white flour
> 1 egg, beaten with 1 tablespoon cooking oil and
>   2 tablespoons milk, salt, white pepper
> 2 cups dry white bread crumbs
>   Cooking oil for deep frying
> 1 recipe Sauce Périgourdine (page 78)

Melt the butter in a saucepan. When foaming, put in the mushrooms and simmer 2 minutes; add shallots, simmer 4 minutes. Add the béchamel and bring to a boil. Remove from heat and add egg yolks; mix thoroughly until yolks are well incorporated. Then add the ham, tarragon, chives, salt, white pepper, nutmeg, cayenne and hard boiled eggs. Mix thoroughly. Pour into a shallow pan to cool. Shape croquettes from this the size of large corks. Roll them in the flour, then dip in the egg-oil-milk mixture and roll in the bread crumbs, keeping the cork shape. Fry in deep fat at 190 degrees for 1 minute or until well browned. Drain on paper towels. Serve périgourdine sauce on the side.

Zéphir d'Oeufs Nouvelle-Écosse

[SALMON CUSTARD NOVA SCOTIA]   FOR 6

> 2 cups Chicken Broth (page 62)
> 6 ounces fresh salmon, puréed through a fine sieve
> 1 tablespoon chopped parsley
> 1 tablespoon chopped chives
> 1 tablespoon chopped tarragon (1 teaspoon, if dry)
>   Salt to taste

¼ teaspoon cayenne pepper
6 whole eggs and 2 egg yolks
¼ cup dry sherry
1 tablespoon chopped truffles
1 recipe Sauce Périgourdine (page 78)
4 tablespoons port

Bring the chicken broth to a boil and mix in the salmon purée with a whisk. Lower heat. Add the parsley, chives, tarragon, salt and cayenne and simmer 2 minutes. In a mixing bowl, beat the eggs and egg yolks gently. With a soup ladle, slowly pour the boiling broth over the eggs so they will not curdle. Blend in sherry, truffles. Pour this mixture into six 4-ounce custard cups. Place them in a deep ovenware dish, with 1½ inches of water in the bottom. Bring the water to a boil on the top of the stove. Cover the dish with the lid and place in a preheated 350-degree oven 20 minutes or until the custards are set. Remove from the oven and let the custards cool until lukewarm. Unmold on a serving platter. Stir the port into the périgourdine sauce and spoon over the custards before serving.

French Fried Eggs

These were served to the Emperor Napoleon at Marengo. I found them very successful when I first became chef on the famed Blue Train that runs between Paris and the Riviera. I had little cooking space and my French Fried Eggs were quick, easy, and when embellished with the fact that Napoleon liked them, very popular.

Put 2 cups of cooking oil into a deep skillet. When hot (400 degrees), drop the egg in. Turn the egg often with a wooden spatula so that it will take on an even brown color. This should take about 3 minutes. Drain the egg on a cloth or paper towel.

5

POISSON—Fish

Fish probably is my favorite food, and when I think back on how I first came to love it, the memory involves the process of becoming a chef. During the early part of World War I, I had been working with the French Red Cross, having left high school to join a field hospital, an old textile factory converted into a hospital by the nuns of the order of Saint Vincent under the supervision of the brilliant Mother Superior Raphael. Because of the culinary interest instilled in me by my grandmother, I was assigned to work in the kitchen under Madame Olivier and Mademoiselle Marie Carraux, both excellent cooks and wonderful women. At the end of 1915, Monsieur Loreaux, Second Chef at the famous Hôtel du Palais d'Orsay in Paris, came to our area recruiting young men to serve their apprenticeship in the kitchens of the hotel. This was the equivalent of a baseball scout on the prowl for talent in the United States, a chance of a lifetime for a young man. Cooking, learning to become a chef, was, and is, one of the highest honors in France. Madame Olivier brought me to Monsieur's attention and I went to Paris at a salary of 15 francs a month.

The boss, Maître Chef Monsieur Étienne, was a most talented man and my early inspiration to scale the heights of chefdom. He had cooked for the Russian Tsar and the German Kaiser, and had come from Moscow in 1898 for the opening of the hotel. There were about 100 of us—apprentices, cooks and chefs, not counting kitchen helpers and porters. After carefully interviewing me, Monsieur Étienne selected me as one of the apprentices who would take the full two-year course, spending approximately three months in each of these departments:

Audierne, Brittany

First Work
Roast, Grill, Frying
Sauce
Fish
Entremets—Vegetables, soups, eggs, pastas
Garde-Manger—Butcher shop, larder room, where meats, poultry
    and fish are prepared for the oven. Aspic dishes and cold hors-
    d'oeuvre are also prepared.
Pastry shop
Commune—Cooking for the help
Banquet kitchen
Pantry—Called the "office." Dairy products, fruits, coffees, teas are
    prepared here.

First Work meant cleaning the working benches, chopping blocks, and carving boards, putting coal in the stoves, cleaning poultry and game, chopping parsley, pounding coarse salt in a mortar and then pushing it through a sieve.

Then I went to the Roast Department, under Chef Raymond Villemony, a tough man built like one of his chopping blocks. He disliked waiters and kept a broomstick dipped in charcoal hidden near his knives. Following an argument with a waiter, he would reach in for the broomstick and hit the waiter across his starched, white shirt, putting him out of action. For the waiter could not do his job with black streaks on his shirt.

Although much of my time was spent pounding and sieving dry bread crumbs, Chef Villemony seemed to like me and gave me special duties which put me ahead of the other apprentices. What the chef really hated was laziness and disobedience. Once, when an apprentice refused to follow an order, the chef grabbed him by the neck and held him over the burning ring plate of a stove where he had sprinkled cayenne. The boy sneezed and coughed and choked, until three of us rushed in and saved him.

Why does all of this remind me that fish is my favorite food? Because I seldom ate in the Roast Department, good as Villemony was to me. It was always too hectic. I went to the Fish Department, which was run by a gentle, thoughtful chef. But such is the human mind that I cannot remember his name; I remember the violent one more clearly.

There in the Fish Department the kitchen was airy, overlooking the Seine River and the Tuileries Gardens. So I cooked, then sat and ate my fish surrounded by beauty, watching the birds and flowers in the garden and the boats on the river, the turmoil and the terror of my Roast Department forgotten. Fish. How wonderful!

If what the famous epicure Anthelme Brillat-Savarin said has any truth—"Tell me what you eat, and I will tell you who you are"— then I should be somewhere swimming in a river, perhaps the Seine. For I eat twice as much fish as anything else. Here I hope you will find several recipes to tempt you into eating—and cooking—fish several times a week.

With a little effort you can get fresh fish. Do it; frozen fish has half its personality removed. America is bountiful in all things. From her streams, lakes, rivers and oceans comes a greater selection of fish and seafood than anywhere else in the world.

Remember, a fresh fish can look you clearly in the eye. If a fish's eye is cloudy, the flesh not firm, do not buy; it has been around too long. Beware of buying fish without heads. The heads have been removed because the eyes betray them. Filets of fresh fish will have absolutely no odor. No fresh fish will. Let your eye and your nose do your fish buying.

Do not despair if you do not live near the sea and cannot get fresh ocean fish. Do not resort to frozen fish, please. Use the fish from your area. Fish, like local wine, is best in its own territory. Your lake, stream and river fish can be used. Fish, as the poet said, is fish. Some are fatter than others, some have more bones; all of them adapt themselves well to these recipes. I, of course, would rather have a turbot than a bluefish, but that is probably because turbot was what I was brought up on. On the other hand, the Maine lobster has no equal, nor do the All-Americans—the brook trout, smallmouth bass and shad.

BLUEFISH

Filets of Bluefish with Mushrooms

FOR 6

6 ounces sweet butter (1½ sticks)
1 pound mushrooms, chopped
1 cup chopped onions
1 cup tomato purée
1 cup dry white wine
1 tablespoon chopped garlic
½ pound boiled ham, diced
½ tablespoon salt
½ teaspoon ground white pepper
1 tablespoon chopped parsley
1 tablespoon chopped tarragon
6 bluefish filets, ½ pound each
1 cup white bread crumbs

Melt 1 stick of the butter in a deep saucepan; add the mushrooms and onions and simmer 5 minutes. Blend in the tomato purée, wine, garlic, ham, salt, pepper and parsley and cook another 5 minutes. Add the tarragon and mix. Place the bluefish filets lengthwise in a shallow, buttered, oval baking dish. Pour the sauce over the fish, spread the bread crumbs and place in a preheated 400-degree oven 15 minutes. Brown under the broiler just before serving.

CABILLAUD—Codfish

Codfish Cakes with Tomato Sauce

FOR 12 CAKES

1 pound salted codfish
4 large baked potatoes
2 three-ounce packages cream cheese
1 teaspoon ground white pepper
4 egg yolks
½ cup grated onion
2 eggs
½ cup milk
2 tablespoons oil
1 tablespoon salt

Pepper
Flour
2 cups white bread crumbs
1 cup cooking oil
6 tablespoons sweet butter
2 cups Sauce Tomate (page 83)

Soak codfish overnight in enough water to cover. Drain, rinse and place in a skillet covered with fresh water. Bring to a boil, then lower heat and simmer 20 minutes. Drain and allow the fish to dry. Scoop the pulp from the baked potatoes and blend thoroughly with the cream cheese, white pepper, egg yolks, grated onion and codfish, which has been broken into lumps. Stir this well on top of the stove 5 minutes. Spread the mixture on a flat pan to cool. Beat the eggs, milk, oil, salt and pepper together with a whisk. Form the cooled codfish mixture into 12 oval, flat cakes, roll them in flour, then in the egg-milk-oil-salt-pepper mixture, then in the bread crumbs. Heat the butter and oil in a skillet which can be put into the oven. When hot, brown the fish cakes well on both sides. Then slide the skillet into a preheated 400-degree oven 5 minutes. Serve with tomato sauce on the side.

NOTE: Salted codfish can be obtained, fileted, in wooden boxes.

Cabillaud Sauté Lyonnaise

[CODFISH SAUTÉED WITH POTATOES AND ONIONS]   FOR 4

1 pound salted codfish
2 medium potatoes, sliced the thickness of a silver dollar
2 medium onions, sliced thin
¼ pound sweet butter
½ cup cooking oil
1 tablespoon chopped garlic
1 teaspoon ground black pepper
¼ cup red wine vinegar
Chopped parsley

Soak codfish overnight in enough water to cover. Drain, rinse and place in a skillet covered with fresh water. Bring to a boil, then lower heat and simmer 20 minutes; drain and allow fish to dry. Sauté the potatoes and onions in a skillet in the butter and oil 10 minutes. Add the fish in lumps and the garlic and cook 10 minutes over a brisk fire, or until the fish, potatoes and onions become a golden brown color. Add the pepper and, if necessary, salt. Sprinkle the vinegar and then the parsley over the dish and serve.

Cabillaud à la Crème

[CODFISH IN CREAM]   FOR 4

> 1 pound salted codfish
> 2 cups heavy cream
>   Salt and cayenne pepper to taste
> 1 teaspoon white flour
> 4 tablespoons sweet butter
> 4 thick slices buttered toast
>   Nutmeg
> 3 hard boiled eggs—yolks and whites chopped separately

Soak the cod overnight in enough water to cover. Drain, rinse and place in a skillet covered with fresh water. Simmer 15 minutes. Drain and allow fish to dry. Heat the cream in a saucepan and add the codfish in lumps; simmer 5 minutes. Check taste; if necessary, add salt and cayenne. Knead the flour and butter into a paste and add gradually to the cod and cream, avoiding lumping. Put the cod mixture on toast, a pinch of nutmeg on this, and sprinkle with chopped egg whites and yolks.

ÉGLEFIN—Haddock

Filets d'Églefin Regina

[HADDOCK FILETS IN CREAM]   FOR 4

This recipe comes from Monsieur Louis Triaurau, my Chef and Professor at the Hotel Regina in Paris.

> 2 pounds haddock filets
> 2 cups heavy cream
> 2 cups milk
> 1 tablespoon salt
> ⅛ teaspoon cayenne pepper
> ½ cup Madeira
> 4 eggs, boiled 6 minutes
> 6 tablespoons sweet butter

Place the filets of haddock in a saucepan with the cream, milk, salt and cayenne. Bring to a boil, then reduce flame and simmer 15 minutes. Drain the liquid from the pan and reduce to half its volume. Add the Madeira. Separate the egg yolks from the whites and mix the yolks with the butter. Add to the milk liquid and blend until thick and smooth. Pour over the filets. Serve tiny boiled new potatoes on the side.

BROCHET—Pike

Quenelles de Brochet Nantua

[PIKE QUENELLES   FOR ABOUT 50 SMALL OR
WITH CRAYFISH]   16 LARGE QUENELLES

Step One: Panade
    1 cup milk
    6 tablespoons sweet butter
    ¾ cup white flour

Bring the milk to a boil in a saucepan, add the butter and flour (which has been sieved). Stir vigorously with a spatula until it will not stick to the spatula. Put into a small crockery kitchen bowl. Brush with melted butter, to avoid crusting, until it has cooled and you are ready to use it.

Step Two: Quenelles
    1 pound pike flesh, put through meat grinder (fine blade)
    4 egg whites
    Salt and cayenne pepper to taste
    Panade (above)
    Pinch nutmeg
  ¼ cup good brandy
  1 cup heavy cream

Place forcemeat of pike in a shallow pan placed on shaved ice so it will remain very cold during the procedure. Add the egg whites one at a time, mixing well after each; add the salt and pepper, then the panade. Stir, blend well with a wooden spatula. Stir in the nutmeg and brandy. Then, slowly, add the cream, stirring gently, until the mixture is light but solid. Butter the bottom of a shallow pan. For small quenelles, take two teaspoons, fill one with this forcemeat and with the other scoop it out and lay it on the bottom of the pan. Align several of these spoon-shaped quenelles and cover with boiling, salted water; simmer 5 minutes. The quenelles should float to the surface. Remove, place in bowl of cold water and use as needed. For a larger quenelle, use two tablespoons as a molding instrument. The quenelles should have an egg shape.

Step Three: Final assembly
Place pike quenelles in a well-buttered, oblong au gratin dish, then into a preheated 350-degree oven 10 minutes. Cover lightly with Sauce Nantua (page 69), circle with diced crayfish or shrimp and diced truffles touched with a small amount of Sauce Hollandaise (page 81). Place in a pre-

heated 400-degree oven 5 minutes. Allow two or three large quenelles for each serving. Serve with Riz Pilaf (page 275) and Fleurons (page 285).

NOTE: Pike quenelles are often served as a garnish. If you prefer not to prepare these yourself, they can be bought in cans exported from France and Switzerland. If too large, cut them into small cubes.

POMPANO

Filets de Pompano au Plat

[FILETS OF POMPANO]   FOR 4

> *6 ounces sweet butter (1½ sticks)*
> *6 large white mushrooms, sliced but not too finely*
> *1 tablespoon coarsely chopped parsley*
> *1 tablespoon finely chopped celery, white part only*
> *1 tablespoon finely chopped shallots*
> *1 bay leaf*
>   *Salt and white pepper*
> *4 pompano filets, 10 ounces each, skin removed*
> *1 cup Fumet (page 62)*
> *2 cups dry white wine (Meursault preferred)*
> *¼ cup lemon juice*
> *1 tablespoon white flour*

Butter the bottom of an ovenproof fish dish with 4 tablespoons of the butter. In the dish, arrange the sliced mushrooms, parsley, celery, shallots and bay leaf and sprinkle with salt and pepper. Lay the filets on this bed and pour in the fumet, wine and lemon juice. Bring to a boil on top of the stove; cover tightly with aluminum foil and place in a preheated 400-degree oven 10 minutes. Drain the liquid from the fish dish into a skillet or deep saucepan; cook to reduce it one-half. Mix the flour with the remaining butter to obtain a soft paste (beurre manié), and add this paste to the liquid, very slowly, in small pieces so it will not lump. Check seasoning. Pour this sauce over the fish, making sure that the bottom of the fish dish is very dry before doing so. Place in a preheated 400-degree oven 5 minutes before serving.

SAUMON—Salmon

Mousse de Saumon Brillat-Savarin

[SALMON MOUSSE] FOR 4

1 pound salmon
2 egg yolks
1 cup white bread crumbs
1 tablespoon salt
Pinch cayenne pepper, or to taste
⅛ teaspoon nutmeg
2 tablespoons brandy
¼ cup dry sherry
1 cup extra heavy cream
2 egg whites
1 ounce black truffles, diced fine
4 tablespoons sweet butter
1 soufflé mold or pyrex dish, 3 inches
   deep by 6 inches in diameter
Sauce Brillat-Savarin (page 67)

Force the raw salmon meat through a fine sieve or the fine blade of the meat grinder. Put in a deep saucepan placed on top of shaved ice and with a wooden spoon or spatula vigorously mix in the egg yolks, bread crumbs, salt, cayenne, nutmeg, brandy and sherry. Add the cream, spoonful by spoonful, until the mixture becomes fluffy. Beat the egg whites until stiff. Fold gradually into the fish mixture, working with slow upward strokes. Add the truffles last. Butter the soufflé mold and fill it with the fish mousse. Place on top of the stove over moderate heat 3 minutes (use an asbestos pad if it is an open gas flame). This starts the heat working from the bottom so the mousse will rise well. Place the mold in a shallow pan with 1½ inches of boiling water and put the pan into a preheated 400-degree oven 20 minutes. Increase heat to 450 degrees for the last 2 minutes. Serve immediately. Pass Brillat-Savarin sauce.

Saumon Farci St. Vincent

[STUFFED SALMON]   FOR 8

Step One: Stuffing
> 1 salmon or salmon trout about 8 pounds
>   (boned without spoiling shape, leave on head)
> ¼ pound sweet butter
> ½ cup chopped shallots
> ½ pound whiting meat put through a fine sieve or
>   fine blade of meat grinder
> 1 cup white bread crumbs
> 1 cup purée cooked spinach (squeezed dry)
> ½ cup purée cooked sorrel
> 1 tablespoon chopped tarragon
> 2 eggs
> 1 tablespoon salt
> ½ teaspoon cayenne pepper, or to taste
> ¼ cup cognac or good brandy
>   Pinch grated nutmeg
> 1 thin slice larding pork

Melt the butter in a saucepan and add the shallots. Sauté slowly 5 minutes; do not brown. Remove from the stove and add the ground whiting, bread crumbs, spinach, sorrel, tarragon, eggs, salt and cayenne. Mix well. Put the mixture on a medium flame 5 minutes, stirring continually. Add the brandy and check seasoning; add nutmeg. Cool. Stuff salmon with this mixture, placing the larding pork in the aperture to help retain the stuffing. Sew the edges of the fish together with a small needle and fine twine. Place the salmon in a well-buttered flame-proof baking dish.

Step Two: Cooking the salmon
> 1 quart dry white wine
> 2 cups Fumet (page 62)
> ½ cup chopped shallots
> ½ cup sorrel, finely sliced (fresh, if available)
> 1 cup finely chopped spinach
> 1 tablespoon chopped tarragon
> 1 tablespoon chopped parsley
> 1 teaspoon chervil
> 6 tablespoons sweet butter
> 1 tablespoon salt
> 1 teaspoon ground white pepper
> 1 cup heavy cream
> 1 cup Fish Velouté (page 66)

Pour wine and fumet around the salmon. Add the shallots, sorrel, spinach, tarragon, parsley and chervil. Dot the fish with small lumps of butter and sprinkle with salt and pepper. Bring the liquid to the boiling point on top of the stove. Cover with aluminum foil and place in a preheated 400-degree oven 45 minutes. Remove and drain the liquid in the baking dish into a saucepan. Simmer 5 minutes; add the cream and simmer an additional 5 minutes, stirring well so the mixture will not stick. Add one cup of fish velouté. Bring to the boiling point, then strain through a fine sieve, forcing the green ingredients through to get flavor and color. The sauce should be light green. If it is not green enough, add a few drops of green vegetable coloring before putting the sauce over the fish, skinning first for easy serving. Remove twine from fish. Pour the sauce over the salmon and bake in a preheated 400-degree oven 5 minutes before serving. Decorate with 3-inch long, crescent-shaped Fleurons (page 285).

Darnes de Saumon Braisées aux Concombres et Crevettes

[BRAISED SALMON STEAKS WITH CUCUMBERS AND SHRIMPS]   FOR 6

Step One
    6 pieces peeled cucumbers cut
      crosswise into 2-inch sections
    1 cup water
    1 tablespoon salt
    ½ pound shrimp, peeled and cooked
    ½ cup Fish Velouté (page 66)

Scoop out the seeds from the centers of the cucumbers with a small spoon to make a well in each. Arrange the cucumbers upright in a small, deep, well-buttered pan. Add the water and salt. Bring to a boil, cover and place in a preheated 350-degree oven 5 minutes, or until just cooked but not too soft. Dice shrimp, mix with fish velouté and simmer 5 minutes. Fill the cucumber wells with the shrimp mixture. Keep warm until ready to use.

Step Two

    3 salmon steaks, 10 ounces each, 1 inch thick
    ¼ pound sweet butter
    2 cups dry white wine
    2 cups Fumet (page 62)
    1 tablespoon salt
    1 teaspoon freshly ground white pepper
    3 tablespoons lemon juice
    1 cup extra heavy cream
    1 cup Sauce Hollandaise (page 81)
    6 slices black truffles (large)
    6 Fleurons (page 285)

Butter an ovenproof oval dish with half of the butter. Place the salmon steaks in it. Add the wine, fumet, salt, pepper and lemon juice. Bring to a boil on top of stove; cover with aluminum foil and place in a preheated 400-degree oven 10 minutes. Drain the liquid into a deep saucepan, add the cream and reduce over medium heat to one-half its volume. Add the hollandaise sauce, mixing thoroughly with the remaining butter. Strain through a fine cheesecloth. Remove center bones and skin from salmon. Pour sauce over fish and encircle with stuffed cucumber cylinders. Put under the broiler 3 minutes. Arrange the truffle slices on top of the steaks. Place fleurons around before serving. Serve ½ steak to each person.

NOTE: Slices of truffle, before being placed on the fish, can be dredged in melted butter to make them shine.

Darnes de Saumon Mâconnaise

[SALMON STEAKS IN RED WINE]   FOR 4

    2 salmon steaks, 1½ inches thick, 12 ounces each
    6 ounces sweet butter (1½ sticks)
    ½ cup finely chopped shallots
    4 sliced white mushrooms
    1 bay leaf
      Pinch thyme leaves
      Salt and pepper
    2 cups red Burgundy from Mâcon
    1 cup Fumet (page 62)
    12 medium-sized white mushroom caps
      Juice of one lemon
    ½ pound salt pork cut into small dice
    1 cup Demi-Glace (page 74)

12 small Quenelles de Brochet (page 117)
1 tablespoon chopped parsley

Using 6 tablespoons of the butter, grease an ovenproof fish dish and arrange the salmon slices in it. Spread the shallots, sliced mushrooms, bay leaf, thyme, salt and pepper over the fish. Add the wine and fumet and bring to a boil on top of the stove. Cover tightly with aluminum foil and bake in a preheated 350-degree oven 20 minutes. In a saucepan, sauté the mushroom caps with the lemon juice and 1 tablespoon of the butter. Cook the salt pork 15 minutes in water; drain and sauté in a skillet 2 minutes. Add the mushroom caps to the pork. Remove salmon to a platter; keep warm. Reduce liquid (and reserved mushroom juice) that the salmon cooked in by half. Stir in the demi-glace and simmer 5 minutes; then add the rest of the butter in small lumps, stirring slowly. Remove the center bone and skin from the salmon steaks. Arrange them on an ovenproof fish platter with the salt pork, quenelles (which have been heated in a little fumet) and mushroom caps around them. Strain the sauce over this. Place in a preheated 300-degree oven 5 minutes before serving. Sprinkle with chopped parsley and serve. Check seasoning often while cooking.

ALOSE—Shad

Filets d'Alose au Four Crémaillère

[STUFFED BAKED SHAD FILETS]   FOR 6

Step One: Stuffing
   4 tablespoons sweet butter
   ¼ cup cooking oil
   1 cup finely chopped shallots
   2 small cloves garlic, chopped
   ½ pound mushrooms, chopped
   1 shad roe, coarsely chopped
   1 cup cooked chopped sorrel (fresh, if possible),
      or substitute fresh spinach
   1 teaspoon chopped fresh thyme leaves or pinch dried
   3 ounces tomato purée
   1 tablespoon salt
   1 teaspoon ground white pepper
      Pinch nutmeg
   ½ cup white bread crumbs
   2 egg yolks
   ¼ cup chopped parsley
   ¼ cup cognac

Put butter and oil in thick-bottomed saucepan. When hot, add shallots and simmer 3 minutes without browning. Add garlic and mushrooms; simmer 3 minutes. Stir in the roe, simmer 2 minutes. Blend in the sorrel, thyme, tomato purée, salt, pepper and nutmeg; simmer 5 minutes. Then add the bread crumbs, egg yolks, parsley and cognac. Cool.

Step Two: Cooking the fish
> *1 five-pound shad (which, when*
>   *boned, will yield 4 pounds)*
> *1 cup dry white wine*
> *1 cup Fumet (page 62)*
> *4 tablespoons melted sweet butter*
>   *Juice of ½ lemon*
> *1 teaspoon tabasco sauce*
> *1 teaspoon salt*

Butter the bottom of a shallow, oval, ovenproof dish; place one shad filet, skin down, in it. Spread the stuffing evenly over the filet, and lay the other filet on it, skin up. Pour the wine and fumet around the fish; cover with aluminum foil. Bring to a boil on top of the stove, then place in a preheated 400-degree oven 30 minutes. Remove foil and raise the heat to 450 degrees and continue cooking 5 minutes. Peel the skin off the top filet and serve the shad with a sauce made with the melted butter, lemon juice, tabasco and salt mixed with the liquid left in the baking dish.

Laitance d'Alose au Gratin à la Royale

[STUFFED SHAD ROE WITH BLINIS]   FOR 4

> *½ cup chopped shallots*
> *¼ pound sweet butter*
> *1 cup dry sherry*
> *1 large pair shad roe*
> *6 ounces Beluga caviar*
> *2 cups heavy cream*
> *1½ teaspoons salt*
> *1 teaspoon white pepper*
>   *Pinch cayenne pepper*
> *½ cup Sauce Hollandaise (page 81)*
> *¼ cup lemon juice*
> *1 recipe Blinis à la Russe (page 281)*

Sauté the shallots in the butter 4 minutes in a shallow ovenproof pan; do not brown. Add the sherry and shad roe. Cover with aluminum foil and place in preheated 400-degree oven 15 minutes. Remove the roes, split them in two; spread the caviar inside the split roes. In the pan the roes were in, add cream and reduce to half. Season with salt, pepper and cayenne; strain through a fine sieve or cheesecloth. Stir in hollandaise sauce, mixing gently with a spoon; then add lemon juice. Cover the stuffed roes with this sauce, and place under the broiler 5 minutes. Serve blinis on the side.

ÉPERLANS—Smelts

Éperlans au Four Florentine

[BAKED BONELESS SMELTS WITH SPINACH] FOR 4

½ cup cooking oil
½ cup chopped shallots
3 slices bacon, diced
2 small cloves garlic, chopped
1 ounce tomato paste
1 tablespoon salt
½ teaspoon ground black pepper
⅛ teaspoon nutmeg
1 cup finely chopped cooked spinach
½ cup white bread crumbs
½ cup grated Swiss cheese
1 whole egg
12 large smelts, boned
½ cup chopped parsley
4 lemon halves

Heat the oil in a deep saucepan. Sauté shallots 2 minutes; do not brown. Add the bacon, cook 2 minutes, then the garlic and tomato paste. Stir and cook 2 more minutes. Blend in the salt, pepper, nutmeg and spinach and cook 3 minutes. Blend in bread crumbs, grated cheese and egg and simmer 10 minutes. Stuff the smelts with this mixture and put in a shallow, oval ovenproof dish that has been oiled. Place in a preheated 450-degree oven 10 minutes. Before serving, place under the broiler 2 minutes. Sprinkle with parsley and serve with lemon halves.

RED SNAPPER

Filets of Red Snapper Oriental Style　　　　FOR 6

> *6 ounces sweet butter (1½ sticks)*
> *2 red snapper filets, 3 pounds each*
> *½ cup sliced shallots*
> *⅓ cup sliced garlic*
> *½ teaspoon cayenne pepper*
> *1 tablespoon salt*
> *1 teaspoon fresh thyme leaves (½ amount if dry)*
> *1 bay leaf*
> *½ cup chopped parsley*
> *1 cup diced celery*
> *1 teaspoon saffron*
> *4 tomatoes, peeled and sliced*
> *2 cups dry white wine*
> *2 cups Fumet (page 62)*
> *6 tablespoons lemon juice*
> *1 cup white bread crumbs*

Butter the bottom of a large, shallow ovenproof fish pan with half the butter and lay the red snapper filets lengthwise. Sprinkle over them the shallots, garlic, cayenne, salt, thyme, bay leaf, parsley, celery, saffron and tomatoes. Add the wine, fumet and lemon juice. Cover securely with aluminum foil and bring to a boil on the top of the stove. Sprinkle the bread crumbs over the fish, dot with the remaining butter, replace foil and put in a preheated 450-degree oven 30 minutes. Remove foil and cook 5 minutes or until the top crusts brown.

SOLE

Filets de Sole Wembley

[POACHED FILETS OF SOLE IN SAUCE]　　　　FOR 8

> *8 sole filets, about 6 ounces each*
> *2 cups dry white wine*
> *2 tablespoons lemon juice*

1 cup Fumet (page 62)
¼ pound sweet butter
1 teaspoon salt
1 cup dry white bread crumbs
2 ounces purée of foie gras, or pork-liver paste
1 cup Sauce Hollandaise (page 81)
1 teaspoonful thyme leaves
   Pinch nutmeg
   Pinch bay leaf
1 teaspoon tarragon (fresh or dry), chopped finely
   Pinch cayenne pepper
   Dash celery salt
6 tablespoons dry sherry

Flatten the filets with the side of a heavy knife or cleaver and fold them along the width. Place them in a shallow, ovenproof oval dish. Add the wine, lemon juice and fumet, dot with butter and sprinkle with salt; cover with aluminum foil. Bring to a boil on top of the stove, then place in a preheated 400-degree oven 10 minutes. Place the filets on a warm fish platter and drain the liquid into a saucepan. To the liquid add, one by one, the bread crumbs, foie gras, hollandaise sauce, herbs and seasonings, keeping the saucepan hot. Check seasoning. When the sauce gets thick, add the dry sherry. Pour sauce over filets and serve.

Filets of Sole Cape Cod

FOR 4

Step One: Fish Mousse
   ¼ pound pike meat
   ¼ pound Pâte à Chou (page 283)
   1 egg
   ½ teaspoon salt
      Pinch red cayenne pepper
      Pinch nutmeg
   ½ cup heavy cream

Chop the pike in a meat grinder (fine blade) or put through a fine sieve, then into a mixing bowl placed on shaved ice. Working with a wooden spoon, beating vigorously, add the chou paste, egg, salt, pepper and nutmeg. Mix well. Then add the cream, slowly, stirring so it will mix well and not lump.

Step Two: Preparation
    8 sole filets, 6 ounces each
        Fish Mousse (already prepared)
    2 cups white wine
    2 tablespoons lemon juice
        Salt and pepper
    1 pound bay scallops
        Sweet butter to cook scallops
    1 pound button mushrooms
    ¼ cup lemon juice (to cook mushrooms)
    1 cup heavy cream
    1 cup Sauce Hollandaise (page 81)
    ¼ cup Madeira

Flatten the filets with the side of a heavy knife or cleaver and coat them with the mousse. Fold along the width and place in a shallow, ovenproof, oval dish. Add the wine and lemon juice and sprinkle with salt and pepper. Bring to a boil on top of the stove. Cover with aluminum foil and bake in a preheated 400-degree oven 15 minutes. Sauté the scallops quickly in a small amount butter 3 minutes; reserve the liquid. Cook the mushrooms in the lemon juice with a sprinkle of salt; reserve the liquid. Transfer the scallops and mushrooms to another pan and keep warm. To the reserved juices, add the liquid from the filets and the cream. Reduce one half and blend in the hollandaise sauce. Stir half this sauce in with the scallops and mushrooms. Place filets on a serving platter with scallops and mushrooms arranged in the center. Check the seasoning of the remaining sauce and blend in the Madeira. Pour the sauce over the filets and serve hot with Fleurons (page 285) or Riz Pilaf (page 275).

Filets de Sole Orly

[FRIED FILETS OF SOLE]   FOR 4

Step One: The batter
    2½ cups sifted white flour
    1 teaspoon cooking oil
    ½ cup beer
    1 teaspoon salt
    ½ cup lukewarm water
    2 egg whites, stiffly beaten
        Pinch cayenne pepper
        Pinch nutmeg

Mix the flour, oil, beer, salt and warm water into a soft batter; keep in a warm place 2 hours. When ready to use, add the stiffly beaten egg whites, mixing gently, then the cayenne and nutmeg.

Step Two: Preparation
>   *2 pounds sole filets, cut lengthwise into 8 pieces*
>   *½ cup lemon juice*
>   *2 tablespoons finely chopped parsley*
>   *1 tablespoon chopped chervil*
>   *Salt and ground white pepper*
>   *Cooking oil, Crisco or lard*
>   *Sauce Tomate (page 83)*

Five minutes before cooking, season the filets with a mixture of the lemon juice, parsley, chervil, salt and pepper. Dry the filets well and dip one by one into the batter and fry in a deep skillet in the hot oil. Let cook 5 minutes; they should be nicely browned and crisp. Serve on a clean white napkin (see note) together with fried parsley (see note) and lemon halves. Also serve very hot tomato sauce, to which you have added 6 tablespoons of soft sweet butter, mixed in by stirring clockwise until incorporated into the sauce. It brings a good flavor and softens.

NOTE: This is served on a white napkin for presentation, and also in order for the sole to be drained of oil. Then the filets will be dished out onto hot plates, with the sauce poured over or on the side of the plate.

Fried Parlsey: Use the curly type, separated from the stem, washed and dried by wrapping in cheesecloth. Fry in oil in a deep skillet until crisp. Drain on paper towel and sprinkle with salt.

Filets de Sole en Gougeons

[FRIED STRIPS OF SOLE WITH HERB SAUCE]   FOR 4

Step One: Sauce Aromates
>   *1 cup cider vinegar*
>   *2 tablespoons finely chopped shallots*
>   *2 teaspoons chopped tarragon*
>   *1 teaspoon crushed white peppercorns*
>   *1 leaf fresh sweet basil*
>   *Pinch rosemary*
>   *Pinch sage*
>   *Pinch thyme leaves*
>   *2 spinach leaves, chopped*
>   *½ teaspoon chervil*
>   *1 cup thick Mayonnaise (page 84)*
>   *1 teaspoon Lea & Perrins sauce*
>   *Salt to taste*
>   *1 teaspoon French mustard (Dessaux)*

Combine all ingredients, up to the mayonnaise, in a saucepan. Cook until well reduced. Cool, then blend with the mayonnaise. Strain through cheesecloth; add the Lea & Perrins sauce, salt and mustard.

Step Two
>   *2 pounds sole filets, cut into small strips*
>   *3½ inches long, ¾ inch wide*
>   *Salt and pepper*
>   *White flour (to roll filets in)*
>   *3 eggs beaten together with ½ cup oil, ½ cup milk*
>   *1 pound white bread crumbs*
>   *4 lemon halves*

Season the filets with salt and pepper. Roll in flour. Shake well so not too much adheres. Dip into the egg mixture, roll each piece in bread crumbs. Be careful that they do not stick to one another. Cook in a skillet in hot oil 3 minutes. Present on a clean white napkin in serving dish, then transfer to hot plates with the aromates sauce and lemon halves on the side.

Filets de Sole Ali Baba

[FILETS OF SOLE WITH EGGPLANT AND
MUSHROOM PURÉE]   FOR 4

>   *4 sole filets, 6 ounces each*
>   *Fish Mousse (see Filets of Sole*
>   *Cape Cod, Step One, page 127)*
>   *2 cups dry white wine*
>   *2 tablespoons lemon juice*
>   *2 cups Fish Velouté (page 66)*
>   *1 cup Sauce Hollandaise (page 81)*
>   *4 small eggplants*
>   *2 tablespoons cooking oil*
> *½ pound mushrooms*
>   *2 tablespoons finely chopped shallots*
>   *4 tablespoons sweet butter*
>   *1 teaspoon chopped garlic*
>   *1 cup tomatoes, peeled, diced*
>   *4 hard boiled egg yolks, put through a sieve*
>   *Pinch nutmeg*
>   *1 tablespoon salt*
> *½ teaspoon white pepper*
>   *Pinch thyme*

Flatten the filets with side of a heavy knife or cleaver and coat them with the mousse. Fold them along the width and place in shallow, ovenproof, oval pan. Add the wine and lemon juice. Bring to a boil on top of the stove. Cover with aluminum foil and bake in a preheated 400-degree oven 15 minutes. Drain the liquid and reduce to half. Add the fish velouté (reserving 2 tablespoons) and simmer until the sauce thickens. Blend in the hollandaise and strain through a cheesecloth. Set aside. Cut eggplants into halves lengthwise. Score the flesh deeply, being careful not to cut the skin. Pour the cooking oil over eggplants and place in a preheated 400-degree oven 15 minutes. Remove the pulp with a soupspoon, being careful not to break skin. Chop this pulp with the mushrooms. In a saucepan, cook the shallots in butter for 2 minutes, then add the garlic and the eggplant-mushroom mixture; simmer 10 minutes. Add the tomatoes, sieved egg yolks, nutmeg, salt, pepper and thyme and moisten with the 2 tablespoons of reserved velouté. Fill the eggplant shells with this mixture and place a filet on top of each. Cover with the sauce and bake uncovered in a preheated 450-degree oven 5 minutes before serving. Present the filets on a round platter arranged like an open fan. A decorated lemon, scooped out basketlike and filled with parsley leaves, is attractive placed in the center of the dish.

Filets de Sole Murat

[FILETS OF SOLE WITH VEGETABLES]   FOR 4

> *8 sole filets cut into small strips 2½ inches*
>   *long, ¾ inch wide*
>   *Salt and white pepper*
>   *White flour*
> *1 cup cooking oil*
> *6 ounces sweet butter (1½ sticks)*
> *1 medium boiled potato, diced in ½-inch cubes*
> *1 teaspoon chopped shallots*
> *2 artichoke bottoms, diced in ½-inch cubes*
> *2 tablespoons lemon juice*
> *2 tablespoons Lea & Perrins sauce*
> *1 tablespoon chopped parsley*

Salt and pepper the filets. Roll them in flour, carefully, so not too much flour adheres. In a heavy-duty skillet, put 4 tablespoons of butter and the oil. When hot, fry the filets quickly (so they will not stick together) 3 minutes. Remove from skillet and drain. Place on a round serving platter; keep warm. In another skillet, put 4 tablespoons of butter; when hot, cook the diced potatoes quickly 3 minutes; add shallots and cook 3 minutes.

Add the artichoke bottoms, sauté 2 minutes, then add the rest of the butter. Sprinkle the lemon juice over the filets, also the Lea & Perrins. Carefully arrange the potatoes and artichoke bottoms over the fish; sprinkle with chopped parsley; place under the broiler in order to serve very hot.

Filets de Sole Palais d'Orsay

[FILETS OF SOLE WITH SHRIMPS]   FOR 4

> 8 sole filets, 6 ounces each
> ¾ cup dry white wine
> ¼ cup lemon juice
>   Salt and pepper
> 1 cup Fish Velouté (page 66)
> 1 cup Sauce Hollandaise (page 81)
> 1 cup Sauce Nantua (page 69)
> ½ pound small grey shrimps or
>   small diced shrimps, cooked
> 8 slices black truffles
> 8 Fleurons (page 285)

Flatten the filets with the side of a heavy knife or cleaver; place in a shallow, ovenproof, oval dish. Add the wine and lemon juice; sprinkle with salt and pepper. Bring to a boil on top of stove. Cover with aluminum foil and cook in a preheated 400-degree oven 10 minutes. Drain the liquid and reduce to one third. Blend in the fish velouté sauce and cook 5 minutes. Divide this sauce between two saucepans. In one, blend the hollandaise sauce; in the other, the nantua sauce. Simmer the sauce with the nantua 5 minutes. Do not cook the hollandaise. Arrange the filets on a round platter, shrimps in the center. Strain the red nantua sauce over the shrimps, the yellow hollandaise mixture over the sole. Place a slice of truffle on each filet and decorate the edge of platter with fleurons.

Filets de Sole l'Horizon

[FILETS OF SOLE WITH CRAYFISH]   FOR 4

¼ pound sweet butter
2 tablespoons chopped shallots
1 teaspoon chopped parsley
8 sole filets, 6 ounces each
2 cups dry vermouth
6 tablespoons lemon juice
1 teaspoon salt
½ teaspoon ground white pepper
  Pinch thyme leaves
1 cup Sauce Hollandaise (page 81)
8 medium mushroom caps
8 medium crayfish
  Court Bouillon for Crayfish (below)
1 cup white bread crumbs

Using 6 tablespoons of butter, liberally butter a shallow ovenproof fish dish. Spread half of the shallots and parsley on the bottom. Lay the filets on them and sprinkle the rest over the fish. Pour the vermouth in and 2 tablespoons of lemon juice. Season with salt and pepper, add the thyme leaves. Bring to boil on top of stove, cover with aluminum foil and place in a preheated 400-degree oven 10 minutes. Drain the liquid and boil to reduce one-half. Add the hollandaise sauce. Strain through cheesecloth. Sauté the mushrooms in another pot with the remaining 4 tablespoons of lemon juice and 2 tablespoons of butter. Simmer the crayfish in a light court bouillon. Place the mushrooms on top of the filets, cover all with the sauce. Sprinkle on the bread crumbs and place in the broiler until brown. Reheat the crayfish in court bouillon. To present, arrange the crayfish around the platter.

Court Bouillon for Crayfish   FOR 3 CUPS

2 cups dry white wine
1 cup water
1 small onion, sliced
  Bouquet garni
1 teaspoon salt
  Pinch cayenne
¼ cup lemon juice

Place all the above ingredients into a deep skillet, simmer 10 minutes; add crayfish, simmer 5 minutes more; leave crayfish in this court bouillon to cool.

Filets de Sole Normande

[FILETS OF SOLE WITH SHRIMPS, SMELTS
AND MUSHROOMS]   FOR 4

8 sole filets, 6 ounces each
6 ounces sweet butter (1½ sticks)
  Salt and pepper
8 medium mushroom caps, fluted
2 cups dry white wine
2 tablespoons lemon juice
2 cups Fish Velouté (page 66)
1 cup heavy cream
  Pinch cayenne pepper
8 small, breaded, fried smelts
4 large shrimps, boiled, cleaned
8 heart-shaped croutons, fried in butter

Lay the sole filets in an ovenproof fish dish which has been buttered with
4 tablespoons of the butter. Salt and pepper. Place one mushroom cap on
each filet. Pour in the wine and lemon juice. Bring to a boil on top of the
stove, cover with aluminum foil and place in a preheated 400-degree oven
10 minutes. Drain the liquid, add the fish velouté, cooking until it thickens.
Stir in the cream, simmering again to thicken, stirring carefully so that it
does not stick to the bottom of the pan. Strain and add remaining butter
in small lumps, stirring slowly with a wooden spoon. Stir in a little cayenne
pepper. Pour over the filets which you have kept hot. Arrange the fried
smelts, shrimp and croutons around the serving platter and serve.

Paupiettes de Sole Cendrillon

[ROLLS OF SOLE STUFFED WITH PIKE MOUSSE
IN BAKED POTATOES]   FOR 4

4 sole filets, 6 ounces each
½ pound Fish Mousse (see Filets of Sole
  Cape Cod, Step One, page 127)
4 strips oiled wax paper to circle each rolled filet
2 cups dry white wine
1 cup Fumet (page 62)
4 large Idaho potatoes, baked
4 tablespoons sweet butter
  Salt and white pepper
4 artichoke bottoms
1 cup Mushroom Purée (see Duxelles, page 308)
½ cup heavy cream

Flatten the filets and spread fish mousse on each. Roll, tightly, so they will look like large corks. Wrap each rolled filet completely with the oiled wax paper. Place the filets, seam side down, in a deep ovenproof saucepan. Pour in the wine and fumet. Bring to a boil on top of the stove, cover with foil and cook 15 minutes in a preheated 400-degree oven. Cut off the top of each potato, reserving the top. Scoop out the pulp and mix with the butter, a pinch of salt and a pinch of pepper. Slice the artichoke bottoms and cover with the mushroom purée. Cover the bottoms of the empty potato shells with the mashed pulp. Put the artichoke bottoms with the mushroom purée on top of the mashed baked potatoes. Remove the wax paper from the paupiettes and arrange them on the potatoes. Put the liquid in which the sole has been cooking in a thick-bottomed saucepan, place on top of the stove and add the cream. Reduce to a thick consistency. Check seasoning. Pour this sauce over the potatoes topped with the paupiettes, which should then be cooked in a preheated 350-degree oven 10 minutes. Replace the potato tops you have reserved and serve each potato in a fancy, folded napkin, to be opened as a surprise dish.

TRUITE—Trout

Soufflé de Truite en Papillote Comtesse de Moucheron

[SOUFFLÉ OF TROUT]   FOR 4

Step One: To make mousse
¼ pound boneless pike or pickerel flesh
1 egg
½ cup heavy cream
¼ teaspoon salt
*   Pinch cayenne pepper*
*   Pinch nutmeg*
2 tablespoons Marc de Bourgogne (brandy from Burgundy)
½ cup white bread crumbs
2 ounces small diced black truffles which have been
*   soaked in Marc de Bourgogne for ½ hour*
⅛ pound shrimp, diced and cooked in sweet butter

Put the fish through a food chopper (fine blade), then into a mixing bowl placed on shaved ice so it will remain cold while working. Stirring vigorously with a wooden spoon, add the egg, then the cream, salt, pepper, nutmeg, brandy and bread crumbs. Blend into this pike mousse the truffles and shrimp.

Step Two
    4 brook trout, ½ pound each, boned, head on
    4 thin slices larding pork
    ¼ pound pike mousse (1 ounce for each fish)
    4 pieces oiled wax paper cut in a heart shape, 10 inches long
        and 10 inches wide or large enough to wrap each fish
    ½ cup lemon juice
    1 cup dry white Burgundy (Meursault best)
        Salt, white pepper
    1 cup Fish Velouté (page 66)
    1 cup heavy cream
    1 cup Sauce Hollandaise (page 81)

Lay 1 slice of larding pork inside each trout, then stuff trout with mousse. Place on the oiled wax paper, pour over each trout 2 tablespoons of lemon juice, ¼ cup of wine and sprinkle lightly with salt and pepper. Make a sort of bag of the papers by folding the edges to enclose the fish. Butter an ovenproof fish platter and lay the wrapped fish in this. Bake in a preheated 350-degree oven 20 minutes. Serve in the paper right on the plate, with the guest unwrapping it himself. Mix the fish velouté, heavy cream and hollandaise together and serve, warm, on the side.

TURBOT

Turbot à la Dubois

[TURBOT WITH SHELLFISH AND
DUCHESSE POTATOES]   FOR 6

Step One
    6 small tomatoes
    1 cup bread crumbs
    1 cup chopped mushrooms
    ½ cup chopped parsley
    ½ cup finely chopped boiled ham

Cut off the tops of the tomatoes and hollow out about half the pulp. Stuff with the mixture of bread crumbs, mushrooms, parsley and boiled ham. Bake in a preheated 450-degree oven 5 minutes. Set aside and keep warm.

Step Two
    24 mussels
    24 oysters
    12 bay scallops

>   2 yellow onions, sliced into rings
>   6 lemon halves

Bread the mussels, oysters and scallops and fry in deep fat. Roll the onion rings in flour and also fry in deep fat. Keep warm. Scallop the lemon halves.

Step Three
>   1 six-pound turbot (split in the center with a sharp,
>   pointed knife; carefully remove center bone)
>   4 teaspoons salt
>   ½ teaspoon ground white pepper
>   1½ cups melted sweet butter
>   ½ recipe Pommes de Terre Duchesse (page 314)
>   Parsley sprigs for garnish
>   Sauce Béarnaise (page 82)

Place the turbot on an oval, well-buttered ovenproof dish. Sprinkle on salt and pepper and cover with melted butter. Place under the broiler 10 minutes, then in a 400-degree oven 15 minutes. Squeeze the duchesse potatoes around the fish with a pastry bag with a fluted tube. Return to the broiler to allow the potatoes to brown; then arrange the tomatoes, mollusks, onion rings, lemon halves and parsley attractively around the fish and potatoes. Serve with a boat of béarnaise sauce on the side.

NOTE: You can substitute halibut for turbot, but it won't be as tasty.

Filets de Turbot à la Normande

[TURBOT FILETS IN CREAM]   FOR 4

Step One: Prepare the garnish
>   12 oysters simmered 1 minute in 2 tablespoons dry white wine (reserve
>   liquid), kept warm
>   24 mussels simmered, covered, 5 minutes in 2 tablespoons dry white wine
>   (reserve liquid), trimmed of tough membrane and kept warm
>   12 medium-sized shrimps, boiled 5 minutes or until pink, kept warm
>   12 medium mushroom caps simmered 3 minutes in a small amount of
>   lemon juice, 2 tablespoons water, pinch of salt and 2 tablespoons
>   sweet butter (reserve liquid), kept warm
>   8 tiny smelts, deep fried, kept warm
>   18 small white cooked onions (jarred)
>   8 heart-shaped croutons
>   Chopped parsley

Step Two

4 filets from one 5-pound turbot
1 cup dry white wine
1 cup Fumet (page 62)
1 tablespoon salt
1 teaspoon ground white pepper
6 ounces sweet butter (1½ sticks)
1 cup extra-heavy cream
1 tablespoon flour
1 tablespoon lemon juice

Place the filets on a flat, well-buttered oval ovenproof dish and add the wine and fumet. Sprinkle with salt and pepper and dot with half the butter. Cover with aluminum foil and bring to a boil on top of the stove, then place in a preheated 400-degree oven 20 minutes. Drain the liquid into a deep saucepan and add the cream and reserved liquids; simmer 10 minutes. Knead the rest of the butter with the flour and add to the liquid slowly to avoid lumping. Blend in lemon juice and check seasoning. Strain through a fine cheesecloth and pour over the filets, arranging around the fish the oysters, mussels, shrimps, onions and smelts. Place three mushroom caps on each filet. Complete the garnish with the croutons just before serving. Sprinkle the parsley over the mollusks and onions. Serve very hot.

NOTE: The bread croutons may spell N O R M A N D E, the letters being cut at least 2 inches high and fried in deep butter or just browned with melted butter under the broiler.

POCHOUSE—Fresh Water Fish Stew

La Pochouse Bourguignonne

[BURGUNDY FISH STEW IN WHITE WINE]   FOR 6

5 pounds your choice of lake and river fish, such as
*   yellow perch, bass, pike, carp, lake trout, bream,*
*   eel and pickerel (cut large fish in steaks, filet small ones)*
*   Salt and pepper*
1 pound lean salt pork, blanched, diced
1 pound yellow Spanish onions, sliced, not too fine
*   Sweet butter*
1 teaspoon fresh thyme or ½ teaspoon dried
2 bay leaves
2 cloves
*   Pinch nutmeg*

1 tablespoon chopped garlic
2 quarts dry white wine
2 cups Fumet (page 62)
   Bouquet garni
¾ cup white flour
¼ pound sweet butter
1 pound small white mushroom caps, cooked 3 minutes
   in 2 tablespoons each sweet butter, lemon juice and
   water, pinch of salt (reserve liquid)
1 cup heavy cream
4 egg yolks
½ cup good brandy
   Croutons
   Quenelles de Brochet (optional, page 117)

Cut the whole fish into 3-inch pieces and salt and pepper. Cook the cubes of salt pork with the onions in a little butter in a deep pot 10 minutes. Let the onions take on a light brown color. Place the fish on top of the onion-and-salt-pork mixture, adding the thyme, bay leaves, cloves, nutmeg and garlic. Pour on the wine and fumet and add the bouquet garni. Bring to a boil and simmer 20 minutes. Remove the fish, place in a casserole and keep warm. In another casserole, mix the butter with the flour to make a roux, cook 10 minutes, allowing it to get a blond color. Strain the wine-and-stock liquid along with the liquid in which you have previously cooked the mushrooms. Add the liquid slowly to the flour-butter mixture, beating with a whisk to avoid lumping. Simmer 20 minutes to make a velouté. Mix the heavy cream with the egg yolks. Blend with the velouté and bring to a simmer (but do not boil), then strain through cheesecloth. Pour this sauce over the fish, add the mushrooms and, optional, small pike quenelles (2 per person). Sprinkle the brandy and serve croutons separately.

NOTE: For the croutons, slice French bread, rub with garlic, and brown in butter.

CRUSTACÉS ET MOLLUSQUES—Shellfish

ESCARGOTS—SNAILS

Escargots Beaujolaise

[SNAILS IN RED WINE]   FOR 4

> ¼ *pound sweet butter*
> 2 *tablespoons chopped shallots*
> 1 *teaspoon chopped garlic*
> 2 *dozen canned snails*
> ¼ *cup cognac or good brandy*
> 2 *cups red Beaujolais or other good red wine*
>   *Bouquet garni*
> 1 *cup Demi-Glace (page 74)*
>   *Salt and pepper*
> 12 *small white mushroom caps*
> 4 *veal quenelles (canned), cut into 12 cubes in all*
> 8 *puff-paste crusts, 4 inches long, 2 inches wide*
>   *(baked with ready-made dough)*
>   *Chopped parsley*

In a shallow pan, with a small amount of butter, sauté the shallots 2 minutes; do not let them take on any color; add the garlic, cook 1 minute, then the snails, which have been drained; simmer 3 minutes. Add the brandy and flambé. Stir in the wine, bouquet garni and demi-glace; sprinkle on the salt and pepper. Cook, covered, 10 minutes. Sauté the mushroom caps separately on a very quick fire with a little of the butter, salt and pepper (they should be lightly browned). Now, add the quenelles and the mushrooms to the snails. Remove the bouquet garni. Add the rest of the butter, in small pieces, moving the pan clockwise so it will mix, without oiling, into the sauce; do not boil. Serve over the puff crusts on hot plates. Sprinkle finely chopped parsley. Check the seasoning by tasting often during the cooking stage.

NOTE: In the last stage, the butter should be well incorporated into the sauce: If too hot, the butter will melt and look like oil. By moving the pan and not stirring, you do not break the substance of the sauce, which should be creamy-smooth.

CRABES—CRABS

Crabe au Gratin Tahitienne

[CRAB MEAT WITH BAKED AVOCADO]   FOR 4

2 ripe avocados, halved
¼ pound sweet butter
1 pound lump crab meat
1 tablespoon chopped shallots
¼ cup sherry
1 cup heavy cream
1 tablespoon salt
⅛ teaspoon cayenne pepper
1 cup Sauce Hollandaise (page 81)
2 tablespoons Dijon mustard

Dot butter over avocados. Bake in a preheated 400-degree oven, uncovered, 10 minutes. Scoop out meat without mashing. Cover and keep warm. Reserve the shells. Place the crab lumps on an ovenproof flat dish and put into a 400-degree oven 3 minutes. Pick out any bones that show in the crab meat. Gently simmer the shallots in a saucepan with the sherry 4 minutes, add the cream and simmer 2 minutes; add the salt, cayenne, hollandaise and mustard. Mix gently; add the crab meat, being careful not to break it up. Fill the avocado shells with the crab-meat mixture, then cover with the avocado meat. Place in a shallow ovenproof serving dish. Put into a preheated 400-degree oven 5 minutes and serve.

Crabe à la Romanoff

[CRAB MEAT WITH CAVIAR]   FOR 4

1 pound lump crab meat
¼ cup Armagnac or other good brandy
¼ cup dry sherry
1 cup heavy cream
1 cup Sauce Hollandaise (page 81)
Salt to taste
½ teaspoon cayenne pepper
6 ounces fresh Beluga caviar
4 thick slices buttered toast

This should be executed at the table in a chafing dish. Place the crab meat under the broiler for 2 minutes so that the bones will come to the surface and can be removed. Bring the crab meat to the table in a chafing dish, and over the flame add the Armagnac. Ignite and flambé. Add the sherry and cream, stirring gently in order not to break the crab lumps. When almost at a boil, add the hollandaise sauce, blending to thicken the sauce. Stir in the salt and cayenne. Just before serving on toast, add the caviar, mixing well, but gently. Plates and toast should be hot.

HOMARD—LOBSTER

Homard à l'Américaine

[LOBSTER AMERICAN STYLE]   FOR 6

3 lobsters, 2½ pounds each
¼ pound sweet butter
1 tablespoon chopped tarragon
2 cups cooking oil
1 cup finely chopped onions
4 coarsely chopped garlic cloves
6 tablespoons cognac or brandy
2 cups dry white wine
2 cups Fumet (page 62)
2 tablespoons tomato paste
4 tomatoes, peeled, seeded, cut in small pieces
1 teaspoon salt
1 tablespoon freshly ground white pepper
  Bouquet garni
1 teaspoon cayenne pepper

Some are squeamish about killing a lobster with a knife, but it is not difficult. Simply place lobster on cutting board, on its back. Hold firmly with left hand to the board, and with a heavy, sharp knife, send the point deeply into area between chest (thorax) and head. If you prefer, cut deeply through area between chest and tail, or simply cut tail from body. (Using latter method, it is just as easy to work with lobster stomach down.) Either way, you will sever the spine, and the lobster will expire immediately. Any motion after that is purely reflex. Or simply cut tail from body. This also will sever the spine. Now cut lobster from head to end of tail, splitting shell casing down the front of the entire body.

Discard stomach and intestinal tract. This means everything but the long, green liver (tomalley) and the reddish roe (coral). Blend these with the butter and force through a sieve. Mix in one half of the tarragon and refrigerate until later.

Remove each tail, cut crosswise in three pieces. Remove and crack claws. Cut the body (chest section) in two lengthwise. Pour the cooking

Killing and Cutting Up a Lobster

(1) *With lobster held on its back on cutting board, pierce area between head and chest (thorax).* (2) *Or, alternatively, cut sharply and quickly downward between chest and tail.* (3) *Split chest lengthwise. Do not cut so deeply that you reach intestines.* (4) *Reserve the greenish liver (tomalley) and the reddish roe (coral). Discard stomach (nutlike sac in head) and intestine (runs along the shell from stomach through tail).* (5) *Cut tail crosswise into three pieces.* (6) *Remove claws, severing at joint.* (7) *Crack claws. Be careful to remove loose pieces of shell so they won't become part of the sauce and strangle a guest.*

oil into a deep pot, preferably one with a heavy bottom. When very hot, add the lobster pieces and sauté until reddish (about 5 minutes). Add onions, cook for 5 minutes, then the garlic and cook 2 minutes. Drain the oil. Add the brandy and flambé. Stir in the wine, fumet, tomato paste, tomatoes, salt, pepper and bouquet garni. Bring to a boiling point. Cover and place in a preheated 400-degree oven 20 minutes. Place on medium heat on top of the stove. Remove the lobster pieces, place in a serving casserole and keep warm. Let liquid reduce until thick; remove bouquet garni, then push through a sieve and stir in mixed tomalley and coral; do not boil. Allow to reach the boiling point. Check seasoning. Add the cayenne (use smaller amount if desired) and more salt if necessary. Pour over the lobster and serve hot. Sprinkle on the remaining chopped tarragon. Riz Pilaf (page 275) should accompany this dish.

Homard au Whisky

[LOBSTER IN WHISKEY SAUCE]   FOR 6

    3 lobsters, 2½ pounds each
    1 cup cooking oil
    1 cup finely chopped shallots
    1 cup finely diced carrots
    ½ cup white flour
    ½ cup Scotch
    1 quart heavy cream
       Special bouquet garni (2 celery stems tied
       together with 2 parsley sprigs and 1 white leek)
    1 teaspoon salt
    1 cup Sauce Hollandaise (page 81)
    ½ teaspoon cayenne pepper
    1 tablespoon lemon juice

Kill and split lobsters as instructed on page 143. Push the tomalley and coral through a sieve and save. Remove the tail and cut into three sections, crosswise. Cut the carcass lengthwise. Remove and crack claws. Heat oil in a deep saucepan. When very hot, add the lobster sections. Cook over high heat 5 minutes. Lower heat and add the shallots and carrots, simmer 5 minutes. Drain the oil. Sprinkle flour over the lobster. Stir. Add the whisky, cream, bouquet garni and salt. Bring to the boiling point, then place in a preheated 400-degree oven, covered, 35 minutes. Remove the lobster sections; place in a serving casserole. Reduce the cream mixture by simmering uncovered to one half its volume. Remove bouquet garni. Add the hollandaise, blend in well, but do not boil. Strain through a fine cheesecloth and add cayenne. Correct seasoning. Stir in the lemon juice and the strained tomalley and coral and pour over the lobster. (For easier handling by the diner, remove the shells before pouring in the sauce.)

Homard à la Moutarde

[LOBSTER IN MUSTARD SAUCE]   FOR 4

2 three-pound lobsters
1 cup cooking oil
1 cup chopped shallots
6 tablespoons Marc de Bourgogne or brandy
2 cups dry white wine
2 cups heavy cream
1 teaspoon salt
2 branches fresh tarragon or
   1 tablespoon dried tarragon leaves
1 cup Fish Velouté (page 66)
4 egg yolks, beaten
2 tablespoons Dijon mustard
½ teaspoon cayenne pepper
4 tablespoons sweet butter

Kill and split lobster as instructed on page 143. Push the tomalley and coral through a sieve and save. Cut the lobster tails crosswise in 3 sections, carcass lengthwise. Remove and crack the claws. Heat the oil in a deep pot. When hot, add the lobster pieces and sauté 5 minutes. Add the shallots, cook 2 minutes. Drain oil. Add 4 tablespoons of the Marc, the wine, cream, salt and tarragon. When at the boiling point, place in a preheated 400-degree oven 35 minutes, covered. Keep the lobster warm and simmer sauce from lobster pan over medium flame on top of the stove; add the fish velouté. When thick, remove from stove and blend in egg yolks, stirring with a whisk so it will not curdle. Stir in the mustard and pepper. Strain through a fine cheesecloth. Return to the top of the stove over low heat, adding butter in small lumps, stirring clockwise, gently. Check seasoning. Stir in the rest of the Marc and the strained tomalley and coral. Pour this mustard sauce over the lobster. Serve hot, encircled with Fleurons (page 285).

Homard en Couronne

[CURRIED LOBSTER MEAT]

FOR 4

½ cup finely chopped onions
¼ pound sweet butter
½ cup peeled, chopped apples
½ cup chopped celery
1 teaspoon chopped garlic
2 tablespoons curry powder
1 cup heavy cream
1 cup Sauce Béchamel (page 71)
   Salt and freshly ground white pepper to taste
1 pound lobster meat, cut in small pieces
¼ cup sweet sherry
1 recipe Riz Pilaf (page 275)

Sauté the onions in the butter 5 minutes in a saucepan; do not brown. Add the apples, celery, garlic and curry powder; sauté 5 minutes. Add the cream and béchamel sauce, salt and pepper. Place the lobster in a shallow saucepan, pour over sherry and put in a preheated 400-degree oven 5 minutes to warm. Strain the sauce over the meat through a fine strainer, forcing the vegetables through. Simmer on top of the stove, being careful not to boil. Pack a savarin mold with the rice pilaf. Unmold on a round platter and fill the center with the lobster curry. Keep warm in the oven until served.

MOULES—MUSSELS

Moules Marinière

[MUSSELS STEAMED IN WINE WITH HERBS]

FOR 4

3 quarts mussels, well cleaned
2 cups dry white wine
1 cup finely chopped shallots or onions
½ cup chopped Italian parsley
1 teaspoon ground white pepper
¼ pound sweet butter
1 cup Sauce Hollandaise (page 81)
2 tablespoons lemon juice
   No salt should be added, as the natural salt
   in the mussels is sufficient

Place the mussels in deep saucepan or skillet, pour in the wine and add the shallots, parsley, pepper and butter. Cover the pan tightly and put on a very hot burner to cook the mussels quickly. After 2 minutes, remove the lid and shake the mussels, so those on the bottom come to the top and all cook evenly. Replace lid and cook 2 minutes more. Take out mussels (but save liquid) and arrange on a flat pan, discarding any that have not opened. Separate the half shells, placing those containing the mussel kernels in a serving casserole, one on top of another. Now reduce the liquid to three quarters of its volume, then blend in the hollandaise sauce, stirring with a wire whisk. Check seasoning. Add lemon juice. To serve, ladle the mussels from the casserole into rimmed soup plates with the sauce over them.

HUÎTRES—OYSTERS

Gratin d' Huîtres Monsieur Young

[OYSTER STEW]   FOR 6

This from Walter Young, famous Chef-Steward during the delightful era of Jack Bowman: the good days of the Hotels Biltmore and Commodore and the Westchester Country Club.

1 quart shucked oysters (reserve liquor)
2 cups heavy cream
1 tablespoon salt
1 tablespoon ground white pepper
¼ teaspoon nutmeg
4 cups saltine cracker crumbs
¼ pound sweet butter

Put oysters and liquor into a skillet and bring to a boil. Remove oysters. Strain liquor through cheesecloth to catch any sand. Return liquor to skillet and add cream, salt, pepper and nutmeg; simmer 5 minutes. Butter a 1½-quart deep ovenproof dish. Spread a layer of cracker crumbs in the bottom of the dish, arrange a layer of oysters over them, then pour in 1 cup of liquid. Repeat layers, making the last layer cracker crumbs. Dot the butter over the top. Place in a preheated 400-degree oven 30 minutes.

COQUILLES—SCALLOPS

Coquilles St. Jacques aux Pommes de Terre Duchesse

[BAY SCALLOPS WITH DUCHESSE POTATOES]   FOR 4

> 1 pound bay scallops
> ½ cup chopped shallots
> 1 cup diced mushrooms
> ¾ cup dry white wine
> ¼ cup lemon juice
> 1 teaspoon salt
> 1 cup Fish Velouté (page 66)
> 1 cup Sauce Hollandaise (page 81)
>   Freshly ground white pepper, if necessary
> ½ recipe Pommes de Terre Duchesse (page 314)

Place the scallops in a shallow saucepan with the shallots, mushrooms, wine, lemon juice and salt. Cook over a very hot burner 2 minutes, stirring so each scallop will cook evenly. Remove scallops and place them on an ovenproof platter. Reduce the liquid 5 minutes. Add the fish velouté and cook 2 minutes; add the hollandaise sauce. Strain through fine cheesecloth. Check seasoning, adding pepper and more salt if necessary. Drain the scallops well, as any liquid accumulated from them greatly changes the taste of the sauce. Add the sauce and mix carefully. Place under the broiler 2 minutes.

NOTE: Before placing under broiler, the serving platter should be edged with a band of duchesse potatoes squeezed through a pastry bag with a fluted tube.

Scallop Pot Pie Boston Style   FOR 6

> 1 pound bay scallops
> ¾ cup dry white wine
>   Salt and pepper
> 6 individual pot pie dishes
> 2 cups Fish Velouté (page 66)
> 1 tablespoon Lea & Perrins sauce
> 1 tablespoon chopped parsley
> 1 teaspoon tabasco

24 small white boiled onions
24 small boiled potatoes, shaped to size of onions
6 hard boiled eggs, quartered
24 small mushroom caps, cooked lightly in lemon juice
2 pounds Puff Paste (*page 284*)

Place the scallops and wine in a deep saucepan and sprinkle in the salt and pepper. Bring to a slight boil. Distribute the scallops in the individual pot pie dishes and keep warm. Simmer the liquid, adding the fish velouté; reduce to half its volume. Add the Lea & Perrins sauce and parsley. Check seasoning. Strain through a fine cheesecloth. Stir in tabasco. Add equal amounts of potatoes, onions, eggs and mushrooms to the pot pie dishes. Fill with sauce and partially cool. Roll the puff pastry dough out to ½-inch thickness and cut 6 round pieces; cover the pot pie dishes. Put them on a flat pastry pan and into a preheated 400-degree oven 15 minutes, or until pastry is brown. Serve immediately.

6

VOLAILLE—Poultry

VOLAILLE—Chicken

The first thing that crosses my mind when I think of chicken is one of my early jobs as a full-fledged chef in Paris. The owner of the restaurant was a renowned penny-pincher, so stingy that he would even paint a mark on the bottles of the cheap, raw cooking wine he supplied so he knew exactly how much was used (an unheard of thing in any professional French kitchen). When he asked me to demonstrate how far I could stretch food, and still make it delicious, it was a dubious but necessary challenge. After I had made the customers happy with a chicken hash made with just the skins of the chickens,* I had also become a staunch friend and admirer of the owner (he removed the marks from the wine bottles).

Although you can't get quite as much from a chicken as you can from a pig, it is an extremely versatile bird. However, as the modern cook turns up his nose at such French delicacies as poached cock's combs, stewed heads and feet (and probably never sees them in a market anyway), it is to the point to reluctantly offer recipes for just the chicken itself, and not its by-products. Even so, the repertoire is large.

When buying a chicken make an all-out effort to get it fresh. It is worth the trouble. Push the chicken's breastbone; if it is pliable and flexible, the bird is young and should be tender. If I am going to poach, boil or braise a bird, I try to get one that isn't overly fat, for *too* much fat can mean that the meat won't be of the best quality. Also, have your butcher pull the sinews from chicken drumsticks (if

* See a chicken hash in this chapter that would cause my old boss to commit suicide.

Château de Faulin, Burgundy

he won't, or doesn't know how, it is time to change butchers); this makes them nearly as tasty as the thighs.

If you are going to prepare a chicken casserole, first brown the whole trussed bird, breast down in foaming hot butter, turning carefully with two wooden forks or spoons so you don't break the flesh, and evenly brown the whole bird. This prevents the flesh from later pulling or shrinking from the bones and reducing juiciness.

I rate the culinary talent of a restaurant (or home) by the way it cooks and serves chicken. Supposedly a simple dish, it is one that is seldom cooked properly. I find it strange that few do well with what I place high on the list of the best of all foods. Probably because chickens are so reasonable in price, too many of us treat them as ordinary when they (and all poultry) are truly extraordinary. Avoid the restaurant that offers a stringy, dry chicken, or one that doesn't carve and serve it with proper respect. What is better than a young chicken, rubbed with sweet butter, hot off a spit, tender, moist, delicious? And how difficult to find!

I classify chickens in five distinct categories:

Chickens of 1 pound: Poussins (Squab Chickens)
Chickens of 2 or 3 pounds: Poulets (Broilers)
Chickens of 4 or 5 pounds: Poulardes (Roasters)
Chickens of 5 pounds and over: Chapons (Capons or Caponettes)
Fowls or stewing chickens: Poules. These are old chickens that have outlived their egg- or chick-producing ability and make by far the richest and tastiest broth. Properly trussed, simmered with celery (leaves too), white onions, carrots and a bay leaf, they produce a glorious aromatic stock. When slow-cooked until tender, their flesh can be used for chicken pies and many other dishes that benefit from rich sauces created from the stock in which the fowl simmered.

When planning a special dinner or entertainment, do as I do: give the first thought to poultry—the simple key to elegant dining.

POUSSINS—SQUAB CHICKENS

Squab chickens are at their best cooked in a casserole, broiled or boned and stuffed. By increasing cooking times, broilers can also be cooked with these recipes.

Poussins Grillés à la Diable

[SQUAB CHICKENS BROILED WITH MUSTARD]

> *1 squab chicken for each person*
> *Cooking oil*
> *Salt and white pepper to taste*
> *1 teaspoon Dijon mustard per bird*
> *1 tablespoon white bread crumbs per bird*
> *Sauce Diable (page 76)*

Split the bird down the back, cut off spinal bone and flatten the bird with a cleaver. Brush oil over each chicken and sprinkle with salt and pepper. Fix tightly between a double grill and then place 6 to 8 inches above the embers of a charcoal fire, 2 minutes on each side. Remove, spread mustard over each bird and cover with bread crumbs. Replace in grill, again over charcoal fire, 10 minutes each side. (Can be cooked in a 400-degree oven if watched carefully.) Serve with sauce diable on the side and garnish the serving platter with watercress. Gaufrette Potatoes (page 315, Note) go well with this dish.

Poussins Grillés à l'Américaine

[SQUAB CHICKENS BROILED WITH VEGETABLE GARNISH]

> *1 squab chicken for each person*
> *Cooking oil*
> *Salt, white pepper and paprika*
> *1 strip crisp bacon per bird*
> *1 whole tomato, broiled (with butter), for each serving*
> *1 teaspoon Beurre Maître d'Hôtel (page 88) per bird*
> *Julienne Potatoes (page 315, Note)*
> *1 bunch watercress on each end of serving platter*

Split the bird down the back, cut off spinal bone and flatten bird with cleaver. Rub with oil and sprinkle with salt, pepper and paprika. Place tightly between a double grill, then 6 to 8 inches above glowing charcoal embers. Allowing 5 minutes on each side, turn for 20 minutes until well browned and crisp. Garnish the birds with the bacon, tomato, maître d'hôtel butter, Julienne potatoes and watercress.

Poussins en Casserole Polonaise

[CASSEROLE-ROASTED SQUAB CHICKENS WITH
BREAD CRUMBS]   FOR 4

> ¼ pound sweet butter
> 4 squab chickens trussed with fine twine
>   Salt and white pepper
> ½ teaspoon dry thyme leaves
> 2 hard boiled eggs, finely chopped
> ½ cup white bread crumbs
> 1 tablespoon lemon juice
> 1 tablespoon chopped parsley

Put half of the butter in an earthenware ovenproof casserole on top of
the stove. When the butter is foaming, salt and pepper the chickens and
cook 5 minutes, turning once so each side will start cooking. Sprinkle with
the thyme leaves. Place in a preheated 450-degree oven, uncovered, 20
minutes, basting often. Pour off the grease and remove the twine. Sprinkle
chopped eggs over the birds. Melt the remaining butter and sauté the
bread crumbs in it until golden; spoon evenly over birds. Sprinkle with
lemon juice and parsley and serve the birds very hot. Each guest carves
his own poussin.

Poussins Farcis Ménagère

[STUFFED BONED SQUAB CHICKENS]   FOR 4

> 4 squab chickens (have butcher bone birds, cutting
>   down the back without slitting the remaining skin)
> ¼ pound sweet butter
> 1 tablespoon cooking oil
> 6 ounces chicken livers
> 1 tablespoon chopped onions
> ½ cup white bread crumbs
> ½ teaspoon thyme leaves
>   Pinch nutmeg
> 1 tablespoon chopped boiled ham
> 1 egg
>   Salt and white pepper to taste
> 4 thin slices larding pork, 4 inches square
> ¼ cup cognac
> ½ cup Demi-Glace (page 74)
> 1 teaspoon Madeira
> 1 teaspoon chopped parsley

Heat the oil with a third of the butter in a saucepan on medium heat. Simmer livers 2 minutes; add onions, cook 3 minutes. Cool; put through a meat grinder with the coarse blade. Melt a second third of the butter in a saucepan. Mix the bread crumbs, thyme, nutmeg and ham well; simmer in hot butter 2 minutes, stir in egg and add salt and pepper. Blend well. Cool before stuffing the bird. Spread birds out, spoon equal amounts of stuffing on each bird. Re-form birds to resemble original shape and sew together with a trussing needle. Wrap 1 slice of larding pork around each poussin; tie with twine. Melt the remaining butter in a deep casserole. When foaming, put in the birds and cook on top of the stove on high fire 2 minutes on each side. Cover the pot and place in a preheated 400-degree oven 30 minutes. Remove the larding pork and brown birds 10 minutes, 5 minutes on each side, without the cover. Remove the birds and keep warm. Pour off the fat and add the cognac and demi-glace; simmer 5 minutes. Stir in the Madeira. Remove the stitching from the birds and place them in a deep serving dish or platter; strain the sauce over, sprinkle with parsley and serve. Wild rice goes well with the dish.

POULETS—BROILERS

This size chicken is at its best roasted or sautéed. To sauté, divide the chicken into pieces: 2 drumsticks, 2 second joints, 2 breasts. The carcass pieces are cooked with the rest (for the cook to taste), but never served. Drumsticks are on the serving platter but seldom offered to guests unless solicited. There are many classic recipes for chicken sautés. Each French province has its own recipe, based on its agricultural and natural products, such as truffles in the Périgord. With today's transportation, however, it is a simple (albeit expensive) matter to have the world's products—poultry, fish, shellfish, meat—flown to your door.

Chickens from Bresse, arriving from Louhans in Paris in early morning, are loaded on a jet at Orly and delivered to New York the same evening, or to O'Hare in Chicago or to Montreal. These are available in a few specialty shops in each of these cities. So it is fitting to offer recipes of French specialties, many of these my own.

Poulet Sauté Grand Siècle

[SAUTÉED CHICKEN WITH AVOCADOS AND FOIE GRAS]   FOR 4

> 6 tablespoons sweet butter
> 1 two- to three-pound chicken, cut in 6 pieces
>   Flour
>   Salt and black pepper
> 2 tablespoons Fine Champagne or cognac
> 2 tablespoons Madeira
> ½ cup Demi-Glace (page 74)
> 2 avocados, halved lengthwise, pits removed
> 1 ounce chopped truffles
> 4 slices foie gras, size of a silver dollar
> 4 very thin slices truffles
> ½ teaspoon salt

Melt 4 tablespoons of butter in a thick-bottomed saucepan. Dredge the chicken pieces in the flour, salt and pepper. When the butter foams, sauté the chicken 2 minutes on each side, turning for 10 minutes. Cover and simmer 15 minutes. Remove the chicken to a serving platter and keep warm. Drain the grease from the saucepan and add the Fine Champagne, Madeira and demi-glace; simmer 10 minutes. Bake the avocados in a preheated 400-degree oven, uncovered, 10 minutes. Scoop out the flesh, mash with a fork and blend in the chopped truffles, remaining butter and ½ teaspoon salt. Put the mashed pulp back into the shells, place a slice of foie gras on top of each and put under the broiler 2 minutes. Strain the sauce over the chicken. Decorate each avocado with a slice of truffle and alternate with 4 heart-shaped croutons (fried crisp in butter) around the chicken.

Poulet Sauté Grande Canarie

[SAUTÉED CHICKEN WITH BANANAS]   FOR 4

2 tablespoons cooking oil
6 tablespoons sweet butter
1 three-pound chicken, cut in 6 pieces
   Flour, salt, white pepper and paprika
1 tablespoon chopped shallots
2 tablespoons Spanish brandy
6 tablespoons Madeira
1 tablespoon Demi-Glace (page 74)
2 tablespoons Sauce Velouté (page 66)
1 cup heavy cream
4 bananas halved lengthwise

Heat the cooking oil with half the butter in a thick-bottomed saucepan. When the butter foams, put in the chicken pieces, which have been dredged in flour and seasoned with salt, pepper and paprika. Brown lightly on all sides 10 minutes. Add the shallots and simmer 3 minutes; cover and simmer 20 minutes. Drain grease. Add brandy and flambé. After the flames die, add the Madeira, demi-glace, velouté and cream. Simmer 20 minutes. Remove chicken to an ovenproof serving casserole, strain the sauce over and simmer 5 minutes before serving. Dredge bananas in flour and sauté in the remaining butter. Place on each guest's plate before serving the chicken. I like a salad of hearts of palm on the side.

Poulet Sauté Louisianne

[FRIED CHICKEN LOUISIANA STYLE]   FOR 4

1 three-pound chicken, cut in 6 pieces
Flour (for dredging)
Salt and white pepper
1 cup Anglaise (page 1)
1 cup white bread crumbs
4 tablespoons sweet butter
¼ cup cooking oil
½ cup white flour
1 cup heavy cream
¼ cup applejack
1 cup Sauce Velouté (page 66)
8 slices broiled bacon

Dredge the chicken in flour, season with salt and pepper, dip in the anglaise and roll in bread crumbs. Fry in a deep pan in butter and oil for 10 minutes, turning to cook both sides. Remove and place in a saucepan, uncovered, in a preheated 350-degree oven 30 minutes. Brown the ½ cup flour in a flat pan in a preheated 400-degree oven 20 minutes, stirring often, until it becomes just light brown. Or brown in a very heavy pan over a low fire, stirring frequently. Remove from the oven, cool 5 minutes and place in a saucepan. Mixing constantly, slowly add the cream, applejack and velouté; simmer 15 minutes. Check seasoning. Arrange the chicken on a warm serving platter. Garnish with bacon. Reduce the sauce to 1 cup, strain and serve in boat for each guest to spoon over the chicken. Corn Fritters (page 300) usually accompany this dish.

Poulet Sauté au Vinaigre

[SAUTÉED CHICKEN IN PIQUANT SAUCE]   FOR 4

4 tablespoons sweet butter
¼ cup cooking oil
1 three-pound chicken, cut in 6 pieces
Salt and white pepper
24 whole shallots
2 tablespoons cognac
¼ cup cider vinegar
¼ cup port
1 cup Demi-Glace (page 74)
Bouquet garni
1 tablespoon chopped fresh tarragon

Heat the cooking oil with the butter in a saucepan. When the butter foams, put in the chicken pieces and sprinkle with salt and pepper. Cook 10 minutes on a brisk fire, turning each piece several times. Add the shallots and simmer 10 minutes on a mild fire. Drain grease, add cognac and flambé. After the flames die, stir in the vinegar, port and demi-glace; add the bouquet garni. Cover and simmer 30 minutes. Remove the bouquet garni and sprinkle on the tarragon. Serve over round or heart-shaped croutons.

Poulet Sauté Riviera

[CHICKEN SAUTÉED WITH SUMMER VEGETABLES]   FOR 4

> ¼ cup olive oil
> 4 tablespoons sweet butter
> ½ cup sliced onions
> 1 cup diced zucchini
> ½ cup sliced green pepper, seeded
> 12 pitted green olives
> 1 cup skinned, seeded, finely chopped tomatoes
> 1 tablespoon finely diced red pimentos (fresh or canned)
> 2 cloves garlic, chopped
> 1 tablespoon diced white celery
> ½ teaspoon dry thyme leaves
> 1 tablespoon coarsely chopped parsley
> 1 bay leaf
> ½ teaspoon sweet basil
> ½ teaspoon dry rosemary
>   Salt and white pepper to taste
> 6 tablespoons dry white wine
> 1 three-pound chicken, cut in 6 pieces

Heat the oil with the butter in a deep ovenproof saucepan. When the butter foams, add all ingredients except the wine and chicken. Simmer 30 minutes, uncovered. Add the wine and arrange the chicken on the stewed vegetables. Bring to a boil, cover with aluminum foil *and* a lid. Place in a preheated 350-degree oven 65 minutes or until chicken is tender.

Poulet Sauté à la Crème Charolaise

[CHICKEN SAUTÉED IN CREAM AND WINE]   FOR 4

> 6 tablespoons sweet butter
> 1 three-pound chicken, cut in 6 pieces
>   Salt to taste
> 1 tablespoon white flour
>   Bouquet garni
> ¾ cup dry white wine
> 1 cup Chicken Broth (page 62)
> 1 cup heavy cream
> 2 egg yolks
> 1 teaspoon lemon juice
>   Pinch cayenne pepper

Melt the butter in a skillet; when foaming, add chicken and cook 15 minutes over a mild fire, turning often so it will not take on color. Sprinkle with salt and flour, cover and cook 5 minutes, turning the chicken several times. Add the bouquet garni, wine and broth, and cook, covered, 20 minutes or until chicken is tender. Remove the chicken to an ovenproof serving casserole. Add the cream to the sauce and cook 15 minutes. Beat the egg yolks with a wire whisk, adding to them 1 cup of the sauce; stir this into the sauce, with the lemon juice and cayenne. Strain over the chicken and bring to the boiling point, but do not boil, as the sauce will curdle. Riz Pilaf (page 275) goes well with this.

Coq au Vin Antoine   FOR 4

This dish I made often (in fact, first learned it) at the famed Hôtel du Palais d'Orsay, built atop the Paris-Orléans railroad station early in the century during a world's fair. I recall that our main kitchen was on the seventh floor, causing the head chef, Monsieur Étienne, to point out frequently that the art of cooking was indeed held on a high plane in *his* place. In most restaurants and hotels, kitchens were on the lower levels. Our main dining room was on the third floor, and I remember every dish being a masterpiece. An all-time favorite was this recipe, which I have worked with and even improved over the years.

> ¼ pound salt pork, diced, blanched 2 minutes
> 4 tablespoons sweet butter

　　1 *three-pound chicken, cut in 6 pieces*
　　　Salt and black pepper
　　　Flour
12 *small white onions*
12 *white medium mushroom caps*
　　1 *teaspoon chopped garlic*
　　2 *cups good red Burgundy (Pommard,*
　　　Chambertin, Nuits St. George)
　　1 *cup Demi-Glace (page 74)*
　　　Bouquet garni
　　2 *tablespoons Marc de Bourgogne or cognac*
　　1 *tablespoon chopped parsley*

Try out (extract grease from) the salt pork in a deep saucepan over a medium-hot fire for about 3 minutes; remove the salt pork and reserve. Add the butter to the pan and, when foaming, add salted, peppered, floured chicken pieces. Cook over a medium-hot fire 10 minutes, turning several times. Add the onions and cook 5 minutes; add mushrooms and cook 5 minutes; add garlic and cook 2 minutes. Drain off the fat and add the reserved salt pork. Cover and simmer 15 minutes. Add the wine, demi-glace and bouquet garni. Cook, covered, 20 minutes or until the chicken is tender. Remove the bouquet garni and place the chicken in a serving casserole. Let the sauce cook, uncovered, 5 minutes. Pour the Marc over the chicken, flambé and stir in sauce. Simmer 3 minutes before serving. Sprinkle with parsley. Serve with heart-shaped croutons and Gnocchi à la Parisienne (page 272).

Côtelettes de Poulet Alsacienne

[CHICKEN CUTLETS STUFFED WITH FOIE GRAS]　　　　FOR 4

　　4 *chicken breasts from two 3- to 4-pound*
　　　birds, boned, skinned, tendons removed
　　4 *slices foie gras, ⅛ inch thick*
　　　Salt and pepper to taste
　　　White flour
½ *cup Anglaise (page 1)*
½ *cup white bread crumbs*
½ *cup clarified butter*
　1 *cup Sauce Périgourdine (page 78)*
¼ *cup Madeira*

Flatten breasts with the side of a heavy knife or cleaver, like thin veal cutlets. Place 1 slice of foie gras on each breast, sprinkle with salt and pepper and fold the breast over the foie gras, enclosing it. Dredge in flour, then dip in anglaise and roll in bread crumbs. Melt the butter in a saucepan; when foaming, put well-sealed cutlets to cook over high heat 5 minutes on each side. Place in a preheated 400-degree oven 15 minutes or until tender. Blend the périgourdine sauce with the Madeira and heat; serve on the side with Nouilles à l'Alsacienne (page 270).

Côtelettes de Poulet à la Russe

[CHICKEN CUTLETS WITH SOUR CREAM]   FOR 4

> 4 chicken breasts from two 3- to 4-pound birds, boned, skinned
> 4 tablespoons sweet butter
>   Salt to taste
> ½ teaspoon cayenne pepper
> 2 tablespoons heavy cream
> ½ cup white bread crumbs
> ½ cup white flour
> ½ cup clarified butter (should be clear as oil)
> ¼ cup vodka
> 1 cup sour cream
> ½ cup Sauce Velouté (page 66)

Chop the chicken very fine, removing the cords and tendons. Add 4 tablespoons of butter to the chicken meat and the cayenne, salt, cream and bread crumbs, gradually blending into a paste. Divide this mixture into four equal parts, shaping into cutlets. Dredge with flour. Heat the clarified butter in a saucepan until foaming. Sauté cutlets 3 minutes on each side, or until brown. Place, uncovered, in a preheated 400-degree oven 10 minutes. Transfer the cutlets to a warm serving platter. Drain grease, add vodka, then blend in sour cream and velouté; simmer 3 minutes. Strain through cheesecloth over cutlets. Serve with Champignons au Gratin Dauphinoise (page 308).

Suprême de Volaille Véronique

[BREAST OF CHICKEN WITH WHITE GRAPES]   FOR 4

A half-breast of chicken, boned and with the skin and tendons removed, is called a suprême. One suprême is usually ample for each person. For this recipe use two 3- to 4-pound chickens, yielding 4 suprêmes.

> 6 tablespoons sweet butter
> 4 chicken suprêmes

½ cup white flour
  Salt and white pepper
¼ cup Madeira
 1 cup Demi-Glace (page 74)
 1 cup seedless white grapes, peeled
 1 teaspoon currant jelly
 4 croutons, ⅛ inch thick, fried in butter

Melt butter in saucepan. When foaming, put in breasts, dredged in flour, salted and peppered. Cook on high heat 5 minutes on each side; cover and cook on a medium fire 15 minutes or until tender. Drain grease, and add the Madeira and demi-glace; cook 5 minutes. Uncover and add grapes; cook 3 minutes. Place the breasts on croutons on warm plates. Stir the currant jelly in the sauce. Pour the grapes and sauce over the breasts. Wild rice goes well with these sauced suprêmes.

POULARDES—ROASTERS

Ballottines de Volaille à la Milanaise

[STUFFED CHICKEN LEGS WITH RICE]   FOR 4

This ballottine is the leg of the chicken from which you (or your butcher) have taken the bone from the second joint. Flatten that flesh with a cleaver and stuff (or coat) it with forcemeat. Close the flesh by overlapping, tie it with a piece of twine and wrap it snugly with a thin slice of larding pork (fat back). This stuffed leg is also called jambonneau, taking the shape of a tiny ham. There are other such recipes, named for the shape, garnish or for the way it is cooked. For instance, this same recipe can be made with veal cutlets and is then called Alouettes sans Têtes (Headless Larks).

Step One: Boning the leg
Remove the legs from two 4-pound chickens (large legs). Many markets sell just the legs or chicken in parts. Remove the second-joint bones with a sharp knife. Pound the meat of the second joint flat.

Step Two: Stuffing for 4 Ballottines
 ¼ pound veal loin
 ¼ pound pork loin
 ⅛ pound boiled ham
 6 tablespoons sweet butter
 1 tablespoon finely chopped shallots
 ½ teaspoon Épices Parisienne (page 2)
  Salt and white pepper to taste
 2 tablespoons cognac
 2 tablespoons Madeira
 2 tablespoons white bread crumbs
 1 egg
 2 teaspoons peeled, chopped truffles (reserve
  peelings and juice from can)
 4 thin slices larding pork

Put veal, pork and ham through fine blade of meat chopper. Melt the butter in a saucepan; when foaming, add shallots and cook 3 minutes. Take off fire and add ground meat, spices, salt, pepper, cognac and Madeira; mix well. Blend in bread crumbs, egg and truffles. Layer the boned, flattened thighs with this stuffing (forcemeat). Tie with twine. Wrap with larding pork. Place in the refrigerator to become firm, 2 or 3 hours, until you are ready to cook them.

Step Three: Cooking
>   *4 tablespoons sweet butter*
>   *½ cup cooking oil*
>   *½ cup sliced onions*
>   *½ cup sliced carrots*
>   *1 clove garlic, crushed*
>   *2 tablespoons cognac*
>   *½ cup dry white wine*
>   *2 cups Demi-Glace (page 74)*
>   *Salt and white pepper to taste*
>   *Bouquet garni*
>   *1 tomato, skinned, seeded, finely diced*
>   *1 tablespoon of trimmings and juice*
>   *reserved from truffles in Step Two*
>   *4 cups Risotto à la Milanaise (page 278)*
>   *Grated Parmesan cheese*

Heat the oil and butter in a saucepan. When foaming, add the onions and carrots and cook 3 minutes, stirring occasionally. Add the garlic and cook 2 minutes. Place the ballottines on top of the vegetables and cook 5 minutes, turning the ballottines every minute. Add the cognac, wine, demi-glace, salt, pepper, bouquet garni, tomato and truffle trimmings. Bring to a boil on top of the stove, cover with a lid and place in a preheated 350-degree oven 1 hour or until tender. Take the ballottines from the pot, remove the larding pork and twine and keep warm. Strain the sauce through a fine wire strainer, forcing the vegetables through with a wooden spoon. Reduce this sauce 5 minutes over medium heat. Check seasoning. Skim fat from top. Stir in 1 tablespoon of truffle juice. Place the cooked rice milanaise in a serving casserole and arrange the ballottines on top of the rice. Cover with the sauce. Serve grated Parmesan cheese separately.

Arroz con Pollo à la Mexicaine

[CHICKEN AND RICE MEXICAN STYLE]   FOR 4 OR 6

> ½ cup cooking oil
> 4 tablespoons sweet butter
> 1 five-pound chicken, cut in 8 pieces,
>   4 from breasts, 4 from legs
>   Salt
> 1 cup sliced onions
> 1 cup sliced green peppers
> 1 tablespoon chopped garlic
> ½ cup diced white celery
> 1½ teaspoons powdered saffron
> 2 tomatoes, skinned, seeded, diced
> ¾ cup dry white wine
> 1 quart Chicken Broth (page 62)
> ½ teaspoon cayenne pepper
> 1 tablespoon salt
> 2 tablespoons red pimentos (canned or fresh)
>   Bouquet garni
> 1½ cups rice
>   Grated Parmesan cheese

Heat the oil and butter in a skillet or casserole. When foaming, put in the salted chicken pieces. Sauté slowly 10 minutes, turning pieces often; do not let them take on color. Add onions and green peppers, cook slowly 10 minutes. Add the garlic, cook 2 minutes; add celery and saffron, simmer 5 minutes. Add the tomatoes, wine, chicken broth, cayenne, 1 tablespoon of salt, pimentos and bouquet garni. Bring to a boil, cover with a lid and cook 35 minutes. Add the rice and stire until boiling again. Cover with aluminum foil *and* a lid. Place in a preheated 350-degree oven 20 minutes or until chicken and rice are tender. Remove bouquet garni and stir, mixing well until smooth. Serve as it comes out of the oven with Parmesan on the side.

Arroz con Pollo à la Péruvienne

[CHICKEN PERUVIAN STYLE]   FOR 4 OR 6

> ½ cup cooking oil
> ¼ pound lean salt pork cut in 1-inch cubes, blanched 5 minutes
> 4 legs from two 5-pound chickens; separate second joints and drumsticks and divide second joints lengthwise, making 8 pieces
> 1 cup sliced onions

1 cup sliced green peppers
½ cup fresh sliced red pimentos
1 tablespoon chopped garlic
½ tablespoon diced white celery
2 tomatoes, skinned, seeded, diced
1 tablespoon salt
½ teaspoon cayenne pepper
1 teaspoon powdered saffron
½ cup dry white wine
1 quart Chicken Broth (page 62)
Bouquet garni
12 chorizos (Spanish sausages)
1½ cups rice
12 large oysters, shucked
12 gambas (Spanish shrimps) or large shrimps
Grated Parmesan cheese

Heat the oil and cook the salt pork in a skillet or casserole 3 minutes. Place the chicken parts in a pot and sauté slowly 10 minutes, turning often to cook on all sides; do not brown. Add the onions, green peppers and pimentos and simmer 10 minutes, stirring often. Add the garlic, cook 2 minutes; add the celery, tomatoes, salt, cayenne, saffron, wine, chicken stock and bouquet garni; bring to a boil, cover and simmer 20 minutes. Brown the chorizos under the broiler 3 minutes on each side. Add the chorizos, rice, oysters and shrimps to the chicken. Bring to a boil, cover with aluminum foil *and* lid. Place in a preheated 400-degree oven 20 minutes. Remove the bouquet garni. Serve cheese separately.

Chicken Fricassee with Rice   FOR 6

6 ounces sweet butter (1½ sticks)
1 five-pound chicken, cut in 8 pieces, 4 from breasts, 4 from legs
1 cup finely chopped onions
Salt and white pepper to taste
12 small mushroom heads (reserve trimmings and stems)
⅓ cup flour
2 cups Chicken Broth (page 62)
Bouquet garni
1 cup white rice
1 tablespoon lemon juice
12 small white onions, boiled
1 cup heavy cream
4 egg yolks
Chopped parsley

Melt half the butter in a skillet. Sauté chicken over medium heat for 15 minutes, turning often so it will cook evenly. Add the chopped onions and sprinkle with salt, pepper and mushroom trimmings; cook 10 minutes. Sprinkle with flour and mix thoroughly. Cover and cook 15 minutes. Add the chicken broth, bouquet garni and rice. Bring to a boil, cover with aluminum foil *and* a lid. Place in a preheated 350-degree oven 25 minutes or until rice and chicken are tender. Simmer the mushrooms in the lemon juice and half of the remaining butter 3 minutes; set aside. Sauté onions in the other half of the remaining butter; set aside. Blend the cream with the egg yolks and, off heat, add slowly to the chicken and rice. Arrange the mushrooms and onions around the chicken and rice in a serving casserole. Sprinkle with parsley and serve very hot.

Volaille Hachée Blind Brook

[CHICKEN HASH]   FOR 4

Step One: To prepare the breast of chicken
    1 quart water
    ¾ cup dry white wine
        Bouquet garni
    1 teaspoon salt
    1 large onion stuck with 2 cloves
    1 whole large chicken breast

Put all ingredients in a pot, cover and simmer 40 minutes. Remove skin and bones and dice the chicken. Save the broth, straining into a container and storing it for other uses.

Step Two: Hash
    2 cups heavy cream
        Boiled chicken breast, diced
        Salt to taste
        Pinch cayenne pepper
        Pinch nutmeg
    4 tablespoons sweet butter
    1 egg yolk
    2 tablespoons dry sherry

Bring the cream to a boil and add diced chicken, salt, pepper and nutmeg. Boil 5 minutes. Knead butter and egg yolk together with a fork. Add to the chicken and cream, stirring in slowly off heat so it will incorporate without lumping. Stir in the sherry at the last moment and heat without boiling until the hash thickens. Serve on dry toast or in patty shells. This recipe is also used for Oeufs Pochés Encore (page 99).

CHAPONS—CAPONS

Chapon Sauté à la Crème

[CAPON SAUTÉED IN CREAM]   FOR 4

It is a historic fact that Prime Minister Lloyd George and President Raymond Poincaré were bitter enemies during the Peace Conference that followed the First World War. I like to think I brought them together at the dinner table when, to their mutual delight, I prepared this simple dish that is a favorite in Poincaré's native Lorraine. With it, I served plain egg noodles and some heart-shaped croutons, well browned under the broiler. A white Moselle was poured —as I remember, Berncasteler and Piesporter, mellow and nicely colored.

¼ pound sweet butter
1 five-pound capon, cut in 6 pieces,
* 2 from breasts, 4 from legs*
* Salt and white pepper to taste*
2 tablespoons white flour
½ cup dry white wine
1 cup Chicken Broth (page 62)
* Bouquet garni*
1 cup heavy cream
4 egg yolks
1 tablespoon lemon juice

Melt the butter in a skillet. When it is foaming, sauté the capon pieces, turning often so they will not brown. Sprinkle with salt and pepper and cook over medium heat 25 minutes. Sprinkle with flour and cook, covered, 10 minutes. Stir in the wine and broth, add the bouquet garni, cover and cook slowly 25 minutes or until tender. Place the capon in a serving dish. Blend the cream and egg yolks well. Stir slowly into cooking pan, off heat to avoid curdling. Stir in the lemon juice and strain the cream sauce through fine cheesecloth. Bring this sauce almost to a boil. Remove from heat, stir well. It should be just thick enough to coat the capon. Spoon it over the pieces of bird and serve. This dish goes well with Riz Pilaf (page 275).

Chapon Poché, Sauce Suprême

[POACHED CAPON WITH CREAM SAUCE]   FOR 6

Step One: Cooking the capon
        3 quarts cold water
        2 cups dry white wine
        1 large onion stuck with 3 cloves
        2 large carrots
        2 cloves garlic, unpeeled
        1 stalk celery
        1 sprig parsley
        1 bay leaf
        ½ teaspoon dry thyme
        2 tablespoons salt
        10 white peppercorns
        1 five-pound capon, needle-trussed with twine
            (reserve wing tips and giblets)

Put the water and wine in a deep pot and add the onion, carrots, garlic, celery, parsley, bay leaf, thyme, salt, peppercorns, wing tips and giblets of the bird. Bring to a boil. Simmer 45 minutes, covered. Put capon in and cook 1½ hours, covered, or until tender.

Step Two: Sauce Suprême
        ¼ pound sweet butter
        ½ cup white flour
        1 quart chicken broth (from cooking the capon)
        1 cup heavy cream mixed with 2 egg yolks

Melt the butter in a skillet. Blend in flour and cook on a mild flame 10 minutes; do not let it take on color. Cool 5 minutes. Slowly add 1 quart of the strained chicken broth, stirring all the while with a wire whisk; simmer 15 minutes. Take off fire, stir in the cream-egg mixture. Check seasoning. Strain through a fine cheesecloth. Carve capon breast into 4 pieces, the legs into 4. Remove skin, arrange on serving platter and cover with sauce suprême. Riz Pilaf (page 275) is an excellent accompaniment.

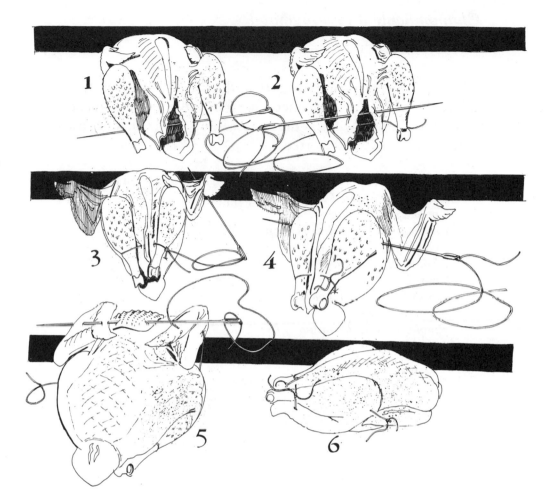

Trussing a Chicken

(1) *Run threaded trussing needle through bottom section of chicken,* under legs. (2) *Bring needle back over one leg, through breastbone tip, over other leg.* (3) *Tie securely.* (4) *Cut off remaining string. Rethread needle. Run needle through joining point of thigh and drumstick. Push through to same point opposite side of chicken.* (5) *Fold chicken wings under. Using same thread, run needle through one wing. Press neckskin against back of chicken. Run needle through neckskin and part of backbone, pinioning it, then through other wing. Pull string together tightly. Tie. Cut off excess cord.* (6) *Compact bird is now ready for cooking.*

Chapon Sauté à l'Estragon

[CAPON SAUTÉED WITH TARRAGON]   FOR 4

Claudette Colbert preferred this dish when she visited La Crémaillère after her performances at the Westport, Connecticut, Playhouse. She began with a dozen escargots and liked browned Parisienne potatoes with the entrée.

> *1 five-pound capon, cut in 8 pieces, 4 from breasts, 4 from legs*
> *½ cup flour, seasoned with salt and pepper*
> *¼ pound sweet butter*
> *½ cup white onions, finely chopped*
> *1 clove garlic, chopped*
> *2 branches fresh tarragon*
> *1 cup dry sherry*
> *2 cups Brown Stock (page 63)*
> *Bouquet garni*
> *1 tablespoon sweet butter*
> *8 fresh tarragon leaves*

Roll the capon pieces lightly in the seasoned flour. Melt the butter in a saucepan. When foaming, add capon on a medium fire, turning often, cooking slowly until pieces are brown. Add the onions, garlic and branches of tarragon and simmer 10 minutes. Stir in the sherry and brown stock and add the bouquet garni; bring to a boil. Cover and place in a preheated 350-degree oven for 45 minutes or until capon is fork tender. Remove the capon to a warm serving platter. Over a brisk fire, reduce the stock by half, stirring often. Strain, stir in the butter in circular strokes with a wooden spoon, then add the tarragon leaves. Pour the sauce over the capon and serve.

Chapon en Casserole Auvergnate

[BRAISED CAPON WITH SAUSAGE AND
CHESTNUT STUFFING]   FOR 6

I needed a change after the Peace Conference, so one fine day I joined my older brother, who was back from the army, and we made a slow journey home. What a pleasure it was traveling through the province of Burgundy, where wines are in every cellar, rich or poor, war or not, and where nearly every housewife is an excellent cook. At one stop our Tante Marie made her specialty, this recipe. With it she served a purée of knob celery. It was better to my taste than the capon I had prepared for the great men at the Peace Conference. When I told my aunt, she flooded the place with wine. I remember a Pommard 1911 that was a poem.

Step One: Stuffing
    ½ pound sausage meat
    ½ cup white bread crumbs
    1 egg
    ¼ cup cognac
      Salt and white pepper to taste
      Pinch nutmeg
    ½ teaspoon dry thyme leaves
    1 pound cleaned chestnuts, cooked in water
      for 10 minutes or canned au naturel
    1 five-pound capon

Mix the sausage meat with the bread crumbs and add the egg, cognac, salt, pepper, nutmeg and thyme leaves. Mix in the chestnuts, trying not to break them. Stuff the capon and sew the aperture with a trussing needle and twine. Truss the bird as for roasting.

Step Two: Cooking
    4 tablespoons sweet butter
    ¼ cup cooking oil
    1 carrot, sliced
    1 onion, sliced
    1 clove garlic
    1 bay leaf
    1 sprig parsley
    1 cup dry white wine
    1 cup Demi-Glace (page 74)
    1 cup Brown Stock (page 63)

Heat the oil and butter in a deep casserole. When foaming, add the carrots, onion and garlic and place the stuffed bird on top. Add the bay leaf and parsley and cook on a moderate flame 10 minutes, turning the capon to cook 5 minutes on each side. Add the wine, demi-glace and brown stock. Cover, bring to a boil and place in a preheated 350-degree oven 1½ hours or until tender. Take the capon from the casserole and remove the twine. Carve the breasts in 4 pieces and legs in 6 pieces (2 from second joint). Remove the stuffing and arrange in the center of a warm serving plate, encircled with capon pieces. Strain the sauce and skim the grease off the top. Check seasoning. Serve on the side.

CORNISH GAME HENS

When the Cornish game hen was introduced in the United States in 1950, I was the first restaurateur to recognize the unique serving possibilities of this succulent, easy-to-cook new bird with the large breast. Of course it can be cooked using the same recipes as for roasting, broiling or grilling squab chickens and squab pigeons. But I was impressed with this first really new food item to appear in this country in many years, and I created original recipes.

Unfortunately, the Cornish hen became a fad that vanished from the fine-food scene too quickly because inferior birds flooded the market. Some producers even offered scrawny white leghorns that were artificially plumped up in the packaging to make them resemble the big-breasted Cornish. Also, too many cooked the delicate little birds improperly and complained that they were tasteless and dry. When the supermarkets entered the scene, bringing price and quality down, the day of the Cornish's popularity among gourmets was ended.

However, there are still good Cornish hens on the market. But try them first before buying in quantity. Private markets where the butcher will skillfully bone them are the preferable places to buy them. Ideally, one Cornish hen of 1 pound or under—never more—should be served to each person (one of the reasons for its original success).

Boned, Stuffed Cornish Game Hens Crémaillère   FOR 4

Step One: Stuffing
    6 tablespoons sweet butter
    1 tablespoon chopped shallots
    1 cup chopped white mushrooms
    6 ounces lean pork loin, chopped fine in meat chopper
    6 ounces hen and chicken livers, finely chopped
    1 tablespoon salt
    ½ teaspoon Épices Parisienne (page 2) or equal mixture
       of dry rosemary, marjoram, bay leaf and thyme
    ½ teaspoon white pepper
    2 tablespoons cognac
    2 tablespoons Madeira
    1 egg

3 tablespoons white bread crumbs
1 teaspoon chopped chives
1 teaspoon chopped chervil
1 teaspoon chopped parsley
4 hens, boned by your butcher

Melt butter in a saucepan. When foaming, add shallots, cook 3 minutes; add mushrooms, cook 3 minutes. Remove from the stove and add the pork, livers, salt, épices Parisienne, pepper, cognac and wine. Stir in the egg, bread crumbs, chives, chervil and parsley and blend well. Stuff the birds, re-forming flesh to its original shape, and sew with a trussing needle and fine twine. Place each bird on a piece of aluminum foil, molding it into a basket to keep bird in shape. Refrigerate until firm.

Step Two: Cooking birds
6 tablespoons sweet butter
¼ cup cooking oil
1 cup sliced onions
1 cup sliced carrots
1 clove garlic
½ teaspoon thyme leaves
1 bay leaf
1 sprig parsley
1 branch celery
1 teaspoon salt
½ teaspoon white pepper
2 tablespoons cognac
6 tablespoons Madeira
2 cups Demi-Glace (page 74)
4 tablespoons sweet soft butter

Heat the oil and 6 tablespoons butter in a deep saucepan. When foaming, add the onions and carrots, cook 5 minutes. Add the clove of garlic, cook 2 minutes. Add the thyme, bay leaf, parsley, celery, salt and pepper. Place birds on top of the mixture, then in a preheated 450-degree oven 15 minutes, uncovered. Baste often so the hens will not get dry. Pour off the grease and add the cognac, Madeira and demi-glace. Bring to boil on top of stove, cover with a lid, reduce oven to 350 degrees and cook 95 minutes or until tender. Remove twine from birds; place in a serving casserole. Simmer sauce on top of the stove to reduce to half. Strain through a fine wire strainer. Blend in the 4 tablespoons of soft butter, stirring slowly with a cooking spoon; do not boil. Pour buttered sauce over the birds. I usually serve buttered fresh spinach with the hens. The touch of green beside the bird is just right.

Boned Cornish Game Hen in Brioche   FOR 4

Step One: Stuffing
> ¼ pound foie gras, cut in 4 pieces
>   1 large peeled truffle cut in 4 pieces (reserve peelings)
> ¼ cup cognac
> ½ teaspoon cayenne pepper
>   1 teaspoon salt
>   1 pinch Épices Parisienne (page 2)
>   2 tablespoons Madeira
> 4 Cornish game hens, boned by your butcher
> 4 four-inch square, thin slices larding pork

In a bowl, marinate foie gras, truffle slices, cognac, pepper, salt, spices, Madeira 1 hour before using. Spread open boned birds; lay a slice of larding pork in each. Place 1 slice of foie gras and 1 slice of truffle on the larding pork. Spoon the marinade over the foie gras and truffle. Reshape the birds and sew with trussing needle and twine. Place each bird on a piece of aluminum foil, molding it into a basket to keep bird firmly in shape. Refrigerate.

Step Two: Cooking birds
>   4 tablespoons sweet butter
> ½ cup cooking oil
>   2 tablespoons cognac
> ½ cup Madeira
>   1 cup Brown Stock (page 63)
>   1 tablespoon peelings from truffle
>   1 teaspoon salt

Heat the oil and butter in a saucepan. When foaming, place birds in pan and cook 2 minutes. Put uncovered in a preheated 400-degree oven 15 minutes, basting birds often. Pour off grease; pour in cognac, Madeira, brown stock, truffle peelings and salt. Bring to a boil on top of stove, reduce heat, cover and simmer 35 minutes or until tender. Remove birds and continue simmering sauce 2 hours; reserve.

Step Three
>   1 recipe Brioche Dough (page 284)
>   1 egg yolk mixed with tablespoon milk (dorure)

Roll brioche dough ½-inch thick. Cut into four 8-inch squares. Lay a bird on top of each square, bringing the dough over to wrap birds well. Seal, brushing cold water around the seam edges of the dough. With a pastry brush, brush dough with dorure to give a golden color to the dough. Place in a preheated 350-degree oven 20 minutes, then raise heat to 400 degrees for 15 minutes or until golden. Serve with Sauce Périgourdine (page 78), using as a base the sauce the birds were cooked in.

Cornish Game Hens in Casserole Crémaillère   FOR 4

6 tablespoons sweet butter
4 Cornish game hens, cleaned, trussed for roasting,
* wrapped in a thin slice of larding pork*
* Salt and white pepper*
½ cup cognac
¼ cup Madeira
1 cup Demi-Glace (page 74)
1 teaspoon currant jelly
4 cups cooked wild rice
4 tablespoons sweet butter

Melt 6 tablespoons of butter in a deep saucepan. Season hens with salt and pepper and cook 10 minutes over medium heat on top of stove. Turn several times with two wooden spoons so the skin will not break and hens will brown evenly on each side. Cover with a lid and cook 40 minutes or until tender. Remove the birds to a serving platter. Pour off the grease and add half the cognac and the Madeira and demi-glace. Stir in currant jelly and strain into a sauceboat. Sauté the rice in 4 tablespoons of butter in a skillet. Bring hens to the table with the sauce and wild rice on the side. On a serving platter, carve each into 4 parts, 2 breasts, 2 legs. Pour over the remaining cognac and flambé. Divide the rice on plates and place the legs of each bird on the rice and the breasts over the legs. Pour sauce over meat.

"Route Nationale"

DINDES—Turkeys

Dinde aux Marrons

[TURKEY STUFFED WITH CHESTNUTS]   FOR 18-POUND TURKEY

Step One: Stuffing
 1 cup chopped onions
 ¼ pound bacon, diced
 1 tablespoon chopped garlic
 1 pound sausage meat
 ½ pound boiled ham, chopped
 2 cups white bread crumbs
 2 eggs
 ½ teaspoon dry thyme
 ½ teaspoon dry sage
 ½ teaspoon dry rosemary
  Salt and pepper
 1 teaspoon Lea & Perrins sauce
 1 tablespoon chopped truffles
 ¼ cup cognac
 1 tablespoon chopped parsley
 ½ cup Demi-Glace (page 74)
 1 pound cooked chestnuts (dry chestnuts soaked
  overnight and cooked in water with a bunch
  of celery until tender)

Sauté the onions with the bacon 5 minutes. Add garlic and cook 2 minutes. Add the remaining ingredients, except for the chestnuts. Mix thoroughly. Add the chestnuts and mix well.

Step Two: Cooking turkey
 Soft sweet butter
 1 pound chipolata sausages (small onion-base sausages)
 ½ cup sherry
 Sauce Périgourdine (page 78)

Stuff turkey. Sew the aperture tightly and truss bird with trussing needle and twine; rub the bird with soft butter and wrap very tightly in aluminum foil. Place in a roasting pan in a preheated 400-degree oven 1 hour. Reduce heat to 350 degrees and cook 2½ hours. Remove foil and leave the turkey in the oven another hour at 350 degrees, or until fork tender. Bake the chipolata sausages in oven for 10 minutes, then sauté them quickly in the pan gravy left from cooking the turkey, to which has been added the sherry. Serve the sausages with the turkey and a boat of périgourdine sauce on the side for the sliced turkey and stuffing.

Médaillons de Monsieur Pernet

[MEDALLIONS OF TURKEY BREAST]   FOR 4

My friend Monsieur Pernet, Head Chef of the famous Réserve de Beaulieu, was named Premier Ouvrier de France in 1966, a high honor few achieve.

These médaillons that he liked to serve are round or oblong, 2½ inches in diameter, ¾-inch thick, and are usually cut from filets of beef. For this unusual dish he used the breast of an 18-pound turkey for 8 médaillons, 4 from each breast.

> 8 médaillons, 2½-inches diameter, ¾-inch thick
>   Salt and white pepper
> 8 thin slices Virginia ham, large enough
>   to wrap a médaillon
> ¼ pound sweet butter
> 1 cup sliced onions
> 1 cup sliced carrots
> 2 tablespoons flour
> ½ teaspoon thyme leaves
> 1 bay leaf
> 1 sprig parsley
> 1 branch celery
> 1 cup sliced white leeks
> 1 cup dry French vermouth
> ½ cup heavy cream
> 1 cup Chicken Broth (page 62)
> 4 cups puréed sweet potatoes
> 1 tablespoon Dijon mustard
> 1 tablespoon chopped chives
> 4 tablespoons sweet butter

Salt and pepper the médaillons. Wrap each in a slice of ham and tie with twine. Melt the ¼ pound butter in a saucepan. When foaming, slowly sauté the onions and carrots 10 minutes; do not brown. Sprinkle flour on the onions and carrots, and lay in the médaillons; add thyme, bay leaf, parsley, celery and leeks. Cover and simmer 5 minutes. Stir in the vermouth, cream and chicken broth. Simmer, covered, 40 minutes or until tender. Remove the twine from the médaillons and place on top of a warm purée of sweet potatoes on a serving platter. Keep warm. Strain sauce through fine wire strainer, pushing the vegetables through with a wooden spoon. Boil, uncovered, until sauce thickens. Remove from fire and slowly stir in the mustard and chives and the 4 tablespoons of butter. Pour over the médaillons.

Médaillons de Dinde en Papillote

[MEDALLIONS OF TURKEY IN FOIL]   FOR 4

> 6 tablespoons sweet butter
> 1 tablespoon chopped shallots
> 1 tablespoon chopped mushrooms
> 1 tablespoon chopped boiled ham
>   Salt and white pepper to taste
> 2 tablespoons cognac
> ¼ cup dry white wine
> 1 cup Demi-Glace (page 74)
> 4 médaillons cut from breast, ¾-inch thick,
>   2½-inches in diameter
> 4 ten-inch-square sheets aluminum foil
> 4 slices Swiss cheese
> 4 slices Virginia ham
>   Sauce tomate (page 83)
> 4 tablespoons sweet butter

Melt the 6 tablespoons of butter in a saucepan. When foaming, add shallots, cook 2 minutes; add mushrooms, cook 3 minutes; add ham, salt, pepper, cognac, wine and demi-glace. Mix well. Place each turkey médaillon on a sheet of aluminum foil; cover with 1 slice of Swiss cheese and 1 slice of Virginia ham. Spoon the ham-mushroom mixture over. Carefully fold foil, sealing edges tightly. Place these papillotes in a shallow pan, then into a preheated 400-degree oven 50 minutes. Open and serve in foil. Over low heat, slowly stir the 4 tablespoons of butter into the tomato sauce. Serve on the side.

Cuisses de Dinde Braisées

[BRAISED SECOND JOINTS OF TURKEY]   FOR 8

> 4 second joints from 18-pound turkeys
>   White flour

Salt and white pepper
½ cup sweet butter
16 small white onions
24 small carrots
2 cloves garlic, crushed
¾ cup dry white wine
*1 cup **Demi-Glace** (page 74)*
Bouquet garni
16 new potatoes, trimmed to size of small eggs
1 cup green peas, fresh or frozen

Dredge the turkey joints in the flour, salt and pepper. Melt butter in a large skillet. When foaming, add turkey thighs and sauté over medium heat 10 minutes on each side. Add onions, sauté 5 minutes; add carrots and garlic, sauté 5 minutes. Add the wine, demi-glace and bouquet garni. Bring to a boil; cover, lower heat and simmer 1½ hours or until tender. Cook potatoes and peas separately in water until tender. After the 1½-hour cooking of the turkey, stir in potatoes and peas. Simmer 10 minutes before serving. Remove bouquet garni. Check seasoning. Serve a half-thigh to each person.

PINTADES—Guinea Hens

These are wild African birds that have been domesticated, or semi-domesticated, and are seen usually in two colors: white and purplish pearl. They are a favorite of mine, with one qualification: They must be fresh. To my taste, the frozen birds lose that famous delicate guinea flavor, with just a touch of the wild, so different from all other fowl. In making the following dish from these historic birds that first came to civilization's roost in Rome, I prefer a bird of 2½ to 3 pounds. One guinea's breast of this size is sufficient for two servings.

I should tell you where you can obtain the best game birds I have been able to find. Oven-ready superb quail, chukkar partridges, baby pheasants, broiler pheasants, adult pheasants, baby and adult guinea hens, wild turkeys and mallard ducks can be had any time of year—just write for a price list to: *Mrs. Howard Capp, Birdcliff, Wingdale, New York*. Mrs. Capp tells me that she successfully ships as far as California, Texas, Florida, and inland Canada.

Filets de Pintade Crémaillère

[BREAST OF GUINEA HEN CRÉMAILLÈRE]   FOR 4

> 6 tablespoons sweet butter
> Salt and white pepper
> 4 half breasts of guinea hen from 2 birds 2½ to 3 pounds
> 1 tablespoon chopped shallots
> 1 cup sliced mushrooms
> 4 thin slices Virginia ham
> ½ cup dry sherry
> Confectioners' sugar
> 4 heart-shaped croutons, fried in butter
> 4 cups steamed wild rice
> 1 cup heavy cream
> ½ cup Sauce Hollandaise (page 81)
> Grated Parmesan cheese

Melt the butter in a saucepan. When foaming, add salted and peppered breasts, skin-side down, and sauté 10 minutes, turning after 5 minutes. Add the shallots and mushrooms. Cover and place in a preheated 400-

degree oven 15 minutes or until tender. In the meantime, place the ham slices in a flat pan; pour over half the sherry and sprinkle with a little confectioners' sugar. Then place under the broiler 2 minutes. Place the ham on croutons in a large au gratin, ovenproof pan. Arrange 1 cup of wild rice on each slice of ham and top with a breast. Keep warm. After removing breasts from saucepan, stir in the remaining sherry and the cream; simmer until the sauce thickens. Remove from fire and add hollandaise, blending with a wooden spoon. Do not boil. Check seasoning. Pour this sauce over the breasts, sprinkle with grated Parmesan cheese and place under the broiler until well browned.

Filets de Pintade Smitane

[BREAST OF GUINEA HEN WITH SOUR CREAM]   FOR 4

Step One: Prepare Purée Soubise
        3 tablespoons sweet butter
        6 ounces white onions, sliced
        ⅔ cup rice
    1⅓ cups Chicken Broth (page 62)
            or White Stock (page 61)
        Salt and white pepper to taste
        ⅓ cup heavy cream

Melt the butter in an ovenproof saucepan and add onions. Simmer slowly 10 minutes; do not brown. Add the rice, chicken broth, salt and pepper; bring to a boil. Cover with aluminum foil *and* lid and place in preheated 350-degree oven 25 minutes or until rice is cooked. Rub through a sieve and stir in the cream.

Step Two
        6 tablespoons sweet butter
        4 half breasts of guinea hen from 2 hens 2½ to 3 pounds
            Salt and white pepper
    12 small mushroom caps cooked 5 minutes in butter and lemon juice
        2 cups soubise (which you have prepared)
    ¼ cup dry sherry
        2 cups sour cream
    1 teaspoon paprika
        1 cup Sauce Hollandaise (page 81)
    ½ cup white bread crumbs
        4 heart-shaped croutons, fried in butter

Melt butter in a saucepan and sauté the breasts over a medium flame 10 minutes, turning after 5 minutes. Sprinkle with salt and pepper, cover and simmer 20 minutes or until tender. Remove breasts, place on top of the soubise in an ovenproof dish. Place mushrooms on top of breasts. Keep warm. Add the sherry to the saucepan, cook 2 minutes; add the sour cream and paprika, cook 5 minutes, mixing well. Do not boil. Off fire, blend in the hollandaise. Check seasoning. Pour the sauce over the breasts, sprinkle bread crumbs on top and brown under the broiler. Arrange croutons around when serving.

PIGEONS—Squabs

Now we come to one of my very favorite birds—the squab. One reason: I met my collaborator and friend, Jack Denton Scott, through squabs. More than a decade ago he came to La Crémaillère in Banksville, New York, with my old friend the late Gaston Lauryssen, then president of the Ritz Carlton. We dined together—on squab, naturally. It was a pleasant evening, Jack and I boring Gaston somewhat with our nonstop conversation, which varied from squabs and the ways to present them to wing shooting and hunting in general, a sport we both love.

Three days later Jack reappeared with a parcel: two huge, beautiful squabs, the largest and the most succulent I have ever had. Thus our friendship was sealed—by squabs. We agreed that any man who has such a love for these birds can't be all bad.

Squab is my favorite bird not only because of my friendship with Jack, but because it happens to be the most delicious, most easily digested, tenderest, juiciest of all foods. The ill, with serious digestive difficulties, are always able to eat squab.

A squab is a young pigeon which is marketed just before it is ready to leave the nest, at 25 or 30 days of age. For nearly a month that squab has sat in the nest and had food pumped into it by its doting mother, a rich predigested food with a wholesome grain base that makes the bird butterball fat in under a month. No muscles develop, only lean, tender meat encased in fat, which ensures juiciness—unless the bird is spoiled in the cooking.

Squabs are excellent grilled, broiled, or in a casserole; they are at their best stuffed and roasted, and great in a pie. I have a pie that I learned during my days as a chef in England, one that Lloyd George liked to have me make when I cooked for him. During that time I also learned and developed a stuffed squab with a bread crumb mixture, a Scotch specialty. So I herewith offer you an English, a Scotch, and, of course, a French recipe.

Squab Pie English Style   FOR 4

Step One: Roasting squabs
        4 squabs, needle-trussed
        4 tablespoons sweet butter
        4 slices bacon
    ½ cup chopped shallots
    ¼ cup dry sherry
        1 cup Demi-Glace (page 74)
    12 pitted green olives
        1 teaspoon Lea & Perrins sauce
            Salt and pepper to taste
        4 hard boiled eggs, cut in half
        1 tablespoon chopped parsley

Roast the squabs in melted butter 35 minutes in a preheated 400-degree oven. Carve them into 4 pieces each: breasts, legs. Cook the bacon with the shallots 5 minutes in a saucepan. Add the carcass bones left after carving the birds and the sherry and demi-glace; simmer 15 minutes. Arrange the squab pieces in a pyrex pie dish. Pour the sauce over, straining through a fine wire strainer. Add the green olives, Lea & Perrins, salt, pepper, hard boiled eggs and parsley; cool 1 hour.

Step Two: Pie dough
    1½ cups white flour
    1½ teaspoons salt
        ⅔ cup lard or Crisco
        4 tablespoons water
        1 beaten egg

Sift flour and salt. Mix in lard with a pastry cutter. When well blended, add water. Mix well. Roll out ⅛-inch thick on floured board. Cover the pie dish with this dough, seal the edges tight and brush the top with beaten egg. Make a hole in the center and place a paper funnel so steam can escape. Place in a preheated 350-degree oven 1 hour. If some of this dish is left over, it can be served cold.

Stuffed Squab Scotch Style

FOR 4

Step One: Stuffing
   4 tablespoons sweet butter
   ½ cup finely diced bacon
   ½ cup chopped onions
   1½ cups white bread crumbs
   ½ teaspoon dry thyme leaves
   ½ teaspoon dry sage
   ½ bay leaf, crushed
      Salt and white pepper to taste
   4 squabs

Melt the butter and sauté bacon 10 minutes on a slow fire. Add onions and simmer 5 minutes. Stir in the bread crumbs, thyme, sage and bay leaf and sprinkle with salt and pepper; blend well. Stuff the squabs. Sew up the aperture securely so no stuffing will escape; truss birds with a trussing needle and twine.

Step Two: Cooking
   ¼ pound sweet butter
   ½ cup port
   1 cup brown gravy
   ½ teaspoon cayenne pepper
      Sauce Diable (page 76)

Melt 4 tablespoons of butter in a casserole, put in the squabs and sauté on top of the stove over medium heat 10 minutes, turning the squabs over several times with two wooden spoons in order not to break the skin. Cover and place in a preheated 400-degree oven 30 minutes. Pour in the port and gravy and simmer in oven 15 minutes. Remove twine from the birds and keep warm. Add the cayenne and the remaining butter to the sauce diable and stir until butter is melted. Serve the sauce on the side with the squabs.

Pigeons aux Petits Pois

[SQUABS WITH BABY PEAS]

FOR 4

   6 tablespoons sweet butter
   4 squabs, trussed
   12 small white onions
   2 slices bacon, diced

1 cup shredded Boston lettuce
1 cup Demi-Glace (page 74)
2 cups shelled peas
  Bouquet garni
  Salt to taste

Melt butter in a deep saucepan and sauté squabs 10 minutes over medium heat. Stir in onions, bacon and lettuce and simmer 15 minutes. Add the demi-glace, peas, bouquet garni and salt. Bring to boil, cover saucepan and simmer 30 minutes or until squabs and peas are tender. Remove twine from squabs and cut them into 4 pieces each. If not enough sauce, add more demi-glace. Check seasoning. Squabs, peas and sauce are served together.

CANETONS, CANARDS—Ducklings, Ducks

Caneton aux Pruneaux

[DUCKLING GARNISHED WITH PRUNES]   FOR 4

Step One: Stuffing
  6 tablespoons sweet butter
  1 cup finely chopped onions
  1 tablespoon chopped garlic
  1 pound sausage meat
    Salt and white pepper to taste
  1 teaspoon Épices Parisienne (page 2)
  2 tablespoons white bread crumbs
  1 egg
  1 tablespoon chopped parsley
  ¼ cup cognac
  1 six-pound Long Island duckling

Melt the butter in a saucepan. When foaming, add the onions and sauté 5 minutes over medium heat; do not brown. Add garlic and cook 2 minutes. Add sausage meat; mix thoroughly. Add salt, pepper, épices Parisienne, bread crumbs, egg, parsley and cognac. One hour before cooking, stuff the duck with this forcemeat. Truss tightly with trussing needle and twine.

Step Two: Cooking
> *1 pound prunes soaked 12 hours;*
> > *simmered 30 minutes in 1 cup red wine,*
> > *2 tablespoons sugar, 1 stick cinnamon*
> *6 tablespoons sweet butter*
> *½ cup sliced onions*
> *½ cup sliced carrots*
> *2 cloves garlic, crushed*
> > *Salt and white pepper to taste*
> *6 tablespoons cognac*
> *¾ cup port*
> *2 cups Demi-Glace (page 74)*
> *½ cup juice from cooked prunes*
> > *Bouquet garni*

Melt the butter in a skillet and sauté stuffed duck 15 minutes, 5 minutes on each breast and 5 minutes on its back. Add onions, carrots, garlic, salt and pepper. Cover and simmer 20 minutes. Add the cognac, port, demi-glace, juice and the bouquet garni. Bring to boil, cover and place in a preheated 400-degree oven 30 minutes or until tender. Remove twine and place duck on serving platter. Strain the sauce through a fine strainer and simmer, uncovered, 10 minutes. Skim. Pit the prunes and arrange around the duck. Check seasoning of simmering sauce, which should be thickening. Pour it over the duck and present the platter to your guests. Carve the duck, taking the legs off and making thin slices of the breast. Spoon the stuffing out (1 full spoonful on each plate) and arrange duck slices over it with the pitted prunes around. Ladle sauce over each serving. The legs will be cut up in 2 pieces; the drumstick is seldom served, unless solicited. Serve Fleurons (page 285) on the side.

Canard à l'Orange Crémaillère

[DUCK IN ORANGE SAUCE]   FOR 4

This is the dish my Grandmother used to serve on Bastille Day, July 14. After the torchlight parades, the dancing in the streets, the sampling of wine in many places, my older brother and I would always end up at Grand'mère's for Canard à l'Orange. With it that grand old lady poured simple but authoritative Pontet-Canet, served chambré, room temperature.

1 six-pound duck, remove wings, neck,
  gizzard; dress, truss with twine
1 cup sliced onions
1 cup sliced carrots
2 cloves garlic, crushed
2 branches celery
1 sprig parsley
½ teaspoon thyme leaves
1 bay leaf
1 tablespoon salt
6 black peppercorns
1 cup orange juice
1 cup Brown Stock (page 63)
2 ounces tomato paste
2 cloves
½ cup Grand Marnier or Cointreau
⅔ cup sugar
1 cup water
4 oranges, peeled, cut into sections
6 tablespoons cognac
1 teaspoon currant jelly

Brown wings, neck and gizzard in a preheated 450-degree oven 15 minutes. Stir in all ingredients through the cloves except duck. Add ¼ cup of the Grand Marnier. Simmer, tightly covered, 1 hour. Cook the sugar and water in a thick-bottomed saucepan until the sugar caramelizes. Strain the above sauce into it and simmer, covered, 20 minutes. Roast duck in a preheated 400-degree oven 1 hour or until tender. Remove twine and place the duck on a serving platter surrounded by orange sections. Stir the cognac into the roasting pan with the remaining ¼ cup of Grand Marnier and the currant jelly; blend. Reduce, uncovered, on medium heat, to a good consistency. Blend with first sauce and spoon half over the duck to present to your guests. Remove the duck to a carving board. Carve the breast in 6 pieces and cut off thighs, leaving drumsticks, which are not served. Heat 3 minutes over a chafing dish before serving. The plates should be hot. Serve quarters of peeled oranges on the side.

Salmis de Canard Grand Veneur

[RAGOUT OF DUCK]   FOR 4

> 1 *five-pound duck, trussed*
> 3 *ounces lean salt pork, cut in small dice*
> 1 *cup sliced onions*
> 1 *tablespoon chopped garlic*
> 6 *tablespoons cognac*
> ¼ *cup port wine*
> ½ *cup red wine*
> 2 *cups Demi-Glace (page 74)*
>   *Bouquet garni*
> 12 *medium mushroom caps*
> 4 *tablespoons sweet butter*
>   *Salt and black pepper to taste*
>   *Liver from the duck, finely chopped*
> 12 *jumbo pitted green olives*
> 1 *tablespoon chopped parsley*
> 6 *heart-shaped bread croutons, each coated*
>   *with canned purée of foie gras*

Roast the duck in a preheated 400-degree oven 1 hour, 20 minutes on each side, and 20 minutes on the back. Baste often. Carve the duck into 4 pieces from the breasts, 4 pieces from the legs. Chop the carcass into 4 pieces. Lightly brown the salt pork in a thick-bottomed saucepan, add the onions and cook 10 minutes. Add the garlic, cook 2 minutes; add chopped carcass, cook 5 minutes. Add cognac and flambé. Stir in the port, red wine, demi-glace and the bouquet garni. Simmer 30 minutes. Sauté mushrooms in butter 3 minutes. Place mushrooms and the duck pieces in a casserole. Strain the sauce over the duck, forcing the ingredients through a fine wire strainer. Season with salt and pepper, cover pot and simmer in a preheated 400-degree oven 20 minutes. Stir the duck liver into the salmis; lightly simmer on top of stove 5 minutes. Add the pitted green olives. Simmer 3 minutes just before serving. Sprinkle with the parsley. Serve croutons on each plate. The duck can be roasted in the morning, the salmis prepared in the evening.

OIE—Goose

Oie Farcie à l'Auvergnate

[GOOSE STUFFED WITH GARLIC]   FOR 6

The French province of Auvergne is noted for its superb geese and exceptional garlic. The plump geese are fed only fine grains and chestnuts, giving them marvelous flavor. The garlic is large, firm, white —and aromatic. At least to me garlic is aromatic—and to the people of Auvergne. They have it on just about everything except strawberries! If you don't like it as we do, reduce the amount of garlic in this recipe. This, however, is the classic dish.

> *1 eight-pound goose*
> *3 ounces goose fat, finely chopped*
> *½ cup finely chopped onions*
>   *Liver from the goose, finely chopped*
> *1 pound sausage meat*
> *¼ cup cognac*
> *¼ cup Madeira*
> *12 jumbo pitted green olives, cut into small pieces*
> *½ cup bread crumbs*
> *1 egg*
> *1 tablespoon salt*
> *1 teaspoon white pepper*
> *½ teaspoon Épices Parisienne (page 2)*
> *24 cloves garlic, peeled*
> *2 thin slices of larding pork (fat back)*
> *1 cup Demi-Glace (page 74)*
> *¼ cup port*

Melt the goose fat in a saucepan. When hot, add the onions, cook 3 minutes; add the chopped liver, cook 2 minutes. Cool. In a bowl, mix the sausage meat with the cooled onions and liver. Add the cognac and Madeira; mix well with your hands, kneading gently. Add other ingredients (up to the larding pork), one by one, mixing after each. Add the cloves of garlic last. Stuff the goose. Lay the larding pork over the apertures and, using a trussing needle and twine, close as tightly as you can. Wrap the goose snugly with aluminum foil. Place in a roasting pan with a pint of water in the bottom, cover, then place in a preheated 450-degree oven 2 hours. If the water evaporates, add more during the cooking time. While the goose cooks, prepare the demi-glace, stirring in the port to use to sauce the goose. Slice the goose's breast with a sharp carving knife into 6 generous slices; the second joints can be served, but not the drumstick. Spoon stuffing from goose, a heaping tablespoonful for each guest. Top the stuffing with a slice of goose. Pass the sauce. I like braised fennel with this goose.

Oie Farcie à l'Alsacienne

[GOOSE STUFFED WITH SAUERKRAUT]   FOR 6

1 eight-pound goose
1 cup chopped goose fat
1 cup chopped onion
1 cup peeled, cored and sliced apples
1 teaspoon chopped garlic
  Liver from the goose, finely chopped
1 cup white bread crumbs
1 egg
1 pound cooked sauerkraut (see note)
1 tablespoon salt
1 teaspoon white pepper
1 pinch cumin seeds
1 teaspoon Épices Parisienne (page 2)
¼ pound blood pudding, cut into small pieces
¼ cup kirschwasser
2 thin slices larding pork, 4 inches square

Melt the goose fat in a saucepan 3 minutes; add chopped onions and cook slowly 5 minutes; do not let onions take on color. Add apple slices, cook 3 minutes; add garlic, cook 2 minutes; add chopped liver, cook 2 minutes. Place this in a mixing bowl. When cooled, mix in bread crumbs, egg, sauerkraut, salt, pepper, cumin seeds, spices, blood pudding and kirschwasser. Blend well. Stuff the goose. Place the larding pork to block the apertures at the cavity and neck. Truss very tightly with a trussing needle and twine. Wrap goose snugly in aluminum foil, place in a roasting pan and pour in 1 pint of water. Cover and roast in a preheated 450-degree oven 2 hours or until fork-tender. Remove stuffing, place on a serving platter. Carve breast in 8 generous slices, cut second joints into 6 pieces. Arrange meat on top of the stuffing for presentation before serving. Serve warmed applesauce on the side, and some plain boiled new potatoes. A good Riesling or Traminer Alsatian wine goes well with this fine Alsatian dish.

NOTE: There are several excellent brands of sauerkraut in cans. There is one, cooked with champagne, which I prefer for this recipe.

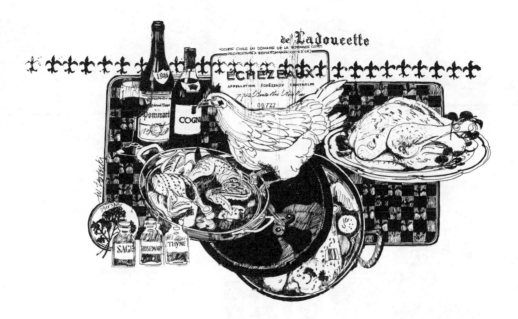

7

VIANDES—Meats

BOEUF—Beef

There is an old chef's saying, "Heaven sends good meats; the Devil sends cooks." Which means that much good meat is ruined by indifferent cooks. I don't like to point a finger in just one direction, but I have seen so many good marbled, aged, prime strip sirloin steaks messed up over American charcoal fires that the thought still distresses me.

The weekend cook, always the man of the house, dons his apron and chef's hat, builds a roaring fire, squirting the charcoal with an inflammable liquid to get it started. Then he and the guests proceed to get smashed on martinis until finally the "cook" goes to work. The steaks go on, the fire and everyone get too high; soberly the wife or junior stands by with a glass of water, hurling it on the fire when commanded by the master of the house, spraying coal ash on the steaks. When the steaks are "done," and I mean done, everyone sits to eat. Usually each person is served a whole steak, which tastes exactly like a cube of charcoal, either overdone or nearly raw, depending upon the strength of the martinis.

Now I don't want to spoil this good American fun. It is enjoyable to cook outdoors over charcoal. The charcoal should be real hardwood charcoal, not the synthetic balls pressed together and formed of coal dust and chemicals, and the fire should be allowed to die to embers before the steaks are cooked, turning often. Some do this; most don't.

Moreover, it is crude to serve a whole steak. A steak should be sliced, and each person given several slices—more, if they ask or indicate that they are hungry.

Colmar, Alsace

I do a steak in hunting camp that is simple and that has a much better flavor than that of burnt charcoal. Take a prime shell or strip steak that has been standing at room temperature for a couple of hours. Melt a tablespoon of butter in a saucepan, add a teaspoon of olive oil to keep the butter from burning. When the butter foams, add the steak and cook over a medium flame, turning very often. Cook until done to your liking, medium rare, rare, or whatever. If in doubt, lift from pan and cut into it a bit to check the color. When done, pour all the grease from the pan. Keep the steak warm. Replace the pan on a mild heat and pour in 2 ounces of a good brandy. With a wooden spoon, stir well into the browned particles that remain in the pan. When it is blended, stir in one small finely chopped black truffle, mixing well. Slice steak, pour hot brandy-truffle sauce over and serve immediately. Have your dinner, and after-dinner drinks, outside by the charcoal fire. Very pleasant.

I lead this chapter off with this comment on beef because it is the world's most popular meat. At least it is in those fortunate areas where it can be obtained without taking out a bank loan. The problem with beef, in my opinion, is that it is nearly always grilled, roasted or broiled, and I get bored eating it cooked the same old ways. Therefore, in this chapter I am listing a few of my own recipes that will help relieve that monotony.

The first recipe is one created by my Grandmother fifty-nine years ago, one that she had me prepare when I was ten. She was such a great cook and had such wonderful results in her kitchen that even then I wanted to one day become a chef as good as she. I haven't realized that ambition, but I am still trying.

Entrecôtes de ma Grand'mère

[STEAK IN HERBED SAUCE WITH AN EGG] FOR 4

An entrecôte is a boned steak cut from between the ribs of the beef, or often from the shell or sirloin.

> ¼ pound sweet butter
> 4 entrecôtes, 12 ounces each
> 1 tablespoon salt
> 1 teaspoon black pepper
> ½ cup chopped shallots

1 teaspoon chopped garlic
½ pound white mushrooms, sliced
2 tomatoes, skinned, seeded, cut into small pieces
¾ cup Madeira
½ cup Demi-Glace (page 74)
1 tablespoon chopped parsley
½ teaspoon dry thyme leaves
½ teaspoon dry rosemary leaves
1 teaspoon fresh chopped tarragon
¼ cup cognac
4 eggs
½ cup Sauce Périgourdine (page 78)

Melt the butter in a thick-bottomed saucepan. When foaming, sauté salted and peppered entrecôtes over a brisk fire so they brown quickly, searing them to retain the blood inside; turn over on each side several times, so they cook evenly (to be medium done they should cook totally 8 minutes). Remove entrecôtes to an oblong, ovenproof serving platter and keep on the side. Sauté shallots slowly 3 minutes, to soften; do not brown. Sauté garlic 2 minutes the same way. Add mushrooms, sauté 2 minutes. Add tomatoes, Madeira, demi-glace, parsley, thyme, rosemary and tarragon. Cook 10 minutes. Drain the steak juice that has run onto the serving platter into the hot sauce; add cognac, blend this into the sauce. Now pour the entire sauce over the entrecôtes. Break 1 egg on each entrecôte. Bake in a preheated 450-degree oven 3 minutes. Pour over each cooked egg 1 tablespoon of périgourdine sauce.

Entrecôtes à la Bercy

[STEAK WITH MARROW SAUCE]   FOR 4

¼ pound sweet butter
4 entrecôtes, 12 ounces each
1 tablespoon salt
1 teaspoon white pepper
½ cup chopped shallots
¼ cup cognac
1 cup dry white wine
½ cup Demi-Glace (page 74)
¼ pound beef marrow, cut in small dice,
    blanched 1 minute
2 tablespoons chopped parsley

Melt butter in a thick-bottomed saucepan. When foaming (do not let brown), sauté salted and peppered entrecôtes over brisk fire, turning often for 6 minutes (medium rare), so they brown evenly. Remove entrecôtes to a serving platter, keep warm. Drain butter, add shallots, cook 3 minutes; add cognac, flambé. Add wine and demi-glace, cook 5 minutes, simmering slowly. This sauce should reduce to half. Add marrow, stirring sauce in a rotating manner, so marrow will be well incorporated and will give a shining appearance. Check seasoning. Pour over entrecôtes. Sprinkle with parsley.

Tournedos à l'Antoine   FOR 4

Monsieur Étienne, night chef or "débrouillard" of the Palais d'Orsay, needed extra help every evening. He would say to us apprentices, "Who has a day off tomorrow?" There were always two of us available and very willing to work extra time with him. First, in order to learn more, but secondly to get a reward, not financial, but an unusual meal of our own conception and cooking. After closing, the night chef would say, "Now, cook anything you wish." Most of the time I cooked a tournedos, a 1½-inch-thick slice cut from the center of the filet, trimmed of fat and circled with butcher's twine to hold it together:

> 6 ounces (1½ sticks) sweet butter
> ¼ cup cooking oil
> 4 tournedos, 1½-inches thick, 3-inches
>   in diameter (about 6 ounces each)
>   Salt
> 2 tablespoons chopped shallots
> ½ pound mushrooms, sliced
> ¼ cup cognac
> ¼ cup Madeira
> 2 medium-sized tomatoes, peeled, seeded,
>   cut up in small cubes
> 1 cup Demi-Glace (page 74)
>   Salt and black pepper to taste
> 4 round croutons, 3-inches in diameter,
>   ¼-inch thick, fried in 4 tablespoons
>   of the butter
> 1 tablespoon fresh chopped tarragon
> 1 tablespoon chopped parsley

Heat the oil and half of the butter in a thick-bottomed saucepan. When foaming, add salted tournedos; sauté 2 minutes at a time on each side, for a total of 8 minutes (medium done) so tournedos brown evenly. Remove tournedos to a serving platter; keep warm. Pour off grease from the tournedos pan and add remaining 6 tablespoons of butter. When this is foaming, sauté shallots 2 minutes. Add sliced mushrooms, sauté 2 minutes. Add cognac, Madeira, tomatoes and demi-glace. Simmer 5 minutes. Season to taste with salt and pepper. Place the tournedos on the croutons on the serving platter, pour the sauce over and sprinkle with chopped tarragon and parsley. I like Pommes de Terre Parisienne (page 313) with this.

Boeuf à la Stroganoff

[BEEF STROGANOFF]   FOR 4

Chefs may not pass out their hard-won knowledge to the customers, but they usually will to other chefs. Thus the stint I had as sauce cook at the Hotel Carlton on the Champs-Élysées in Paris was time well spent. Several talented chefs there had cooked in many parts of the world and taught me a number of foreign dishes. One had cooked this for the late Tsar of Russia.

    2 pounds beef tenderloin, in small slices,
       3-inches long, ½-inch thick
       Salt and pepper
    ¼ pound sweet butter
    2 cups finely chopped white onions
    2 cloves garlic, chopped
       Bouquet garni
    2 ounces tomato paste
    1 cup Beef Bouillon (page 64)
    1 cup heavy cream

Sprinkle salt and pepper liberally on the beef slices. Melt the butter. When foaming hot, sauté beef over a medium fire 2 minutes, turning the slices often. Add the onions, simmer 5 minutes. Add the garlic, bouquet garni, tomato paste, beef stock and cream. Simmer, uncovered, until this sauce is thickened. Remove beef. Strain stock. Pour over beef slices and serve piping hot. We always served boiled new potatoes and a good chilled rosé with it.

Filet Mignon Haché Madame Sue

[CHOPPED STEAK]   FOR 4

    ¼ pound sweet butter
    ½ cup chopped shallots
     2 tablespoons cognac
    ½ cup cold water
  1½ teaspoons salt
    ½ teaspoon pepper
     1 tablespoon Lea & Perrins sauce
     1 tablespoon Dijon mustard
     2 pounds lean beef filet, put through
       medium blade of meat chopper
    ½ cup white bread crumbs
      Sauce Fleurette (page 89)

Melt half the butter in a saucepan, add shallots and simmer 3 minutes until soft but without color. Add cognac, water, salt, pepper and Lea & Perrins. Place in a mixing bowl; add mustard, chopped beef, bread crumbs and remaining butter, which should be soft. Mix thoroughly. Taste for seasoning. Mold 4 patties, 3 inches in diameter, 1¼-inch thick. Place these in the refrigerator 2 hours before ready to use. Sauté in butter in a thick-bottomed saucepan. Cook to your own taste, rare or medium. Serve with fleurette sauce.

Emincé de Filet de Boeuf Bordelaise

[TENDERLOIN TIPS WITH MARROW SAUCE]   FOR 4

    ½ cup cooking oil
    ¼ pound sweet butter
     2 pounds tenderloin tips, cut in strips
      2-inches long, 1½-inches wide
      Salt and pepper
     2 tablespoons chopped shallots
     2 cups sliced mushrooms
     2 cups Sauce Bordelaise (page 76)
     2 tablespoons chopped parsley

Heat the oil and half the butter in a thick-bottomed saucepan. When foaming, sauté the salted and peppered strips of beef over a brisk fire 5 minutes. Drain the grease. Place the beef strips in a deep saucepan. Keep warm. Melt the remaining butter in the pan in which beef was cooked. When foaming, add the shallots, cook 2 minutes; add the mushrooms, cook

3 minutes; stir in the bordelaise sauce, simmer 10 minutes. Pour the sauce over the beef and bring to a boil. Sprinkle with parsley and serve with French Fried Onions (page 310).

Filet de Boeuf à la Normande

[BEEF FILET WITH CALVADOS SAUCE
AND GARNISHES]   FOR 6

> *1 five-pound whole beef filet, trimmed*
> *of fat and sinews, larded with small*
> *strips of fat back put lengthwise every*
> *3 inches. Tie filet every 4 inches with*
> *medium butcher's twine, roundwise.*
> *Salt and pepper*
> *1 teaspoon celery salt*
> *¼ pound sweet butter*
> *1 cup sliced onions*
> *1 cup sliced carrots*
> *1 clove garlic, crushed*
> *6 tablespoons Calvados*
> *½ cup Madeira*
> *1 tablespoon tomato purée*
> *1 cups Demi-Glace (page 73)*
> *1 ounce truffles, chopped*
> *Garnishes (page 203)*

Rub larded, tied filet with salt, pepper and celery salt. Melt the butter in a roasting pan. When foaming, sauté filet on hot fire 2 minutes on each side. Place in a preheated 500-degree oven 10 minutes; turn filet and cook another 10 minutes. Add onions, carrots, garlic, cook 5 minutes. Remove from oven, drain grease. Place cooked filet on an oblong platter, preferably silver. Keep warm. Now add to the roasting pan the Calvados, Madeira, tomato purée and demi-glace. Simmer on top of the stove 10 minutes or until vegetables are soft. Strain, pushing vegetables through a fine strainer; add the truffles, simmer 5 minutes. Check seasoning. Arrange garnishes around the filet with watercress at each end. Make the presentation at the table. The host will slice the filet ¼ of an inch thick. The sauce is served on the side.

NOTE: Larding used to be a necessity when meats were tougher and leaner and needed help to keep moist. Although it is not essential today, it is still always desirable. All meats benefit from seasoned strips of fat, adding additional flavor, tenderness and moistness. Especially improved are veal, lean beef roast and filets.

You need a needle—a *lardoire*—to insert strips of fat into meat. This is a hollow steel tube with a curly flexible fishtail on one end, the point on the other. I prefer this to the popular, but difficult, open steel trough.

The fat is *lard gras*, fresh pork fat back. If you can't get fat back, then use raw strips of fat from a pork roast or pork chops. In an emergency you can use bacon or even salt pork if you parboil to remove salt. No harm in buying several needles; they are inexpensive.

Pork fat back when cut in a strip for larding is called a *lardoon*. Cut the strips to fit your particular needle. Roll them in small amounts of chopped fresh parsley, thyme, garlic, salt and pepper; place them in the freezer until stiff. This will make it easier to put them in the needle.

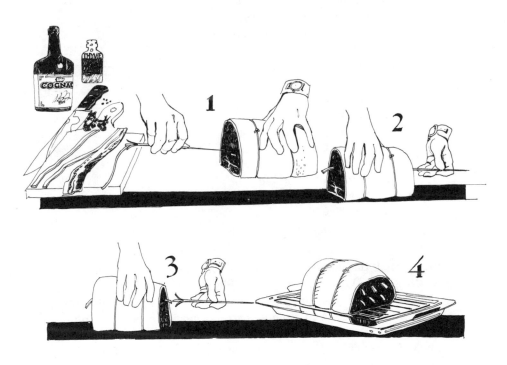

Larding a Roast

Insert a frozen strip of lard into the needle. Push the needle firmly, but gently, without any jabbing or yanking motions, into and through the meat. Draw the needle straight through. As it emerges from the other side, pull needle out. Easy does it. When you see the pork fat, pull needle one way, the pork fat the other, toward the meat, to keep the fat in the meat, and not have it come out with the needle. Insert as many strips as you please. Here, six strips do the job.

Garnishes

These can be cooked and kept warm while the filet is cooking:

> *6 artichoke bottoms (may be canned)*
> *heated with 2 tablespoons sweet butter*
> *2 cups small round carrots (canned)*
> *2 cups Pommes de Terre Parisienne (page 313)*
> *6 small Soufflés d'Épinards (page 317)*
> *6 tablespoons sweet butter for the carrots and potatoes*
> *1 bunch fresh watercress*

Rumstecks Carbonnade à la Flamande

[RUMP STEAKS IN BEER]   FOR 6

> *6 ounces sweet butter (1½ sticks)*
> *1 pound onions, sliced*
> *6 rump steaks, 1-inch thick*
> *(1 pound each)*
> *½ cup cooking oil*
> *2 cloves garlic, chopped*
> *1 tablespoon salt*
> *1 teaspoon pepper*
> *6 tablespoons brandy*
> *1 quart dark beer*
> *2 cups Beef Bouillon (page 64)*
> *Bouquet garni*

Melt the butter in a deep saucepan. Sauté onions 15 minutes, until brown. In another saucepan sauté rump steaks in the cooking oil, browning both sides. Drain. Place the steaks on top of the onions in their saucepan and add the garlic, salt and pepper. Pour on the brandy and flambé. Add the beer, beef stock and bouquet garni, bring to a boil and cover; place in a pre-heated 400-degree oven 1½ hours. Remove steaks to a serving platter. Cook sauce uncovered over brisk fire 10 minutes to thicken; remove bouquet garni. Check seasoning. Serve with small boiled new potatoes.

Boeuf à la Mode

[BRAISED BEEF WITH CHAMBERTIN WINE]   FOR 6

Step One: Marinade
        1 five-pound piece top round or rump, larded with
            eight ½-inch-wide strips of larding pork
        2 bottles Chambertin wine (red Burgundy)
        2 cups Brown Stock (page 63)
        1 cup cooking oil
        1 cup sliced carrots
        1 cup sliced onions
        1 cup sliced celery
        2 sprigs parsley
        1 bay leaf
        1 teaspoon thyme leaves
        ¼ teaspoon nutmeg
        4 cloves
        12 black peppercorns
        1 tablespoon brown sugar
        2 cloves garlic, crushed
        3 tablespoons salt

Place the beef in a large crock. Pour in the wine, stock and oil. Add all remaining items. Weight beef with a heavy plate to keep it submerged. Refrigerate 48 hours. Oil will float to the top. When ready to cook, remove beef from marinade onto a wire grate and drain 1 hour. Wipe dry.

Step Two: Cooking beef
        ½ pound fat back, cut into ¾-inch squares
        1 cup sliced carrots
        1 cup sliced onions
        1 tablespoon chopped garlic
        2 ounces tomato purée
        2 cups Demi-Glace (page 74)
        ½ cup Marc de Bourgogne or cognac
            Bouquet garni
        2 calf's feet

In a roasting pan large enough to hold beef and marinade, sauté fat back for 5 minutes. Brown beef over brisk fire for 10 minutes, turning often so it will color evenly. Add carrots, onions, cook 5 minutes. Add garlic, cook 2 minutes. Strain marinade and add to beef pot. Add tomato purée, demi-glace, Marc de Bourgogne, bouquet garni and calf's feet. Bring to a boil on top of the stove, cover tightly and place in a preheated 350-degree oven 3 hours or until tender.

Step Three: Vegetables
  24 small white onions
   6 tablespoons sweet butter
   1 pound small mushroom caps
  12 new potatoes (trimmed and
     shaped like pullet's eggs)
     Chopped parsley

While the meat is in the oven, prepare the above vegetables. Brown onions in butter 10 minutes. Sauté mushrooms 5 minutes. Boil potatoes 10 minutes, then drain. Keep these three items on the side. Transfer the beef to a serving casserole, straining the liquid over it. Add the whole onions, mushrooms and potatoes. Cut the meat from the calf's feet into 1-inch squares and add to the casserole. Bring to a boil on top of the stove 15 minutes or until onions and potatoes are tender. Before serving, skim grease from the top of the casserole and sprinkle with parsley. Serve with heart-shaped croutons fried in butter. Leftover beef can be served cold.

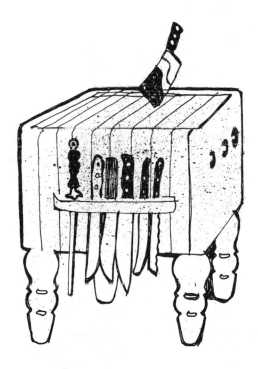

Boeuf en Daube Charolaise

[BRAISED BEEF CASSEROLE]   FOR 4

Although the French didn't develop fine beef cattle as early as the English, we did make up for lost time by coming into the competition with one of the very best, the Charolais, named after the section in my home place of Burgundy where they originated. The cattle, the color of clotted cream, contentedly cropping rich pasture, are one of that area's contributions to France's natural beauty. Breeders in the United States have also done well with the Charolais, and their meat is becoming increasingly popular among epicures. This recipe is a favorite in the Charolais region.

3 pounds shoulder of beef, cut in 2-inch cubes
½ pound onions, sliced
½ pound carrots, sliced
1 tablespoon chopped garlic
1 bay leaf
1 teaspoon thyme leaves
*   Pinch nutmeg*
1 celery stalk
1 sprig parsley
1 leek, white part only
2 tablespoons salt
1 teaspoon black pepper
3 cloves
1 quart red Burgundy
2 tablespoons Marc de Bourgogne or cognac
1 cup Demi-Glace (page 74)
½ pound lean salt pork, cut in 1-inch cubes
2 tablespoons chopped parsley

Put all the above ingredients except for the salt pork and chopped parsley into an earthenware casserole, large enough so the meat will be well submerged. Marinate in refrigerator 12 hours. Remove the beef cubes, drain well. Sauté the salt pork in a skillet 5 minutes. Add the beef pieces. On a brisk fire, brown beef, turning often, 10 minutes. Drain grease, pour the marinade over and bring to a boil. Replace beef and marinade in the casserole. Cover and seal tight with an abaisse (see note). Place in a preheated 350-degree oven 4 hours. Remove the abaisse and put the beef in a separate container. Strain the sauce over beef, pushing the vegetables through the strainer. Place meat and sauce in a serving casserole. Boil 5 minutes before serving. Sprinkle with chopped parsley. Serve croutons, browned in butter, on the side.

NOTE: An abaisse is made by mixing 1 pound of white flour with enough water to obtain a solid dough. Roll like a long sausage; cement it around the casserole lid, wetting it so it will stick and make the casserole airtight. This is also called repère. The dough is not edible.

Boeuf à la Bourguignonne

[BEEF STEW IN BURGUNDY WITH ONIONS]   FOR 4

Along with the memory of a glass of red wine mixed with a lump of sugar that I drank as a child before I went to bed, is this stew made by my grandmother (who walks strongly through this book). It was one of her favorites, and she served it often when we visited. During her later years, she always had a bottle of rare wine derrière les fagots (hidden in the wood pile) for us. As I remember, it was usually a Pommard, Beaune or Corton of a good vintage that we would drink with her stew.

3 tablespoons cooking oil
2 pounds beef, sirloin, chuck, or round,
  cut in good bite-size cubes
1 tablespoon flour
3 cloves garlic, chopped
3 cups red Burgundy
1 cup water
  Bouquet garni
  Salt and pepper to taste
½ pound lean salt pork, diced
24 small white onions

Heat the oil in a saucepan and brown the beef well over a brisk fire. Drain off the oil, sprinkle in the flour and mix well. Cook until the flour is brown, being careful not to burn, then add the garlic, wine, water, and bouquet garni; season with salt and pepper, stir well and bring to a boil. Cover the pot and place in a preheated 350-degree oven 2 hours or until beef is tender. Sauté the salt pork in a saucepan, add the onions. Remove the bouquet garni from the stew pot and stir in the salt pork and onions. Mix in well. Skim the grease from the top. Simmer and serve piping hot. My grandmother served heart-shaped fried croutons with her stew.

Boeuf à la Ficelle

[BEEF HUNG WITH A STRING]   FOR 6

I first had this dish on the famous French ship *Normandie*. It was created by Gaston Magrin, a great chef, strict not only with his own crew, but with the passengers. If they were not ready when his special dishes were ready, he became outraged, and justly so, for many a superb dish is ruined by tardy diners. Boeuf à la Ficelle must be eaten the moment it is ready, otherwise it is overdone.

Step One: Cook beef
  6 quarts Beef Bouillon (page 64)
  12 medium-sized carrots
  2 large onions, stuck with 4 cloves
  6 celery stalks, well cleaned
  4 leeks, white parts only,
    5 inches long, well cleaned
  2 cloves garlic, unpeeled
  3 tablespoons salt
  12 peppercorns
  5 pounds beef, rump or sirloin
  12 new potatoes, shaped as eggs, boiled separately

Place the stock in a large pot and add the carrots, onions, celery, leeks, garlic, salt and peppercorns. Bring to boil, simmer 45 minutes. Remove vegetables; keep warm. Tie the piece of beef with butcher's twine and hang it from a crossbar (a large wooden spoon works well) over the pot, so the meat will not touch the sides, but is suspended in the beef stock. Cover snugly with foil and boil 18 minutes per pound (90 minutes). Beef will be medium rare and very tender. Arrange the vegetables around the beef and serve immediately with the potatoes. Beef should be sliced against the grain, ½- to 1-inch thick, and should be pink, not rare. The sauce served with this dish is a combination of mustard and horse-radish:

Step Two: Prepare sauce
  ½ cup white wine or cider vinegar
  2 tablespoons Dijon mustard
  ½ cup Sauce Velouté (page 66)
  ⅓ cup olive oil
  ½ tablespoon salt
  ⅓ cup grated horse-radish (fresh, if possible)

Bring the vinegar to a boil, add the mustard and stir 2 minutes. Add the velouté and stir in oil very gradually, as for making mayonnaise. Add the salt and grated horse-radish. It should be a very smooth sauce, lukewarm when served.

Plat de Côtes Bourgeoise

[SHORT RIBS OF BEEF WITH CARROTS AND ONIONS]   FOR 4

Step One: Short ribs
    ½ pound salt pork, diced
    4 pounds short ribs
      Salt
    1 cup sliced onions
    1 cup sliced carrots
    2 cloves garlic, crushed
    4 ounces tomato purée
    2 cups Demi-Glace (page 74)
    2 cups dry white wine
      Bouquet garni
    1 teaspoon black pepper

Sauté the salt pork in a skillet. Salt the short ribs and add when the salt pork is foaming hot. Brown ribs 15 minutes, turning often so they color evenly. Add the onions and carrots, cook 10 minutes. Add garlic, cook 2 minutes. Pour off the grease. Add the tomato purée, demi-glace and wine. Bring to a boil, add the bouquet garni and sprinkle with pepper. Cover the skillet and place in a preheated 350-degree oven 3 hours. When ribs are tender, take from oven, remove bones and place the meat in a serving casserole. Over a brisk flame, reduce the sauce remaining in the skillet, cooking about 10 minutes. Strain over the meat and add the following prepared vegetables:

Step Two: Vegetables
    ¼ pound sweet butter
    24 small white onions
    1 teaspoon brown sugar
    2 cups small round carrots (canned)
    2 cups cooked green peas (may be frozen)
      Salt

Melt the butter in a saucepan. When hot, add the onions and simmer 15 minutes until nicely browned. Add sugar, carrots and peas. Simmer 5 minutes. Add salt to taste. Pour off the grease, then add to the beef casserole and simmer 5 minutes before serving. Au gratin noodles or boiled parsley potatoes are excellent with the ribs.

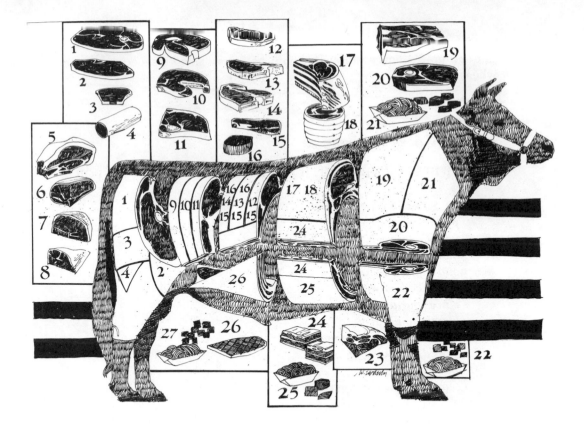

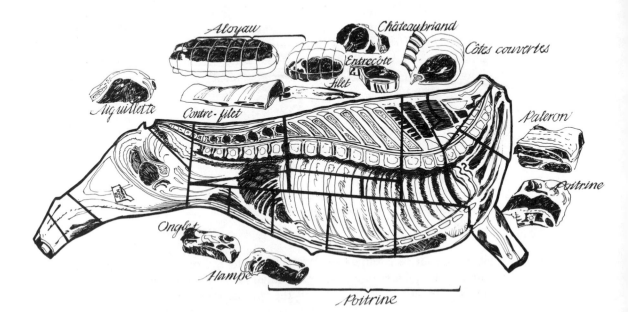

French Cuts of Beef

American Cuts of Beef

Round
- (1) Round steak
- (2) Top round steak
- (3) Bottom round steak
- (4) Eye of round
- (5) Rump roast
- (6) Standing rump
- (7) Sirloin tip roast
- (8) Heel of round

Loin end
- (9) Pin-bone sirloin
- (10) Flat-bone sirloin
- (11) Wedge-bone sirloin

Short loin
- (12) Club steak
- (13) T-bone steak
- (14) Porterhouse steak
- (15) Strip-loin steak
- (16) Filet mignon

Rib
- (17) Standing rib roast
- (18) Rolled roast

Chuck
- (19) Chuck roast (blade)
- (20) Chuck roast (arm)

Foreshank
- (21) Ground meat and stewing meat

Brisket
- (22) Ground meat and stewing meat
- (23) Brisket, corned beef

Plate
- (24) Short ribs
- (25) Ground meat and stewing meat

Flank
- (26) Flank steak
- (27) Ground meat and stewing meat

Plat de Côtes Grillés à la Diable

[DEVILED SHORT RIBS OF BEEF]   FOR 4

    4 pounds short ribs
    1 cup Dijon mustard
    1 cup white bread crumbs
    ½ cup cooking oil
    2 tablespoons salt
    2 tablespoons crushed pepper
      Sauce à la Diable (page 251)

Roast short ribs in a preheated 350-degree oven 1 hour. Meanwhile mix the mustard, bread crumbs, oil, salt and pepper into a paste. Spread the mustard paste evenly over the top side of ribs; roast 1 more hour. When ready to serve, place the ribs under the broiler. Cook slowly 10 minutes, then on higher heat 5 minutes to make a crust. Remove bones; carve into 4 portions and serve with potato chips and sauce à la diable on the side. A purée of celery knobs goes well with this dish.

Queue de Boeuf à la Prince of Wales

[OXTAIL STEW]   FOR 6

At the British Officers' Mess in Boulogne, where I worked with Paul Escoffier, a frequent visitor was the Prince of Wales, a thoughtful gentleman whose dinner or luncheon requests often preceded him. One day he sent a message that he would like oxtails for dinner. Monsieur Escoffier sent a man on a motorcycle to scout up the tails. I cooked them.

    4 tablespoons lard
    8 pounds oxtail, cut in 4-inch pieces
    ⅓ cup white flour
    2 cloves garlic, minced
    2 cups dry white wine
    1 quart Beef Bouillon (page 64)
      Bouquet garni
    6 tomatoes, peeled, seeded, quartered
    2½ cups cubed carrots
    12 small white onions
    1 cup peas, cooked
    1 pound potatoes, shaped like eggs, steamed

Heat the lard in a large, deep saucepan. Brown the oxtail on all sides, sprinkle with flour, add garlic and brown 2 minutes. Add the wine, stock, bouquet garni and tomatoes. Bring to a boil, cover and place in a pre-heated 400-degree oven 30 minutes. Brown the carrots and onions and stir into oxtail pot. Return, covered, to the oven 45 minutes. Remove bouquet garni. Check seasoning. Stir in peas and potatoes and simmer on top of the stove 5 minutes. Serve in a warm earthenware casserole. Be a prince, too, and drink a good bottle of Beaune with it. The Prince of Wales also liked crusty, freshly-baked French country bread with his oxtail.

VEAU—Veal

Mignonnettes de Veau, Park Imperial

[VEAL FILETS WITH TOMATOES]   FOR 4

> 2 tablespoons olive oil
> 1 cup chopped sweet onions
> 2 tablespoons chopped garlic
> 3 tomatoes, peeled, seeded, cut in ½-inch slices
> 1 tablespoon salt
> 1 teaspoon white pepper
> 1 teaspoon chopped thyme leaves (½ teaspoon if dry)
> 1 teaspoon chopped sweet basil (½ teaspoon if dry)
> ¼ pound sweet butter
> 2 pounds veal, from loin or filet, cut in 2-inch squares, ¼-inch thick
> ¾ cup Madeira
> ½ cup Demi-Glace (page 74)
> ½ cup grated Swiss cheese
> 1 tablespoon chopped parsley

Heat the oil in a thick-bottomed saucepan over a low fire. Add onions, cook 5 minutes; do not brown; add garlic, cook 2 minutes; add tomatoes, salt, pepper, thyme and basil, cook 10 minutes. Place this in a deep au gratin dish (pyrex or other). In a heavy saucepan, melt half the butter. When foaming, sauté veal rapidly over a quick fire, turning the pieces often so each will get a slight color (5 minutes should be enough). Place the veal mignonnettes on top of the tomato mixture in the au gratin dish. Drain the grease from the saucepan, add the Madeira and demi-glace, cook 4 minutes. Remove from fire and add remaining butter in small lumps, stirring slowly with a kitchen spoon. Check seasoning. Pour over veal and sprinkle with grated cheese and parsley. Place in a preheated 400-degree oven, uncovered, 8 minutes or until meat is tender. Serve new boiled potatoes or Riz Pilaf (page 275) on the side.

Picatta Maître d'Hôtel

[VEAL IN LEMON BUTTER]   FOR 4

Picatta are small 3-inch-square pieces of veal, ⅛-inch thick, cut from the loin or filet. Serve three pieces per person, one pound of meat for 4 persons.

1 one-pound loin of veal, cut in twelve
   3-inch squares, ⅛-inch thick
   Salt and white pepper
1 cup white flour
½ cup cooking oil
¼ pound sweet butter
 2 tablespoons chopped parsley
¼ cup lemon juice

Salt and pepper the picattas and dredge in flour. Heat the oil in a skillet and sauté the picattas 10 minutes, turning often. Remove picattas to a shallow serving platter. Keep warm. Drain fat from skillet, melt butter, add parsley and lemon juice, blend, pour over picattas. Sauce should be very warm but not boiling. Serve with a purée of broccoli.

Médaillons de Veau Hongroise

[VEAL MEDALLIONS WITH PAPRIKA]   FOR 4

A médaillon is a slice of veal, 1-inch thick, 3 inches in diameter, cut from the loin or filet, trimmed of fat and sinews.

¼ pound sweet butter
 3 tablespoons cooking oil
 4 veal medallions, each 6 ounces
½ cup finely chopped onions
 1 teaspoon salt
 1 tablespoon paprika
 1 cup heavy cream
 1 cup Sauce Velouté (page 66)
½ teaspoon cayenne pepper

Melt half of the butter in a thick-bottomed saucepan, add oil. When foaming, cook medallions 3 minutes on each side. Add onions, sprinkle with salt and cook slowly 10 minutes, occasionally turning the veal. Sprinkle with paprika, cook 3 minutes. Remove medallions to a serving plate. Drain oil and add the cream and velouté. Simmer, stirring, 5 minutes. Strain through a fine strainer, pushing onions through with wooden spatula. Add cayenne and remaining butter. Bring to a simmer, but do not boil. Pour lightly over the medallions. Serve with boiled new potatoes or noodles.

Paupiettes de Veau à la Milanaise

[VEAL ROLLS STUFFED WITH MUSHROOMS
AND HAM]

FOR 6

Step One: Stuffing for 6 veal paupiettes
> 6 tablespoons sweet butter
> 2 tablespoons cooking oil
> ½ cup finely chopped onions
> 1 teaspoon chopped garlic
> 1 cup chopped mushrooms
>   Salt and white pepper to taste
> 2 tablespoons tomato purée
> ½ cup finely chopped boiled ham
> ¼ cup cognac
> ½ cup Demi-Glace (page 74)
> 1 teaspoon fresh thyme leaves
> 2 tablespoons white bread crumbs
> 2 egg yolks

Melt the butter in a heavy-bottomed saucepan. When foaming, add the oil and onions, cook 5 minutes; add the garlic, cook 2 minutes. Add the mushrooms, salt and pepper, tomato purée and ham, simmer 4 minutes; add the cognac, demi-glace and thyme, simmer 2 minutes. Remove from stove and add the bread crumbs and egg yolks. Mix well. Cool 2 hours

Step Two: To stuff and cook paupiettes
> 6 loin veal steaks, 6 ounces each,
>   flattened to 6 by 4 inches, ¼-inch thick
> 6 thin slices from 6-ounce square of
>   fat back, 6 by 4 inches (save skin)
> 6 tablespoons sweet butter
> ½ cup sliced onions
> ½ cup sliced carrots
> 1 clove garlic
>   Skin of 6-ounce square of fat back (see above)
> 2 cups dry white wine
> ½ cup tomato purée
> ½ cup Demi-Glace (page 74)
>   Salt and white pepper to taste
>   Bouquet garni

Cover veal steaks with the stuffing, then roll veal to resemble a large cork. Wrap the thin slices of larding pork around the veal and tie these with twine. Melt butter in skillet. When foaming, put in onions, carrots, garlic and fat-back skin. Simmer 5 minutes. Place the paupiettes on top of the vegetables, cook 10 minutes, turning veal several times, so each side will start to cook. Add wine, tomato purée, demi-glace, salt, pepper and bouquet garni. Bring to a boil, cover and place in a preheated 350-degree oven 90 minutes. Take out paupiettes, remove twine and place the rolls in a casserole. Keep warm. Push the sauce through a fine strainer, boil 5 minutes or until thickened. Check seasoning. Pour over paupiettes, simmer 3 minutes before serving. Serve with Risotto à la Milanaise (page 278).

Émincé de Veau à la Neuchâteloise

[MINCED VEAL IN CREAM SAUCE]   FOR 4

> 2 pounds veal, loin or filet, sliced in strips
>   2 inches long, ½-inch thick
>   Salt and white pepper
> ½ cup white flour
> 2 tablespoons sweet butter (more, if needed)
> 2 tablespoons cooking oil (more, if needed)
> ½ cup minced shallots
> ¾ cup Neuchâtel wine
> 1½ cups heavy cream
>   1 egg yolk
>   1 tablespoon lemon juice

Salt and pepper strips of veal, dredge in flour. Heat the oil and butter in a thick-bottomed saucepan. When foaming, sauté the veal strips over a high fire 5 minutes; add shallots, cook 2 minutes. Stir in the rest of the flour, cook 3 minutes. Add wine, simmer 1 minute; add cream, cook 5 minutes. Remove strips of veal to a warm serving dish. Remove sauce from fire, mix egg yolk with a little sauce, then add slowly to sauce, stirring rapidly so egg will not scramble. Stir in lemon juice. Strain with a very fine strainer or cheescloth over the veal. This dish goes well with Spetzli (page 271).

Bitokes de Veau à la Russe

[VEAL PATTIES IN SOUR CREAM]   FOR 4

¼ pound sweet butter
2 tablespoons cooking oil
½ cup chopped onions
1 tablespoon salt
1 cup white bread crumbs
½ teaspoon cayenne pepper
1½ pounds veal, loin or filet, all fatty parts removed,
  run through fine blade of meat chopper
2 egg yolks
White flour
½ cup vodka
1 cup sour cream
1 cup Sauce Hollandaise (page 81)

Heat the oil and half the butter in a saucepan. When foaming, add onions, cook 5 minutes without browning. Add salt and bread crumbs; remove from the stove and add cayenne; mix in the veal and egg yolks, blend thoroughly. Cool. Make 4 patties 3 inches in diameter, 1½ inches thick. Refrigerate 2 hours before using. Dredge in the flour. Melt the remaining butter in a saucepan; when hot, cook the bitokes (patties) slowly, 10 minutes on each side. Remove to a warm serving dish. Drain fat from pan, add the vodka, stir in the sour cream and simmer 5 minutes. Remove from fire and blend in the hollandaise sauce. Heat, but do not boil. Strain over the bitokes. Steamed cucumbers are excellent with this dish.

Côtes de Veau à la Paiva

[VEAL CHOPS IN CREAM SAUCE WITH
MUSHROOMS AND ARTICHOKE BOTTOMS]   FOR 4

½ pound white mushrooms
2 tablespoons lemon juice
Salt
4 tablespoons sweet butter (more, if necessary)
4 veal chops, 1-inch thick
4 slices foie gras, ½-inch thick
1 cup white bread crumbs
2 cups heavy cream
4 artichoke bottoms, cut in quarters, cooked
  (may be obtained in jars)

2 egg yolks
Salt and white pepper
1 tablespoon chopped parsley
1 teaspoon chopped tarragon (½ teaspoon if dry)

Place cleaned mushrooms in a deep saucepan, add lemon juice and salt and simmer 2 minutes. Drain and set aside. Melt the butter in a saucepan; when foaming, add chops. Brown on each side, turning often, 10 minutes. Remove and cool slightly. Make an incision in the side of each chop with a sharp knife. Insert a slice of foie gras and close the aperture with fine twine and needle. Roll the chops in bread crumbs and sauté in their saucepan 8 minutes, turning often. Place the chops in an ovenproof serving dish, remove twine. Keep warm. Drain the butter from the veal saucepan, add cream and cook to reduce to half its volume. Add the artichokes and mushrooms, bring to a boil, remove from fire and add egg yolks, salt and pepper to taste. Place artichokes and mushrooms in the center of serving dish, arranging the chops around. Spoon the cream-egg yolk sauce lightly over the vegetables and chops; place in a preheated 350-degree oven 5 minutes before serving. Fit each chop with a frill to decorate and sprinkle with parsley and tarragon.

Côtes de Veau à la Soubise

[VEAL CHOPS WITH ONION PURÉE]   FOR 4

1 cup white rice
2 cups sliced onions
3 cups White Stock (page 61)
2 egg yolks
Salt and white pepper to taste
4 tablespoons sweet butter
4 veal chops, 1 inch thick, salted and peppered
2 cups Demi-Glace (page 74)
2 tablespoons truffle juice (liquid from the tin)
4 tablespoons cognac
1 cup Sauce Béchamel (page 71)
1 cup heavy cream
½ cup Sauce Hollandaise (page 81)
4 slices black truffles

Cook the rice and onions in a deep saucepan in the white stock; when boiling, put a lid on the pan and place in a preheated 400-degree oven for 30 minutes or until rice is tender. Force through a sieve and mix well with the egg yolks, salt and pepper; set aside. Melt the butter in a skillet. When foaming, add veal chops and cook 20 minutes, turning often (chops should be tender); remove to flat serving dish. Drain the butter from the skillet and stir in demi-glace, truffle juice and cognac. Over medium heat, reduce 5 minutes, strain into a sauce boat, keep warm. Coat the top of each chop with a ½-inch layer of soubise (rice-onion mixture). Mix the béchamel with cream, simmer 5 minutes. Off heat, blend in the hollandaise, mixing well. Spread over the veal chops and soubise. Place under the broiler to brown. Put a truffle slice on top of each chop. Serve with sauce boat on the side.

Côtes de Veau en Casserole Lucullus

[VEAL CHOP CASSEROLE WITH MACARONI] FOR 4

> 6 tablespoons sweet butter
> 3 tablespoons cooking oil
> 4 lean veal chops, ½ pound each
>   Salt
>   White flour
> 1 cup mushrooms, sliced julienne
> ¼ cup Madeira
> 1 cup Demi-Glace (page 74)
> 1 tablespoon smoked beef tongue, sliced julienne
> 1 tablespoon black truffles, sliced julienne
> 2 cups elbow macaroni, boiled 10 minutes, drained
> 1 tablespoon foie gras purée
> 1 teaspoon white pepper
> 4 thin slices boiled ham
>   Grated Swiss cheese

Heat the oil and half the butter in a thick-bottomed saucepan. When foaming, add chops, which have been salted and dredged in flour. Cook chops 5 minutes on each side or until light brown in color. Cover and simmer 15 minutes or until tender. Place chops in a casserole. Keep warm. Drain fat from the saucepan and melt the remaining butter; add mushrooms, cook 3 minutes. Add the Madeira, demi-glace, smoked tongue and truffles, cook 3 minutes. Add the elbow macaroni, mix thoroughly and add the foie gras, keeping the pan on low fire so it is hot. Sprinkle with pepper. Mix all well. Place ham under the broiler 1 minute, then slip a slice under each chop in the casserole. Pour the macaroni mixture over the chops and bring to the boiling point before serving. Serve grated Swiss cheese on the side.

Côtelettes de Veau à la Landaise

[VEAL CUTLETS WITH FOIE GRAS]   FOR 4

Landes is an old province in the southwest of France abounding in sand dunes and pine forests. It is renowned for its foie gras. This is one of the area's favorite dishes.

> *1 cup Anglaise (page 1)*
> *6 tablespoons sweet butter*
> *8 veal cutlets, 4-inches square, ¼-inch thick*
> *4 slices foie gras, 2-inches square, ¼-inch thick*
> *4 thin slices black truffles*
> *¼ cup Madeira*
> *Salt and white pepper*
> *White flour*
> *2 cups white bread crumbs*
> *1 cup clarified butter*

Melt butter in a heavy saucepan. When foaming, cook veal 3 minutes on each side, very quickly. Remove from pan, cool. Marinate foie gras and truffles in Madeira 30 minutes. When veal cutlets are cold, place 1 slice of foie gras and 1 slice of truffle on each of the 4 cutlets. Salt and pepper and then cover with the other 4 cutlets. Dredge in flour, dip into the anglaise, then dredge in bread crumbs, so the edges will be sealed with the crumbs. Heat clarified butter in a skillet, cook cutlets 5 minutes on each side. Place in a preheated 350-degree oven 15 minutes before serving. Serve Sauce Périgourdine (page 78) on the side.

Côtelettes de Veau Château Mireille

[BREADED VEAL CUTLETS] FOR 6

6 veal cutlets, 6 ounces each flattened to ⅛-inch thickness
  Salt and white pepper
1 cup white flour
2 cups Anglaise (page 1)
2 cups white bread crumbs
½ cup cooking oil
12 anchovy filets
12 stuffed green olives
½ cup capers
1 hard boiled egg, chopped
2 tablespoons lemon juice
6 tablespoons sweet butter
2 tablespoons chopped parsley
3 cups Sauce Tomate (page 83)

Season veal cutlets with salt and pepper, dredge in white flour, dip into the anglaise, then into the white bread crumbs. Pour the oil into a thick-bottomed pan (add more, if needed). When hot, cook cutlets 5 minutes, turning, then place in a preheated 400-degree oven 15 minutes. Remove to serving platter. Keep warm. Arrange anchovy filets on cutlets, making a ring; place two olives in each ring, spread the capers over this, then the chopped egg. Sprinkle with lemon juice. Melt the butter in a skillet and let it get a light brown (noisette). Pour over the cutlets and sprinkle with chopped parsley. Serve very hot with the tomato sauce on the side.

Daube de Veau Bonnevay

[BRAISED VEAL STEW] FOR 6

Monsieur Bonnevay was the proprietor of a most famous hotel at Paray-le-Monial, in Burgundy. He inherited the hotel and its traditions from a long line of famed chefs and restaurateurs. The two most famous contemporary chefs, the late Monsieur Fernand Point from the Pyramid at Vienne, and Monsieur Alexandre Dumaine from the Côte d'Or at Saulieu, served their apprenticeships with Monsieur Bonnevay. I sometimes worked with Monsieur Bonnevay when he was short-handed. Here is one of his popular veal recipes. Daube is well-cooked meat or poultry, braised in a special casserole having a cover which seals the contents, almost like a pressure cooker but with less heat.

6 tablespoons sweet butter
½ pound salt pork, cut up in small dice,
    blanched 2 minutes, dried
1 three-pound round roast of veal
18 small white onions
2 cloves garlic, crushed
18 carrots, shaped like small walnuts
18 potatoes (new if possible), shaped like walnuts
1 cup diced white celery
1 teaspoon thyme leaves
1 bay leaf
2 sprigs parsley
    Salt and white pepper to taste
2 cups dry white Burgundy
2 cups Demi-Glace (page 74)
    Abaisse (see note under Boeuf en
    Daube Charolaise, page 206)

Melt the butter and sauté the salt pork in a skillet. When foaming, brown veal on all sides over moderate heat 15 minutes. Place the onions around, brown 3 minutes; add garlic, simmer 2 minutes. Place the veal in an earthenware casserole large enough to hold the meat, vegetables and liquid. To this casserole add the onions, carrots, potatoes, celery, thyme, bay leaf, parsley, salt and pepper, wine and demi-glace. Bring to a boil on a slow fire, so the casserole will not break. Put the lid on and seal with an abaisse. Place in a preheated 350-degree oven 3 hours. Break open the abaisse when ready to serve.

Blanquette de Veau à l'Ancienne

[VEAL STEW WITH ONIONS AND MUSHROOMS]   FOR 6

During the week in much of rural France (especially in Burgundy), people sit over their breakfast of café au lait (hot coffee with hot milk poured over toasted bread in a large bowl) and wonder aloud what they are going to have for lunch. Then, after that, they start thinking about dinner. This is a favorite lunch in Burgundy.

3 pounds veal breast, cut in 2-inch dice
½ pound lean salt pork, blanched 2 minutes, dried
6 ounces sweet butter (1½ sticks)
1 cup diced onions
1 tablespoon chopped garlic
½ cup white flour
¾ quart White Stock (page 61)
Bouquet garni
1 tablespoon salt
2 cloves
2 egg yolks
Pinch nutmeg
½ teaspoon cayenne pepper
2 cups heavy cream
2 tablespoons lemon juice
18 small whole white onions
1 pound button mushrooms

Blanch the veal pieces 2 minutes, rinse under cold water to wash off foam; dry veal. Sauté salt pork in a skillet with ¼ pound of the butter 4 minutes. Add the veal, cook 5 minutes on a hot fire, stirring often; add the diced onions, cook 5 minutes; add garlic, cook 2 minutes. Sprinkle on the flour, mix thoroughly and put in a preheated 400-degree oven 10 minutes. Put back on top of the stove. Reserve 1 cup of white stock to cook the whole onions and add the rest to the veal skillet along with the bouquet garni, salt and cloves. Bring to a boil and put back in a 350-degree oven, covered, for 90 minutes or until tender. Remove the veal (but not the sauce) to a deep ovenproof serving platter. Keep warm. Mix egg yolks, nutmeg, cayenne and 2 tablespoons of cream. Add the remaining cream to the sauce that the veal has cooked in, cook 15 minutes on top of the stove, uncovered, to reduce. Remove from fire so that it is not boiling, then whisk in egg yolk mixture very slowly so as not to lump. Stir in 1 tablespoon of lemon juice, put cream-egg mixture through fine strainer or cheesecloth. Check seasoning. In another pot, cook small whole onions in the remaining 2 ounces of butter and 1 cup of white stock for 30 minutes or until tender. Sauté mushrooms in 1 tablespoon lemon juice 3 minutes. (Mushrooms and onions may be cooked while veal is in oven.) Add mushrooms and onions to the veal, pour the sauce over, heat almost to a boil. Serve with fried heart-shaped croutons, Riz Pilaf (page 275) or plain boiled new potatoes.

Quenelles de Veau aux Champignons

[VEAL QUENELLES WITH MUSHROOMS] FOR 6

Shaped like dumplings, quenelles are made of forcemeat. In this recipe they are made with veal and baked with fresh mushrooms.

Step One: Veal quenelles
> *1 pound lean veal*
> *1 pound veal kidney suet, trimmed of all membranes*
> *1 tablespoon salt*
> *½ teaspoon cayenne pepper*
> > *Pinch nutmeg*
> *2 tablespoons cognac*
> *2 eggs*
> *1 cup heavy cream*
> *1 quart White Stock (page 61)*

Grind veal and kidney suet fine in meat chopper. Put into a mixing pan on top of another pan filled with crushed ice so the bottom of the top pan will be cold. Stirring vigorously with a wooden spatula, add salt, pepper, nutmeg, cognac and eggs and mix thoroughly. Then add cream very slowly, mixing without stopping for 10 minutes. This mixture should be of light consistency. Butter the bottom of a flat pan large enough to hold 18 quenelles. Mold this forcemeat with 2 tablespoons dipped in warm water so the meat will detach easily from the spoons. Each should be the size of a large egg. Place in buttered pan. Pour over 1 quart of boiling white stock, simmer 5 minutes, or until quenelles rise to the surface. Remove quenelles and keep warm and dry in an au gratin dish.

Step Two: Mushrooms and sauce for the quenelles
> *4 tablespoons sweet butter*
> *½ pound button mushrooms*
> *1 teaspoon salt*
> *6 tablespoons dry white wine*
> *1 tablespoon lemon juice*
> *1 cup Sauce Béchamel (page 71)*
> *1 cup heavy cream*
> *½ teaspoon cayenne pepper*
> *1 egg yolk*
> *½ cup grated Swiss cheese*

Melt the butter in thick-bottomed saucepan. When foaming, add the mushrooms, sprinkle with salt and cook 3 minutes over a high flame. Add wine and lemon juice, then béchamel sauce, cream and pepper, cook 5 minutes. Remove mushrooms and place them around the quenelles. Strain sauce through fine strainer or cheesecloth and add egg yolk, mixing well. Pour the sauce over the quenelles and mushrooms and sprinkle with grated cheese. Place in a preheated 400-degree oven 10 minutes, then under the broiler 2 minutes before serving.

AGNEAU—Lamb

There are two kinds of lamb, spring and baby. Anything else is mutton. Spring lamb is under a year old. Legs, loins and saddles are best roasted. Baby lamb can be a few weeks or a few months old and its legs and saddles are also preferred roasted. The neck and breast are used for stews. Roast baby lamb should always be served pink to retain its moisture, tenderness and delicate flavor.

All lamb is improved by inserting slivers of garlic into slits in the meat before roasting. Roasting time should be 15 to 18 minutes per pound, in a 450-degree oven. Rib chops should also be served pink.

Loins, when boned and cut in 3-ounce pieces, are called noisettes; two are right for one portion. Shoulders should be boned and stuffed, rolled, tied with twine and pot roasted, or braised. Serve with vegetables or pastas.

A whole lamb is impressive roasted on a spit; the Arabs call this mechoui (roast). The lamb is roasted over an ember fire and basted often with melted butter, to serve fifteen to twenty.

The most popular lamb dish in France is Gigot Rôti Boulangère. Like Lapereau à la Boulangère, for which there is a recipe on page 360, it takes its name from the rural custom of housewives bringing their all-ready-for-the-oven casseroles to the neighborhood baker (boulanger). After his last bake has come out of the wood-burning oven, he will cook the women's roasts. Dishes so roasted are much tastier than those cooked in ordinary ovens.

Gigot Rôti Boulangère

[ROAST LEG OF LAMB WITH ONIONS
AND POTATOES]   FOR 4

> 1 four-pound leg of lamb,
>   with pelvis bone removed
> 4 slivers garlic
> ¼ pound sweet butter
> ½ pound onions, sliced
> ½ pound potatoes, sliced the
>   size of silver dollars
>   Salt and white pepper
> ¼ cup dry white wine
> 1 cup White Stock (page 61)

Insert garlic slivers with a sharp, pointed knife in various parts of the leg; tie around 4 times with twine. Sauté the onions with half the butter 5 minutes, stirring well to prevent coloring. Mix with the potatoes and place in an earthenware cooking vessel large enough to hold the leg of lamb. Sprinkle with salt and pepper and add the wine and white stock. Put aside. Place the leg of lamb with the remaining butter in a roasting pan on top of the stove 2 minutes to brown, turning. Cook in your own oven, preheated to 450-degrees, 5 minutes on each side. Remove and place the leg on top of the vegetables in the earthenware pot. Cover with aluminum foil and bring it to your baker, or, using your own 400-degree oven, bake 35 minutes after the potatoes have started cooking.

Gigot Poché aux Aromates

[LEG OF SPRING LAMB POACHED WITH HERBS]   FOR 4

    1 four-pound leg of lamb
    1 quart White Stock (page 61)
    1 quart water
    1 quart dry white wine
    2 fresh basil leaves or ⅓ teaspoon dry
    ⅓ teaspoon rosemary
    ⅓ teaspoon sage
    ⅓ teaspoon dry mint
    2 cloves garlic
    2 large yellow onions
    2 cloves
        Bouquet garni
    2 tablespoons salt
    12 black peppercorns
    2 tablespoons arrowroot
    2 tablespoons freshly grated horse-radish

Tie the leg of lamb with 4 rounds of twine. Place it in a roasting pan or casserole; pour the liquids over; add all the above items except the arrow-root and horse-radish. Bring to a boil, skim off top, cover and simmer 70 minutes. Remove the lamb and place on an oblong serving platter. Keep warm. Through a fine cheesecloth, strain 2 cups of the bouillon in which the lamb cooked. Mix the arrowroot with 1 cup cold water, stir into the bouillon and cook 5 minutes or until thickened. Check seasoning and consistency. If too thick, add more bouillon. Stir in the horse-radish. Slice the leg crosswise. Serve this horse-radish sauce and a purée of broccoli on the side.

Gigot Bouilli à la King George V

[BOILED LEG OF LAMB]   FOR 6

In March 1918, when I was still cooking for the British Officers' Mess under Monsieur Paul Escoffier (son of Auguste), George V, King of England, came to France, landing at Boulogne-sur-Mer and staying at the Hôtel Metropole. The proprietor, Monsieur Heynon, knowing that we had plenty of food and knew what to do with it, got in touch with us, and I was sent to help do the cooking for the King. It was a big thrill for me, and I went two days beforehand to prepare the welcoming dinner. The menu was elaborate, but the King of England preferred simple foods. One of the first dishes I prepared for him proved to be one of his favorites:

1 six-pound leg of lamb, wrapped in cheesecloth
1 tablespoon salt
  Bouquet garni
8 carrots, 2 inches long
4 white turnips, halved, 2 inches long
2 small whole bunches celery, tied with cord
10 small white onions
1 medium head Savoy cabbage, cut in 8 parts
  Sauce Câpre (page 68)

Place lamb in a pot and cover with cold water. Bring to a boil and simmer 30 minutes. Add salt, bouquet garni and all the vegetables. Cover the pot and simmer 1 hour, until lamb and vegetables are tender. Remove cheesecloth. Serve the leg of lamb surrounded by the vegetables and pass a sauce boat of caper sauce. His Majesty drank a claret, a Mouton-Rothschild 1904, but he had influence. A lesser wine won't detract from this kingly lamb.

Selle d'Agneau Maurice de Talleyrand

[SADDLE OF LAMB WITH CHESTNUT PURÉE]   FOR 4

6 tablespoons sweet butter
½ cup sliced onions
1 cup sliced carrots
1 stick celery
1 sprig parsley
1 bay leaf
1 clove garlic
1 five-pound saddle of lamb
  (remove kidneys)
  Salt
½ teaspoon cayenne pepper
¼ cup Madeira
1 cup Demi-Glace (page 74)
2 tablespoons chopped truffles
1 pound chestnut purée (obtainable
  in jars, marrons au naturel)
2 egg yolks
1 cup Sauce Mornay (page 73)
2 tablespoons grated Swiss cheese

Melt the butter in a deep saucepan. When foaming, add the onions, carrots, celery, parsley, bay leaf and garlic, cook slowly 5 minutes. Place the lamb saddle on top of this, sprinkle with salt and cayenne. Cover and place in a preheated 450-degree oven 45 minutes, basting often. Remove the saddle to a platter. Cool 20 minutes. Meanwhile, add the Madeira to the saucepan, cook 3 minutes. Strain this and stir in the demi-glace. Cook 5 minutes, add the truffles and skim off the fat. Heat the chestnut purée, blend in the egg yolks and stir over medium fire until the mixture thickens to a heavy paste. Check seasoning. Carve the filets on both sides of the saddle, lengthwise. Make four ½-inch-thick slices. Coat each with chestnut purée and replace the slices to keep the original shape of the saddle. Heat the mornay sauce and spread it over the saddle. Sprinkle the grated cheese on top and place in a 450-degree oven 10 minutes. Before serving, brown under the broiler. Serve the Madeira-truffle sauce on the side and accompany the dish with Laitues Braisées (page 304).

Côtelettes d'Agneau Soufflées Jurassienne

[SOUFFLÉED LAMB CHOPS]   FOR 6

> 4 tablespoons sweet butter
> 12 loin lamb chops, 1-inch thick
> 1 cup boiled rice
> ½ cup chicken liver purée
> 2 tablespoons chopped boiled ham
> 2 teaspoons salt
> 1 teaspoon white pepper
>   Pinch nutmeg
> 2 eggs, beaten
> 2 tablespoons cognac
> 1 cup Sauce Velouté (page 66)
> ½ cup heavy cream
> 1 egg yolk
> 2 tablespoons grated Swiss cheese
> 2 tablespoons white bread crumbs

Melt the butter in a saucepan. When foaming, cook lamb chops 2 minutes on each side. Remove to ovenproof platter. Keep warm. Drain fat from the pan and add the rice, chicken liver purée, chopped ham, salt, pepper and nutmeg. Mix well over a medium fire 5 minutes. Mix in eggs well, cook 2 minutes; blend in cognac. Mixture should be paste-like. Coat the chops with this paste, forming a dome on each chop. Simmer the velouté with the cream 2 minutes; off fire, add the egg yolk, stirring with a whisk so it will not lump. Strain this sauce over chops, mix cheese and bread crumbs, sprinkle over the sauced chops. Place in a preheated 500-degree oven 6 minutes or until brown. Serve with Gaufrette Potatoes (page 315, Note).

Noisettes d'Agneau à l'Estragon

[NOISETTES OF LAMB WITH TARRAGON]   FOR 4

Noisettes (boned loin meat cut in 3-ounce pieces, 1-inch thick) should be cooked when you are ready to eat them and never be allowed to stand after being prepared. They should be sautéed in butter or broiled under a brisk fire and kept pink, not overdone. Classic names some cookbooks give noisettes are mostly names of the garnishes or sauces.

> 8 noisettes
>   Salt and white pepper
> ¼ pound sweet butter
>   2 tablespoons chopped shallots
> ½ cup coarsely chopped fresh tarragon
> ¼ cup Madeira
>   1 cup Demi-Glace (page 74)
> 16 whole fresh tarragon leaves
>   8 croutons, heart-shaped, fried in butter

Salt and pepper the noisettes. Melt half of the butter in a thick-bottomed saucepan. When foaming, cook the noisettes over a high fire 2 minutes on each side, then again 2 minutes on each side. Remove to a serving platter. Keep warm (not hot). Drain fat from the pan and add remaining butter. Cook shallots 2 minutes, add chopped tarragon, Madeira and demi-glace. Simmer 5 minutes. Strain through a fine cheesecloth. Dip tarragon leaves in hot water 30 seconds, drain and place 2 leaves on each noisette. Arrange noisettes on croutons, pour sauce over without disturbing the leaves on the noisettes (do that by holding them in place with a spoon while you pour the sauce). Serve Pommes de Terre Parisienne (page 313) on the side.

Filets d'Agneau de Lait Sautés Minute

[SAUTÉED BABY LAMB FILETS] FOR 4

6 tablespoons sweet butter
2 pounds baby lamb filets, cut in
  small strips, 1-inch square
  Salt and white pepper
½ cup chopped shallots
2 tablespoons cognac
¼ cup Madeira
½ cup Demi-Glace (page 74)
1 tablespoon chopped parsley
1 tablespoon finely chopped tarragon

Melt the butter in a deep saucepan. When foaming, add salted and peppered filets. Cook 3 minutes over brisk fire, turning often. Add the shallots, cook 2 minutes. Remove the lamb and add the cognac, Madeira and demiglace to the saucepan, cook 3 minutes. Put the lamb back into the saucepan and add the parsley and tarragon. Blend over medium heat without boiling. Serve with heart-shaped croutons fried in butter. Your guests should be ready to sit down to this dish as soon as it is ready.

Cari d'Agneau à la Bharatpur

[CURRY OF BABY LAMB] FOR 6

3 pounds lamb, cut into 1½-inch cubes
  (from neck or shoulder)
  Salt
½ teaspoon cayenne pepper
6 tablespoons sweet butter
2 cups chopped onions
1 tablespoon chopped garlic
1 cup peeled, chopped apples
2 tablespoons flour
2 tablespoons curry powder
½ cup dry white wine
2 cups White Stock (page 61)
2 tomatoes, peeled, seeded, finely diced
  Bouquet garni

Salt and pepper the lamb. Melt the butter in a skillet. When foaming, sauté lamb 10 minutes, stirring often so pieces will cook evenly. Add the onions and garlic, simmer 15 minutes. Add the apples and sprinkle with flour and curry powder, mix thoroughly. Add the wine, stock, tomatoes and bouquet garni. Bring to a boil, cover and place in a preheated 350-degree oven 1 hour or until lamb is tender. Remove meat to a serving casserole. Strain the sauce through a fine strainer into a separate saucepan, pushing all the ingredients through, simmer 5 minutes. Check seasoning; add more pepper if you like it sharper. Skim fat off the top, pour over the lamb, bring to a boil and serve. Serve Riz Pilaf (page 275) or plain boiled rice and shredded coconut and chutney.

Épaule d'Agneau Farcie Provençale

[ROLLED SHOULDER OF LAMB STUFFED WITH HERBS]

FOR 6

Step One: Stuffing
- *¼ pound sweet butter*
- *2 tablespoons chopped onions*
- *1 teaspoon chopped garlic*
- *2 tablespoons chopped boiled ham*
- *2 tablespoons purée of spinach*
- *1 teaspoon sweet basil*
- *1 teaspoon thyme leaves*
- *½ teaspoon rosemary*
- *1 tablespoon salt*
- *1 teaspoon white pepper*
- *Pinch nutmeg*
- *1 cup white bread crumbs*
- *2 eggs, beaten*
- *½ cup boiled rice*

Cook the onions in butter 5 minutes; do not brown. Add the garlic and ham, cook 2 minutes; add the spinach, herbs, salt, pepper and nutmeg, cook 2 minutes. Add the bread crumbs, eggs and rice, cook 3 minutes, stirring with a wooden spatula so eggs will not lump. Cool before stuffing the lamb shoulder.

Step Two: Cooking lamb
> *1 three-pound boned shoulder of lamb,*
>   *flattened with side of a cleaver*
> *3 large thin slices fat back (larding pork)*
> *4 tablespoons sweet butter*
> *1 cup sliced carrots*
> *1 cup sliced onions*
> *1 teaspoon coarsely chopped garlic*
> *2 cups dry white wine*
> *2 cups Demi-Glace (page 74)*
> *¼ cup Sauce Tomate (page 83)*
>   *Salt and black pepper*
>   *Bouquet garni*

Line the lamb shoulder with larding pork and spread the stuffing on this. Roll tightly and sew compactly with a trussing needle and twine. Melt the butter in a deep saucepan. When foaming, brown lamb shoulder evenly on a hot fire 10 minutes, turning meat several times. Add the carrots and onions, cook 5 minutes or until brown; add the garlic, cook 2 minutes. Add the wine, demi-glace, tomato sauce, salt, pepper and bouquet garni. When boiling, cover and place in a preheated 350-degree oven 75 minutes or until tender. Remove from pot into a serving casserole. Keep warm. Strain the sauce through a fine strainer, pushing the vegetables through. Simmer 10 minutes. Check seasoning. Serve the sauce on the side, also a garniture of Ratatouille Niçoise II (page 303).

Ragoût d' Agneau aux Primeurs

[LAMB RAGOUT WITH SPRING VEGETABLES]　　　FOR 6

Step One: Cooking lamb
> *6 tablespoons sweet butter*
> *4 tablespoons lard*
> *3 pounds lamb, cut in 1½-inch cubes*
>   *(from neck or shoulder)*
> *2 cups diced onions*
> *2 cups diced carrots*
> *1 tablespoon chopped garlic*
> *½ cup white flour*

    1 cup dry white wine
    1 quart Brown Stock (page 63)
    1 cup diced white celery
      Bouquet garni
    1 tablespoon salt
    2 whole tomatoes, peeled,
      seeded, cut in quarters
    2 ounces tomato purée

Melt the butter and lard in a skillet. When very hot, sauté lamb for 10 minutes or until brown, turning often. Add the onions and carrots and let them take on color. Add the garlic, cook 2 minutes; sprinkle with flour, cook 3 minutes. Add the wine, brown stock, celery, bouquet garni, salt, tomatoes and tomato purée. Bring to a boil, cover and place in a preheated 350-degree oven 1 hour until almost tender (the dish will cook 20 minutes later). While cooking, prepare the vegetables.

Step Two: Preparing primeurs
    24 small white onions, cooked 15 minutes in 2 tablespoons sweet butter
    24 small carrots, trimmed and shaped the size of large green olives,
      cooked 10 minutes in water, drained
    24 small white turnips, cooked same as carrots
    12 new potatoes, trimmed to shape of pullet eggs, cooked in water 10
      minutes, drained
    1 cup fresh or frozen peas, cooked 5 minutes, drained
    1 tablespoon caramel coloring
    Chopped parsley

Transfer the lamb from the skillet to a casserole and cover with the drained vegetables. Strain lamb sauce into the casserole, bring to a boil on top of the stove and simmer, uncovered, 20 minutes or until lamb and vegetables are tender. Skim fat from the top. Check seasoning. Add coloring and stir in well. Sprinkle with chopped parsley and serve.

Côtelettes de Mouton Rôties à la Champvallon

[ROASTED MUTTON CHOPS]   FOR 4

    4 thick mutton chops with ribs (8 ounces each)
    Salt and white pepper
    6 tablespoons sweet butter
    ½ pound onions, sliced
    ¾ cup dry white wine
    1 cup Demi-Glace (page 74)
    ½ pound potatoes sliced the size of silver dollars
    2 tablespoons white bread crumbs

Salt and pepper the chops. Melt the butter in a thick-bottomed saucepan. When foaming, add the chops and cook 5 minutes on each side over a high flame. Remove the chops to a baking dish (earthenware or pyrex). Cook the onions in the saucepan 6 minutes. Add the wine and demi-glace and bring to a boil. Stir in the potatoes and pour over the chops. Bring to a boil on top of stove, cover with aluminum foil and cook 1 hour or until tender in a preheated 350-degree oven. Skim the fat, sprinkle with bread crumbs and place under the broiler 2 minutes to brown.

PORC—Pork

Côtes de Porc Charcutière

[PORK CHOPS WITH GHERKINS]   FOR 4

> 4 pork chops, 6 ounces each, trimmed of fat
>   Salt
> 4 tablespoons sweet butter
> ½ cup chopped onions
> 2 tablespoons Madeira
> 1 cup Demi-Glace (page 74)
> 1 tablespoon Dijon mustard
> ½ cup sliced sour gherkins
> 1 teaspoon brown sugar
> ½ teaspoon black pepper

Salt chops and let stand 10 minutes. Melt the butter in a thick-bottomed saucepan. When foaming, put chops in. Sauté chops 3 minutes on each side over a high fire. Add the onions and cook 5 minutes on a lower fire. Drain the grease and add the Madeira, demi-glace, mustard and gherkins. Simmer 30 minutes or until tender. Place chops on a serving platter. Keep warm. Add sugar and pepper to sauce and cook 5 minutes. Pour the sauce over the chops and serve very hot. French-fried sliced bananas go well with this.

Carré de Porc à la New Orleans

[ROAST LOIN OF PORK WITH SWEET POTATOES]   FOR 6

> 1 three-pound loin of pork (6 ribs)
>   Salt and white pepper
> 1 teaspoon fresh thyme leaves (½ teaspoon if dry)

½ teaspoon rosemary
4 tablespoons sweet butter
24 small onions, blanched 2 minutes
2 cloves garlic, unpeeled
12 carrots, shaped like small eggs, blanched 5 minutes
1 pound sweet potatoes, boiled in skin,
   then trimmed and shaped the size of eggs
½ cup dry white wine
1 cup White Stock (page 61)
1 tablespoon chopped parsley

Place the pork loin in an ovenproof cooking dish. Sprinkle with the salt and pepper, thyme and rosemary leaves. Dot with small lumps of butter. Place in a preheated 450-degree oven 35 minutes, then turn pork and cook another 35 minutes, basting several times. Arrange the onions around the loin and roast 10 minutes. Add the garlic cloves, carrots and sweet potatoes and roast 10 minutes more or until the vegetables are tender. Remove from oven and add the wine and stock. Bring to a boil on top of the stove and cook 5 minutes. Remove the pork to a warm platter and arrange the vegetables around it. Reduce liquid to half. Remove garlic, skim fat from gravy. Slice the meat ½-inch thick, sprinkle with parsley and serve with gravy on the side.

Carré de Porc à la Créole

[LOIN OF PORK WITH PEPPERS AND TOMATOES]   FOR 6

1 three-pound loin of pork (6 ribs)
½ cup cooking oil
2 cups sliced onions
4 cloves garlic, chopped
   Salt and white pepper
2 cups sliced green peppers
1 cup red pimentos
4 fresh tomatoes, peeled, seeded, cut into quarters
3 ounces tomato paste
1 cup dry white wine
1 tablespoon fresh chopped thyme leaves
   Bouquet garni
1 cup sliced okra
2 tablespoons Major Grey's Chutney
½ cup sliced sour gherkins

Heat the oil in a deep saucepan. Brown the pork, turning frequently. Add the onions and lightly brown them. Add the garlic, salt and pepper and simmer 15 minutes. Add the green peppers, pimentos, tomatoes, tomato paste, wine and thyme leaves. Bring to a boil, add the bouquet garni, cover and put in a preheated 450-degree oven 1½ hours. Remove the loin, carve into chops and place on a serving platter. Keep warm. Remove the bouquet garni and skim off the oil. Add the okra and chutney to the sauce in the pan and simmer 10 minutes. Add the sour gherkins to this sauce and pour lightly over the chops. Serve hot with Riz Pilaf (page 275).

Carré de Porc Fumé à la Mandarin

[SMOKED LOIN OF PORK WITH ORANGES]   FOR 6

> 1 three-pound smoked loin of pork (6 ribs)
> 1 onion stuck with 4 cloves
>   Bouquet garni
> 1 tablespoon black peppercorns
> 1 tablespoon salt
> ¾ cup brown sugar
>   Pinch nutmeg
> 6 oranges, peeled, sliced ½-inch thick
> 1 cup fresh orange juice
> 1 cup Demi-Glace (page 74)
> ½ cup Cointreau or Triple Sec

Put the loin of pork in a deep skillet, cover with cold water and add the onion, bouquet garni, peppercorns and half the salt. Cover and cook over medium heat 1 hour. Remove pork from the liquid and trim off most of the fat. Place in a roasting pan; coat with the brown sugar, which has been mixed with the nutmeg and remaining salt. Arrange the orange slices on top and pour in the orange juice, demi-glace and Cointreau. Bring to a boil, cover and bake 30 minutes in a preheated 450-degree oven. Remove the loin to a serving platter. Reduce the liquid in the pan to half and strain through a fine strainer. Check seasoning. Serve the sauce on the side. A purée of chestnuts or sweet potatoes goes well with this.

Fricadelles Flamande

[PORK MEAT BALLS]   FOR 6

> ¼ pound sweet butter
> ½ cup chopped shallots

2 cloves garlic, chopped
1 tablespoon salt
1 teaspoon black pepper
  Pinch nutmeg
2 pounds loin of pork (trimmed, no fat),
  put through medium blade of meat chopper
3 egg yolks, beaten
3 cups white bread crumbs
3 egg whites, stiffly beaten
½ cup cooking oil
24 small white onions
12 potatoes, trimmed to size and shape of eggs
½ cup dry white wine
 2 cups Chicken Broth (page 62)
  Bouquet garni
½ cup chopped parsley

Melt half the butter and cook shallots slowly 3 minutes. Do not brown.
Add garlic and cook 2 minutes. Place in a mixing bowl with the salt,
pepper, nutmeg, meat and egg yolks. Mix thoroughly, add bread crumbs
and mix well. Blend in the stiffly beaten egg whites. Shape the mixture
into 12 balls, each the size of a large egg. Heat the cooking oil in a skillet
and brown the meat balls (about 3 minutes), turning often so they color
evenly. Brown the onions in the remaining butter. Place the meat balls in
a deep saucepan, surround them with the onions and potatoes and pour
in the wine and chicken broth. (There should be enough to cover the
ingredients.) Bring to a boil, add the bouquet garni and cover and place
in a preheated 400-degree oven 40 minutes or until potatoes are done.
Bake approximately 30 minutes covered, 10 minutes uncovered. Check
seasoning. Remove bouquet garni before serving. Place on a serving platter and sprinkle with parsley. (The cooking liquid is not used in this recipe.)

8

ABATS—Variety Meats

Here are those choice, unusual meats many of us overlook or, because of a lack of knowledge or experience, frown upon; but we French hold them in high esteem: livers, hearts, kidneys, sweetbreads, brains, calf's head, feet, tongue, testicles, and more. To my way of thinking, not only are abats highly nutritious, but they are among the tastiest in our French cuisine—delicate in flavor, a delight to cook and serve. For our extremely competitive dining world today, these are truly "different" recipes. Yet they are time-proven. In fact, peasant-proven, which to me is always the true test of fire. The first recipe I offer could be called "Lamb Delights"; truly they are the ultimate that an animal can offer.

ANIMELLES—Testicles

Animelles d'Agneau Bonne-Mère

[SAUTÉED LAMB TESTICLES]   FOR 4

1 pound lamb testicles
6 tablespoons sweet butter
1 tablespoon chopped shallots
½ pound mushrooms, sliced
6 tablespoons dry white wine
2 tablespoons dry sherry
½ cup heavy cream
1 cup Sauce Béchamel (page 71)
   Salt and white pepper to taste
1 tablespoon chopped parsley
½ cup Sauce Hollandaise (page 81)

Farmhouse, Normandy

Soak the testicles 2 hours in enough cold water to cover. Drain. Add the same amount of fresh water in a deep saucepan with the testicles and boil 2 minutes. Rinse under cold running water, remove the outer skin and slice each in four pieces. Melt the butter in another saucepan. When foaming, sauté the shallots 3 minutes; do not brown. Add the mushrooms, sauté 2 minutes; add the testicles, sauté 5 minutes. Pour in the white wine, sherry, cream and béchamel sauce and add the salt, pepper and parsley; simmer 5 minutes. Add the hollandaise sauce, stir gently. Place in a baking dish and brown under the broiler before serving.

CERVELLES—Brains

This blanching technique should be used in cooking all brain dishes: Soak brains in cold salted water for four hours. Drain. Remove outer skin or membrane and blood spots, but leave brain intact without cutting it. Wash well in cold water and place in a deep skillet with enough cold water to cover. Add ½ cup cider vinegar for each quart water; 1 bay leaf, 1 teaspoon dry thyme leaves and 2 tablespoons salt. Bring to a boil. Simmer 15 minutes. Cool in the liquid for 25 minutes. Brains then can be kept in refrigerator and used as needed.

Cervelles d'Agneau au Beurre Noir

[LAMB BRAINS WITH BLACK BUTTER]   FOR 4

    2 lamb brains, blanched
    ¼ pound sweet butter
    ½ cup wine vinegar
        Salt and white pepper to taste
    2 tablespoons capers
    1 tablespoon chopped parsley

Split brains in two lengthwise and dry of all liquid. Place in a baking dish, then in a preheated 400-degree oven 7 minutes. Melt the butter in a skillet until well browned. Spoon over the brains. Bring the vinegar to a boil in a skillet, and pour over the brains. Season with salt and pepper. Sprinkle on the capers and parsley just before serving.

Frittos de Cervelles Portugaise

[FRIED CALF'S BRAINS WITH PORTUGUESE SAUCE]   FOR 4

Step One: Marinade
> 2 calf's brains, blanched, cut into 8 pieces
> 1 tablespoon salt
> 1 tablespoon white pepper
> 4 tablespoons lemon juice
> 2 tablespoons cooking oil
> 2 tablespoons chopped parsley

Make a marinade of the salt, pepper, lemon juice, cooking oil, parsley. Soak the brains in this for 1 hour before cooking.

Step Two: Cooking the brains
> 1 cup white flour
> 1 egg
> 1 teaspoon salt
> ¼ cup beer
> ¼ cup heavy cream
> 2 tablespoons melted sweet butter
> Oil for deep frying
> Sauce à la Portugaise (page 79)

Blend the flour, egg, salt, beer, cream and melted butter into a batter. Let this rise on the stove shelf for one half hour before using. When ready, drain the pieces of brain. Dip each into the batter separately. Deep fry at 370 degrees until well browned. Drain pieces on dry cloth or paper towels. Serve with sauce à la portugaise.

TÊTE DE VEAU—Calf's Head

Tête de Veau Vinaigrette

[CALF'S HEAD WITH VINAIGRETTE SAUCE]   FOR 6

Step One
Cut a medium calf's head into 8 pieces. Blanch brain and reserve. Soak
the pieces of head in cold water, completely submerged, for 24 hours. Then
place the head pieces in a deep skillet with fresh cold water to cover, bring
to boil, cook 4 minutes and rinse under running cold water. Trim off most
of the fat. Rub pieces with halves of lemon to keep them white.

>   *1 gallon cold water*
>   *½ cup white flour, blended with enough*
>   *cold water to make a smooth paste*
>   *Tongue from the head*
>   *1 large onion stuck with 2 cloves*
>   *2 cloves garlic*
>   *1 stalk celery, white parts only, chopped*
>   *1 bay leaf*
>   *White of one leek*
>   *1 teaspoon thyme leaves*
>   *¼ cup lemon juice*
>   *4 tablespoons salt*
>   *¼ cup tabasco sauce*

Make a blanc, a form of court bouillon, by combining all the above ingredients. Reserving the brains, put the pieces of calf's head into the
blanc. Bring to boil, being careful not to let the calf's head stick to the
bottom of pot and burn. Simmer 2 hours. (After 1 hour, test tongue for
tenderness, pressing tip between forefinger and thumb. If not yet done,
cook longer.) Cool in its own liquid. Cook the brain on the side as suggested in the recipe for Cervelles d'Agneau au Beurre Noir (page 242).

Step Two
Warm as many pieces of calf's head as you need in the liquid in which
it cooked, adding some of the tongue and brain. Simmer 3 minutes. Drain.
Serve some plain boiled potatoes on the side. Each helping should have a
boneless slice of head, a piece of brain, 1 slice of skinned tongue. Serve
with Sauce Vinaigrette (page 325) and Sauce Gribiche (page 327) on
the side.

Tête de Veau en Tortue

[CALF'S HEAD IN TURTLE SAUCE]   FOR 6

>   1 calf's head, cooked and cut into twelve 2-inch cubes
>   2 cups Demi-Glace (page 74)
>   2 cups Sauce Tortue (page 80)
>   ½ cup Madeira
>   ¼ cup dry sherry
>   6 medium mushrooms, simmered in 6 tablespoons lemon
>   juice, ¼ cup water, 1 teaspoon salt 3 minutes (reserve juice)
>   12 pitted green olives
>   6 one-inch squares of the precooked tongue
>   12 small quenelles of chicken (recipe follows)
>   Heart-shaped croutons fried in butter (for garnish)

Place the calf's head in deep saucepan with the demi-glace, turtle sauce, Madeira and sherry. Bring to boil and simmer 10 minutes. Add the mushrooms and juice they were cooked in, olives, tongue and quenelles. Simmer to reduce liquid to half the original volume. Serve with heart-shaped croutons around the platter.

Quenelles de Poularde

[CHICKEN QUENELLES]   FOR ABOUT 16 QUENELLES

>   1 cup white bread crumbs
>   1 cup boiling milk
>   1 teaspoon salt
>   Pinch nutmeg
>   Pinch cayenne pepper
>   1 egg
>   1 pound white meat of chicken
>   1 cup heavy cream
>   White of 1 egg
>   Salt and white pepper to taste

Place white bread crumbs in a deep saucepan with milk. Add the salt, nutmeg and cayenne. Stir well over a moderate fire into a smooth consistency. Turn off heat and add the whole egg, mix well. Cool, place in refrigerator (this is called panade). Put the chicken meat through the fine blade of the meat chopper; rub this chopped meat through a fine sieve. Mix the chicken meat with the panade in a shallow pan, over a bed of shaved ice, in order to keep the mixture very cold. Mix vigorously with a wooden spatula, adding gradually the heavy cream and egg white.

Add salt and pepper to taste. Mold forcemeat with two teaspoons to the size of large olives. Drop these in a well-buttered, shallow saucepan. Pour 1 pint of boiling water over and let simmer 5 minutes over a low fire or until quenelles rise to the surface of the liquid. The water should cover the quenelles while cooking. Remove quenelles to a bowl filled with cold water. Dry them as you need them before using.

COEUR—Heart

Coeur de Veau Farci Bourguignon

[STUFFED CALF'S HEART IN WINE SAUCE]   FOR 4

Step One: Stuffing
    ¼ pound sweet butter
    1 cup chopped onions
    1 cup white bread crumbs
    1 tablespoon chopped garlic
    ½ cup chopped parsley
    ½ tablespoon white pepper
    1 tablespoon salt
        Pinch sage powder
    ½ pound sausage meat
    1 egg

Melt the butter in a saucepan, add onions, cook 5 minutes. Add bread crumbs, garlic, parsley, pepper, salt and sage. Mix the sausage meat and egg into the mixture.

Step Two: Cooking
    2 calf's hearts
    2 slices larding pork
    2 tablespoons cooking oil
    2 carrots, sliced
    1 onion, diced
    1 clove garlic
    1 celery stalk
    1 bay leaf
    1 teaspoon thyme leaves
    2 cups red Burgundy
    2 cups White Stock (page 61)

Stuff the hearts and cover the aperture with larding pork; sew with a trussing needle and twine. Brown the hearts in hot cooking oil in a deep saucepan. Stir in the sliced carrots, onion, garlic, celery, bay leaf and thyme. Pour in the wine and stock. Bring to a boil on top of the stove, cover with a lid and put into a preheated 350-degree oven 1 hour or until tender. Remove hearts and place in a serving casserole. Strain the sauce over the hearts and simmer 5 minutes on top of the stove before serving. Slice the hearts at table. Serve with plain boiled potatoes or Riz Pilaf (page 275).

ROGNONS—Kidneys

There are three ways to cook kidneys: whole, after trimming the suet; split in half and broiled, sautéed or in casserole; cut into small pieces to sauté for pies or pudding.

Lamb and veal kidneys are more tender than beef; therefore they will cook faster. It also makes a difference if the kidneys come from a young animal or an old one; this changes the cooking time. Ask your butcher, or test in cooking.

Rognons d'Agneau Turbigo

[LAMB KIDNEYS WITH MUSHROOMS AND SAUSAGES]   FOR 6

2 cups Demi-Glace (page 74)
1 cup dry white wine
12 mushroom caps (reserve stems and peelings)
½ cup cooking oil
6 kidneys, trimmed, divided; cut out fat at
   bottom and remove membrane
¼ pound sweet butter
½ cup chopped shallots
1 teaspoon salt
½ teaspoon pepper
¼ cup cognac
12 heart-shaped croutons, fried in butter
½ pound small pork chipollata sausages,
   baked 5 minutes in a 450-degree oven
½ cup beef marrow, mashed into a paste
   Chopped parsley

Cook demi-glace with wine and mushroom stems and peelings 10 minutes to reduce liquid to one-third of its volume. Meanwhile, heat cooking oil in a thick saucepan. When hot, add kidneys and sauté quickly 3 minutes, turning each twice so it will fry on each side. Empty pan into a colander; drain. This will eliminate kidney odor. Sauté mushroom caps 3 minutes in a small amount of the butter. Set aside. Melt the remaining butter in the same pan you sautéed kidneys. When hot, return kidneys to the pan with the shallots and sauté together 3 minutes. Add salt and pepper. Pour in the cognac and flambé. Place each half kidney on a crouton with 1 mushroom cap on top of each kidney. Arrange on a serving platter, with sausages fanned in the center of the platter. Bring demi-glace-and-wine sauce to a boil and add the mashed marrow, blending gently with a kitchen spoon. Check seasoning. Strain through a fine cheesecloth over the kidneys. The sauce should be of a good consistency. Sprinkle the dish with chopped parsley. Serve Riz Pilaf (page 275) on the side.

Rognons d'Agneau à la Richebourg

[LAMB KIDNEYS WITH SWEETBREADS, ONIONS AND MUSHROOMS]   FOR 6

½ pound lamb sweetbreads, blanched
6 ounces (1½ stick) sweet butter
1 teaspoon salt
½ teaspoon white pepper
1 cup Demi-Glace (page 74)
1 cup Richebourg red wine or other good red Burgundy
24 small white onions, well browned in some of the butter
6 lamb kidneys
½ cup cooking oil
12 medium mushroom caps, peeled, quartered
2 shallots, chopped
1 clove garlic, minced
¼ cup Marc de Bourgogne or cognac
½ tablespoon chopped chervil
½ tablespoon chopped parsley
12 Fleurons (page 285)

Melt 4 tablespoons of the butter in a saucepan, add sweetbreads and sprinkle with half the salt and pepper. Stir in half the demi-glace and all the wine. Simmer 5 minutes or until sauce is of good consistency. Add the browned onions, simmer 10 minutes. Set aside. Cut each kidney in 8 pieces, peeling off the membrane and coring out white centers. Heat the oil in a saucepan. Sauté the kidney pieces 2 minutes, turning all pieces once. Drain well in a strainer or colander. Melt the remaining butter in the pan the kidneys were sautéed in. Add mushrooms, shallots and garlic, simmer 3 minutes. Stir in the kidneys. Pour in the Marc de Bourgogne and flambé. Add the remaining demi-glace and bring to a boil. Add the sweetbreads, simmer 10 minutes. Check seasoning. Serve in a hot casserole bordered with fleurons and sprinkled with chervil and parsley.

Rognons de Veau en Casserole Grand'mère

[VEAL KIDNEY CASSEROLE]   FOR 6

> *½ pound lean salt pork, cut in ¾-inch cubes*
> *6 veal kidneys (trim most fat off, leaving a small*
>   *amount around the kidney so it won't dry in cooking)*
> *24 medium mushroom caps*
> *24 small white onions, browned in sweet butter 3 minutes*
>   *1 clove garlic*
> *¼ cup cognac*
> *½ cup sherry*
>   *2 cups Demi-Glace (page 74)*
>   *1 teaspoon salt*
> *½ teaspoon pepper*
> *½ cup chopped parsley*
>   *1 bay leaf*
> *½ teaspoon dry thyme leaves*
> *24 Pommes de Terre Parisienne (page 313)*
>   *1 recipe Abaisse (see note*
>   *under Boeuf en Daube Charolaise, page 206)*

Put the salt pork in a skillet, cover with cold water and bring to a boil; simmer 2 minutes. Place under cold running water 5 minutes. Drain. Place the salt pork in a thick-bottomed saucepan on a medium flame, simmer 3 minutes. Add the whole kidneys, cook for 10 minutes, or until brown, turning often. Add mushrooms, simmer 3 minutes; add browned onions, simmer 3 minutes; add garlic, simmer 2 minutes. Pour off grease. Add the cognac and flambé. Stir in the rest of the ingredients except the abaisse. Check seasoning. Put into an earthenware casserole. Cover and seal with the abaisse. (Wet the edges of the casserole and press the abaisse around, sealing the lid.) Place the casserole in a preheated 400-degree oven for one half hour. This dish should be served immediately on coming out of the oven; unseal the cover at the table so your guests can appreciate the aroma.

Rognons de Veau Flambés

[VEAL KIDNEYS IN MUSTARD CREAM SAUCE]   FOR 4

> ½ cup cooking oil
> 4 veal kidneys, cut into pieces 1-inch
>   square; remove all fat, membranes
> 4 tablespoons sweet butter
> ½ cup chopped shallots
> 1 teaspoon salt
> ½ teaspoon white pepper
> ¼ cup cognac
> ½ cup sherry
> 2 cups heavy cream
> 2 egg yolks, beaten
> 1 tablespoon Dijon mustard
> 1 teaspoon Lea & Perrins sauce

Heat the oil in a thick-bottomed saucepan. Add the kidneys, sauté 3 minutes over high fire. Remove to a colander, draining oil and blood. Let kidneys stand 5 minutes. Melt butter in the same saucepan. When foaming, sauté kidneys and shallots, adding salt and pepper, for 3 minutes. Add cognac and flambé. Blend in the sherry and cream. Mix the egg yolks with mustard. Remove the kidneys to a serving dish. Simmer cream to reduce to one half. Remove from fire and add the egg yolk-mustard mixture, stirring quickly with a kitchen spoon (if the cream is too hot, the eggs will curdle). The saucepan may be put back on the flame again, but do not boil. Before serving, blend in the Lea & Perrins and strain sauce over the kidneys. Serve with Riz Pilaf (page 275) and Fleurons (page 285).

Rognons de Veau Grillés au Poivre

[BROILED PEPPERED VEAL KIDNEYS
WITH SAUCE À LA DIABLE]   FOR 4

> 2 veal kidneys, split in half, leaving some fat on
> 1 cup white bread crumbs
> ½ cup Dijon mustard
> ¼ cup crushed black peppercorns
> 1 teaspoon salt
>   Pinch nutmeg
> ½ teaspoon dry thyme leaves
>   Sauce à la Diable (following)

Grill kidneys under broiler 3 minutes on each side. Remove, drain. Mix the bread crumbs with the rest of the ingredients to make a paste. Spread this paste over the kidneys; place them under a very hot broiler 3 minutes on each side. Serve with sauce à la diable on the side and hot potato chips.

Sauce à la Diable

½ cup chopped shallots
¼ cup Madeira
1 cup Demi-Glace (page 74)
1 teaspoon salt
½ teaspoon pepper
2 tablespoons Lea & Perrins sauce
1 tablespoon Dijon mustard
1 tablepsoon chopped fresh tarragon
(or ½ teaspoon dry)
2 tablespoons cognac
6 tablespoons sweet butter

Simmer shallots in the Madeira 5 minutes. Add demi-glace, simmer 5 minutes. Add salt, pepper, Lea & Perrins, mustard and tarragon, cook 2 minutes; stir in cognac. Strain through fine strainer. Mix the butter into the sauce slowly *just* before serving, so the sauce will be smooth and the butter flavor at its best.

FOIE—Liver

Foies de Volaille en Couronne Régence

[CHICKEN LIVERS IN A RICE CROWN]   FOR 4

Step One: For a crown of rice 8 inches in diameter
  6 tablespoons sweet butter
  ½ cup chopped onions
  1 cup rice
  2 cups boiling White Stock (page 61)
  1 teaspoon salt
  ½ teaspoon white pepper
    Bouquet garni
  1 cup grated Parmesan cheese
  1 eight-inch buttered crown mold

Melt the butter in a skillet, add onions, cook 5 minutes; do not brown. Stir in the rice, sauté 2 minutes. Add hot stock, salt, pepper and bouquet garni. Bring to a boil on top of the stove, cover with aluminum foil *and* lid and place in a preheated 400-degree oven 20 minutes or until rice is tender. Remove bouquet garni, stir in cheese and pack the rice in a mold. Keep very hot.

Step Two: Chicken livers
  6 ounces sweet butter (1½ sticks)
  1 pound chicken livers, well cleaned,
    trimmed of membranes
  2 tablespoons chopped shallots
  2 tablespoons cognac
  ½ cup Madeira
  1 cup Demi-Glace (page 74)
  1 teaspoon salt
  ½ teaspoon white pepper
  2 ounces black truffles, cut in ⅛-inch dice
  1 tablespoon chopped parsley

Melt ¼ pound butter in a saucepan. When foaming, add chicken livers. Sauté quickly 3 minutes, browning livers well. Remove livers, drain grease. In the same saucepan, melt the remainder of the butter, add shallots and cook 2 minutes. Replace the livers in the pan, pour in the cognac and flambé. Add the Madeira, demi-glace, salt and pepper, simmer 3 minutes. Add truffles, blend. Invert the rice crown on the serving dish to unmold and pour liver mixture in the center of the ring. Sprinkle with chopped parsley.

Foies de Volaille en Brochette Lucifer

[CHICKEN LIVERS ON SKEWERS WITH
LUCIFER SAUCE]   FOR 4

¼ pound sweet butter
12 medium mushroom caps
1 teaspoon salt
½ teaspoon white pepper
2 cups white bread crumbs
2 tablespoons Dijon mustard
1 teaspoon fresh chopped thyme leaves, or ¼ teaspoon dry thyme
1 teaspoon fresh chopped sweet basil, or ¼ teaspoon dry basil
½ pound chicken livers
8 slices bacon, cut in 2-inch squares

Melt the butter in a saucepan, add mushrooms and sprinkle with salt and
pepper, sauté 2 minutes. Mix the liquid obtained from the mushrooms with
the bread crumbs, mustard, thyme and basil. Cut the chicken livers in half
and divide equally on 4 skewers (wood or metal), alternating bacon and
mushrooms. Roll the filled skewers in the bread crumb mixture. Place them
under the broiler 3 minutes, turn for another 3 minutes. Serve the skewers
on a bed of Riz Pilaf (page 275) with Sauce Lucifer (below) on the side.

Sauce Lucifer

4 tablespoons sweet butter
½ cup chopped shallots
1 tablespoon chopped garlic
½ cup chopped green peppers
½ cup chopped red pimentos
1 cup Demi-Glace (page 74)
¼ cup brandy
½ cup Sauce Tomate (page 83)
1 tablespoon Lea & Perrins sauce
¼ cup sherry
1 teaspoon salt
Pinch cayenne pepper
1 tablespoon chopped fresh sweet
basil or ½ teaspoon dry

Simmer shallots with butter 5 minutes. Add garlic, cook 1 minute. Stir in
peppers and pimentos, simmer 5 minutes. Blend in the rest of the ingredients and simmer 6 minutes before serving.

Soufflé de Foie de Veau à l'Italienne

[SOUFFLÉ OF CALF'S LIVER WITH TOMATO SAUCE]   FOR 4

> ¾ pound calf's liver
> ¼ pound sweet butter
> ½ cup flour
> ¼ cup chopped shallots
> ¼ cup cognac
> 2 egg yolks, lightly beaten
> 1½ teaspoons chopped fresh sweet basil
> 1 tablespoon salt
> ½ teaspoon white pepper
> 1½ teaspoons chopped fresh tarragon
> 4 egg whites, stiffly beaten
> 1 tablespoon chopped parsley

Put the calf's liver through the meat chopper with fine blade. Melt the butter in a heavy-bottomed saucepan, saving about 2 tablespoons to butter the soufflé dish. When melted, stir in the flour and shallots, simmer 4 minutes; do not brown. Add the liver, blend well over fire 2 minutes. Add cognac. Over a very low fire, stir in the egg yolks, then the basil, salt, pepper and tarragon. Cool. Then blend stiffly beaten egg whites and parsley into mixture. Butter an 8-inch soufflé mold and pour the liver mixture in. Place in a pan with 2 inches of boiling water and into a preheated 400-degree oven 35 minutes or until the soufflé rises and browns. Serve with Sauce Tomate (page 83) on the side. A soufflé should be served as soon as it comes out of the oven.

RIS DE VEAU—Sweetbreads

Before using sweetbreads, they should be soaked and blanched in the same manner as brains (page 242).

Ris de Veau en Casserole Clamard

[SWEETBREADS WITH PEAS AND ONIONS]   FOR 4

> ½ pound salt pork, cut in 1-inch dice
> 2 pairs calf's sweetbreads, blanched,
>   divided into 4 portions
> ¼ cup dry sherry
> 1 head Boston lettuce, washed and cut into strips

24 *small white onions, browned in butter*
1 *pound shelled new green peas*
1 *teaspoon salt*
½ *teaspoon white pepper*
1 *lump sugar*
2 *cups Demi-Glace* (*page 74*)
Small bouquet garni
6 *tablespoons sweet butter*

Blanch salt pork 2 minutes, rinse under running water 5 minutes, dry. Put in a saucepan, sauté 3 minutes. Add sweetbreads to the salt pork in the saucepan and sauté 5 minutes, turning the sweetbreads often. Add the rest of the ingredients except the butter. Cover the saucepan, bring to a boil and put in a preheated 400-degree oven 35 minutes. Remove bouquet garni. Check seasoning. Stir in butter. Serve immediately.

Ris de Veau en Meurette Mâconnaise

[SWEETBREADS WITH CHICKEN QUENELLES]   FOR 4

2 *pairs calf's sweetbreads, blanched,*
   divided into 4 portions
½ *pound lean salt pork, cut into 1-inch dice*
24 *small white onions*
4 *cloves garlic, peeled*
½ *pound mushroom caps*
2 *cups red Burgundy*
1 *cup Demi-Glace* (*page 74*)
Bouquet garni
Salt and white pepper to taste
24 *Chicken Quenelles* (*page 243*)
8 *heart-shaped croutons, ½-inch thick, fried in butter*
Chopped parsley

Blanch the sweetbreads the evening before. Cut each pair in half and place between two plates with a weight on top to keep them firm until used; refrigerate. Blanch salt pork cubes 2 minutes, then put under cold running water and dry. Sauté salt pork in a skillet 3 minutes. Add onions and sweetbreads, sauté 5 minutes, turning several times to brown sweetbreads evenly. Add garlic and mushrooms, simmer 3 minutes. Add wine, demi-glace, bouquet garni, salt and pepper and bring to a boil. Cover pan and put in a pre-heated 400-degree oven 45 minutes. Remove bouquet garni. Check seasoning. Serve 1 portion of sweetbreads to each person, placing the croutons and quenelles around the plates. Pour the sauce, which should be of a good consistency, over all. Sprinkle with chopped parsley.

Ris de Veau à la Crème Dom de Champagne

[SWEETBREADS IN CHAMPAGNE SAUCE]   FOR 4

> 4 tablespoons sweet butter
> 2 pairs calf's sweetbreads, blanched,
>   divided into 4 portions
> ¼ cup Fine Champagne or cognac
> ¾ cup dry champagne
> 1 cup heavy cream
> 1 teaspoon salt
> ¼ teaspoon cayenne pepper
>   Bouquet garni
> ½ cup White Stock (page 61), if needed
> 2 cups Duxelles (mushroom purée), kept warm (page 308)
> 4 Bread Croustades (see Crevettes Cape Cod, page 10)
> 2 egg yolks
> 1 tablespoon chopped chervil
> 1 tablespoon chopped parsley

Melt the butter in a saucepan. When foaming, sauté sweetbreads 5 minutes on each side, browning lightly. Add the brandy, flambé. Add the champagne, cover and simmer 5 minutes; add the cream, salt, cayenne and bouquet garni. Cover, simmer on a low fire 20 minutes (if liquid becomes too thick, add white stock). Remove sweetbreads. Spoon the mushroom purée into the croustades. Place one portion of sweetbreads on top of each croustade. Reduce sauce to a good consistency. Off fire, stir in egg yolks (be sure sauce is not boiling, as eggs will curdle). Strain over the sweetbreads and place in a preheated 350-degree oven 10 minutes before serving. Sprinkle with chervil and parsley.

Champagne

Tourte de Ris de Veau Armoricaine

[SWEETBREAD TART WITH VEAL QUENELLES]   FOR 6

I could not resist including this classic recipe for those who can get to a really *complete* fine food store or perhaps live in farm country.

Step One: Tourte (Pastry Shell)
Fill the bottom of a round tart mold, 8 inches in diameter, with a ¼-inch layer of Puff Paste (page 284). With a medium, plain pastry tube, push a circle of Pâte à Chou (page 283) 1-inch wide around the mold, making a shell. Bake in a preheated 350-degree oven 18 minutes.

Step Two: Quenelles de Veau (Veal Quenelles)
For about 12 quenelles
   ½ pound lean veal
   ½ recipe Panade (see Quenelles de Brochet, page 117)
    2 egg whites
   ½ cup heavy cream
    1 teaspoon salt
   ½ teaspoon cayenne pepper
      Pinch nutmeg

Put veal through the fine blade of the meat chopper. Add the panade and egg whites. Mix well. Place on a bed of chopped ice, blend with cream (adding a little at a time), sprinkle in salt, pepper, nutmeg. Mix well. Mold with two dessert spoons on a deep buttered pan, pour boiling water over, simmer until quenelles rise to the surface. Remove from water and drain on a cloth.

Step Three: Sweetbreads
   ¼ pound sweet butter
    2 pairs sweetbreads, blanched, cut into 8 pieces
   24 medium mushroom caps
    1 teaspoon salt
   ½ teaspoon white pepper
    1 cup dry white Meursault
    6 tablespoons Madeira
    1 cup heavy cream
   12 cocks' combs (available in cans or jars)
    4 ounces cocks' testicles (available in cans or jars)
    1 cup Sauce Hollandaise (page 81)
    2 ounces black truffles, cut in ¼-inch dice
   12 veal quenelles (already prepared)
      Tourte (already prepared)

Melt butter in a heavy-bottomed saucepan; when foaming, sauté sweet-breads 5 minutes, turning to brown evenly. Add mushrooms, salt and pepper, simmer 4 minutes. Pour in the wine, Madeira and cream, simmer 15 minutes. Add cocks' combs and testicles, simmer 5 minutes. Remove sweetbreads, mushrooms, cocks' combs and testicles and add hollandaise to pan. Blend but do not boil. Strain sauce and stir in truffles. Keep separate from the sweetbreads until ready to serve. Place the sweetbread mixture and quenelles in the tourte, pour the sauce over and put in a preheated 400-degree oven 5 minutes before serving.

Médaillons de Ris de Veau Lucullus

[MEDALLIONS OF SWEETBREADS] FOR 4

> 1 pair sweetbreads; blanched, cut into 4 portions
>   Salt and white pepper
> ¼ pound melted sweet butter
> 2 cups white bread crumbs
> 4 artichoke bottoms (available in cans or jars)
> 4 slices foie gras, ½-inch thick
> 2 cups Sauce Bâtarde (page 82)
> 2 cups Sauce Périgourdine (page 78)

Salt and pepper the sweetbreads; roll them in half the melted butter, then in white bread crumbs; salt and pepper again. Heat the remaining butter in a saucepan. Sauté sweetbreads 10 minutes, turning them often (they should not get too dry). Warm the artichoke bottoms. Place a slice of foie gras on each and put in a preheated 400-degree oven 3 minutes. Place 1 portion of sweetbread over each slice of the foie gras, cover with the sauce bâtarde, place under the broiler to brown. Serve the medallions of sweetbreads and the périgourdine sauce separately.

LANGUE—Tongue

Langue de Veau ou de Boeuf St. Germain

[CALF OR BEEF TONGUE WITH SPLIT PEA PURÉE] FOR 6

Step One: Blanc for a 3-pound tongue
    2 quarts cold water
    ½ cup white flour mixed with enough
      cold water to make a smooth paste

  3 tablespoons salt
  1 whole onion stuck with 2 cloves
  1 bay leaf
  1 sprig parsley
  1 stalk celery
  1 sprig thyme leaves
  1 clove garlic
 12 peppercorns
  1 three-pound fresh tongue

Mix the above ingredients, except the tongue, together and bring to a boil. Put in the tongue and simmer until tender (calf's tongue will take 1 hour, beef's tongue 2 hours, maybe more, depending on the quality of the animal). Remove the skin from the tongue.

Step Two: Purée St. Germain (Purée of Peas)
 ½ pound dry green split peas
  1 tablespoon salt
  6 tablespoons softened sweet butter

Cover peas with cold water and soak for about 12 hours. Pour off water peas have soaked in and cover with fresh cold water (about 1 quart). Add salt. Cook 1 hour, or until tender. Drain. Put through a fine sieve, strainer or food mill. Keep warm. Spread warm butter over the top so the purée will not crust.

Step Three: Sauce St. Germain
  6 ounces (1½ sticks) sweet butter
 ½ cup chopped shallots
  1 cup chopped mushrooms
  6 tablespoons Madeira
  2 cups Demi-Glace (page 74)
  1 teaspoon salt
 ½ teaspoon white pepper
  1 cup chopped boiled ham
  1 tablespoon chopped fresh tarragon
   (½ teaspoon dry)
 ½ cup chopped parsley
  1 tablespoon chopped fresh chervil
   (½ teaspoon dry)

Melt the butter in a shallow saucepan. Add the shallots, cook 3 minutes; add mushrooms, cook 3 minutes; add Madeira, demi-glace, salt and pepper, simmer 5 minutes; add ham, tarragon, parsley and chervil. Bring to a boil, mixing well. Check seasoning.

Step Four: Final assembly
    Purée St. Germain (already prepared)
    6 slices tongue (already prepared)
    Sauce St. Germain (already prepared)
    1 cup fried white bread crumbs
    ½ cup grated Parmesan cheese

Put the purée of peas on a serving platter. Lay the slices of tongue over the peas and pour the sauce over the tongue. Sprinkle bread crumbs and cheese over the sauce. Put in a preheated 400-degree oven 5 minutes before serving.

"Route Nationale"

Langue de Boeuf Charcutière

[SMOKED BEEF TONGUE WITH CHARCUTIÈRE SAUCE]

FOR 6

Step One: Prepare tongue
Simmer a 2½-pound smoked tongue in deep water for 3 hours or until tender. Remove skin, keep warm.

Step Two: Sauce Charcutière
    4 tablespoons sweet butter
    ⅓ cup chopped shallots
    1 cup Demi-Glace (page 74)
    2 tablespoons Madeira

¼ cup sherry
½ cup white wine vinegar or cider vinegar
1 tablespoon salt
1 teaspoon white pepper
½ cup chopped sour gherkins
1 tablespoon Dijon mustard
1 tablespoon Lea & Perrins sauce

Melt the butter in a saucepan and cook shallots 5 minutes. Add the demi-glace, Madeira, sherry, vinegar, salt and pepper. Cook 5 minutes. Add the gherkins and mustard. Mix well, but do not boil. Keep hot until serving. Slice cooked tongue into 1½-inch-thick slices. Arrange on a serving platter. Stir Lea & Perrins into the sauce just before pouring over tongue. Put in a preheated 400-degree oven 3 minutes before serving. Serve with mashed or au gratin potatoes.

TRIPE

Tripes à la Normande

[TRIPE WITH CALF'S FEET]   FOR 6

5 pounds honeycomb tripe, well-washed,
*   drained, cut in 3-inch squares*
3 calf's feet
1 quart dry white wine
1 quart White Stock (page 61)
2 yellow onions, stuck with 3 cloves
4 leeks, white part only
3 cloves garlic
2 stalks celery
2 large carrots
1 bay leaf
1 branch thyme or ½ teaspoon dry thyme leaves
2 tablespoons salt
1 teaspoon white pepper
¼ cup Calvados

Place all ingredients in a deep earthenware casserole. Bring to a boil on top of the stove, cover and place in a preheated 350-degree oven 4 hours or until tripe and calf's feet are tender. Remove tripe and peel meat from calf's feet; cut in 2-inch-square pieces. Place in a serving casserole. Reduce liquid to a good consistency by cooking, uncovered, on top of the stove for one half hour. Strain it over the tripe and meat from calf's feet. Add the Calvados and simmer, covered, 20 minutes. Check seasoning. Should be served very hot, with boiled new potatoes, Dijon mustard and pepper milled over it.

Tripes à la Mode de Caen   FOR 8

My dear departed friend Gaston Lauryssen, the famous president of the Carlton House in New York City and a Belgian epicure of note, used to drive to La Crémaillère in Banksville two Sundays a month and join me in lunching on this, perhaps the greatest of abat dishes. Often he was accompanied by my co-author, Jack Denton Scott, and his wife Maria Luisa. Both Scotts are cooks par excellence, and Mary Lou, as we call her, has often joined me while we worked as a team, doing everything from chopping leeks for this dish to boning squab and fluting mushrooms. I dedicate this dish to that memory, and to Gaston Lauryssen, who loved it so much.

> 2 pounds fresh honeycomb tripe
> 2 pounds beef rennet (lining of fourth stomach)
> 2 calf's feet, bones split
> ½ pound larding pork, sliced in leaves
> 1 tablespoon salt
> 3 medium carrots
> 2 medium Bermuda onions, stuck with 4 cloves
> 2 cloves garlic
> ¼ teaspoon thyme, pinch rosemary, ½ bay leaf and 1 teaspoon white peppercorns, wrapped in cheesecloth
> 1 sprig parsley, 1 large white stalk of celery and ½ pound leeks (white part only), tied together with butcher's twine
> 2 quarts dry white wine
> 1 quart Chicken Broth (page 62)
> 3 tablespoons Calvados V.S.O.P.
> Dijon mustard

Soak tripe, rennet and calf's feet in cold water 4 hours, changing water every hour. Drain, dry well. Cut tripe and rennet in 2-inch pieces. Break bones of calf's feet into 2 pieces each. Line the bottom of a roasting pan with the lard leaves. Place the tripe, rennet and feet on this. Add the salt, carrots, onions, garlic, the herbs in cheesecloth, parsley, celery and leeks. Cover with wine and chicken broth. Bring to a boil on top of the stove. Tie foil snugly around the pan, then cover. It should be tightly sealed (an abaisse can be used, see note under Boeuf en Daube Charolaise, page 206). Simmer in a preheated 300-degree oven 10 hours. Remove, place tripe and rennet in an earthenware casserole. Bone the feet, cutting the meat in 1-inch cubes, and add to the tripe. Keep warm. Pour the liquid through a fine strainer, discarding all ingredients. Bring strained liquid to a boil in a skillet; reduce to 1½ quarts. Skim off the fat. Stir in the Calvados and pour over the tripe mixture. Simmer 30 minutes. Check seasoning. Serve in hot soup plates with the mustard and French bread on the side. Plain boiled new potatoes are also good with it.

9

PASTA, RIZ, ET CRÊPES ET PÂTES—Pasta, Rice, and Pancakes and Doughs

PASTA

Spaghetti Castiglione FOR 6

While working as Second Chef at the Hotel Castiglione in Paris, I was elected by the owner, Monsieur Borgo, an Italian by birth, as his private chef. This meant that besides my many duties, I had to cook for him and his numerous guests. I created a number of recipes especially for him, with samples for the Wine Steward so that he could select the right wine to be poured with the dish. The advantage of the dubious honor of being the boss's private chef was that the Wine Steward always gave me a sample of the wine that was served and I had the chance to experiment, an opportunity welcomed by all chefs worthy of their hats. Monsieur Borgo was a gentleman, a gastronome with a splendid red nose resulting from his finely developed taste for the good food and wines he could have at the snap of a finger. One of the spaghetti dishes I created was:

Château de Tanlay, Burgundy

Castiglione Sauce
   4 tablespoons sweet butter
   1 tablespoon chopped onions
   1 teaspoon chopped garlic
   ½ cup thinly sliced mushrooms
   ¼ cup Marsala
   1 cup heavy cream
   ½ tablespoon salt
   1 teaspoon white pepper
   1 tablespoon shredded smoked beef tongue
   1 tablespoon shredded boiled ham
      Pinch nutmeg
   2 egg yolks
   1 tablespoon Sauce Hollandaise (page 81), optional

   1 pound spaghetti, cooked in a deep pot
      filled with boiling water and
      1 tablespoon salt 10 minutes,
      rinsed under cold running water,
      drained in a colander
   1 ounce shredded black truffles
   2 tablespoons grated Parmesan or Asiago cheese

Melt the butter in a saucepan. When foaming, add chopped onions, simmer 3 minutes; do not let brown. Add garlic, simmer 2 minutes; add mushrooms, simmer 3 minutes; add Marsala, cream, salt and pepper, simmer 2
minutes. Add tongue, ham, nutmeg, egg yolks and hollandaise. Mix well.
Stir in the spaghetti and truffles. Butter a deep au gratin dish and pour in
the spaghetti mixture; sprinkle with the grated cheese. Place, uncovered,
in a preheated 400-degree oven 15 minutes. The top should be well
browned. If not, place under the broiler 1 minute.

Spaghetti à la Marinare

[SPAGHETTI WITH SEAFOOD SAUCE]   FOR 6

Marinare Sauce
   ½ cup olive oil
   2 tablespoons chopped onions
   1 tablespoon chopped garlic
   1 tomato, peeled and seeded, diced
   1 cup cooked cherrystone clams (canned
      acceptable), chopped coarsely
   1 tablespoon chopped anchovy filets
      Salt to taste

Freshly ground white pepper to taste
1 tablespoon Demi-Glace (page 74)
1 teaspoon finely chopped sweet basil

1 pound spaghetti, cooked in a deep pot
   filled with boiling water and
   ½ tablespoon salt 15 minutes,
   rinsed under cold running water,
   drained in a colander
½ cup grated Parmesan or Asiago cheese

Heat the olive oil in a saucepan. Simmer onions 3 minutes; add garlic, simmer 2 minutes; add tomato, simmer 3 minutes. Add the clams, anchovies, salt, pepper, demi-glace and basil. Using wooden forks, mix spaghetti with this sauce over low heat until well blended. Add half the grated cheese just before serving. Serve remaining cheese on the side.

Spaghetti à la Bolognaise

[SPAGHETTI WITH TOMATO AND MEAT SAUCE]   FOR 6

Bolognaise Sauce
  ¾ cup olive oil (more if needed)
   1 cup coarsely chopped onions
   1 tablespoon chopped garlic
  ½ pound chopped raw filet of beef (chopped with
    sharp knife, not with meat chopper)
  ½ cup Sauce Tomate (page 83)
  ½ cup Demi-Glace (page 74)
   1 teaspoon salt
   1 teaspoon white pepper
   1 tablespoon dry mushrooms (soaked
    1 hour in water, drained, diced)
  ¼ cup dry white wine
   2 tablespoons Marsala

1 pound spaghetti, cooked in a deep pot
   filled with boiling water and
   1 tablespoon salt 10 minutes,
   rinsed under cold running water,
   drained in a colander
½ cup grated Parmesan or Asiago cheese

Heat half the oil in a saucepan. Add the onions, cook 10 minutes; do not brown. Add the garlic, simmer 2 minutes; add the chopped beef, simmer 10 minutes. Blend in the tomato sauce, demi-glace, salt, pepper and mushrooms, simmer 15 minutes, adding white wine and Marsala gradually. Heat the remaining oil in a skillet; add the spaghetti and sauté 5 minutes or until the spaghetti is hot. Place on a warm serving platter or directly onto warm individual plates. Pour Bolognaise over each serving. Pass the grated cheese.

Timbale de Vermicelle des Antilles

[TIMBALE OF VERMICELLI AND SEAFOOD]   FOR 4

    ½ cup cooking oil
     1 cup chopped onions
    ½ cup coarsely chopped green peppers
     1 tablespoon chopped pimentos
     1 teaspoon chopped garlic
    ½ cup diced mushrooms
  1½ teaspoons salt
    ½ teaspoon cayenne pepper
    ¼ teaspoon saffron
    ½ cup diced tomato, peeled and seeded
     2 tablespoons dry sherry
     1 tablespoon Demi-Glace (page 74)
    12 cooked mussels, meat halved
    12 steamed soft-shell clams, meat halved
    ½ cup cooked, diced shrimp
    ½ cup clam and mussel juice

    ½ pound vermicelli, cooked in boiling water
        with 2 teaspoons salt 7 minutes,
        rinsed under cold running water,
        drained in a colander
     1 tablespoon grated Parmesan or Asiago cheese

Heat the oil in a saucepan. Simmer the onions and green peppers 10 minutes; add the pimentos and garlic, simmer 3 minutes. Add the mushrooms, salt, cayenne, saffron and tomatoes, simmer 5 minutes. Add the wine and demi-glace, simmer 5 minutes. Stir in the mussels, clams, shrimp and the clam and mussel juice, blending well. With a wooden fork, gently stir in the vermicelli; keep on low heat 3 minutes. Add grated cheese, mix. Fill a 1-quart earthenware timbale with the vermicelli mixture; place, uncovered, in a preheated 400-degree oven 15 minutes before serving.

NOTE: Earthenware timbales can be found in stores that specialize in French cooking utensils.

Elbow Macaroni Lucullus

[MACARONI WITH LIVER SAUCE]   FOR 4

Sauce Lucullus
>   *4 tablespoons sweet butter*
>   *1 tablespoon chopped shallots*
>   *2 tablespoons Madeira*
>   *1 cup Demi-Glace (page 74)*
>   *1 tablespoon chopped black truffles*
>   *1 tablespoon salt*
> *½ teaspoon white pepper*
>   *2 tablespoons foie gras paste*

> *½ pound elbow macaroni,*
>   *cooked in boiling water*
>   *with 2 teaspoons salt 15 minutes,*
>   *rinsed under cold running water,*
>   *drained in a colander*
> *⅛ pound fresh chicken livers, cut in ¼-inch pieces*
> *1 tablespoon cooking oil*
> *½ cup grated Parmesan or Asiago cheese*

Melt the butter in a casserole. Add the chopped shallots, simmer 5 minutes. Add Madeira, demi-glace and truffles, simmer 5 minutes; season with salt and pepper. Blend in the foie gras. Stir in the elbow macaroni, blending with a wooden fork; simmer 5 minutes. Sauté the chicken livers in oil 2 minutes. Drain. Stir into the casserole just before serving. Serve the grated cheese on the side. This dish may also be used as a garnish for roast veal or chicken casserole.

Macaroni au Gratin

[MACARONI WITH CHEESE]   FOR 4

> *½ pound elbow macaroni,*
>   *cooked in boiling water*
>   *with 2 teaspoons salt 15 minutes,*
>   *rinsed under cold running water,*
>   *drained in a colander*
> *½ cup heavy cream*
> *1 tablespoon Sauce Béchamel (page 71)*
> *1 teaspoon salt*
>   *Pinch white pepper*
>   *Pinch nutmeg*
> *1 tablespoon white bread crumbs*
> *½ cup grated Parmesan or Asiago cheese*

Place the macaroni in a saucepan with the cream, béchamel, salt, pepper and nutmeg, simmer 3 minutes. Add half of the cheese, mix. Butter an au gratin dish, pour in the macaroni and sprinkle the top with the remaining cheese and bread crumbs. Place in a preheated 450-degree oven 4 minutes. Put under the broiler 1 minute to brown.

Noodles Mexican Style

FOR 4

½ cup cooking oil
½ cup chopped onions
½ cup small diced green peppers
1 tablespoon red pimentos, chopped
½ cup chopped mushrooms
1 teaspoon chopped garlic
Salt and pepper to taste
½ teaspoon paprika
¼ teaspoon saffron
1 cup heavy cream
2 egg yolks
½ pound egg noodles,
cooked in boiling water
with 2 teaspoons salt 10 minutes,
rinsed under cold running water,
drained in a colander
¼ cup grated Parmesan or Asiago cheese

Heat the oil in a saucepan, add the onions, green peppers and red pimentos, simmer 15 minutes; do not brown. Add the mushrooms, garlic, salt, pepper, paprika and saffron, simmer 3 minutes. Add cream, simmer 3 minutes; off fire, stir in the egg yolks (avoid overheating or they will curdle). Stir in the noodles, place in a deep, buttered baking dish. Sprinkle cheese on top. Place in a preheated 450-degree oven 10 minutes before serving. If top is not brown enough, place under the broiler until well browned.

Nouilles à l'Alsacienne

[NOODLES WITH FOIE GRAS]

FOR 4

½ pound egg noodles,
cooked in boiling water
with 2 teaspoons salt 10 minutes,
rinsed under cold running water,
drained in a colander

2 tablespoons sweet butter
1 tablespoon Demi-Glace (page 74)
1 teaspoon diced black truffles
1 teaspoon salt
  Pinch white pepper
  Pinch nutmeg
4 tablespoons purée of foie gras

Place the noodles in a saucepan with the butter, demi-glace, truffles, salt, pepper and nutmeg; simmer 3 minutes. Before serving, blend in the purée of foie gras, mixing the noodles upward with a spaghetti fork so the foie gras will be evenly mixed into the noodles.

Spetzli   FOR 6

2 cups white flour
3 eggs
1 tablespoon cold water
1 teaspoon salt
  Pinch white pepper
  Pinch nutmeg
  Pinch thyme powder

Mix the flour, eggs and water, stirring vigorously with a wooden spoon 10 minutes. Blend in the salt, pepper, nutmeg and thyme. Bring 2 quarts of water to a boil. With a small knife or steel spatula, cut off ½-inch bits of the batter and drop into the boiling water. Simmer 5 minutes. Drain the spetzli on paper towels or a cloth, or store in cold water until ready to use. Serve with butter or a sauce of your choice.

Gnocchi à la Parisienne   FOR 4

Step One: Gnocchi
>   1 cup milk
>   4 tablespoons sweet butter
>   ½ teaspoon salt
>   Pinch nutmeg
>   1 cup sifted white flour
>   4 eggs
>   Pinch cayenne pepper

In a saucepan, bring the milk with the butter, salt and nutmeg to a boil. Add the flour all at once, mixing vigorously with a wooden spatula on the stove 2 minutes or until the mixture will not stick to the pan. Remove from the stove. Add the eggs, one by one, mixing very quickly; add the pepper. Cool 30 minutes. Fill a 2-quart pot with water, add 1 tablespoon salt and bring to a boil. Reduce to a steady simmer. Fill a pastry bag with the above batter. Using a plain nozzle ¾ inches in diameter on pastry bag, push the dough through, cutting it off every 1¼ inches with a sharp knife. Drop these little dumplings into the simmering water. Cook 5 minutes, or until each one rises to surface. Remove, dry on cheesecloth. Keep warm.

Step Two: Sauce
>   1 cup Sauce Velouté (page 66)
>   ½ cup heavy cream
>   1 teaspoon salt
>   ½ teaspoon white pepper
>   4 tablespoons sweet butter
>   1 tablespoon Sauce Hollandaise (page 81)
>   ½ cup grated Parmesan or Asiago cheese

Bring the velouté to a boil. Add the cream, simmer 3 minutes; add the salt and pepper. Remove from fire. Blend in the butter and hollandaise. Spoon half of the sauce in the bottom of an au gratin dish. Place the gnocchi dumplings on top and cover with the remaining sauce. Sprinkle with cheese and place, uncovered, in a preheated 400-degree oven 10 minutes. Serve immediately.

Gnocchi à la Romaine   FOR 4

>   2½ cups milk
>   1 teaspoon salt
>   Pinch white pepper
>   Pinch nutmeg
>   1 cup semolina or white grits
>   1 egg
>   ¼ pound sweet butter
>   ½ cup grated Parmesan or Asiago cheese

In a deep saucepan, bring the milk to a boil. Add the salt, pepper and nutmeg. Blend in all the semolina, stirring well with a wooden spatula; simmer 15 minutes, stirring constantly. Remove from the stove, add the egg and half of the butter; mix well. Pour into a flat dish, spreading the mixture ¾-inch thick. Cool 2 hours. Cut into rounds, 2 inches in diameter. Place on a buttered, shallow baking dish. Sprinkle with cheese and dot with the remaining butter. Place in a preheated 350-degree oven 15 minutes. If not browned, place under the broiler 2 minutes before serving.

Gnocchi à la Niçoise   FOR 4

>   1 pound potatoes
>   ½ cup white flour
>   1 teaspoon salt
>   1 teaspoon white pepper
>   Pinch nutmeg
>   2 tablespoons olive oil
>   1 cup Sauce Tomate (page 83)
>   2 tablespoons dry white wine
>   2 tablespoons sweet butter
>   ½ cup grated Parmesan or Asiago cheese

Peel the potatoes and boil in water as for making mashed potatoes. Drain well and push through a fine strainer. Replace over low flame to dry thoroughly; do not burn. Remove from heat and add flour, salt, pepper, nutmeg and oil; mix well. Make small, walnut-size balls from this paste. Press each ball against the back of a fork to give it a cylindrical shape. Drop into a skillet of simmering, salted water 3 minutes. Dry on cheesecloth. Heat the tomato sauce, wine and butter together, then spoon a coating in a deep au gratin dish. Arrange the gnocchi in layers, spooning tomato sauce over each layer. Sprinkle with cheese and place in a preheated 350-degree oven 15 minutes. Before serving, place under the broiler 2 minutes to brown.

Gaudes à la Bourguignonne

[CORNMEAL PUDDING AU GRATIN]   FOR 4

        1½ cups sifted fine cornmeal
          2 cups milk
          1 cup water
          1 teaspoon salt
          1 egg, beaten
        ½ cup grated Swiss cheese
          1 cup heavy cream
          2 tablespoons dry white wine
          1 tablespoon white bread crumbs
          2 tablespoons melted sweet butter

Blend the cornmeal with the milk and water; let stand at room temperature 1 hour. Add the salt and cook in a double boiler 1 hour, stirring often to avoid lumping. Stir in the egg. Spread evenly, 1½-inches thick, on a baking dish. Blend the cheese, cream and wine; pour over the gaudes. Then sprinkle with bread crumbs and dribble with melted butter. Place in a preheated 450-degree oven 10 minutes. Put under the broiler 2 minutes before serving. Cut in portions for 4. Gaudes is an excellent garniture for a rabbit or hare stew.

A word about cheese: You will note that I have suggested Parmesan or Asiago cheese in these pasta recipes. It is not always possible to get good, aged, imported Italian Parmesan. The domestic, the South American, and other versions are not what they should be, and do not add proper flavor to your pasta dishes. Asiago is far superior to these, and in the opinion of many cheese epicures (including my co-author), is at least the equal of Italian Parmesan. Produced by the famous Frigo family in the Asiago area of northern Italy for generations, it also has been made by that same illustrious, award-winning family here in the United States, in Wisconsin, for well over a half a century. Asiago is a grana type, actually with a more subtle flavor than Parmesan—if it has been properly aged. Unaged, it is tasty as a table cheese with fruit or salad, but not proper for grating with pastas. It should be bought as *vecchio* (old), or better still, as *stravecchio* (very old). Thus aged, it is golden, with a distinctive flavor held by no other cheese, and goes extremely well with all pasta and rice dishes. Carefully aged Asiago can be obtained from the fine Frigo Food Products Company, Inc., 109 South Main Street, Torrington, Connecticut, 06790.

RIZ—Rice

Riz Pilaf

[RICE PILAF]   FOR 4

> ¼ *pound sweet butter*
> ½ *cup chopped onions*
> 1 *cup rice*
> 2 *cups Beef Bouillon (page 64)*
> *Bouquet garni*
> *Salt and white pepper*

Simmer the onions slowly in half of the butter; do not brown. Add the rice, sauté 3 minutes. Add the broth, bouquet garni, salt and pepper. Bring to a boil, cover with aluminum foil *and* a lid and place in a 400-degree oven 20 minutes or until rice is done. Stir with a fork and add the remainder of the butter. Remove the bouquet garni. Each grain should be separate.

Pilaf de Foies de Volaille à l'Orientale

[CHICKEN LIVER PILAF WITH MUSHROOMS
AND GRAPES]   FOR 4

Step One: Rice Pilaf (for this recipe)
  4 tablespoons sweet butter
  ½ cup chopped onions
  2 cups rice
  5 cups boiling Chicken Broth (page 62) or
    White Stock (page 61)
  1 tablespoon salt
  ½ teaspoon white pepper
    Bouquet garni

Melt the butter in a saucepan and simmer the onions 3 minutes; add the
rice, mix well over low heat 2 minutes. Add the hot stock, salt, pepper and
bouquet garni. Bring to a boil, cover with aluminum foil *and* a lid and
place in a preheated 350-degree oven 20 minutes or until tender. Remove
and stop further cooking by stirring rice with a fork. Keep warm.

Step Two: Chicken livers
  1 cup Demi-Glace (page 74)
  1 tablespoon Sauce Tomate (page 83)
  ¼ cup dry sherry
  1 teaspoon salt
  ½ teaspoon white pepper
  ¼ pound sweet butter
  ½ pound chicken livers, cut bite-size
  8 small mushroom caps
    Pinch thyme leaves
  1 tablespoon chopped parsley
  1 tablespoon cognac
  ½ cup grated Asiago or Parmesan cheese
  24 white grapes, peeled and seeded

Heat the demi-glace in a saucepan with the tomato sauce, sherry, salt and
pepper. Set aside; keep warm. Melt half of the butter in a skillet. When
foaming, add the chicken livers and cook briskly, turning, 3 minutes.
Remove the livers to a colander. Sauté the mushrooms in the same
skillet 3 minutes. Stir mushrooms and livers into the warm demi-glace
mixture. Add and mix thyme, parsley and cognac. Check seasoning. Stir
the remaining butter and cheese into the rice and mix well over low heat.
Fill a crown mold with the rice, pressing down with a cooking spoon.
Unmold the rice on a warm, round serving platter. Add the grapes
to the chicken liver mixture and bring almost to a boil. Fill the center of
the rice crown with the chicken livers, mushrooms, grapes and sauce.

Soufflé de Riz

[RICE SOUFFLÉ]   FOR 4

> 4 tablespoons sweet butter
> 1 tablespoon grated onion
> 1 cup rice
> 2½ cups boiling White Stock (page 61)
> 1 cup heavy cream
> 1 teaspoon celery salt
> Pinch nutmeg
> ½ teaspoon white pepper
> Salt to taste
> ½ cup cooked, diced mushrooms
> 1 teaspoon chopped chives
> 4 egg yolks
> 1 tablespoon grated Asiago or Parmesan cheese

Melt the butter in a saucepan, add the grated onions and rice. Mix over a low heat 2 minutes. Add boiling stock, cover with aluminum foil *and* a lid and place in a preheated 400-degree oven 20 minutes or until tender. Remove from oven and keep warm. Heat the cream in a saucepan. Blend in the celery salt, nutmeg, pepper, salt (test first, as you already have celery salt), mushrooms and chives; mix well, remove from heat. Beat yolks. Stir yolks slowly into the heated cream (if cream is too hot, yolks will curdle). Mix the cream-egg yolk mixture into the rice with a wooden spoon. Add the cheese and mix again. Spoon into a buttered soufflé dish and place in a pan of boiling water. Put in a preheated 400-degree oven 30 minutes. The top should be well browned and crisp.

Croquettes de Riz à l'Auvergnate

[CHESTNUT-FLAVORED RICE CROQUETTES]   FOR 4

> 1 cup Sauce Béchamel (page 71)
> ½ cup heavy cream
> 2 cups boiled rice, drained, dried
> 1 teaspoon salt
> ½ teaspoon cayenne pepper
> Pinch nutmeg
> 4 egg yolks
> 2 tablespoons chestnut purée (canned au naturel)
> ½ cup white flour
> 1 recipe Anglaise (page 1)
> ½ cup white bread crumbs
> Hot oil or lard for deep frying

Blend the béchamel in a saucepan with the cream. Bring to a boil and add the rice, salt, cayenne and nutmeg; simmer 10 minutes. Beat the egg yolks, stir into the rice and bring to a simmer. Mix in the chestnut purée. Cool. (The rice can be prepared to this point hours before serving.) When ready to use, form rice into croquettes shaped like large corks. Roll in flour, then in anglaise, then in bread crumbs. Fry in oil or lard at 390 degrees until brown. Remove, drain and place in a preheated 400-degree oven 5 minutes before serving. These go well with prime ribs of beef, roast chicken or veal.

Risotto à la Milanaise

[SAFFRON RICE]   FOR 6

> 4 tablespoons sweet butter
> ½ cup chopped onions
> ¼ teaspoon saffron powder
> 1 cup rice
> 2 cups White Stock (page 61)
> 1 teaspoon salt
>   Bouquet garni made up of 1 bay leaf,
>   1 sprig parsley, 1 stalk celery,
>   ½ teaspoon thyme leaves
> 1 cup grated Asiago or Parmesan cheese

Melt the butter in a saucepan. Simmer the onions 5 minutes; stir in the saffron and rice, simmer 3 minutes. Add the white stock, salt and bouquet garni. Bring to a boil, cover with aluminum foil *and* a lid and place in a 350-degree oven 20 minutes or until tender. Remove the bouquet garni; stir in cheese. Excellent with Paupiettes de Veau à la Milanaise (page 216) and other meat and chicken dishes.

Risotto à la Castiglione

[RICE WITH MUSHROOMS AND TRUFFLES]   FOR 4

> 4 tablespoons sweet butter
> ¼ cup olive oil
> 1 tablespoon coarsely chopped onions
> 1 tablespoon coarsely chopped white celery
> 1 tablespoon diced green peppers
> 1 tablespoon diced red pimentos
> 2 cloves garlic

> 1 *teaspoon salt*
> ½ *teaspoon white pepper*
> ⅓ *teaspoon saffron*
> 1 *tablespoon dry mushrooms (soaked 4 hours*
>   *in cold water, drained), chopped fine*
> 1 *cup Piedmont rice*
>   *Bouquet garni*
> 4 *cups boiling White Stock (page 61)*
> 1 *tablespoon finely chopped white truffles*
> ½ *cup grated Asiago or Parmesan cheese*
> ¼ *cup fresh tomato purée*

Heat half the butter with the olive oil in casserole. When foaming, add the onions and simmer 5 minutes. Add the celery, green peppers, pimentos, garlic, salt, pepper and saffron; simmer 10 minutes. Add the mushrooms and rice, simmer 3 minutes. Add the bouquet garni and 1 cup of stock, stirring for 5 minutes. Add more stock as the rice absorbs it. Cover and stir every 2 minutes with a wooden fork. Add the remaining white stock. Cooking time should be 25 minutes, *after* you have added all the stock. Remove the bouquet garni, blend in truffles, cheese, the remaining sweet butter and the tomato purée, which has been heated. Mix well. Check seasoning. Keep very hot and serve with grated cheese on the side. Risotto should be very smooth, not dry.

CRÊPES ET PÂTES—Pancakes and Doughs

Gaufres à la Lyonnaise

[WAFFLES WITH CHICKEN HASH]   FOR ABOUT 6 WAFFLES

Waffles are versatile, excellent with much more than the usual sweet toppings. Here is a favorite of mine.

> *Step One: Waffles*
> 1 *cup sifted white flour*
> 3 *eggs, separated*
> 1½ *cups milk*
> 1 *teaspoon salt*
>   *Pinch nutmeg*
> ¼ *cup melted sweet butter*

Blend the flour and egg yolks, stirring with a wooden spatula until smooth and without lumps. Pour in the milk gradually, stirring constantly. Add the salt, nutmeg and half the melted butter; mix well. Beat the whites of the eggs until very stiff. Add to the batter, mixing slowly. Heat the waffle iron; brush some of the melted butter over each side of the iron. Add enough of the mixture to cover the iron. Make waffles nicely browned and crisp.

Step Two: Waffle topping
    1 recipe Volaille Hachée Blind Brook
        (page 168), substitute Madeira for Sherry
    2 tablespoons grated Swiss cheese

Bring hash to a simmer. Blend cheese in well. Arrange waffles on a large, flat, ovenproof serving platter. Spread hash evenly over each waffle. Put in a preheated 450-degree oven 5 minutes, or until brown.

Matefaim de Sarazin

[BUCKWHEAT PANCAKES]   FOR 4

    1 cup sifted buckwheat flour
    ½ cup sifted white flour
    2 eggs
    1 teaspoon salt
        Pinch white pepper
    2 cups milk
    2 tablespoons beer
    ½ cup sour cream
    ½ cup grated Swiss cheese
    1 teaspoon grated onion
    2 tablespoons shredded boiled ham

Blend the buckwheat and white flour and the eggs slowly with a wooden spatula. Stir in the salt and pepper. Gradually add the milk and beer. Mix well into a smooth batter. Let stand 2 hours in a cool place. On greased griddle, make 1 dozen medium pancakes, ¼-inch thick. Arrange these on a large, buttered ovenproof dish. Combine the sour cream, cheese, grated onion and boiled ham, mixing well. Spoon evenly over Matefaim cakes. Place in a preheated 400-degree oven 15 minutes. Serve immediately.

Blinis à la Russe

[SOUR CREAM PANCAKES]   FOR 4, OR ABOUT 16 BLINIS

> *2 cups buckwheat flour*
> *1 cup sour cream*
> *½ cup melted sweet butter*
> *¼ cup beer*
> *1 teaspoon salt*
> *2 egg whites, beaten stiff*

Mix the flour, cream, butter, beer and salt and blend well. Place on top of the stove to keep warm 30 minutes. Then add the egg whites, stirring in slowly with an upward motion. Cook on a pancake griddle. They should be small and thin.

Pannequets à la Mode du Jura

[CHEESE PANCAKES]   FOR 4

Make this batter 5 hours before using.

> *1 cup sifted white flour*
> *2 eggs*
> *½ cup milk*
> *½ cup heavy cream*
> *1 teaspoon salt*
> *Pinch white pepper*
> *¼ cup melted sweet butter*
> *1 cup grated Swiss cheese*
> *2 cups kirschwasser*

Add the eggs to the flour in mixing bowl one at a time, stirring vigorously after each addition with a wooden spatula until the mixture is smooth. Add the milk and cream slowly, as you continue stirring, then the salt and pepper and half the melted butter. Blend well. Keep in a cool place, not the refrigerator, 5 hours. When ready, use a 2½-inch diameter, thick-bottomed crêpe pan. Heat the crêpe pan and brush with melted butter. Spread 1 tablespoon of batter evenly around the bottom of the pan. Cook over medium heat, 1 minute on each side. After all batter is used, put the pannequets into a preheated 400-degree oven 5 minutes. Remove and place on an ovenproof serving dish. Sprinkle with cheese and kirschwasser. Place under the broiler 2 minutes before serving.

Crêpes au Gratin Cordon Bleu

[SAUCED PANCAKES STUFFED WITH MUSHROOMS, HAM AND HERBS]

FOR 4, OR AT LEAST 12 CRÊPES

Step One: Crêpes
       1 cup sifted white flour
       2 eggs
    1½ cups milk
      ½ teaspoon salt
          Pinch cayenne pepper
          Pinch nutmeg
       4 tablespoons sweet butter

To the flour in large mixing bowl, add one egg; mix clockwise with a wooden spatula, stirring vigorously. Then add the second egg, mixing well to avoid lumping. Blend in the milk, in small quantities at first, until very smooth; then stir in the salt, pepper and nutmeg. This should be done 2 hours before using. When ready to use, melt the butter in a 5-inch crêpe pan until slightly browned; mix into the batter. Make very thin pancakes. Oil pan lightly, or rub with fat, before cooking each crêpe. Place them on top of one another so they will stay moist until used.

Step Two: Stuffing
       4 tablespoons sweet butter
       1 tablespoon finely chopped shallots
       1 cup chopped white mushrooms
      ½ cup chopped lean boiled ham
       1 teaspoon salt
       1 teaspoon white pepper
          Pinch nutmeg
       1 teaspoon chopped tarragon
       1 teaspoon chopped chervil
       1 teaspoon chopped parsley
       1 tablespoon chopped sorrel (fresh, if available)
      ¼ cup Madeira
       2 eggs, beaten
       1 tablespoon white bread crumbs
       1 tablespoon Sauce Velouté (page 66)

Melt the butter in a saucepan. When foaming, add shallots, simmer 3 minutes; add mushrooms, simmer 3 minutes; add ham, salt, pepper and nutmeg and blend well over low heat 2 minutes. Stir in the herbs, mix well over heat 2 minutes. Add the Madeira, eggs, bread crumbs and velouté and simmer 3 minutes, stirring constantly. Cool. When ready to use, spread stuffing, ⅛-inch thick, on each crêpe. Roll and place side-by-side in a well-buttered oblong baking dish.

Step Three: Sauce to cover crêpes
 ½ cup Sauce Velouté (page 66)
 ½ cup heavy cream
 ½ cup grated Parmesan or Asiago cheese
 ½ cup Sauce Hollandaise (page 81)
 2 tablespoons sweet butter

Bring the velouté to a boil, add the cream and simmer 3 minutes. Add two-thirds of the cheese. Bring to a simmer and blend in the hollandaise; do not boil. Pour the sauce evenly over the crêpes. Sprinkle with the remaining cheese and dot with butter. Bake, uncovered, in a preheated 400-degree oven 15 minutes before serving. Place under the broiler to brown.

Pâte à Chou

[CREAM PUFF PASTE]   FOR ABOUT 4 CUPS

 2 cups milk
 ½ teaspoon salt
  Pinch nutmeg
 ¼ pound sweet butter
 2 cups sifted white flour
 8 eggs

In a saucepan, put milk, salt, nutmeg and butter; bring to a boil. Remove from the fire and add the flour all at once, stirring vigorously with a wooden spatula. Replace on medium heat and continue stirring until the paste does not stick to the pan. Off the heat, add the eggs 2 at a time, mixing very fast so they will become thoroughly incorporated. Place in a bowl and cover with soft butter and foil so the top will not crust before the batter is ready to use. Will keep in refrigerator 4 days, or can be frozen.

Brioche Dough
FOR ABOUT 10 BRIOCHES

2 cups sifted white flour
1 yeast cake
2 tablespoons lukewarm water
4 eggs
1 teaspoon salt
1 tablespoon granulated sugar
¼ pound sweet butter, softened

Blend into a dough ½ cup of the flour with the yeast cake and 1 table-spoon of the lukewarm water. Place in a small bowl, cover with a cheesecloth and keep in a warm place to ferment and double its volume. Pour the remaining flour on a large pastry board, making a well in the center. Place one of the eggs and remaining tablespoon of lukewarm water in the well and sprinkle with salt and sugar. Blend well. Then incorporate the butter. After thoroughly mixed, add the remaining eggs, one by one. Now blend well with the yeast mixture. Place this dough in a deep bowl. Cover and keep in a warm place. Four hours later (after it has risen), beat the dough down in an overlapping, kneading motion. Keep in a cool place until ready to use. It does well resting overnight in the refrigerator. Bake in buttered brioche molds on a baking sheet in a preheated 475-degree oven 15 minutes; turn heat down to 350 degrees and cook another 25 minutes. Test by running a knife down center. If it comes out clean, dough is done. Hollow and stuff or sauce as an appetizer, or have with butter or jam for breakfast.

NOTE: The unbaked dough may also be used as a covering, or crust, for pâtés, roasts or as in Cornish Game Hen in Brioche (page 176).

Puff Paste
FOR 1 POUND OF DOUGH

2 cups sifted white flour
¾ pound sweet butter
¾ cup water
1 teaspoon salt

Blend the flour well with the butter, water and salt, avoiding lumps. Place the dough in the refrigerator 2 hours. Roll the dough flat in a rectangular shape, ½-inch thick. Fold over once; roll into a rectangular sheet 1-inch thick. Fold again; roll once more 1-inch thick. Fold the sheet over. During this folding operation, use fresh flour for dusting the dough before rolling so sheets will not stick together. When ready to use, roll the dough to 1-inch thickness. Let rest for 1 hour in the refrigerator. From this point you can cut up the dough in any shape that you want.

Fleurons

[CRESCENT PASTRY]   FOR ABOUT **14**

> *1 beaten egg*
> *1 recipe Puff Paste (page 284)*

Using a lightly floured board and much muscle, roll the dough to ¼- to ⅛-inch thickness. The classic fleuron is a crescent. You can buy a crescent pastry cutter. Or you can use your round fluted pastry cutter, a 2- or 3-inch one: Cut a half-circle from the dough. Now, where you cut out that circle, put the round cutter 1 inch above the blank space in the dough and cut a crescent. When you have cut the number of crescents desired, place them 1 inch apart on a pastry sheet (dampen the pastry sheet or cover with wax paper) and rest them in a cool place 1 hour. Brush the tops of the crescents with the beaten egg and place in a preheated 400-degree oven 15 minutes, or until puffy and golden.

10

LÉGUMES—Vegetables

ARTICHAUTS—Artichokes

Whenever I see an artichoke, I recall the maestro Leopold Stokowski sitting in my restaurant wearing green gloves and eating that vegetable. He wasn't wearing the gloves out of fastidiousness, or to match the color scheme, although they were about the same shade as the artichokes. He always wore them—I suppose to protect those matchless hands that had coaxed forth and commanded such superb music. Or perhaps to attract attention. But he didn't need green gloves for that. That lion head and fierce, demanding eyes were enough. He also liked and understood the artichoke, one of my favorite vegetables. Many people don't. Perhaps these recipes will tempt them to change their minds.

Artichauts Farcis Grand'mère

[GRANDMOTHER'S STUFFED ARTICHOKES]   FOR 4

Step One: Preparing the artichokes
    4 large fresh artichokes

Trim the tips of the leaves with a scissors. To keep compact, tie twine around the middle of the artichoke, then up over it, and knot the cord underneath. Place in a skillet with water to cover, bring to boil and simmer 10 minutes. Take from water. Cool. Remove the center leaves and scrape out the fuzzy choke with a spoon, leaving a hollow space for the stuffing.

Parthenay, Poitou

Step Two: Stuffing
>   6 tablespoons sweet butter
>   2 tablespoons chopped onions
>   1 teaspoon chopped garlic
>   2 cups finely chopped leftover roast: lamb,
>   beef, veal or chicken
>   ½ cup finely chopped boiled ham
>   ½ cup finely chopped cooked smoked tongue
>   1 egg
>   1 tablespoon chopped parsley
>   1 teaspoon chopped chives
>   1 teaspoon salt
>   1 teaspoon white pepper
>   ½ teaspoon Épices Parisienne (page 2)
>   ¼ cup cognac
>   ½ cup white bread crumbs
>   4 very thin slices larding pork, 4 inches square

Melt the butter in a saucepan. When foaming, simmer the onions 4 minutes; do not brown. Add garlic, cook 2 minutes; add leftover chopped meat, simmer 5 minutes. Add all the other ingredients, except larding pork, and mix thoroughly. Check seasoning. Divide this stuffing evenly to fill hollowed artichokes. Tie a slice of larding pork on the top of each artichoke.

Step Three: Cooking stuffed artichokes
>   4 stuffed artichokes
>   2 cups Brown Stock (page 63)
>   ½ cup dry white wine

Place the artichokes in a roasting pan and pour in the brown stock and white wine. Cover, bring to boil on top of the stove and place in a preheated 400-degree oven 1 hour or until leaves pull off easily. Remove the twine and arrange the artichokes on a warm serving platter. Cook the sauce until it is reduced by half. Strain through a fine wire strainer and serve on the side.

Artichauts Frits à la Flamande

[ARTICHOKES FRIED IN BEER BATTER] FOR 4

>   2 cooked artichokes with leaves,
>   cut into quarters, choke removed
>   2 cups sifted white flour
>   ½ cup beer

>   *1 tablespoon cooking oil*
>   *1 tablespoon salt*
>   *½ teaspoon white pepper*
>   *Pinch nutmeg*
>   *1 egg yolk*
>   *1½ cups Sauce Tomate (page 83)*

Mix the beer into the flour and add the oil, seasonings and egg yolk. Blend well. Dip the artichokes in this batter and fry until golden in deep fat at 380 degrees. Dry on paper towels. Serve tomato sauce separately.

FONDS D'ARTICHAUTS—Artichoke Bottoms

For fresh artichoke bottoms, use a very sharp knife, trimming the edges until all the leaves have been cut off. Work the knife around, cutting the center leaves from the thick bottom. Rub half a lemon over to keep the bottom white. In 3 cups boiling water, for 4 bottoms, add 4 teaspoons lemon juice and 2 teaspoons salt. Cook until a sharp pointed knife will pierce the artichoke bottom easily. The cooking time depends on the age and variety of artichoke. It could be as long as 45 minutes.

When ready to use, remove the choke with a teaspoon. Place the artichoke bottom on an oiled or buttered serving platter. (Canned artichoke bottoms are easier to prepare and some brands are very good. They are cleaned, the choke out. To use these, just drain, place on a well-buttered platter and fill them with the ingredients given in the recipe.)

Fonds d'Artichauts Florentine

[ARTICHOKE BOTTOMS WITH SPINACH PURÉE]   FOR 4

> 4 croutons, ⅛-inch thick, 3-inches diameter,
>   fried in butter
> 4 thin slices Parma ham
> ¼ cup sherry
> 4 artichoke bottoms, prepared as previously instructed
> 1 cup cooked, drained purée of spinach
> 4 tablespoons sweet butter
> 1 cup Sauce Mornay (page 73)
> 1 tablespoon grated Swiss cheese

Arrange the ham on croutons, sprinkle with sherry and place under the broiler 3 minutes. Place the artichoke bottoms on the ham. Simmer the spinach in butter 5 minutes. Fill the bottoms with the spinach purée. Cover with the mornay sauce and sprinkle with cheese. Place in a preheated 450-degree oven 10 minutes. If not browned enough, place under the broiler.

Fonds d'Artichauts Brésilienne

[ARTICHOKE BOTTOMS WITH TOMATOES]   FOR 4

> 4 artichoke bottoms, prepared as previously instructed
> 6 tablespoons cooking oil
> 1 tablespoon chopped onions
> ½ teaspoon chopped garlic
> 4 fresh tomatoes, peeled, seeded, cut into quarters
> ½ teaspoon dry thyme leaves
> ¼ teaspoon bay leaf powder
> 1 teaspoon salt
> ½ teaspoon white pepper
> 2 tablespoons white bread crumbs
> 2 tablespoons grated Swiss cheese
> 4 tablespoons sweet butter

Heat the oil in a saucepan, add the onions and simmer 5 minutes; add garlic, simmer 2 minutes; add tomatoes, simmer 15 minutes. Add the thyme, bay leaf powder, salt, pepper and bread crumbs and mix well. Fill the artichoke bottoms with this mixture. Sprinkle with cheese and dot with butter. Place under the broiler 3 minutes before serving.

Fonds d'Artichauts à la Moelle

[ARTICHOKE BOTTOMS WITH MARROW]   FOR 4

> 4 tablespoons sweet butter
> 4 artichoke bottoms, prepared as previously instructed
> 12 slices beef marrow, ⅛-inch thick
> 1 cup Sauce Bourguignonne (page 75)
> 2 tablespoons cognac
> 1 teaspoon chopped fresh tarragon
> 1 tablespoon chopped fresh parsley
> 1 teaspoon salt
>   Pepper to taste

Butter an ovenproof serving platter with all of the butter. Arrange the artichoke bottoms on this. Place in a preheated 400-degree oven 5 minutes. Immerse the marrow slices in boiling water 1 minute. Remove, drain and arrange the marrow on top of the artichoke bottoms. Bring the bourguignonne sauce to a boil and stir in the cognac, tarragon, parsley, salt and pepper. Spoon over the bottoms just before serving.

Fonds d'Artichauts à la Paiva

[ARTICHOKE BOTTOMS WITH MUSHROOMS]   FOR 4

> 4 artichoke bottoms, prepared as previously instructed
> 6 tablespoons sweet butter
> ½ pound white mushrooms, thinly sliced
> 1 tablespoon chopped shallots
> ¼ cup cognac
> 1½ teaspoons salt
> ½ teaspoon cayenne pepper
> 1 cup heavy cream
> 1 tablespoon Sauce Hollandaise (page 81)
> 1 tablespoon grated Parmesan cheese

Place the artichoke bottoms on an ovenproof serving platter. Keep warm. Melt the butter in a saucepan. When foaming, add mushrooms and cook 5 minutes on a brisk fire; add shallots, cook 3 minutes. Add the cognac, salt, cayenne and cream, simmer 3 minutes or until thickened. Remove from stove and add hollandaise, mixing gently with a wooden spoon. Fill the bottoms with this mixture. Sprinkle with grated cheese and place under the broiler 2 minutes before serving. This dish should be well browned and is excellent served with a veal roast or chicken breasts.

Fonds d'Artichauts à la Strasbourgeoise

[ARTICHOKE BOTTOMS WITH FOIE GRAS]   FOR 4

> *1 pound Puff Paste (page 284)*
> *4 artichoke bottoms, prepared as previously instructed*
> *4 slices foie gras, ⅛-inch thick*
> *1 cup Sauce Périgourdine (page 78)*
> *1 egg, beaten*

Roll the puff paste to ½-inch thickness. Cut into four 6-inch squares. Place an artichoke bottom on each square and arrange one slice of foie gras on top of each. Spread 1 tablespoon of périgourdine sauce over the foie gras, fold over the puff paste, seal the edges and brush with beaten egg. Place on a baking sheet. Put in a preheated 400-degree oven 25 minutes or until golden. After 15 minutes, place a second baking sheet under the first one so the bottom of the pastry will not burn. Serve these artichokes around a roast of veal or lamb.

ASPERGES—Asparagus

Fresh asparagus should be peeled or scraped from below the tip to ¾ the length of the stem. Wash well in cold water to remove sand particles inside the spear head. Tied in portions with butcher's twine, the stalks will cook together evenly and are easier to remove from the skillet and serve.

To retain their color and firmness, green asparagus should be placed in boiling salted water. The cooking time will vary according to the quality of the asparagus. After 10 minutes of cooking, check the firmness with a sharp, pointed knife. When cooked properly, the knife will pierce the asparagus easily. Do not let the asparagus get too soft. They are at their best when firm and will also bear reheating, if you wish.

Cold asparagus should be served with:

Sauce Vinaigrette (page 325)
Sauce Gribiche (page 327)
Mayonnaise (page 84)
Mayonnaise Verte (page 85)

Hot asparagus should be served with:

Sauce Hollandaise (page 81)
Sauce Mousseline (page 82)
Melted sweet butter

Asperges Crémaillère au Gratin

[ASPARAGUS AND HAM WITH CHEESE SAUCE]   FOR 4

> 32 asparagus stalks
> 4 thin slices boiled York ham
> ¼ cup dry sherry
> 1 teaspoon confectioners' sugar
> 4 slices toast
> 4 tablespoons sweet butter
> 1 cup Sauce Mornay (page 73)
> 2 tablespoons grated Parmesan cheese

Tie the asparagus in four portions and prepare as previously instructed. Dry on cheesecloth. Broil the ham 3 minutes. Pour the sherry over the ham and sprinkle evenly with sugar. Put under the broiler for another 2 minutes. Butter toast and arrange one slice of ham on each piece; place 8 stalks on top of each slice of ham, spread evenly with the mornay sauce and sprinkle with cheese. Place under the broiler 3 minutes or until brown.

Asperges Polonaise

[ASPARAGUS WITH BREAD CRUMBS]   FOR 4

> 32 asparagus stalks
> 4 tablespoons sweet butter
> ½ cup white bread crumbs
> 2 chopped hard boiled eggs
>   (yolks and whites separate)
> 1 tablespoon salt
> 1 teaspoon white pepper
> 1 teaspoon chopped chives
> 1 tablespoon chopped parsley
> 1 tablespoon lemon juice

Tie the asparagus in four portions and prepare as previously instructed. Melt the butter in a frying pan on a quick fire. When foaming, add the bread crumbs. Sauté until golden. Place the well-drained asparagus on a serving platter and sprinkle the eggs over the tips. Sprinkle with salt and pepper. Spread the bread crumbs over the asparagus. Before serving, sprinkle with chives and parsley and the lemon juice.

AVOCATS—Avocados

The avocado is commonly used in a salad, or to add flavor and appeal to cold fish and other cold dishes. Here are two of my recipes in which they are served hot.

Baked Avocados with Fresh Tomatoes   FOR 4

> 4 tablespoons cooking oil
> 1 tablespoon chopped shallots
> 2 whole tomatoes, peeled, seeded, diced
> 1 tablespoon white bread crumbs
> 4 tablespoons sweet butter
> 2 avocados, cut in half lengthwise
> 1 tablespoon salt
> 1 teaspoon white pepper
> 1 tablespoon grated Parmesan cheese

Heat the cooking oil in a saucepan. Sauté the shallots on a slow fire 3 minutes. Add the tomatoes, simmer 5 minutes; add the bread crumbs, mix thoroughly. Place 1 tablespoon of butter in the hollow of each avocado half. Bake in a preheated 450-degree oven 15 minutes. Remove. Sprinkle with salt and pepper. Fill each avocado half with the tomatoes. Sprinkle with grated cheese and place under the broiler 2 minutes before serving.

Avocados Stuffed with Sorrel   FOR 4

2 avocados, cut in half lengthwise
4 tablespoons sweet butter
1 cup sorrel purée (jarred or canned)
1 tablespoon salt
½ teaspoon white pepper
  Pinch nutmeg
1 egg yolk
1 cup Sauce Mornay (page 73)
1 tablespoon grated Parmesan cheese

Place 1 tablespoon of butter in the hollow of each avocado half. Bake in a preheated 400-degree oven 15 minutes. Scoop out the flesh from the baked avocados and mash with the sorrel, salt, pepper, nutmeg and egg yolk. Stir over medium heat until firm. Fill the shells of the avocados with this purée; cover with the mornay sauce. Sprinkle with grated cheese and place under the broiler 2 minutes or until brown.

CHOU—Cabbage

Chou Jurassienne

[CABBAGE WITH SALT PORK]   FOR 4

1 two-pound Savoy cabbage
½ pound lean salt pork, diced
1 cup sliced white onions
1½ teaspoons chopped garlic
1 teaspoon salt
1 teaspoon white pepper
1 tablespoon chopped parsley

Cook the cabbage in 2 quarts of boiling water 45 minutes. Drain well and chop. Sauté the salt pork in a skillet over medium heat 5 minutes. Add the onions, sauté 10 minutes; add garlic, sauté 2 minutes; add cabbage and sauté on a quick fire 10 minutes or until cabbage is tender. Sprinkle with salt and pepper. Sprinkle with chopped parsley before serving.

Chou Farci

[CABBAGE DOLMA]   FOR 4

Step One: Stuffing leaves
>   *1 two-pound green cabbage*
>   *4 tablespoons cooking oil*
>   *1 tablespoon chopped onions*
>   *1 teaspoon chopped garlic*
>   *1 cup ground leftover roast lamb*
>   *2 tablespoons tomato purée*
>   *Salt and pepper to taste*
>   *2 tablespoons cognac*
>   *½ teaspoon chopped parsley*
>   *½ teaspoon thyme leaves*
>   *½ cup cooked rice*
>   *1 egg, beaten*

Separate the cabbage leaves and blanch in boiling water 5 minutes. Drain. Dry on cheesecloth. If leaves are large, make four portions of each leaf. Heat the oil in a saucepan. Sauté the onions 4 minutes; do not brown. Add the garlic, sauté 2 minutes. Stir in the remainder of the ingredients, except the egg, and simmer 5 minutes. Mix in the egg. Cool. Put some stuffing in each cabbage leaf and fold the leaves into large balls. Tie with butcher's twine.

Step Two: Cooking stuffed cabbage leaves
>   *4 thin slices larding pork, 4 inches square*
>   *1 carrot, sliced*
>   *1 onion, sliced*
>   *1 clove garlic*
>   *Bouquet garni*
>   *1 teaspoon salt*
>   *½ teaspoon white pepper*
>   *½ cup dry white wine*
>   *1 cup Brown Stock (page 63)*

Lay the larding pork in the bottom of an ovenware pot. Add all other ingredients. Arrange the balls of stuffed cabbage leaves on top of this. Bring to a boil on top of the stove, cover and put into a preheated 400-degree oven 1 hour. Remove the cabbage balls. Remove the butcher's twine and arrange the balls on a serving platter. Strain the sauce and skim off the fat. Boil 5 minutes before serving and pour over the cabbage balls.

CAROTTES—Carrots

Carottes à la Vichy

[GLAZED CARROTS]   FOR 4

>   4 cups carrots, sliced the thickness of silver dollars
>   2 cups water
>   4 tablespoons sweet butter
>   1 teaspoon salt
>   ½ teaspoon sugar
>   ½ bay leaf
>   ¼ teaspoon bicarbonate of soda
>   1 tablespoon chopped parsley

Place the carrots in a deep saucepan and add all other ingredients, except the parsley. Cover and simmer 20 minutes. Remove cover; simmer until liquid has evaporated. Sprinkle with the chopped parsley before serving.

Carottes à la Beaujeu

[GLAZED CARROTS AND ONIONS]   FOR 4

>   4 cups carrots, trimmed and
>   shaped like jumbo olives
>   24 small white onions
>   4 cups water
>   1 tablespoon salt
>   1 teaspoon sugar
>   6 tablespoons sweet butter
>   Small bouquet garni
>   1 clove garlic, unpeeled
>   1 tablespoon chopped parsley

Place the carrots and onions in a skillet. Add all other ingredients, except the parsley. Cover and simmer 40 minutes. Remove cover. Remove bouquet garni. Reduce liquid over medium heat until the carrots are almost candied. Sprinkle with the chopped parsley before serving.

CÉLERI-RAVE ET CÉLERIS—Celeriac and Celery

Céleri-Rave Fondants

[CELERIAC IN SAUCE]   FOR 4

> 2 large knobs celeriac (also called celery knobs
>   or roots), peeled, trimmed, shaped like 8 large eggs
> 4 tablespoons sweet butter
> 1 teaspoon salt
> ½ teaspoon white pepper
> 1 cup Demi-Glace (page 74)
> ¼ cup Madeira
>   Small bouquet garni
> 1 teaspoon chopped parsley

Blanch the celery knobs in boiling water 15 minutes. Cool under cold running water. Dry. Using half the butter, grease an oval au gratin dish. Add the celery knobs and sprinkle with the salt and pepper; add the demi-glace and Madeira. On top, place the bouquet garni and dot with the remaining butter. Cover with aluminum foil and place in a preheated 400-degree oven 30 minutes; baste every 10 minutes. Remove the foil and bouquet garni 5 minutes before the end of the 30 minutes. Sprinkle with parsley just before serving.

Céleris à la Crème au Gratin

[CREAMED CELERY AU GRATIN]   FOR 4

> 12 stalks cooked celery (white as possible)
> 1 cup heavy cream
> 1 tablespoon salt
> ½ teaspoon white pepper
> ¼ teaspoon nutmeg
> 1 tablespoon Sauce Béchamel (page 71)
> 2 tablespoons grated Swiss cheese
> 1 egg yolk, beaten
> 4 tablespoons sweet butter
> 1 tablespoon white bread crumbs

Scrape the best portion of the celery stalk with a sharp vegetable peeler. Slice in 3-inch pieces. Boil in water 15 minutes. Drain well. Place the cream into a saucepan. When simmering, add celery pieces; cook 3 minutes. Add the seasonings, then stir in the béchamel sauce, cheese and egg yolk. Using all of the butter, grease an ovenproof serving dish. Pour the celery in, sprinkle with bread crumbs and place in a preheated 400-degree oven 20 minutes.

Pieds de Céleris Braisés à la Romaine

[BRAISED CELERY WITH HAM]   FOR 4

> 4 small bunches celery (white as possible),
>   cut 5 inches long
> 4 thin slices prosciutto
> ½ cup sliced carrots
> ½ cup sliced white onions
> 1 teaspoon salt
>   Pinch white pepper
>   Pinch nutmeg
>   Bouquet garni
> 2 cups White Stock (page 61) or
>   Chicken Broth (page 62)
> ½ cup grated Parmesan cheese

Blanch the celery in boiling water 10 minutes. Cool under running cold water 5 minutes, washing off any sandy or soil particles inside the celery stalks. Dry. Wrap each with a slice of prosciutto tied in place with a piece of twine. Place the carrots and onions in a deep saucepan with the salt, pepper, nutmeg, bouquet garni and stock. Put the celery on top. Bring to a boil, cover with aluminum foil and a lid and put into a preheated 350-degree oven. Cook 1 hour; remove twine. Place celery in an au gratin dish. Reduce the liquid in the saucepan to half its volume. Strain through a fine strainer and pour over the celery. Sprinkle with grated cheese and place under the broiler until brown.

MAÏS—Corn

Corn Fritters

FOR 8 FRITTERS

> 1 cup white flour
> 1 cup cooked corn, grated from cob
> 1 teaspoon salt
>   Pinch white pepper
>   Pinch nutmeg
> 1 teaspoon grated white onion
> 2 egg yolks
> ¼ cup beer
> 1 tablespoon cooking oil
> 1 cup cooking oil

Blend the flour and corn thoroughly. Add the seasonings and grated onion. Stir in the yolks, beer and the tablespoon of oil. Place in the refrigerator 2 hours. Heat the 1 cup of oil in a deep saucepan to 365 degrees. Drop the corn batter in with a tablespoon, 3 or 4 spoonfuls at a time. Fry 2 minutes on each side; drain on absorbent paper. Place the fritters on a flat pan in a preheated 350-degree oven 3 minutes before serving. They should be well browned and crisp, not greasy.

Succotash Mexican Style

FOR 4

> 4 tablespoons sweet butter
> 2 tablespoons green peppers, cut in small dice
> 1 tablespoon red peppers, cut in small dice
> ½ teaspoon paprika
> ½ cup heavy cream
> ½ cup Sauce Velouté (page 66)
> 1 tablespoon salt
> ½ teaspoon white pepper
> 2 cups cooked lima beans
> 2 cups corn kernels
> 2 egg yolks

Melt the butter in a saucepan. When foaming, slowly sauté the green and red peppers 5 minutes. (If you use canned peppers, add just before going into oven.) Add the paprika, cream, velouté, salt and pepper and simmer 4 minutes. Stir in the lima beans and corn, simmer 5 minutes. Mix the egg yolks in thoroughly and pour into a baking dish. Place in a pan of boiling water and put in a preheated 400-degree oven 30 minutes. The top should be crisp; if it is not, place under the broiler 1 minute to obtain a crusty, brown top.

CONCOMBRES—Cucumbers

Concombres à la Crème

[CUCUMBERS IN CREAM]   FOR 4

> 4 cups cucumbers, peeled,
>   trimmed into walnut shapes
> 6 tablespoons sweet butter
> 1 tablespoon salt
> ½ teaspoon cayenne pepper
> ½ teaspoon paprika
> ½ cup heavy cream
> 1 tablespoon chopped parsley

Melt the butter in a saucepan. When foaming, sauté cucumbers on a slow fire 5 minutes. Add salt, cayenne and paprika. Cover and simmer 3 minutes. Remove the lid, add cream and simmer 5 minutes. Remove the cucumbers, avoiding mashing. Simmer the sauce until thickened. Add cucumbers. Check seasoning. Stir in chopped parsley and serve very hot.

AUBERGINES—Eggplants

Eggplants can be broiled, stewed with tomatoes or breaded and fried with garlic and parsley. But, in my opinion, the best way is baked, stuffed with mushrooms.

Aubergines Farcies aux Champignons

[EGGPLANTS STUFFED WITH MUSHROOMS]   FOR 4

2 small Italian eggplants, split in half lengthwise
2 tablespoons cooking oil
6 tablespoons sweet butter
1 tablespoon chopped shallots
½ pound mushrooms, finely chopped
1 teaspoon chopped garlic
1 tablespoon Sauce Tomate (page 83)
1 tablespoon salt
1 teaspoon white pepper
4 tablespoons white bread crumbs
1 egg, beaten
1 tablespoon chopped parsley
1 tablespoon grated Parmesan cheese

Sprinkle the cooking oil over the eggplant halves; bake, uncovered, in a preheated 400-degree oven 15 minutes. Melt the butter in a saucepan. When foaming, add the shallots, sauté 5 minutes; do not brown. Add the mushrooms, sauté 5 minutes; add the garlic, sauté 2 minutes. Stir in the tomato sauce, salt and pepper. With a spoon, remove the eggplant pulp. Chop finely, add the mushroom mixture and blend over the fire. Mix in the bread crumbs, egg and parsley. Fill the eggplant shells with this mixture. Sprinkle with grated cheese and place in a preheated 450-degree oven 10 minutes or until brown.

Aubergines Crémaillère

[EGGPLANTS WITH HAM, TOMATOES AND CHEESE]   FOR 4

6 tablespoons cooking oil
4 tablespoons sweet butter
4 slices eggplant, ¾-inch thick, 4-inches square

1 *tablespoon salt*
4 *thin slices cooked Virginia ham*
¼ *cup dry sherry*
1 *cup drained stewed tomatoes (fresh or canned)*
½ *teaspoon thyme leaves, added to the tomatoes*
4 *slices American cheese, ¼-inch thick, 4-inches square*
1 *teaspoon paprika*

Heat the oil with the butter in a skillet. When foaming, brown the eggplant on both sides; salt both sides. Arrange the slices on an oblong ovenproof serving platter. With the sherry sprinkled on top of each slice grill the ham under the broiler 3 minutes. Place the slices of ham on top of the eggplant, the tomatoes on top of the ham, and the cheese on top of the tomatoes. Sprinkle with paprika. Place under the broiler 5 minutes or until the cheese is melted and has taken on a nice brown color.

Ratatouille Niçoise (II)

[EGGPLANT, ZUCCHINI, PEPPERS AND
TOMATO CASSEROLE]   FOR 6

½ *cup olive oil*
4 *cups peeled eggplant, cut in 1-inch cubes*
4 *cups green zucchini, cut in 1-inch cubes*
½ *cup green peppers, cut in 1-inch squares*
¼ *cup fresh red peppers, cut in 1-inch squares*
½ *cup coarsely chopped onions*
2 *tablespoons chopped garlic*
4 *whole tomatoes, peeled, seeded, cut into quarters*
  Pinch thyme leaves
1 *bay leaf*
1 *teaspoon sweet basil*
  Pinch rosemary
1 *tablespoon salt*
1 *teaspoon white pepper*
½ *cup pitted small black olives*
½ *cup dry white wine*
2 *tablespoons chopped parsley*

Heat the olive oil in a saucepan. Sauté the eggplant and zucchini on a brisk fire 5 minutes. Add the green and red peppers, then the onions, and simmer, uncovered, 5 minutes. Add garlic, simmer 2 minutes. Add tomatoes, herbs, salt and pepper. Stir in the black olives and wine. Cook, covered, 20 minutes in a preheated 350-degree oven. Sprinkle with the chopped parsley before serving.

ENDIVES, LAITUES, POIREAUX ET AIL—Endive, Lettuce, Leeks and Garlic

Endives Meunière

[BRAISED ENDIVE]   FOR 6

Step One: Precooking endive
  6 medium endives
  1 cup water
  2 tablespoons lemon juice
  4 tablespoons sweet butter
  1 teaspoon salt
  1 lump sugar

Combine all the ingredients in skillet. Bring to a boil, cover with aluminum foil *and* a lid and place in a preheated 350-degree oven 40 minutes. Keep endives in a vessel covered with the cooking liquid until ready to use.

Step Two: Braising endive
  6 medium precooked endives
  6 tablespoons sweet butter (for 6 endives)
   Chopped parsley

Melt the butter in a thick-bottomed skillet. When foaming, add the endives, cooking until they turn color. Turn them over until they color on the other side. Sprinkle with parsley before serving.

Laitues Braisées

[BRAISED LETTUCE]   FOR 4

  4 heads Boston lettuce
  4 quarts water
  4 thin slices larding pork
  1 cup thinly sliced carrots
  1 cup thinly sliced onions
  1 tablespoon salt
  2 cups or more Brown Stock (page 63)
   Bouquet garni
  1 clove garlic

Bring water to a boil, add lettuce and blanch 15 minutes. Remove. Wash under running cold water to remove all sand particles. Wrap a slice of larding pork around each head; tie in place with twine. Place the carrots and onions in a deep saucepan with the lettuce on top. Add the salt, brown stock and bouquet garni. Bring to a boil, cover with aluminum foil *and* a lid and place in a preheated 350-degree oven 1 hour. Remove the twine and larding pork. Open the lettuce and fold. Strain the cooking sauce over the heads. Check the amount of brown stock at the beginning and during the cooking procedure, adding more if necessary.

Poireaux au Gratin

[WHITE OF LEEKS AU GRATIN]   FOR 4

> *4 whole leeks, white portion only, split, washed,*
> *   and tied together with butcher's twine,*
> *   cooked in boiling water 20 minutes or until tender*
> *1 cup Sauce Bâtarde (page 82)*
> *½ cup heavy cream mixed with 1 egg yolk*
> *½ cup grated Swiss cheese*
> *1 teaspoon salt*
> *¼ teaspoon cayenne pepper*
> *4 tablespoons sweet butter*

To the sauce bâtarde, add the cream-and-egg-yolk mixture and the cheese, salt and cayenne. Mix well. Check seasoning. Butter an au gratin dish with all of the butter. Drain the leeks, remove the twine and place in the au gratin dish. Pour the sauce bâtarde mixture over the leeks. Put, uncovered, in a preheated 400-degree oven 20 minutes. If not brown, place under the broiler.

Ail en Casserole

[GARLIC IN WINE]   FOR 4

> *6 tablespoons cooking oil*
> *24 cloves garlic, unpeeled*
> *1 teaspoon salt*
> *½ teaspoon white pepper*
> *¾ cup dry white wine*
> *4 slices toast buttered with*
> *   4 tablespoons sweet butter*
> *1 tablespoon chopped parsley*

Heat the oil in an earthenware casserole. Sauté cloves of garlic 3 minutes. Add the salt, pepper and wine. Bring to a boil, cover and simmer 15 minutes. Place the toast slices on a serving platter. Squeeze the garlic between forefinger and thumb out of its skin and onto the toast; pour the wine sauce over. Sprinkle with chopped parsley and give two turns of a pepper mill with white pepper.

"Route Nationale"

FLAGEOLETS

Flageolets can be bought dry or in cans at quality food stores. Dry flageolets should be soaked overnight, covered with cold water. Four ounces of dry beans (½ cup) make about 3 cups after they have been soaked, enough for 4 people. Remove from the water; place in a skillet; cover with cold water. Bring to a boil; simmer 2 hours or until beans are soft, but not mushy. It depends on the quality of the beans. Drain, keep in a cool place until ready to be used.

Flageolets à la Bretonne

[FLAGEOLETS WITH TOMATOES]   FOR 4

> 2 tablespoons sweet butter
> 1 tablespoon chopped onions
> 1 teaspoon chopped garlic
> ½ cup cooked fresh tomatoes, skinned,
>   seeded, diced
> 1 tablespoon tomato purée
> 1 tablespoon Demi-Glace (page 74)
> 1 teaspoon salt
>   Pinch white pepper
> 3 cups cooked flageolets
> 1 teaspoon chopped parsley

Melt the butter in a saucepan. Simmer onions 3 minutes until soft. Add garlic, simmer 1 minute; stir in cooked tomatoes, simmer 3 minutes. Blend in the tomato purée, demi-glace, salt and pepper. When the mixture boils, add the flageolets. Simmer, stirring one or twice without breaking the beans, 3 minutes. Sprinkle with parsley just before serving.

Flageolets Panachés au Gratin

[FLAGEOLETS WITH STRING BEANS AU GRATIN]   FOR 4

    1 cup heavy cream
    1 teaspoon grated white onions
    1 teaspoon salt
    1 teaspoon white pepper
    1 teaspoon chopped parsley
    1 cup cooked flageolets
    1 egg yolk, beaten
    1 cup cooked tiny string beans
    2 tablespoons sweet butter
    1 tablespoon white bread crumbs

In a saucepan, bring the cream to a boil. Stir in the grated onions, salt, pepper and parsley; simmer 3 minutes. Add the flageolets, simmer 2 minutes. Off heat, stir in the egg yolk; do not let scramble. Add the string beans; mix upward slowly, in order not to break the beans. Butter an au gratin dish and add bean mixture. Sprinkle with bread crumbs and place in a preheated 450-degree oven 4 minutes. If not brown, place briefly under the broiler.

Flageolets Washington Style   FOR 4

    1 cup heavy cream
    1 cup cooked flageolets
    1 cup corn kernels
    1 teaspoon salt
    Pinch paprika
    1 egg yolk, beaten
    2 tablespoons sweet butter

In a saucepan, bring the cream to a boil. Stir in the flageolets, corn, salt and paprika; simmer 4 minutes. Off heat, stir in the egg yolk. Butter an au gratin dish and add the bean-corn mixture. Place under the broiler until the top is brown.

CHAMPIGNONS—Mushrooms

Duxelles

[PURÉE OF MUSHROOMS]   FOR ABOUT 2 CUPS

4 tablespoons sweet butter
1 pound mushrooms
  Pinch salt
1 tablespoon lemon juice

Melt butter in a saucepan. When foaming (do not brown), add mushrooms. Sauté 5 minutes, adding salt and lemon juice. Cool. Force through the fine blade of the meat grinder. Return to pan and fire; simmer until almost dry. This purée will be used with other recipes or as a garnish.

Champignons au Gratin Dauphinoise

[MUSHROOMS IN CREAM AU GRATIN]   FOR 4

4 tablespoons sweet butter
1 tablespoon chopped shallots
1 pound mushrooms, sliced thin
2 tablespoons Madeira
1 cup heavy cream
1 tablespoon Sauce Béchamel (page 71)
1 tablespoon Sauce Hollandaise (page 81)
1 tablespoon salt
½ teaspoon white pepper
1 tablespoon white bread crumbs
1 tablespoon grated Swiss cheese

Melt the butter in a deep saucepan. When foaming, add shallots and simmer 5 minutes. Add the sliced mushrooms, simmer 5 minutes. Pour in the Madeira and cream, simmer 5 minutes; stir in the béchamel, simmer 3 minutes. Remove from heat and blend in the hollandaise. Sprinkle with salt and pepper and stir. Pour into a baking dish, sprinkle with bread crumbs and cheese and place in a preheated 450-degree oven 5 minutes. Before serving, brown under the broiler 2 minutes.

OIGNONS ET PETITS POIS—Onions and Peas

Oignons Farcis Barigoule

[ONIONS STUFFED WITH SAUSAGE
AND MUSHROOMS]   FOR 4

Step One: Prepare onions
> 4 *large white or Bermuda onions*

Blanch the onions in boiling water with 1 tablespoon salt 10 minutes. Drain. Remove centers (to make space for the following stuffing) and reserve.

Step Two: Stuff and cook onions
> 4 *tablespoons sweet butter*
> 1 *tablespoon chopped onions*
>   (*from centers of blanched onions*)
> 1 *cup chopped mushrooms*
> 1 *teaspoon chopped garlic*
> 1 *tablespoon tomato purée*
> 1 *teaspoon salt*
> 1 *teaspoon white pepper*
>   *Pinch thyme leaves*
>   *Pinch oregano leaves*
> 1 *tablespoon chopped parsley*
> ½ *pound sausage meat*
> 1 *egg*
> ½ *cup white bread crumbs*
> 1 *tablespoon Demi-Glace (page 74)*
> 4 *thin slices larding pork (fat back)*
> 2 *tablespoons sweet sherry*
> 1 *cup demi-glace*
> 1 *tablespoon grated Parmesan cheese*

Melt the butter in a saucepan. When foaming, add the chopped onions and mushrooms, simmer 5 minutes; do not brown. Add the chopped garlic, simmer 2 minutes. Stir in tomato purée, salt, pepper, thyme leaves, oregano and parsley; simmer 2 minutes. Add the sausage, egg, bread crumbs, and the tablespoon of demi-glace. Mix well. Check seasoning. Fill the centers of the onions with this stuffing. Line the bottom of an oven-proof pot with the slices of larding pork. Pour in the sherry and the cup of demi-glace. Place the stuffed onions on top and sprinkle with grated cheese. Place, covered, in a preheated 350-degree oven 1 hour. Baste every

10 minutes. Before serving, place under the broiler 2 minutes to brown the tops of the onions.

French Fried Onions   FOR 4

> 4 large Bermuda or white onions
> 1 cup milk, to which you have added 1 tablespoon salt
> 2 cups white flour
> 2-quart deep frying pan, filled with cooking oil

Slice the onions in ⅛-inch-thick rings; do not break the rings. Place them in the bowl with the salted milk and marinate 20 minutes. Remove from the milk and dry with cheesecloth or a paper towel. Dredge in flour. Place in a wire frying basket and dip into cooking oil heated to 380 degrees. Shake the basket so the rings will not stick together. Cook until nicely golden and crisp. This should be done just before serving. To serve, spread the onion rings on a dry napkin. Sprinkle with more salt if necessary.

Soubise au Gratin

[PURÉE OF ONIONS AU GRATIN]   FOR 6

> 6 tablespoons sweet butter
> 1 pound Bermuda onions, sliced thin
> 1 cup rice
> 3 cups boiling Chicken Broth (page 62)
>   or White Stock (page 61)
> 1 tablespoon salt
> 1 teaspoon white pepper
>   Pinch nutmeg
>   Bouquet garni
> ½ cup heavy cream, mixed with 2 eggs

Melt the butter in a deep saucepan. Sauté the onions on a moderate flame 20 minutes; do not brown. Add the rice, cook 2 minutes; stir in the hot stock. Continue stirring and add the salt, pepper, nutmeg and bouquet garni. When boiling, cover with aluminum foil *and* a lid and place in a preheated 350-degree oven 25 minutes or until rice is cooked. Remove the bouquet garni. Push the rice and onions through a fine sieve and stir into the egg-and-cream mixture, blending well. Butter a soufflé dish and pour in this soubise. Place in a pan of boiling water in a preheated 450-degree oven 20 minutes. The top should be crusty; if not, brown under the broiler 2 or 3 minutes.

Petits Pois à la Française

[PEAS WITH ONIONS AND LETTUCE]   FOR 4

> 4 tablespoons sweet butter
> 2 ounces lean salt pork, cut into small strips
> 1 cup shredded Boston lettuce
> 12 very small white onions
> 2 cups green peas
> ½ teaspoon salt
> 1 cup White Stock (page 61)
> 1 lump sugar
> Small bouquet garni

Melt the butter in a saucepan. When foaming, add the strips of salt pork. Sauté, turning, 10 minutes on a low fire. Add the lettuce, sauté 5 minutes. Stir in the onions, peas, salt, white stock and sugar and simmer, covered, 10 minutes. Remove cover and simmer, stirring occasionally, until the vegetables are cooked and the liquid has evaporated. Remove the bouquet garni before serving. Check seasoning. These peas are excellent with braised sweetbreads, roast of veal and squabs. At serving time, arrange them in the casserole with the meat and its brown sauce.

POMMES DE TERRE—Potatoes

We can thank the Spaniards for the potato. When they invaded South America in 1524, they found a large number of varieties and species under cultivation. A monk, Hieronymus Cardan, brought the potato from Peru to Spain. From there, it went to Italy, then Austria,

Germany and Switzerland, finally reaching France. It first appeared on Louis XVI's table in 1775, I am told.

The French may have been among the last to receive it, but we have treated it kindly, and, in my opinion, with imagination. Where else but in France, for example, would Purée de Pommes de Terre (mashed potatoes) be treated with such reverence? In some Parisian restaurants, a cart is wheeled in with the boiled potatoes in their pot. Before your eyes they are drained, mashed and whipped with cream and butter. It is usually a two-man job. And the teamwork is as serious as that of a nurse handing a surgeon his instruments. A waiter stands attentively beside the maître d'hôtel giving him items as he needs them. The masher. The whisk. The butter. The cream, warmed over the chafing dish at tableside. The salt. The white pepper. The lowly potato grows in stature as you watch the performance.

My Grandmother also had great respect for the tuber, and prepared it in several imaginative ways. One is:

Pommes de Terre Grand'mère

[GRANDMOTHER'S POTATOES]   FOR 4

> 3 ounces larding pork, diced
> 1 cup sliced onions
> 1 clove garlic, peeled
> ½ cup Sauce Tomate (page 83)
> 6 tablespoons dry white wine
>   Bouquet garni
> 1 teaspoon salt
> 1 teaspoon white pepper
> 1 pound early rose potatoes, peeled or
>   scraped, cut in 1-inch squares
> 3 ounces boiled ham, diced
> 1 tablespoon chopped parsley

Render the larding pork in a skillet 5 minutes to obtain sufficient fat. Add the onions and garlic, sautéing until soft. Tomato sauce, wine, bouquet garni, salt and pepper go in next. Bring to a boil and add the potatoes and boiled ham, keeping on the boil. Cover and place in a preheated 350-degree oven 40 minutes or until potatoes are cooked. Remove the bouquet garni. Check seasoning. Place in a serving dish and sprinkle with chopped parsley before serving.

Pommes de Terre Parisienne

[POTATOES PARISIENNE] FOR 6

> 10 medium new potatoes
> 3 tablespoons sweet butter
> 1 tablespoon olive oil
> ½ teaspoon salt
> 3 tablespoons soft sweet butter
> 1 tablespoon glace de viande
> 1 tablespoon minced parsley

Peel and scoop potatoes into balls with a ¾-inch-diameter potato-baller; even better if smaller. Heat oil and melt the 3 tablespoons of butter in a 10-inch saucepan or skillet, large enough to hold all the potatoes without layering. Reduce the heat to medium. When the butter and oil stop foaming, add the potatoes. Cook three minutes, testing heat, regulating so it is not too high. The butter and potatoes should not become brown; potatoes should be a golden hue. Cook potatoes about eight minutes, shaking pan, or turning potatoes with a wooden fork and spoon, so they are evenly colored. Salt potatoes. Cover the pan and cook the potatoes slowly 10 minutes, checking that they do not stick to the pan and burn and that they are still getting an even color. Remove from heat. Pour the fat off the potatoes. Spoon the 3 tablespoons of soft butter into the potatoes in the pan, shaking the pan and rolling the potatoes around in the butter. The idea is to coat the potatoes and make them shine. Chop the glace de viande so it will melt quickly. Stir it into the pan with the potatoes; place over medium heat, stirring the potatoes into the glace de viande and butter until they are coated. Sprinkle with the parsley.

Crêpes de Pommes de Terre

[POTATO PANCAKES] FOR ABOUT 8 PANCAKES

> 2 medium potatoes, peeled
> 1 cup white flour
> 1 tablespoon salt
> 1 teaspoon white pepper
> Pinch nutmeg
> 2 tablespoons beer
> 2 eggs, beaten
> 1 tablespoon grated onions
> 1 teaspoon chopped parsley
> 4 tablespoons sweet butter
> ¼ cup cooking oil

Grate the potatoes into a mixing bowl. Add the flour, salt, pepper and nutmeg and mix thoroughly. Blend in the beer, eggs, onions and parsley. Heat the oil and butter in a skillet. When foaming, drop the batter in with a large cooking spoon, three or four spoonfuls at a time, depending on the size of the skillet. Cook 3 minutes on each side. The pancakes should be well browned. Arrange on an ovenproof platter and place in a preheated 400-degree oven 3 minutes before serving.

Pommes de Terre au Gratin Savoyarde

[SCALLOPED POTATOES]   FOR 4

> 4 medium potatoes, sliced
>   to shape of silver dollars
> 6 tablespoons sweet butter
> 1 tablespoon salt
> ½ teaspoon white pepper
>   Pinch nutmeg
> 1 cup heavy cream
> 1 cup White Stock (page 61)
> 1 tablespoon grated onions
> 2 eggs, beaten
> ½ cup grated Swiss cheese

Dry the sliced potatoes. Using half the butter, butter a deep baking dish and arrange the potatoes in it. Sprinkle with salt, pepper and nutmeg. In a saucepan, bring the cream and white stock to a boil. Add the onions, simmer 3 minutes. Remove from fire and cool slightly before stirring in the eggs (to avoid curdling). Pour the mixture over the potatoes and sprinkle with cheese. Place, uncovered, in a preheated 400-degree oven 1 hour. If not brown and crisp, place under the broiler. Use the remaining butter to fleck top of the gratin 2 minutes before serving.

Pommes de Terre Duchesse

[DUCHESSE POTATOES]   FOR ABOUT 4 CUPS

> 4 cups boiled, mashed baking potatoes
> 2 egg yolks, beaten
>   Pinch nutmeg
> ¼ pound sweet butter
> 1 tablespoon salt
>   White pepper to taste

First, be sure that potatoes have had all water cooked off before mashing. They should be very dry. Add the egg yolks to the potatoes while they are still hot. Mix quickly so the eggs will not cause lumps. Then add the nutmeg, butter, salt and pepper. These potatoes can be put through a pastry bag with a fluted tube to decorate the edge of a serving platter or to form shells that may be used instead of vol-au-vent.

Pommes de Terre Soufflées

[SOUFFLÉED POTATOES]   FOR 4

Have two deep-fat pans on the stove, one 350 degrees, the other 450 degrees. Peel enough Idaho potatoes to get 24 slices, $\frac{1}{16}$ inch thick, 3 inches in length, 2 inches wide. Wash these slices under cold water; dry each carefully on a dry white cloth. One by one, put slices of potatoes in the 350-degree fat, very quickly, rotating the pan clockwise, so the potatoes will not stick together; fry 3 minutes. Increase the heat to 400 degrees, still moving the pan, 2 minutes. Then, with a wire skimmer, transfer the potatoes to the 450-degree fat. In this fat, the potatoes will blow up evenly. Remove each slice onto paper toweling or a white cloth. Keep separated until ready to use. They can be prepared 2 hours, or 2 days, ahead.

When ready to serve, have the 450-degree pan hot on the stove. Place the amount of potatoes that you want into this very hot pan, turning them with the skimmer, so each side will get crisp. It will take only 1 minute. Remove to drain on a dry white cloth or paper towels. Arrange around the meat or fish that you are serving, or display them on a separate dish, in the center of a well-folded napkin. Sprinkle with salt. If you don't succeed the first time, try again. It can be mastered. It just seems difficult.

NOTE: In some recipes, the following potatoes are called for:

Gaufrette Potatoes: These are small wafers (smaller than potato chips), sliced very thin and deep fried until crisp.
Julienne or Allumette Potatoes: These are cut matchstick size and deep-fried until crisp.

Pommes de Terre au Four Crémaillère

[STUFFED BAKED POTATOES]   FOR 4

> *4 large Idaho potatoes, wrapped in aluminum foil,*
> *   baked in a 400-degree oven 1 hour or until cooked*
> *1 tablespoon chopped chives*
> *1 teaspoon fresh chopped tarragon*
> *1 teaspoon salt*
> *1 teaspoon white pepper*
> *   Pinch nutmeg*
> *1 tablespoon shallots, chopped and simmered*
> *   5 minutes in 4 tablespoons sweet butter*
> *¼ cup heavy cream*
> *1 small package Liederkrantz cheese*
> *1 tablespoon white bread crumbs*

Take the potatoes from the oven and, laying them flat, cut off and save the tops. Remove pulp with a spoon and place empty potato shells on a baking dish. In a bowl, mash the pulp, mixing in the ingredients (except the bread crumbs) one by one to make a purée. Check seasoning. Fill the potato shells with this purée and sprinkle with the bread crumbs. Place in a preheated 450-degree oven 5 minutes or until heated through. Replace tops and serve.

ÉPINARDS—Spinach

Épinards en Branches

[CHOPPED SPINACH]

Cut the center stems from fresh spinach and discard. Blanch the spinach in salted boiling water 5 minutes. Cool under cold water. Drain and chop coarsely. Melt some butter in a saucepan. When foaming, add the chopped spinach and sauté 2 minutes. Add salt, pepper and nutmeg to taste. Prepare amounts needed.

Épinards à la Crème

[CREAMED SPINACH]   FOR 2

1 cup puréed spinach
2 tablespoons Sauce Béchamel (page 71)
2 tablespoons sweet butter

Combine the spinach, béchamel and butter; sauté 5 minutes. Season to taste. Increase proportions according to the number of people being served.

Soufflés d'Épinards

[SPINACH SOUFFLÉS]   FOR 6

½ cup Sauce Velouté (page 66)
1 teaspoon grated white onion
1 pound fresh spinach (1 package frozen)
   cooked until tender in small amount of water,
   dried well (must be free of water)
   and puréed through a fine sieve
1 teaspoon salt
   Pinch nutmeg
   Pinch cayenne pepper
2 eggs, separated
2 tablespoons sweet butter
6 baba molds or ramekins

Heat the velouté in a saucepan and stir in the grated onions; simmer 2 minutes. Add the spinach, salt, nutmeg and pepper; simmer 5 minutes. Off the fire, add the egg yolks, stirring rapidly to avoid scrambling. Beat the egg whites until very firm and stir into the spinach. Check seasoning. Butter the baba molds with all the butter and fill with the spinach mixture. Place in a pan of boiling water in a preheated 400-degree oven 15 minutes.

TOMATES—Tomatoes

Tomates Farcies Provençale

[TOMATOES STUFFED WITH GARLIC AND HERBS]   FOR 4

    4 medium tomatoes
    ¼ cup olive oil
    1 tablespoon chopped shallots
    ½ cup chopped mushrooms
    1 teaspoon chopped garlic
    1 teaspoon fresh thyme leaves
      (¼ teaspoon dried)
    ½ teaspoon sweet basil

Pinch sage
Pinch rosemary leaves
1 teaspoon salt
½ teaspoon white pepper
1 tablespoon tomato purée
1 egg
½ cup white bread crumbs

Cut the tops off the tomatoes about 1½-inches in diameter and save. Remove pulp. Place tomatoes in an oiled baking dish. Heat the olive oil in a saucepan; sauté the shallots 3 minutes, until soft. Stir in the chopped mushrooms, then the garlic, simmer 3 minutes. Add the remaining ingredients, except the egg and bread crumbs. Mix well over heat, simmer 3 minutes, stirring constantly. Take off the heat, blend in egg and bread crumbs. Check seasoning. After the stuffing has cooled, fill the tomatoes. Replace the tops. Place in a preheated 400-degree oven 15 minutes. Cover with aluminum foil and let bake another 20 minutes.

Tomates Farcies à l'Anglaise

[TOMATOES STUFFED WITH HERBED BREAD
CRUMBS AND BACON]   FOR 4

4 tomatoes, halved, pulp removed, drained
2 strips lean bacon, finely chopped
½ cup finely chopped onions
½ cup heavy cream
1 cup white bread crumbs
½ tablespoon salt
Pinch cayenne pepper
½ teaspoon thyme leaves
Pinch sage
Pinch rosemary
½ teaspoon chopped parsley
1 egg yolk
Olive oil

Place the tomato halves on an oiled oblong baking dish. Sauté the bacon in a saucepan, add the onions, simmer 3 minutes. Add the remaining ingredients, except the egg yolk and olive oil. Over low heat, blend in the egg yolk. Stuff tomatoes with this mixture, cover with aluminum foil and place in a preheated 400-degree oven 15 minutes. Remove foil, sprinkle olive oil lightly over each tomato and bake, uncovered, another 5 minutes. The top of the tomatoes should be crusty. If not, place under the broiler 1 minute before serving.

COURGETTES—Zucchini

Courgettes à la Florentine

[ZUCCHINI WITH SPINACH]   FOR 4

Zucchini are sometimes called courgettes or green squash. The Italians have popularized this tasty vegetable. I like it best cooked with another vegetable—tomato, eggplant, or, in this case, spinach.

> 1 pound tender, small zucchini, unpeeled, sliced,
>   shaped like 25-cent pieces
> ½ cup olive oil
> 1 tablespoon finely chopped onions
> 1 teaspoon minced garlic
> 1 cup fresh cooked Épinards en Branches (page 317)
> 1½ teaspoons salt
> ½ teaspoon white pepper
>   Pinch nutmeg
> 2 tablespoons grated Parmesan cheese
> ½ cup white bread crumbs
> 4 tablespoons sweet butter

Heat the oil in a skillet. Sauté the zucchini 4 minutes, turning them over so every slice will become crisp. Add the onions and garlic, simmer 1 minute. Drain oil from the zucchini. Place the spinach in a well-buttered deep baking dish; lay the zucchini on top of it. Season both spinach and zucchini with salt, pepper and nutmeg. Sprinkle with cheese, then with bread crumbs, and dot with butter. Place in a preheated 400-degree oven 20 minutes or until brown.

Courgettes Frites à la Française

[FRENCH FRIED ZUCCHINI]   FOR 4

> ½ pound zucchini
> 2 cups milk
> 1 tablespoon salt
> ½ teaspoon white pepper
>   White flour
>   Cooking oil for deep frying

Wash the zucchini and dry well. Cut into sticks, 2-inches long, ¼-inch thick. Place these in the milk, to which you have added the salt and white pepper. Marinate 5 minutes. Drain the zucchini sticks and dredge in flour. Keep them well separated. Place in a wire frying basket and into a deep frying pan filled with cooking oil heated to 380 degrees. Fry for 3 minutes or until zucchini are very crisp. They should be served immediately, placed on a dry napkin or cheesecloth to absorb excess oil.

11

SALADES—Salads

Often a salad can make the meal memorable. Well prepared with fresh ingredients and a tasty dressing, served with a bird hot and crusty from the spit or with a nice rare, larded filet of beef, it can mean the difference between dining and simply eating. When Alexandre Dumas had his famous fifteen friends gather for dinner at his home every Wednesday at midnight, he said of salads, "It is the task of the master or mistress of the house, if they are worthy of such priestly duty, to attend personally to the seasoning of salads. It should be done an hour before the salad bowl is to be broached. The salad should be turned over three or four times during that hour." When his friend Ronconi couldn't attend a dinner, he sent a servant for his share of the salad. If it rained, it was carried to Ronconi under an umbrella so its superb flavor would not be diluted.

Brillat-Savarin, who gave very little space to vegetables in his gastronomic writings, said of salads, "They freshen without enfeebling, and fortify without irritating."

To simplify, salads called plain salads are either green or composed of vegetables in season. They are served raw, or if cooked, they usually contain just one vegetable. Either way, I like to serve them with a roast, hot or cold. If the salads are more involved, with numerous ingredients, I serve them by themselves, or with elegant cold dishes—meat, fish or chicken mousses.

Served with cheese, a good red wine and crusty French bread, they are a favorite course of mine before dessert. For this, of course, only French cheese will do. Brie is my first choice, but many others are superb: Coulommiers, Camembert, Purecrem, Bibress, Fondue aux Raisins ("grape" cheese), Carré de l'Est, Neufchâtel. There are more than one hundred types of French cheese sold in the United States.

St.-Tropez, Riviera

Among these fine cheeses are Boursault, Boursin, Gervais, Triple Crème Parfait, Petit-suisse, Saint-Florentin, Fontainebleau, Pithiviers au foin (hay-ripened), Epoisses, Valmeuse, Bonbel, Pont l'Évêque, Port-Salut, Reblochon, Livarot, Pamproux, Banon, Chabichou, Chevrotins, Montrachet, Saint-Marcellin, Tonnelets, Pyramide. Roquefort is the king of blue cheeses, made only from ewe's milk and aged in the caves of Roquefort. But it is not the only good blue: Pipo Crème, Fourme Bleu, Bleu de Bresse, Bleu d'Auvergne, Fourme d'Ambert. Hard cheeses I like are Cantal and Cancoillotte, and the fine-textured cooking cheeses, Mimolette, which looks like an Edam and tastes like cheddar, Comté and the nutty Beaumont. Only space restricts me from continuing this list of excellent French cheeses. A rule of thumb is that red wine (or rosé) is usually served with cheese.

An excellent idea is to serve several varieties of cheese on a cheese board and let your guests cut what they want.

Cheese must be served at room temperature; its flavor is lost when it is taken from the refrigerator and served immediately. It should be out at least two hours before serving; twice that time is even better. Round cheese—Brie or Camembert—should be cut from the center out, in wedges. So should square cheese—Pont l'Évêque or Carré de l'Est—but usually in squares rather than wedges.

I will drop some salad hints here at the beginning, and probably repeat them, for they are important: treat your salad bowl as you do your omelette pan. It should be seasoned, perfumed from many salads, of plain wood, unvarnished and untreated. It should never be washed. When through using it, wipe it out well with a dry cloth or paper towel.

Use only a fine grade of wine vinegar and never overdo it; go sparingly. If you use pepper, make sure it is freshly milled into the salad. Olive oil should be the finest, of the first pressing. Wash salad greens well under *cold* water. Do not cut the leaves up but break them carefully with your fingers into bite-size pieces. Wrap them in a dry cloth and place in the refrigerator for an hour to become firm and crisp.

I am often asked the best type of lettuce to use in a salad. My reply usually involves some slight criticism, and a question. "How can Americans survive if they continue to use iceberg lettuce as the base of their salads?" Man does not live on what he eats, but on what he digests. Iceberg lettuce is indigestible. If this monstrous salad habit continues in the United States we need not fear destruction from student riots, hydrogen bombs or nuclear attack. Iceberg lettuce will take care of it. Answer to the original question: I like Boston, or Bibb. The salad, however, involves much more than lettuce.

It must be plainly stated: Salads are those dishes seasoned with oil, vinegar, lemon juice or anything sour. To a few, some sugar may be added. Jellos, cottage-cheese-and-pears and the remaining weird women's-magazine concoctions must be called something else. I will not use the word I have in mind. Suffice it to say, they are not salads. To call them such is as confusing as calling a pickle a "sweet" pickle. Pickle means sour, salty, acid, vinegary—those ingredients used to preserve whatever is going to be pickled. So let us prepare salads with sense and stay classic. Here, except for my Chef's Salad, I will not give recipes for meat, fish or poultry salads, but will stay with raw or cooked vegetables.

The heart of any salad is the dressing.

VINAIGRETTES—Oil and Vinegar Dressings

Sauce Vinaigrette

[FRENCH DRESSING]   FOR ABOUT ½ CUP

Use, as stated, good vinegar (not bargain price or the already mixed freaks, with strange herb and seasoning additions)—wine or cider. If you can't get wine vinegar, use Dijon mustard and first-quality olive oil. Most dressings can be made ahead and kept in the refrigerator or a cool place. I, however, like to make the dressing in an unvarnished wooden salad bowl one hour before being used. The quantity should be according to your number of guests. One caution: Do not use too much dressing; the salad should not be liquid.

> 1 tablespoon Dijon mustard
> 1 teaspoon salt
>   Dash freshly ground white pepper
> 2 tablespoons wine vinegar
> 2 tablespoons olive oil

In the wooden salad bowl, put mustard, salt, pepper and vinegar; blend thoroughly. Now blend in the olive oil, a little at a time. (For garlic dressing, crush garlic clove against the inside of the wooden bowl with a wooden salad spoon; press it into the salt and pepper, so the garlic will completely blend into the dressing.) Now add the salad greens to the bowl. They should be thoroughly dried in cheesecloth or well shaken in a wire salad basket. Herbs of your choice can be added; but last, over the other greens in the bowl, not to the dressing.

Sauce Vinaigrette Royale

[ROYAL FRENCH DRESSING] FOR ABOUT ½ CUP

Same as the previous French Dressing, adding 1 beaten egg yolk for the same amount of dressing, 1 teaspoon chopped shallots, 1 teaspoon chopped chives and 1 teaspoon chopped tarragon.

Sauce Anchoyade

[ANCHOVY DRESSING] FOR ABOUT ½ CUP

  2 cloves garlic
  ½ teaspoon salt
    Pinch white pepper
  2 ounces anchovy filets (1 small can)
  1 hard boiled egg yolk
  2 tablespoons vinegar
  1 teaspoon Dijon mustard
  ¼ cup olive oil
  1 teaspoon chopped parsley

Crush the garlic cloves with the salt and pepper in a wooden salad bowl. Add the anchovies and crush them against the wall of the bowl. Add the egg yolk and mix well to obtain a paste. Stir in the vinegar with a wooden spoon. Slowly add the mustard, olive oil and finally the chopped parsley. This dressing is used for celery whites and knobs, white stems or cardoons, raw artichokes or hearts of palm.

Sauce Gribiche

[GRIBICHE DRESSING]   FOR ABOUT 3½ CUPS

2 hard boiled eggs
1 tablespoon Dijon mustard
2 teaspoons salt
1 teaspoon white pepper
1 cup wine vinegar
2 cups olive oil
1 tablespoon chopped capers
1 tablespoon chopped parsley
1 tablespoon chopped shallots
1 teaspoon chopped tarragon
1 teaspoon chopped chervil

Cut the whites of the hard boiled eggs lengthwise in tiny strips; set aside. Mash yolks with mustard. Add salt, pepper and vinegar. Blend; slowly add oil. When well mixed, add all other ingredients, except strips of egg white; mix again. At the last moment, gently stir in strips of egg white. Used with cold eggs, calf's head, calf's brains, asparagus, celery knobs.

Sauce Roquefort

[ROQUEFORT DRESSING]   FOR ABOUT ½ CUP

Some believe this is American. Not true. It comes from south-western France, in the region around Roquefort where the famous cheese is made. I suppose it becomes American when an inordinate amount of domestic blue cheese, iceberg lettuce and ordinary salad oil are mixed together. But with the proper ingredients, in exact quantities, it is as French as the cheese for which it was named. And a formidable taste-bud tantalizer.

1 teaspoon salt
½ teaspoon white pepper
1 teaspoon Dijon mustard
1 tablespoon white wine vinegar
2 tablespoons olive oil
½ teaspoon grated horse-radish
2 tablespoons Roquefort cheese
1 tablespoon sour or heavy cream

In a wooden salad bowl, mix the salt, pepper and mustard thoroughly. Add the vinegar, mix well. Add the oil slowly. Add the horse-radish and, last, the Roquefort cheese in lumps together with the cream. This dressing should be smooth and not kept in the refrigerator.

Cape Cod Dressing
FOR ABOUT ½ CUP

Make the above Sauce Roquefort, substituting Danish Blue Cheese and blending in 1 teaspoon paprika and 1 teaspoon chopped chives.

Russian Dressing
FOR ABOUT 1 CUP

½ teaspoon dry English mustard (Colman's)
1 teaspoon white vinegar (cider or wine)
1 teaspoon grated horse-radish
1 teaspoon chopped green peppers
1 teaspoon chopped red peppers
1 teaspoon finely chopped onions
1 teaspoon salt
Pinch cayenne pepper
1 teaspoon chopped parsley
1 teaspoon chopped white celery
1 tablespoon chili sauce
1 cup Mayonnaise (page 84)
1 teaspoon vodka

Mix the mustard with the vinegar and add all but the last three ingredients. Blend thoroughly. Add the chili sauce and then the mayonnaise. Just before serving, stir in the vodka. Mix well.

Thousand Island Dressing
FOR ABOUT 1 CUP

Use the Russian Dressing recipe and sprinkle the top of the salad first with the white of one chopped hard boiled egg, then with the chopped yolk.

Creole Dressing
FOR ABOUT ¾ CUP

1 tablespoon chopped green peppers
1 teaspoon chopped red pimentos
1 teaspoon grated onions
1 teaspoon chopped white celery
1½ teaspoons chopped capers

1½ teaspoons chopped sour gherkins
½ teaspoon Dijon mustard
1 teaspoon grated horse-radish
1 teaspoon salt
Pinch cayenne pepper
1 tablespoon white wine vinegar
2 tablespoons olive oil
1 teaspoon Escoffier Sauce Diable
1 teaspoon Lea & Perrins sauce

Mix all but the last four ingredients together thoroughly in a wooden salad bowl. Then blend in the vinegar, oil, sauce diable and Lea & Perrins. Mix well.

Sauce Grand'mère

[GRANDMOTHER'S DRESSING]   FOR ABOUT ¼ CUP

1 teaspoon Dijon mustard
1 egg yolk
1 teaspoon salt
Pinch white pepper
1 tablespoon lemon juice
2 tablespoons heavy cream
1 teaspoon chopped chives
1 teaspoon chopped chervil

Blend the mustard and egg yolk with a wooden salad spoon. Stir in the salt and pepper; add the lemon juice, then the cream. Spread over or toss with whatever salad you want to serve, sprinkling with chives and chervil last. This goes especially well with Boston lettuce or hearts of palm.

Sauce Ravigote

[VINAIGRETTE WITH ONIONS,
CAPERS AND HERBS]   FOR ABOUT ¼ CUP

1 teaspoon salt
Pinch white pepper
1 teaspoon Dijon mustard
1 tablespoon wine vinegar
2 tablespoons olive oil
½ teaspoon each chopped onions, capers, chives and parsley
1 teaspoon mixed chopped chervil and tarragon

Mix the salt, pepper and mustard and blend in the vinegar. Stir in the oil, small amounts at a time, then all the other ingredients. Mix well.

Sauce Vinaigrette Paysanne

[BACON VINAIGRETTE]   FOR ABOUT 1¼ CUPS

> 1 teaspoon Dijon mustard
> 1 teaspoon salt
>   Pinch white pepper
> 1 cup wine vinegar
> 1 tablespoon grated onion
> ½ teaspoon chopped garlic
> 2 strips bacon, diced
> 1 teaspoon chopped parsley

Mix the mustard, salt, pepper and vinegar thoroughly in a wooden salad bowl. Stir in the onions and garlic. Sauté the bacon in a skillet 2 minutes. When crisp, drain well and mix into the sauce. Toss in chopped parsley.

Sauce Méridionale   FOR ABOUT 3 CUPS

This is an herb sauce, typical of southeastern France.

> 2 tablespoons each finely chopped sweet basil, sage,
>   rosemary, chervil, tarragon, chives, shallots, garlic, parsley
> ½ cup wine vinegar
> 2 cups olive oil
> 2 teaspoons salt
> 1 teaspoon Dijon mustard
> ¼ teaspoon white pepper

Mix the herbs. Blend in the vinegar, olive oil, salt, mustard and pepper. This may be kept in a cool place and used as you need it. It goes well on raw vegetables and can be used on pastas and cold fish.

Lemon Dressing

> 1 tablespoon lemon juice
> ½ teaspoon Dijon mustard
> 1 teaspoon salt
> Pinch cayenne pepper
> 2 tablespoons olive oil
> ½ teaspoon chopped chervil
> ½ teaspoon chopped tarragon

Mix the lemon juice, mustard, salt and pepper thoroughly. Add the oil and herbs; blend into a smooth sauce.

Chapons

Chapons are slices from the heel of French bread, 1-inch in diameter, well-rubbed with garlic. Added to salads, they impart a subtle garlic flavor and can be eaten or discarded. Since they are very tasty after being mixed in the dressing, only the anti-garlic school discards them.

SALADES—Salads

Salade de Fonds d'Artichauts et d'Asperges

[ARTICHOKE BOTTOMS WITH ASPARAGUS]   FOR 4

> 4 cooked artichoke bottoms
>   Bunch cooked green asparagus tips
> 4 medium Boston lettuce leaves
>   Sauce Vinaigrette (page 325)
> 1 tablespoon chopped parsley

Place the artichoke bottoms on the lettuce leaves, fill with the vinaigrette. Cut up the asparagus tips and place over the artichokes. Sprinkle with parsley before serving.

Salade d'Avocat

[AVOCADO SALAD]

An avocado, skinned, stone out, is sliced in eight pieces of equal thickness. Arrange four of these slices per person on a lettuce leaf and place a slice of red pimento between the avocado slices, letting the color show. Season with Sauce Grand'Mère (page 329) and sprinkle with chopped fresh chervil.

Salade de Haricots Blancs Secs

[MARROW BEAN SALAD]   FOR 4

> 1 cup dry marrow beans
> 1 tablespoon chopped shallots
> 1 teaspoon chopped parsley
> ½ teaspoon chopped garlic
> 2 tablespoons Sauce Vinaigrette (page 325)
>   Boston lettuce leaves

Soak the beans overnight in 1 quart cold water. Drain the water and add the same amount of fresh water to a skillet with the beans. Simmer 2 hours or until the beans are cooked, still firm, but tender. Drain. When still warm, add the shallots, parsley, garlic and vinaigrette. Mix well. Place in the refrigerator 30 minutes before serving. Serve on lettuce leaves.

Salade de Betteraves

[BEET SALAD]

Beets are at their best when washed clean and baked in a preheated 400-degree oven 1 hour or until a sharp knife pierces easily. Peel while still warm and slice. Season with Sauce Vinaigrette Royale (page 326). Sprinkle with chopped fresh parsley.

Salade de Chou

[GREEN CABBAGE SALAD]

Green cabbage (the amount depending upon your requirements) should be finely shredded and salted one hour before using. Drain the liquid, squeezing it through a cheesecloth. Place cabbage in a salad bowl. Sauté until crisp sufficient strips of bacon for your needs (2 strips for 4 persons). Cut the bacon into bite-size pieces and add, with its fat, to the cabbage. Mix well. Add Sauce Vinaigrette Paysanne (page 325), minus the bacon, which you have already added. Blend thoroughly and serve immediately.

Salade de Céleri-Rave

[CELERIAC SALAD]

Celeriac, also called celery knobs or roots, can be prepared raw—peeled and cut in julienne, soaked in a little lemon juice 10 minutes and dried on fine cheesecloth. They are then seasoned with 2 parts Mayonnaise (page 84), 1 part Dijon mustard, and salt and white pepper to taste. Quantities depend on the amount of salad being served.

These knobs can also be prepared by peeling and cooking in water, adding 2 tablespoons lemon juice to 1 quart water. A sharp, pointed knife will pierce the knobs easily when done. Cool and slice the thickness of a silver dollar. Arrange on a serving dish. Season with Sauce Gribiche (page 327).

Salade de Concombres

[CUCUMBER SALAD]   FOR 4

4 medium cucumbers
1 tablespoon chopped chives
1 tablespoon lemon juice
 Pinch cayenne pepper
1 tablespoon sour cream

Peeled, cut lengthwise, and seeds scraped out, cucumbers should be sliced thin and salted and placed in the refrigerator 4 hours. Squeeze their liquid gently out through cheesecloth. Blend all ingredients well in a salad bowl. Should be served very cold.

Salade de Pissenlits

[DANDELION GREENS SALAD]

Place Sauce Vinaigrette (page 325) in a wooden salad bowl; the amount depends on the number of persons to be served. Fill the bowl with dandelion greens, well cleaned and dried. Sauté 1 slice diced bacon per person. When crisp and *very hot*, mix, fat and all, with the dandelion greens. Serve immediately with 1 chopped hard boiled egg for each person on top of the greens.

Salade d'Oeufs à la Mayonnaise

[HARD BOILED EGGS WITH MAYONNAISE]   FOR 4

1 teaspoon chopped onions
1 teaspoon chopped white celery
1 teaspoon chopped parsley
1 teaspoon chopped chives
½ teaspoon chopped tarragon
½ teaspoon salt
 Pinch cayenne pepper
½ teaspoon Lea & Perrins sauce
½ teaspoon Dijon mustard
4 tablespoons Mayonnaise (page 84)
4 Boston lettuce leaves
4 large hard boiled eggs,
 sliced with an egg slicer

Combine and blend well all the ingredients, except the eggs and lettuce leaves, saving a little of the parsley and chives to sprinkle over the top. Arrange the sliced eggs on the lettuce leaves and spread the sauce over the eggs. Sprinkle the sauce with the remaining parsley and chives just before serving. All ingredients should be freshly cooked and freshly chopped.

Salade d'Endives et de Betteraves

[ENDIVE AND BEET SALAD]

Endive should be cut in quarters, lengthwise, or in smaller sizes and strips, soaked in cold water 10 minutes, dried well and kept in the refrigerator 1 hour before using. Endive should be crisp when ready to use.

Make a salad of endive and beets, using two-thirds endive and one-third beets. Add one chopped hard boiled egg for every 2 persons. Blend well just before serving with Lemon Dressing (page 331).

Salade d'Endives et de Pamplemousse

[ENDIVE WITH GRAPEFRUIT SALAD]

Cut the endive in quarters, lengthwise, and clean in cold water. Dry and refrigerate 1 hour. Place on Boston lettuce and arrange fresh grapefruit sections crosswise. If available, sprinkle with some fresh chopped chervil Season with Lemon Dressing (page 331).

Salade de Mâche et de Betteraves

[FIELD SALAD AND BEETS]

Field salad is a delicate green with a sweet flavor. It is found in the markets in fall and spring. Prepare with an equal amount of cooked beets cut in long, matchstick-sized strips and mix well with Sauce Vinaigrette (page 325).

Salade de Champignons

[WHITE MUSHROOM SALAD]   FOR 4

Wash 12 large, firm white mushrooms well in cold water. Peel the skin; cut in long, match stick-sized strips. Season with 1 tablespoon lemon juice, 2 tablespoons sour cream and 1 tablespoon freshly grated horse-radish. For larger portions, follow the same proportions: 2 parts cream for 1 lemon juice and 1 horse-radish. Mix gently but well; serve on a Boston lettuce leaf. Sprinkle with finely chopped parsley.

Salade de Pommes de Terre

[POTATO SALAD]   FOR 4

Potato salad is at its best when seasoned while the potatoes are still warm. Early rose potatoes (2 potatoes per person) should be cooked in their skins in salted water until soft, but not mushy (about 40 minutes). Remove the skin and slice the potatoes the size you like them. I prefer them the size of silver dollars. Place them in a salad bowl and blend in ½ cup hot White Stock (page 61) and ¼ cup dry white wine for 4 portions. Then add ½ cup Sauce Vinaigrette (page 325) and 1 tablespoon chopped parsley and chives mixed together. The same amount of garlic and chopped onions can be added if you prefer. Serve warm immediately, or cold later.

Salade de Romaine Milanaise

[ROMAINE SALAD WITH ANCHOVIES,
CHEESE AND CROUTONS]   FOR 4

*1 large head romaine lettuce, cleaned and soaked in cold
  water ½ hour, dried in cheesecloth, cut in 4-inch lengths
1 clove garlic*

1 teaspoon salt
½ teaspoon white pepper
1 tablespoon wine vinegar
½ teaspoon Dijon mustard
2 medium anchovy filets
2 tablespoons olive oil
1 teaspoon grated onion
2 eggs, boiled 2 minutes
½ teaspoon chopped sweet basil
1 tablespoon grated Parmesan cheese
½ cup croutons, cut in ½-inch cubes, fried in oil

Crush the garlic against a wooden salad bowl with the salt and pepper. Add the vinegar and mustard and mix. Mash the anchovies with these ingredients. Stir in the oil. Add the onion, eggs and basil and mix well. Add the romaine, sprinkle with cheese and croutons and mix well, but gently.

Salade de Tomates

[TOMATO SALAD]

As a salad ingredient, the tomato is king, the most versatile and colorful of all. Do *not* use hot-house tomatoes. They are innocuous in appearance and taste and add nothing to a salad. When you can, buy fresh, native tomatoes; that is the time to use them. At their best, they should be dead ripe, peeled and seeded. And they should be room temperature, not refrigerated. Quartered or sliced and mixed with any salad dressing recipe here, they stand up well by themselves. Tossed with crisp Boston, Bibb, romaine or other greenery (except the fibrous and weed-tough iceberg) and doused with a salad dressing, they hold that salad together with their personality. They are also excellent with other vegetables in a salad.

With tomatoes, I suggest you exercise your own judgment. Their uses are too numerous to list here. Do remember, however, that for that summertime cold platter, fish, poultry or meat, there is nothing that adds a dash of color and flavor like a tomato garnish. Or hollow out a nice ripe tomato and fill it with cooked vegetables mixed with a salad dressing; serve it with a slice of beef filet and you have a meal.

Salade de Légumes à la Russe

[FRESH VEGETABLE SALAD RUSSIAN STYLE]   FOR 4

> ½ cup each of the following vegetables, cut into ¼-inch cubes, cooked
>   in salted, boiling water until tender: carrots, white turnips, potatoes,
>   celery knobs, string beans, green asparagus tips
> ½ cup green peas, cooked
> ½ cup Sauce Vinaigrette (page 325)
>   4 Boston lettuce leaves
>   1 small head cauliflower, cooked
>   1 tablespoon Mayonnaise (page 84)

Drain the cubed vegetables and peas well and mix with the vinaigrette. Arrange them in the lettuce leaves on a platter, leaving room for the cauliflower in the center. Divide the cauliflower into 4 portions. Place in the center of the lettuce leaves; put mayonnaise on top of the cauliflower. Serve very cold.

Salade de Cresson

[WATERCRESS SALAD]

Watercress should be washed well in cold water, dried in cheesecloth or a wire salad basket and kept wrapped in a dry cloth in the refrigerator until ready to serve. The dressing (amount depending upon the number of guests to be served) should be: 2 parts wine vinegar, 1 part oil and 1 part chopped parsley, seasoned to taste with salt and white pepper. Place the dressing in a wooden salad bowl, add the watercress and toss rapidly and thoroughly. Serve immediately or the watercress will become soggy and wilted.

Chef's Salad Crémaillère   FOR 4

This salad can be the main course for a summer lunch. Ideally, the salad bowl should be of olive wood carved from the heart of the tree (but any unvarnished wooden bowl will serve), well-seasoned by garlic and other ingredients. Your salad bowl should never be used for anything but salads. I am repeating myself now because it is important: Good oil and vinegar should be used, the mustard should be French and chapons should be cut from a loaf of French bread. The green base can be Boston, Bibb, romaine, chicory or endives, washed, dried and broken up into 3-inch pieces. Boston, Bibb and endive make an especially tasty combination. Use lettuce in amounts needed to serve your guests.

> *1 clove garlic*
> *1 tablespoon salt*
> *1 teaspoon white pepper*
> *1 teaspoon Dijon mustard*
> *Dash Lea & Perrins sauce*
> *1 tablespoon tomato purée*
> *1 tablespoon wine vinegar*
> *2 tablespoons olive oil*
> *1 teaspoon each chopped fresh tarragon, parsley, chives*
> *Salad greens mentioned above (amount*
> *depending on appetites of guests)*
> *1 jumbo hard boiled egg, cut in long strips*
> *1 tablespoon boiled ham, cut in julienne*
> *1 tablespoon smoked beef tongue, cut in julienne*
> *1 tablespoon white chicken meat, cooked and cut in julienne*
> *1 tablespoon Gruyère cheese, cut in julienne*
> *8 chapons (page 331)*

Crush the garlic clove against the wooden bowl with a wooden salad spoon. Add the salt, pepper, mustard, Lea & Perrins and tomato purée; mix thoroughly. Pour in the vinegar, then the oil; mix in the chopped herbs. When well blended, add the salad greens and toss well with a wooden salad fork and spoon. Add the egg, ham, tongue, chicken and cheese. Then add chapons and toss well.

NOTE: Quarters of fresh peeled and seeded tomatoes and avocado may be added. If you want to be very fancy, hearts of palm and hearts of artichoke may be added.

Favorite Peasant Dishes

I have never been asked point blank which type of cooking I prefer. Probably because it is a superfluous question. But if asked, I would shiftily say "French," avoiding style or region. I am not sure, however, that the food served by the simple farm people of France does not rank as high as any, including the haute cuisine that we rattle on about. If taste, imagination, originality and simplicity are the prime ingredients of fine cookery, go thou gourmet to the peasant as I have and discover all of these qualities. Then make your own decision, whether you would prefer lunch or dinner at the elegant Lasserre in Paris or at home with farmer Pierre near Dijon at his oak table scrubbed oyster white or at his country inn, eating the favorite dish of the region and drinking the local wine from a carafe.

I did this not long ago in Burgundy, with a farmer with whom I had visited the local market. Rabbits were in abundance there, fat from the rich grass and clover of the region, and we had one for lunch, à la Boulangère, as listed in this chapter. My farmer friend, his face as red from sun and wine as the sweet strawberries from his patch, fat as a squab from his wife's superb cooking, insisted that we follow local custom: With the rabbit we must eat a dish of white onions, simmered in sweet farm butter and flamed with a good brandy. This, he said, was sound insurance, enabling one to drink wine from noon to dusk without a wobble. It didn't work with me, for I was not of that region. But it seemed to do the job for the farmer.

That rabbit dish was so delicious that I would like to honor those underrated animals with a few words. Their meat is white, tender and nutritious, less fat than chicken or any fowl. The domestic rabbits of France (and the U.S.) are fed only natural, wholesome foods—grass, clover and grains from the fields. And the wild rabbits of France that are now coming back after having been destroyed by a madman, select only the purest and best of wild plants and grains. I will not attempt to compare the diet of the chicken with the rabbit, for this book is designed to build appetites, not destroy them. Suffice it to say that the rabbit is the superior creature in natural selection of its foods. For those among you who have not had the privilege of dining on rabbit, buy one at your local market, fresh or frozen, and try one of the recipes in this chapter. You are in for a new dining pleasure.

It should be noted that a number of the recipes in the Abats chapter are also true peasant dishes. But there are so many that they demanded a category of their own. Here, I have assembled just my favorites. The peasant dishes of France would make a thick book of their own.

POTAGES—Soups

Nettle and Leek Soup   FOR 6

If you are in the country during the summer when nettles (use only white dead nettle, blind nettle or lamium album) are everywhere, this soup is worth trying. It is a French peasant staple, and a favorite. It is also delicious.

> ½ pound blanched salt pork, cut in 1-inch cubes
> 2 cups shredded leeks (white part only)
> 2 cups shredded nettles
> 1 teaspoon chopped garlic
> 2 medium potatoes, sliced
>   Stalk celery
>   Sprig parsley
> 1 quart White Stock (page 61)
> 2 cups heavy cream
> 1 tablespoon salt
> 1 teaspoon white pepper
> ¼ teaspoon nutmeg
>   1 egg yolk
> ½ cup chopped chives

In a skillet, sauté the salt pork 3 minutes; add the leeks and nettles, simmer 15 minutes; do not brown. Add the garlic and cook 2 minutes. Add the potatoes, celery, parsley and white stock and simmer 20 minutes or until vegetables are tender. Strain through a coarse strainer, pushing the vegetables through. Add the cream, salt, pepper and nutmeg to this purée; cook 5 minutes. Skim fat from top. Check seasoning. Just before serving, off fire, stir in the egg yolk mixed with the chives.

Potage Purée de Potiron et Poireaux

[PUMPKIN AND LEEK SOUP]   FOR 8

4 tablespoons sweet butter
2 cups shredded leeks (white part only)
1 quart White Stock (page 61)
2 cups milk
  Stalk celery
  Sprig parsley
1 cup diced potatoes
2 cups diced pumpkin
1 tablespoon salt
½ teaspoon white pepper
  Pinch nutmeg
1 tablespoon minute tapioca
1 egg yolk
2 cups heavy cream
1 tablespoon finely chopped chives

Melt the butter in a saucepan, add the leeks and simmer 15 minutes; do not brown. Add the white stock, milk, celery and parsley, the latter two tied together; cook 3 minutes. Add the potatoes, pumpkin, salt, pepper and nutmeg and cook 20 minutes or until vegetables are soft. Remove the celery and parsley. Push the remainder through a fine sieve. Stir in the tapioca; simmer over medium heat 2 minutes. Off fire (liquid should not be boiling), blend in egg yolk and cream, which you have mixed together. Check seasoning. Reheat before serving, but do not boil. Sprinkle the chopped chives on the soup before serving. This soup will be a bit thick. It is also good cold, stirring in a small amount of extra cream before serving.

PORC ET JAMBON—Pork and Ham

Ragoût de Porc aux Marrons

[RAGOUT OF PORK WITH CHESTNUTS]   FOR 6

> ½ pound salt pork, blanched, cut in 1-inch strips
> 2 pounds fresh pork shoulder, cut in 2-inch cubes
> 1 tablespoon salt
> 1 teaspoon white pepper
> 1 cup white flour
> 1 clove garlic, chopped
> 2 cups dry white wine
> 2 cups White Stock (page 61)
>   Bouquet garni
> ¼ cup tomato paste
>   Stalk celery
> 12 small white onions
> 6 tablespoons sweet butter
> 1 pound chestnuts, peeled, cooked in water and salt
>   until tender but not mushy, about 2 minutes

Sauté the salt pork in a deep saucepan 5 minutes. Add the cubes of pork and brown 10 minutes, stirring frequently. Add the salt, pepper and flour; blend thoroughly. Place in a preheated 400-degree oven 5 minutes, stirring 2 or 3 times. Add the chopped garlic, cook 2 minutes. Add the wine, white stock, bouquet garni and tomato paste; bring to a boil on top of stove and add the celery. While the liquid is heating, brown the onions in the butter; add them to the pork pot. Place, covered, in a 350-degree oven to simmer 1 hour or until pork is tender. Stir in the chestnuts; simmer in oven another 10 minutes. Check seasoning. Remove bouquet garni and celery before serving.

Saupiquet de Jambon Morvandelle

[HAM WITH PEAS AND MUSHROOMS IN SAUCE]   FOR 8

In the Morvan district of my home province of Burgundy, tender, pink, mild hams are a specialty. This recipe, and a variation, jambon à la morvandelle, are available on any given day. I like boiled new potatoes with it, and a prime red Burgundy to wash it down.

Step One: Preparing ham
>   *1 precooked 6-pound smoked ham*
>   *¼ pound sweet butter*
>   *1 pound carrots, sliced*
>   *1 pound onions, sliced*
>   *Bouquet garni*
>   *2 cloves garlic, unpeeled*
>   *1 quart dry white wine*
>   *2 quarts White Stock (page 61)*
>   *1 tablespoon salt*

Soak the ham in cold water 24 hours. Place in a large pot of fresh, unsalted water. Simmer, covered, 1½ hours. Remove from the liquid, skin and trim off much of the fat. In a roasting pan large enough to hold the ham, melt the butter. Add the carrots and onions and simmer 10 minutes; do not brown. Place the ham on top of the carrots and onions and add the bouquet garni and garlic. Pour in the wine and white stock. Bring to a boil, cover and simmer 1 hour. Place the ham on a serving platter; keep warm. Reduce liquid to half its volume and press through a strainer. Add salt and set aside.

Step Two: Sauce
>   *¼ pound sweet butter*
>   *2 pounds white mushrooms, thinly sliced*
>   *6 tablespoons Marc de Bourgogne*
>   *1 quart heavy cream*
>   *Sauce the ham was cooked in*
>   *1 pound small peas (canned)*
>   *2 egg yolks*
>   *¼ cup dry sherry*
>   *1 teaspoon cayenne pepper*
>   *Salt, if necessary*
>   *½ cup chopped parsley*

Melt the butter in a shallow saucepan. Add mushrooms, cook 5 minutes. Add the brandy, flambé, then stir in the cream and the reserved sauce. Simmer 15 minutes. Add peas, cook 5 minutes. Beat egg yolks lightly with sherry and blend in at the last moment. Avoid curdling. Add cayenne and check seasoning for salt. Carve the ham in ½-inch slices. Arrange on a platter with the mushrooms, peas and sauce in the center. Space heart-shaped croutons fried in butter between the slices of ham. Sprinkle with parsley.

Pommes de Terre au Lard

[POTATOES WITH SALT PORK]   FOR 6

This dish is typical of east-central France. The peasants are so fond of it that they say: "Who do you like best, your mother or your father?" The answer, "I like lard best; with potatoes."

> 1 pound salt pork, boiled 1½ hours,
>   cut in 1-inch pieces
> 2 cups coarsely chopped onions
> 4 cloves garlic
> ½ cup Sauce Tomate (page 83)
> 1 quart White Stock (page 61)
> 2 cups dry white wine
> 1 tablespoon salt
> 1 teaspoon white pepper
>   Bouquet garni
> 2 pounds potatoes, cut in 2-inch cubes

Place the pork in a skillet, cook 5 minutes. Add the onions, cook 15 minutes; add the garlic, cook 2 minutes. Stir in the remainder of the ingredients. Simmer, covered, ½ hour or until potatoes are cooked. Skim off fat, remove bouquet garni. Check seasoning.

Jarrets de Porc Ménagère

[PIG'S KNUCKLES WITH BEANS]   FOR 6

> 4 pig's knuckles
> 1 large onion, stuck with 4 cloves
> 2 large carrots
> 2 cloves garlic, unpeeled
>   Bouquet garni
> 1 teaspoon white pepper
> ¼ teaspoon nutmeg
> 1 quart dry white wine
> 3 quarts water
> 1 pound marrow beans, soaked
>   in cold water 6 hours
> 1 tablespoon salt
> 1 cup bread crumbs

Place all ingredients, except the water, beans, salt and bread crumbs, in a large pot. Simmer, covered, 1½ hours or until knuckles are tender. Drain beans and put into a cooking casserole. Add the 3 quarts of water (do not salt beans for salt might harden them) and simmer, covered, ½ hour or until slightly underdone. Drain the knuckles, strain and save the liquid they were cooked in. Remove knuckle meat from bones and cut into a total of 12 pieces. Drain the beans; place them and the knuckle meat into the liquid you saved. Simmer, covered, ½ hour. Check the beans. They should be tender, but not mushy. Skim fat off the top, add salt, remove any excessive liquid and sprinkle with bread crumbs. Bake in a preheated 450-degree oven 10 minutes or until crumbs are brown. Serve immediately.

Pieds de Porc Grillés à la Moutarde

[DEVILED PIG'S FEET]   FOR 4

Step One: Preparing pig's feet
4 quarts water
4 tablespoons salt
1 teaspoon thyme leaves
2 cloves
12 peppercorns
1 onion
1 stalk celery
1 bay leaf
4 pig's feet

Make a court bouillon of the above ingredients and simmer the pig's feet in it 2 hours or until tender. When done, split the feet in half and dry well.

Step Two: Final cooking
6 tablespoons sweet butter
4 cups dry bread crumbs
2 tablespoons Dijon mustard
1 tablespoon celery salt
1 tablespoon white pepper

Melt the butter and blend in bread crumbs, mustard, celery salt and pepper. Roll pig's feet in this mustard mixture and place under the broiler 4 minutes on each side. The feet should be well browned. Serve with French fried potatoes or hot potato chips.

Baeckaoffa

[CASSEROLE OF PORK, LAMB AND BEEF WITH
ONIONS AND POTATOES]   FOR 6

1 pound pork shoulder, cut in large cubes
1 pound lamb shoulder, cut in large cubes
1 pound beef rump steak, cut in large cubes
6 medium white onions, sliced
3 cloves garlic, sliced
1 tablespoon salt
½ teaspoon black pepper
1 quart dry Riesling wine
   Bouquet garni
2 pounds potatoes, sliced the
   thickness of silver dollars

Mix the meat cubes, onions, garlic, salt and pepper well in a deep casserole. Add the wine and bouquet garni. Refrigerate, covered, 36 hours. Place half of the potatoes with half of the onions from the marinade in the bottom of a large earthenware casserole. Add half of the marinade, then the meats. Arrange the remaining potatoes and onions to fill the casserole. Pour in the rest of the marinade. Cover the casserole. In France it is cooked in a baker's oven (à la boulangère), but 2½ hours in your oven at 400 degrees will do a good job. Check seasoning before serving.

METS À LA CRÈME—Cream Dishes

Pieds de Veau à la Normande

[CALF'S FEET IN CREAM AND CIDER]   FOR 6

Step One: Preparing calf's feet
  3 calf's feet
  3 tablespoons salt
   Bouquet garni
  ¼ cup lemon juice
  2 cloves

Put all ingredients in a deep saucepan, cover with water and simmer, covered, 2½ hours or until meat is tender. When cooled, remove all meat from bones, cut into 2 inch squares.

Step Two: Sauce Normande
  1 pound small mushrooms
  ¼ pound sweet butter
  ¼ cup lemon juice
  ½ cup sweet cider
  1 cup heavy cream
  3 calf's feet (already prepared)
  2 egg yolks
  1 cup White Stock (page 61)
  24 small white onions, cooked (canned
   are also satisfactory)
  3 tablespoons chopped parsley
  2 tablespoons chopped fresh chives
  1 teaspoon white pepper
  1 tablespoon salt
  6 heart-shaped croutons

Simmer mushrooms in butter and lemon juice 3 minutes. Add the sweet cider and cream, simmer 10 minutes. Add pieces of calf's feet, simmer 5 minutes. Blend in egg yolks mixed with cool stock. Do not let the sauce boil or the eggs will curdle. Add the onions, half of the parsley and the chives, pepper and salt. Thicken the sauce slowly so it will not curdle. Serve on warm plates, arranging croutons on each. Sprinkle with the remaining parsley.

Haricots Rouges à la Crème

[PORK AND KIDNEY BEANS IN CREAM]   FOR 4

> ½ pound kidney beans, soaked in cold water 6 hours
>   Bouquet garni
> 1 pound salt pork, simmered 2 hours in water
> 6 tablespoons sweet butter
> 1 cup chopped white onions
> 1 cup heavy cream
> 1 tablespoon salt
> ½ teaspoon white pepper
> ¼ teaspoon nutmeg
> 2 egg yolks, lightly beaten
> 1 tablespoon chopped parsley

Cook the beans in fresh water to cover with the bouquet garni 1½ hours or until tender. Cut the cooked salt pork in 1-inch cubes. Melt the butter in a saucepan, add onions, cook 5 minutes; do not brown. Add salt pork, cook 3 minutes; stir in cream, simmer 2 minutes. Add the kidney beans, salt, pepper and nutmeg and simmer 5 minutes. Before serving, off fire, add the egg yolks slowly to avoid curdling; let thicken 2 minutes. Sprinkle with parsley.

BOEUF—Beef

Potée Bourguignonne

[BOILED BEEF, SAUSAGE AND SALT PORK
WITH VEGETABLES]   FOR 6

> 5 pounds beef shoulder (1 piece)
> 1 one-and-a-half-pound garlic sausage
> 1 pound salt pork
> 1 bay leaf
>   Branch thyme
> 2 tablespoons salt
> 12 black peppercorns
> 4 stalks celery
> 6 carrots
> 2 large white onions, stuck with 3 cloves
> 1 two-pound Savoy cabbage
> 6 white turnips, trimmed to the size of eggs
> 1 parsnip

6 leeks (white part only)
6 new potatoes, trimmed to the size of eggs

Blanch the beef, sausage and salt pork 3 minutes. Rinse in cold water. Place in a stock pot with water to cover. Bring to a boil, simmer 2 hours. Add all other ingredients except the potatoes, cover and simmer ½ hour. Add the potatoes, simmer another ½ hour or until all vegetables are cooked. Check seasoning. The beef, pork and sausage should be tender. Serve the broth as a soup; follow with the beef, sausage, salt pork and vegetables. Serve with croutons, horse-radish, Dijon mustard and sour gherkins on the side.

Pot-au-Feu

[BOILED BEEF]   FOR 6

Just about every Sunday, the country people of France serve this dish. It is versatile, with several uses. On Sunday the beef and vegetables are eaten. The broth is used as consommé, as petite marmite or in a number of ways that you will find in this book. The leftover beef is used in some of the dishes that follow.

2 pounds beef shin, brisket or shoulder
2 pounds beef knuckles
4 quarts cold water
6 carrots, peeled
4 white turnips, peeled
2 onions, stuck with 4 cloves
1 bunch celery
1 parsnip, peeled
3 cloves garlic, unpeeled
2 leeks (white part only)
2 branches parsley
1 bay leaf
1 teaspoon dried thyme leaves, or 1 branch fresh
6 peppercorns
3 tablespoons salt

Place the beef and beef knuckles in a deep stock pot, cover with the cold water and bring to boil. Remove scum from the top. Add all the vegetables, herbs and seasonings. Simmer, uncovered, 30 minutes; remove vegetables and keep on the side. Continue to simmer meat and bones uncovered 15 minutes more. Then cover and simmer 2 hours or until the meat is tender, adding the vegetables toward the end to reheat. Strain and save the broth to use some other time; serve the beef, sliced, with the vegetables. Horse-radish sauce goes well with this dish, as do sour gherkins, Dijon or English mustard or tomato sauce.

Boeuf Miroton

[STEW OF LEFTOVER BEEF WITH ONIONS]   FOR 6

    ½ pound yellow onions, thinly sliced
    6 tablespoons sweet butter
    1 cup Sauce Tomate (page 83)
    1 cup Brown Stock (page 63)
    1 cup dry white wine
    1 tablespoon salt
    ½ teaspoon black pepper
    3 pounds boiled beef, sliced
    ½ cup bread crumbs

Sauté the onions in butter 10 minutes or until slightly brown. Add the tomato sauce, brown stock, wine, salt and pepper; simmer 20 minutes. Check seasoning. Lay the slices of beef in a shallow, buttered baking dish. Pour the sauce over them and sprinkle evenly with the bread crumbs. Place, uncovered, in a preheated 350-degree oven 15 minutes. The top should be crusty.

Boeuf Sauté à la Lyonnaise

[LEFTOVER BEEF FRIED WITH ONIONS]   SERVES 6

> ¼ pound sweet butter
> 1 pound yellow onions, sliced
> ½ cup dry white wine
> 2 cups Demi-Glace (page 74)
> ½ cup wine vinegar
> ½ cup cooking oil
> 2 pounds boiled beef, sliced in 1-inch squares
> 1 teaspoon chopped garlic
> 1 tablespoon salt
> 1 teaspoon white pepper
>   Pinch nutmeg
> 2 tablespoons chopped parsley

Melt the butter in a skillet, add the onions and cook 10 minutes until slightly browned. Stir in the wine, demi-glace and vinegar; cook 10 minutes. In another skillet, heat the oil and cook the beef quickly on a hot fire, browning the slices. Add the garlic, salt, pepper and nutmeg. Drain the fat, add the beef to the onion pan and simmer 10 minutes. Check seasoning. Sprinkle with chopped parsley before serving.

Hachis de Boeuf Parmentier

[BEEF HASH WITH MASHED POTATOES]   FOR 6

> ¼ pound sweet butter
> 1 cup finely chopped Bermuda or Spanish onions
> 1 clove garlic, chopped
> 3 pounds boiled beef, put through the meat chopper
> 2 cups Sauce Tomate (page 83)
> ½ cup catsup
> 2 cups Demi-Glace (page 74)
> 1 teaspoon salt
> 1 teaspoon white pepper
> ½ cup white bread crumbs
> 4 cups mashed potatoes
> ¾ cup grated Swiss cheese

Melt the butter in a saucepan, add onions and simmer 15 minutes; do not brown. Add garlic, cook 2 minutes; add beef, mix well. Stir in the tomato sauce, catsup, demi-glace, salt and pepper. Add bread crumbs. Blend well. Check seasoning. Place, uncovered, in a preheated 350-degree oven 20 minutes. Butter a shallow baking dish and spoon in the beef mixture. Spread a 1-inch-thick coat of mashed potatoes over it. With a spatula, make a fluted design. Sprinkle with the grated cheese and place under the broiler until well browned. Serve tomato sauce on the side.

Salade de Boeuf

[BOILED BEEF SALAD]   FOR 4

> 1 pound boiled beef, sliced in 1-inch squares
> 1 cup sliced white onions
> 1 cup chopped celery
> 1 cup sliced green peppers
> ½ cup chopped parsley
> 1 tablespoon Dijon mustard
> 1 tablespoon salt
> 1 teaspoon black pepper
> ¼ cup wine vinegar
> 6 tablespoons olive oil
> 2 tomatoes, peeled, quartered
> 2 hard boiled eggs, quartered

Blend the beef with all the above ingredients except the tomatoes and eggs. Check seasoning. Add more oil, vinegar, salt or pepper to taste. Lightly toss in the tomatoes and eggs just before serving.

CANARD, OIE—Duck, Goose

Cassoulet à la Paysanne

[GOOSE OR DUCK, SAUSAGE AND BEAN CASSEROLE]   FOR 8

Although this dish is famous around Toulouse (the goose country in southwestern France where it originated), my maternal grandmother was expert at making it. She taught me to do it passably well at the age of ten. I do so much chatting about my grandmother in these pages, I hope you will bear with me. She was a great cook, actually a Cordon Bleu, and she had that rare genius of communicating enthusiasm for her art. She fascinated me with the mysteries of the kitchen, and so impressed me with her skill when she came to take care of our household after my mother died when I was ten, that even at that age I knew I wanted to become a chef.

A tiny woman, with the flutter and the perkiness of a sparrow and the strength of a team of oxen, my grandmother was born in the Jura Mountains, a bleak and rugged region. During the cold winters, hearty, well-prepared food came first in everyone's thoughts, and a woman who couldn't put it on the table didn't last long. The Jura doesn't hold a candle to Burgundy as a wine-producing area, but they do bottle a good rosé and an excellent straw-colored wine. It is heavy-bodied, resembling a light sherry. The grapes are ripened by spreading them on wooden racks in the sun to increase their sugar content before pressing. My grandmother missed these wines when she lived with us, also the fresh fish of the quick, cold Jura streams, and the sweet corn on the cob, and the flour made from it. It is the only region in France that grows sweet corn for the table.

During the Prussian War of 1870, my grandmother's home was occupied for three years by several German officers. When she wanted to make sure the Germans were in a good mood, she served them this Cassoulet. In her late sixties, when she came to our home, she was so full of vitality that she kept me and my younger brother hopping to keep up with her demands in the kitchen. Ah, grandma, how I wish you were here, so you could sit in your chair by the stove and let me cook you Cassoulet à la Paysanne for a change.

Step One: Preparation of beans
> *1 pound marrow beans*
> *2 quarts White Stock (page 61)*
> *2 cups dry white wine*
> *1 large yellow onion, stuck with 2 cloves*
> *1 large carrot*
> > *Bouquet garni*
> *1 clove garlic*
> > *About a tablespoons salt*

Soak the beans in enough cold water to cover for 6 hours. Drain, add white stock and wine, onion, carrot, bouquet garni and garlic. Cover, bring to a boil and place in a preheated 350-degree oven to simmer 1½ hours. Beans should be undercooked. Check seasoning and add salt. Remove from the oven and keep aside.

Step Two

 1 six-pound duckling (or 6 pounds goose meat)
 1 one-and-a-half-pound garlic sausage
 1½ pounds lean salt pork
 1 cup chopped onions
 ¼ pound sweet butter
 ½ cup chopped garlic
 1 cup Sauce Tomate (page 83)
 2 cups Demi-Glace (page 74)
 1 tablespoon salt
 1 teaspoon black pepper
 Pinch nutmeg
 1 cup bread crumbs

Roast the duckling in a preheated 450-degree oven 1¼ hours. Place the garlic sausage and salt pork in a skillet, cover with water and simmer 1½ hours. Cut the duck in 8 pieces, 4 from the legs and 4 from the breast (meat may be boned, if desired). Cut the carcass in 3 pieces. Cook the onions in butter 5 minutes; do not brown. Add the garlic, cook 2 minutes; add tomato sauce, then the demi-glace, salt, pepper and nutmeg. When boiling, add the duck meat and carcass. Simmer, covered, 15 minutes. Remove the duck and add the marrow beans (drained, but with the liquid they were cooked in reserved). Simmer 10 minutes. Check seasoning. Now place a layer of beans in an earthenware casserole. Put half of the duck on the beans. Slice the sausage in 16 slices, the salt pork in 8 slices. Arrange 6 slices of sausage on top of the duck. Spoon on another layer of beans, the rest of the duck and 6 slices of sausage. Cover with the remaining beans and arrange the rest of the sausage and the sliced salt pork on top. Pour in the sauce in which you simmered the duck. Sprinkle with bread crumbs. Place the casserole in a baking pan with 2 quarts of water. Bring the water to a boiling point on top of the stove, then place in a preheated 400-degree oven 45 minutes. It should be crusty and brown before serving. If too dry, add some of the reserved liquid from the cooked beans.

The late Charles Laughton, a steady guest at La Crémaillère, was fond of this cassoulet. He often said to me, "Patron, when are you going to make your grandmother's famous cassoulet?" "Whenever you like," was my answer. I welcomed the opportunity to honor my grandmother's talent.

Pâté de Canard

[DUCK PÂTÉ]   FOR 4 QUARTS

This is the pride of many a French countryman's kitchen, the mark of his or his wife's culinary ability. It often sits on the sideboard in the place of honor, signaling that you are about to dine at the table of a knowledgeable man. Many a haute cuisine restaurant in the large cities of France and America cannot offer a pâté or a terrine (named for the dish in which it is cooked) to compare with some of the creations of the farmers in regions where it is a specialty. This dish can also be made with rabbit, chicken, pheasant or other birds.

Step One

Skin and bone a 5-pound duck, saving the boned breast intact. All meat from the bird, with the exception of the breast, will be put through the grinder with the other meats. Reserve the carcass.

Step Two

Meat from bird (except breast), cut in 1-inch cubes
½ *pound lean veal (loin preferred), cut in 1-inch cubes*
½ *pound pork loin, cut in 1-inch cubes*
1 *cup diced carrots*
2 *tablespoons Épices Parisienne (page 2)*
3 *tablespoons salt*
1 *tablespoon white pepper*
1 *bay leaf*
Stalk celery
Sprig parsley
½ *cup cognac or good brandy*
½ *cup Madeira or sherry*
½ *pound pork fat, cut in 1-inch cubes*
½ *pound pork liver, cut in 1-inch cubes*
1 *cup diced onions*
1 *tablespoon chopped garlic*
2 *eggs, beaten*
2 *large black truffles, cut in small dice (reserve juice)*
2 *slices boiled ham*
1 *large sheet larding pork*

Place all ingredients through the Madeira in a large earthenware crock. Blend well so each piece of meat will be well seasoned. Marinate, covered, in refrigerator 2 days. Sauté pork-fat cubes with the liver, onions and garlic. Do not brown onions or garlic or overcook liver—it should be pink; cooking time about 2 minutes. Drain the marinade, reserving the liquid and discarding the vegetables; put all the meats, including the liver mixture but excepting the breasts, through the grinder. Mix this meat well in a bowl; add marinade sparingly (the mixture should not be too soggy) and all of the canned truffle juice and blend the beaten eggs in well. Check seasoning and consistency. A good test is to fry a small patty of the ground meat in butter and taste it. The forcemeat should be of a firm consistency, a bit lighter and fluffier than chopped beef.

Cut the ham in strips 1-inch wide the length of a 4-quart terrine. Cut several strips of larding pork the same size as the ham strips. Also, from the larding pork, cut 12 thin slices, or bardes. Wrap the reserved breasts with some of the bardes and line the bottom and sides of the terrine with the rest, saving one to lay on top. Place a layer of the ground meat to fill one-third of the terrine. Then lay the wrapped bird's breasts on top of this. Arrange the strips of boiled him and larding pork around them and scatter the diced truffles. Fill the terrine with the remaining chopped meat, pressing it down, shaping it. The terrine should be well filled, the mixture rising a little above the top. Cover with a slice of larding pork. Seal tightly with aluminum foil, tying it securely with twine around the sides of the terrine. Place the terrine in a roasting pan filled with 3 inches of boiling water, then bake in a preheated 350-degree oven 2½ hours. To test the pâté, run a trussing needle into the center of the meat for 30 seconds. Then place the center of the withdrawn needle to your lips. If the needle is hot, the pâté is done. Remove from oven. Place a plate that fits the top of the terrine on the foil. Put a 3-pound weight on this to press the pâté into a compact shape while it cools. Keep in a cool place while doing this. When cool, but not cold enough so that the grease congeals, pour off the grease. Fill with the same amount of aspic. (This should be made from stock derived by cooking the duck carcass.) Refrigerate 24 hours before cutting. As a variation, you can substitute canned foie gras, smoked beef tongue and pistachio nuts, duck or chicken livers for the breasts. Served cold in slices, this pâté, or terrine, is excellent as a luncheon entrée with hot French bread and cornichons, as a first course for dinner or as an hors-d'oeuvre.

LAPEREAU—Rabbit

Lapereau en Casserole aux Olives

[RABBIT CASSEROLE WITH GREEN OLIVES]   FOR 4

  ½ *pound salt pork, cut in 1-inch cubes, blanched*
  1 three-pound rabbit, cut in 8 pieces
  2 large yellow onions, diced

1 *tablespoon chopped garlic*
2 *cups dry white wine*
1 *cup Chicken Broth (page 62)*
  Stalk celery
1 *teaspoon dry thyme leaves, or 1 branch fresh*
1 *bay leaf*
2 *sprigs parsley*
1 *tablespoon salt*
1 *teaspoon white pepper*
24 *queen green olives, pitted, marinated in 6 tablespoons Madeira*
¼ *pound sweet butter, kneaded with ½ cup white flour*
  Chopped parsley

Sauté the salt pork in a saucepan 3 minutes; add the rabbit pieces. Over medium heat, brown on all sides, turning often. Add the onions, simmer 3 minutes; add garlic, cook 2 minutes. Blend in the wine, broth, celery, thyme, bay leaf, parsley, salt and pepper. Bring to a boil, cover and place in a preheated 350-degree oven 30 minutes or until rabbit is tender. Remove the rabbit pieces to a serving casserole. On top of the stove simmer the sauce in which the rabbit cooked. Add the olives and Madeira. Then, slowly, in small pieces, add the kneaded butter, avoiding lumps and mixing with a wooden spatula. Check seasoning. When simmering, spoon the sauce over the rabbit in the serving casserole, sprinkle with chopped parsley and serve. Croutons can be served with this, or slices of French bread browned under the broiler.

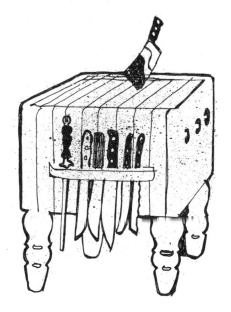

Lapereau à la Boulangère

[RABBIT BRAISED WITH ONIONS AND POTATOES]   FOR 4

The word *boulangère* (baker's wife) comes from an old French custom: After the local baker has taken the last loaf of bread from his oven, for a small fee his wife will put the housewife's casseroles or baking platters in the still-hot oven.

> 6 tablespoons sweet butter
> 1 three-pound rabbit
> ¾ pound larding pork (fat back), sliced paper thin
> 18 small white onions
> 12 small new potatoes, trimmed to pullet-egg size
> 1 tablespoon salt
> 1 teaspoon white pepper
>   Stalk celery
> 1 bay leaf
> 2 cloves garlic, peeled
>   Branch fresh thyme, or 1 teaspoon dry leaves
> 1 cup Chicken Broth (page 62)
> 2 tablespoons finely chopped parsley

Coat an oval baking dish or casserole evenly with all the butter. Wrap the rabbit in larding pork, then lay in the baking dish. Arrange the onions and potatoes around the rabbit. Sprinkle with salt and pepper and add the celery, bay leaf, garlic and thyme. Pour in the chicken broth. Bring to a boil on top of the stove, cover with aluminum foil and place in a preheated 400-degree oven 45 minutes or until rabbit and potatoes are tender. Remove the foil, and cook for another 5 minutes at 450 degrees. Check seasoning. Sprinkle with chopped parsley and serve.

Civet de Lapereau

[RAGOUT OF RABBIT WITH ONIONS AND MUSHROOMS]   FOR 4

> ½ pound salt pork, cut in 1-inch cubes, blanched
> 1 three-pound rabbit, cut in 8 pieces
> ½ cup white flour
> 1 tablespoon salt
> 1 teaspoon black pepper
> 12 small white onions
> 1 tablespoon chopped garlic

6 tablespoons Marc de Bourgogne or other good brandy
2 cups red Burgundy
1 cup Brown Stock (page 63)
    Bouquet garni
12 medium mushroom caps
4 tablespoons sweet butter

Sauté the salt pork in a skillet 3 minutes. Roll the rabbit pieces in flour, salt and pepper and add to skillet. Brown over a quick fire 5 minutes, turning the pieces often so each piece will get brown on all sides. Add the onions, simmer 3 minutes; add the garlic, stir well on fire 2 minutes. Sprinkle with the flour that remains after dredging the rabbit. Mix well over the fire 1 minute, pour in the Marc de Bourgogne and flambé. Then add the wine, brown stock and bouquet garni. Bring to a boil, cover and place in a preheated 350-degree oven 35 minutes or until rabbit is tender. Meanwhile, cook the mushrooms in butter in a separate skillet 3 minutes. Take the rabbit stew from the oven, add the mushrooms and cook uncovered on top of the stove 3 minutes. Check seasoning. Remove bouquet garni before serving. The sauce should be smooth and thick. Serve croutons on the side, or slices of French bread browned under the broiler.

Lapereau à la Moutarde

[RABBIT IN MUSTARD SAUCE]   FOR 4

¼ pound sweet butter
4 tablespoons white flour
1 three-pound rabbit, cut in 8 pieces
1 tablespoon salt
1 teaspoon white pepper
2 tablespoons chopped white onions
1 clove garlic, chopped
½ cup dry white wine
2 cups Chicken Broth (page 62)
2 cups heavy cream
    Bouquet garni
2 tablespoons Dijon mustard
2 egg yolks, beaten
6 medium mushroom caps, cooked separately in
    2 tablespoons lemon juice 3 minutes (reserve juice)
    Pinch cayenne pepper (optional)
1 tablespoon chopped parsley

Melt the butter in a skillet. Add the flour, mix well into a smooth roux and simmer 3 minutes; do not brown. Add the rabbit pieces, salt and pepper and simmer on top of the stove 5 minutes, turning to avoid burning. Add the onions, simmer 5 minutes; add the garlic, simmer 2 minutes. Pour in the wine, chicken broth and cream. Add the bouquet garni, cover and simmer 30 minutes or until rabbit is tender. Remove the bouquet garni. Place the rabbit pieces in an ovenproof serving casserole. Pour the liquid through a fine strainer and reduce to a good sauce consistency. Mix the mustard with the beaten egg yolks and add the mushroom juice to that. Off fire, slowly mix into this sauce, avoiding curdling. Check seasoning. Place the mushrooms in the serving casserole with the rabbit and pour the sauce over. Bring to a boiling point before serving and add the cayenne if you like a sharp sauce. Sprinkle with parsley before serving.

OTHER PEASANT DISHES

Pipérade

[OMELETTE WITH PEPPERS, ONIONS AND TOMATOES]   FOR 4

This is a peasant dish from the Basque region of southwestern France and northern Spain.

4 tablespoons sweet butter
6 tablespoons cooking oil
1 cup thin strips green peppers
1 cup thin strips red peppers
½ cup thinly sliced onions
1 tablespoon salt
1 teaspoon white pepper
2 tomatoes, peeled, seeded, diced
8 eggs, beaten as for an omelette
2 ounces anchovy filets (optional)

In a thick-bottomed saucepan, melt the butter with the oil. Add the green and red peppers, onions, salt and pepper. Simmer 15 minutes, stirring occasionally so vegetables will cook evenly without taking color. Add tomatoes, simmer 5 minutes. Pour the beaten eggs over the vegetables and scramble until firm but fluffy. Stop stirring and cook for 2 minutes until the bottom has a 1-inch thickness. Turn out, like a cake, on a round serving platter. If anchovies are desired, they should be cut into small strips and added to the eggs before cooking. Anchovies are salty, so season accordingly.

Tartar Boreck

[TURKISH RAVIOLI]   FOR 6

This is a Turkish peasant dish, which I learned with the assistance of a Turk. An attractive blonde.

Step One: The dough
1½ cups white flour
1 tablespoon salt
1 teaspoon white pepper
6 tablespoons cooking oil
2 eggs
1 cup lukewarm water

Make this 6 hours ahead; keep in a cool spot, but not in the refrigerator. Sift the flour with the salt and pepper into a mixing bowl. Add the oil, then the eggs and start to incorporate the water gradually (you may not need all of it), avoiding lumping. Place the dough on a pastry board and keep working it into a ball. It should not be too firm; if too firm, add more water at your discretion, depending on the quality of the flour. Keep aside, covered with cheesecloth, in a cool place.

Step Two: The filling
> *2 pounds ground beef or lamb*
> *½ pound white onions, finely chopped*
> *1 tablespoon chopped garlic*
> *½ cup chopped parsley*
> *1 tablespoon salt*
> *1 teaspoon white pepper*
> *¼ teaspoon nutmeg*
> *1 egg*

Mix all the above ingredients very thoroughly with your hands. Check seasoning. When ready to cook, roll the dough ⅛-inch thick and cut into 3-inch squares. Fill each square with 1 tablespoon of the meat mixture. Moisten the edges with a pastry brush and fold over, sealing well. Place these boreck on a paper towel.

Step Three: Cooking
Bring to a boil 4 quarts Chicken Broth (page 62) in a deep pot and put the stuffed boreck in the simmering broth. Stir to avoid the pastry sticking. When gently boiling, reduce to a simmer, cover and cook 1 hour. Serve in a soup plate with the broth, which at this stage will have become slightly thick.

Moussaka à la Turque

[TURKISH MOLDED EGGPLANT AND
LAMB CASSEROLE]   FOR 6

Step One: Lining the serving dish
Cut 1 large eggplant into quarters, lengthwise. Trim the inside, reserving the pulp, and leaving a shell ⅛-inch thick. Blanch the skin 3 minutes in boiling water. Put aside to cool. When cool, line a buttered, deep pyrex or soufflé dish with the purple skin against the side of the dish. Set aside to fill with the following stuffing.

Step Two: Stuffing
> *¼ pound sweet butter*
> *6 tablespoons cooking oil*
> *1 cup chopped onions*
> *1 tablespoon chopped garlic*
> *½ pound mushrooms, chopped*
> *Eggplant pulp, diced*
> *1 cup finely diced potatoes*
> *3 ounces tomato purée*

1 cup Demi-Glace (page 74)
2 tablespoons salt
1 teaspoon white pepper
¼ teaspoon nutmeg
½ cup chopped parsley
2 pounds roast lamb, ground through
*   coarse blade of meat grinder*
2 eggs, beaten
½ cup bread crumbs

Heat the oil and butter in a skillet, add onions and cook 10 minutes. Add garlic, cook 2 minutes. Add all of the remaining ingredients except the eggs and bread crumbs. Bring to a simmer, cover and place in a pre-heated 350-degree oven 1 hour, stirring occasionally to prevent sticking. Remove. Check seasoning. Stir in the eggs and pour this stuffing into the eggplant-lined soufflé dish. Sprinkle with bread crumbs. Place in a pan of boiling water in a 400-degree oven ½ hour. Unmold on a round platter, upside down. This should look like a big cake with the eggplant skin serving as decoration. A whole peeled tomato is usually placed on top. If preferred, tomato sauce may be served.

13

ENTREMETS—Desserts

I think it was Dumas who said, in discussing appetites, "The third type of appetite is that roused at the end of a meal when, after normal hunger has been satisfied by the main courses, and the guest is truly ready to rise without regret, a delicious dish holds him to the table with a final tempting of his sensuality."

He of course was referring to a dessert that would keep even an epicure expectantly in his seat. I *know* that it was Alexandre Dumas in *Le Grand Dictionnaire de Cuisine* who thus described that epicure:

Take the pit out of an olive and replace it with an anchovy. Put the olive into a lark, the lark into a quail, the quail into a partridge, the partridge into a pheasant. The pheasant in its turn disappears inside a turkey, and the turkey is stuffed into a suckling pig. Roasted, this will present the quintessence of the culinary art, the masterpiece of gastronomy. But don't make the mistake of serving it whole, just like that. The epicure eats only the olive and the anchovy.

I will not in this chapter try to satisfy such precious epicurean tastes. In desserts, I lean toward the simple. Here I offer my own favorites, hoping that some will appeal to you.

SOUFFLÉS

A dessert soufflé is simple to make and extremely satisfying to eye and taste. For some inexplicable reason, a mystique seems to have been deliberately created about its preparation. If you can crack

Strasbourg, Alsace

an egg and read a recipe, you can make a soufflé. Its base, and its success, depends upon the "appareil," a mixture of eggs, flour, milk and sugar. To that is added the flavor—fruit purée, chocolate, coffee, liqueurs, vanilla, to name a few. Let us take this dessert in easy steps.

Appareil

[SOUFFLÉ BASE]   FOR 6

> 6 egg yolks (reserve egg whites)
> 1 cup sugar
> ½ cup sifted flour
> 2 cups boiling milk
>   Dash vanilla extract

Place the yolks and sugar in an electric mixer; beat at moderate speed until the mixture becomes thick and forms a ribbon. Remove the bowl from the mixer; add the flour very slowly, mixing by hand with a wooden spatula. Slowly add the boiling milk, a little at a time, avoiding lumping. Stir in the vanilla extract. Place this appareil in a heavy-bottomed pan and cook over moderate heat 2 minutes, or until it thickens, stirring constantly; do not boil. Cool. It can be made 2 hours before using.

Purée de Fruits

[FRUIT PURÉE]

Crush fresh fruits or berries through a fine sieve. Simmer this purée in a shallow pan until it becomes thick. Cool before using. The texture should be fine, not too liquid. The quantity used is up to the cook. It can be made in large amounts and stored in the refrigerator.

Soufflé aux Fruits

[FRUIT SOUFFLÉ]   FOR 6

> 1 recipe Appareil (above)
> 1 cup purée of strawberries or raspberries
> 6 egg whites (those you reserved)
> ½ cup very fine sugar
>   Well-buttered soufflé mold
>   Confectioners' sugar to sprinkle on top

Butter and sprinkle soufflé dish with granulated sugar. Mix the fruit purée into the appareil. Beat the egg whites until very firm, then add the very fine sugar, a little at a time. Mix the appareil into the egg whites, working gently upward with a wooden spatula. Pour mixture into the soufflé mold, filling it to the top. Place on a baking sheet, which you have heated first on top of the stove 2 minutes. When soufflé starts to rise, place in a pre-heated 400-degree oven 20 minutes until well puffed and beginning to brown. Two minutes before removing from the oven, sprinkle confection-ers' sugar over the top (quickly so soufflé will not fall) to get a sugar crust. The soufflé should be served immediately after taking from oven. A fruit syrup can be served on the side. Such syrups can be found at fine food stores in jars.

Frozen Soufflé Crémaillère   FOR 6

> 1 cup water
> 1 cup sugar
> 8 egg yolks
> 2 cups heavy cream
> ½ cup candied fruit (in small dice, soaked in
>   2 tablespoons Grand Marnier 30 minutes)
> 1 teaspoon finely grated orange rind
> 6 tablespoons Grand Marnier
>   A 1-quart soufflé mold and a strip of oiled wax paper,
>   2½ inches wide, which will be tied around the top
>   of the soufflé mold as a high collar

Boil the water and sugar to make a syrup (about 5 minutes). Beat the yolks lightly with a wire whisk. Pour the syrup over the yolks slowly, stirring rapidly so the eggs do not scramble. Place in a double boiler over boiling water and continue stirring until yolk and syrup become very thick. Remove, place on top of cracked ice and keep stirring until cold. Whip the cream until firm, add slowly to egg yolk mixture, mixing upward with a wooden spatula. Stir in the candied fruits, orange peel and the rest of the Grand Marnier. Pour in the soufflé mold. The mixture will rise above the top of the mold and be held in place by the paper collar. Place the mold in the freezer 4 hours. When ready to serve, remove the collar. Decorate the top with whipped cream pushed through a fluted tube. The flavor of the soufflé can be varied by using Chartreuse or other liqueurs in place of the Grand Marnier.

SORBETS—Ices

Soufflés de Mandarines Réserve de Beaulieu

[TANGERINE SOUFFLÉS]   FOR 6

Step One: Preparing tangerines
>   6 tangerines
>   1 quart orange sherbet

Cut the tops off the tangerines. Scoop out the inside, leaving an empty shell. Fill the shells with orange sherbet and keep in freezer until ready to use.

Step Two: Soufflé
>   4 eggs, separated
>   ½ cup very fine sugar
>   ½ cup sifted white flour
>   1 cup milk
>   ¼ cup Grand Marnier
>   2 tablespoons confectioners' sugar
>   1 teaspoon lemon juice

Mix the very fine sugar and yolks together with a wooden spatula. Add the flour and mix well with a wire whisk. Boil the milk and pour slowly into the above mixture, stirring quickly to avoid lumps. Add the Grand Marnier, mix well, set aside in a large bowl. Cool 2 hours, but not in the refrigerator. Whip the egg whites with an electric beater until very stiff. Add the confectioners' sugar (reserving enough to sprinkle over the tangerines before putting them in the oven). Mix in lemon juice. Blend the whites with the cooled egg yolk base, using a wooden spatula and working upward slowly. Place the mixture in a pastry bag with a fluted tube, and flute it on top of the sherbet-stuffed tangerine shells, making a 2-inch thick coating. Sprinkle with the reserved sugar. Place the tangerines on a flat, ovenproof serving platter on top of cracked ice. Put in a pre-heated 450-degree oven 10 minutes. Tops should be brown.

Baked Alaska Crémaillère   FOR 8

>   12 lady fingers
>   ½ pint chocolate ice cream, slightly softened

½ pint vanilla ice cream, slightly softened
½ pint strawberry ice cream, slightly softened
4 eggs, separated
½ cup very fine sugar
3 tablespoons confectioners' sugar
2 teaspoons fresh lemon juice
¼ cup Fine Champagne, warmed

Lay the lady fingers on a flat, oblong, ovenproof serving dish, one alongside the other. Spread a layer of chocolate, a layer of vanilla and then a layer of strawberry ice cream over the lady fingers. Put in the freezer so the ice cream will harden. With a whisk, blend the egg yolks with the very fine sugar until the mixture forms a ribbon. Beat the egg whites stiff; slowly add 2 tablespoons confectioners' sugar and continue beating. Add lemon juice. Mix in the yolks, slowly working upward with a wooden spatula. Then beat. The mixture may become more liquid at first, but will become fluffy as you beat. Spoon the beaten egg mixture over the ice cream, saving enough to decorate the top. Smooth this egg mixture to form an oval mound. Using a pastry bag, decorate the mound with the remaining egg mixture, using your own imagination. Sprinkle the rest of the confectioners' sugar over the top. Place in a preheated 500-degree oven 3 minutes or until well browned. Bring to the table, pour over the warmed Fine Champagne and flambé. Cut crosswise with a cake server, so each guest will get an even portion of Baked Alaska.

Sorbet de Framboises au Rhum

[RASPBERRY SHERBET WITH RUM]

This is a dessert I believe I invented. After an involved meal, it is light and very refreshing. I use it more than any other. The Maharaja of Bharatpur was intrigued with the raspberry sherbet and light white rum when he dined with me a few years ago.

Fill a cold sherbet glass with raspberry sherbet that has been removed from the freezer a few minutes before serving so that it is creamy, not frozen solid. With the end of a spoon, dig a hole ½-inch in diameter in the center (depth depending upon how much sherbet you have in the glass). Fill this with white Martinique Rum. Other liqueurs may be substituted.

CRÈMES—Custards

Oeufs à la Neige

[FLOATING ISLAND]

FOR 8

> 2 cups milk
>   Peel of one orange
> 4 eggs, separated
> ¼ cup confectioners' sugar
> 1 teaspoon lemon juice
> ½ cup sugar
>   Drop vanilla extract
>   Pinch salt

Bring the milk to a boil with the orange peel in a shallow pan. Meanwhile, beat the egg whites stiff. Slowly add the confectioners' sugar and the lemon juice, beating 1 minute. With a tablespoon, scoop out the beaten whites, molding them into large egg shapes. Reduce the heat under the milk to a simmer. Drop two or three spoonfuls of the whites in this (they will expand as they cook). Cook 1 minute on each side, turning carefully. Remove with a slotted spoon and drain on cheesecloth or a white towel. Repeat until all the whites are used. Blend the yolks with the granulated sugar, vanilla and salt, using a wooden spatula. Slowly pour the hot milk over, stirring rapidly with a wire whisk to prevent curdling. Simmer on a low fire 3 minutes, stirring constantly. Watch carefully. The custard should be thick enough to coat the back of the spoon; do not overcook or it will curdle. Strain through a fine strainer into a deep serving dish of glass or porcelain. When cold, arrange the egg whites on top. Decorate each egg white with a maraschino cherry or candied fruit. At La Crémaillère, we also spread lightly spun sugar caramel (recipe follows) over them.

Sugar Caramel

> 1 cup water
> ½ cup sugar

Boil the sugar and water until the syrup becomes dark blonde in color. If the sugar burns and the syrup becomes too dark, it will be bitter. Dip a fork into the syrup and carefully spread over the floating islands in strings 10 minutes before serving.

Sabayon à l'Italienne

[ZABAGLIONE]   FOR 6

> 6 egg yolks
> ½ cup very fine sugar
> 6 tablespoons Marsala
> 1 teaspoon finely grated lemon rind
> 1 tablespoon Strega

Blend all the ingredients well in the top of a double boiler. Place over simmering water. Beat constantly with a wire whisk until it has the fine, light consistency of a ribbon of whipped cream. Serve in stem tulip glasses. Lady Fingers or Champagne Biscuits should be served with this delicate dessert.

Pots de Crème   FOR 6

Pots de crème are attractive little porcelain crocks. The cream served in them is like a custard but much richer, lighter and finer.

> 2 cups milk
> 8 egg yolks
> 1 cup sugar
> ½ teaspoon vanilla extract,
>   1 tablespoon coffee extract
>   or ½ cup cocoa

Bring the milk to a boil. Mix the yolks and sugar with a whisk. Add the chosen flavor and blend well. Pour the boiling milk over the egg mixture, a little at a time to prevent curdling. Do not let it lump, but do not stir too vigorously. Strain through a fine strainer. Fill each pot to the top and skim off the bubbles. Place the pots in a shallow pan with 1½ inches of boiling water. I line the bottom of the shallow pan with a sheet of ordinary paper. The wet paper acts as an anchor and prevents the pots from tipping over. Put in a preheated 275-degree oven 45 minutes or until no pocket forms on top of the pots when slightly tipped. The pot de crème custard should be of a very fine consistency. Serve 1 hour after it is made, or keep in the refrigerator for a few hours. Can be served the next day, but is better when freshly made.

Crème Anglaise

[CUSTARD SAUCE]   FOR ABOUT 2½ CUPS

> 2 cups milk
> 1 teaspoon vanilla extract or ½ vanilla bean
> 4 egg yolks
> ½ cup sugar

Bring the milk to a boil with the vanilla extract or vanilla bean. Meanwhile, mix the yolks with the sugar in a bowl. Pour the milk very gradually over the eggs, stirring with a wire whisk. When well mixed, place in a saucepan on top of low fire, stirring constantly with a wooden spoon. When thick enough, the sauce should coat the back of the wooden spoon evenly. It should not be too thick. Remove to a cool place until ready to use. This sauce is used to accompany many sweets.

Mousse au Chocolat

[CHOCOLATE MOUSSE]   FOR 8, OR ABOUT 2 CUPS

Step One: Coulis de Chocolat
> 6 squares bitter chocolate, shredded
> 1¼ cups sugar
> 1 quart milk
> 4 tablespoons sweet butter
> 1 tablespoon sifted white flour

Blend the chocolate and sugar with the milk. Bring to a boil, simmer 5 minutes. Melt the butter in small skillet; blend in the flour. Stir the butter-flour paste into the milk mixture, a little at a time to avoid lumping. Boil, stirring, 2 minutes. Strain through a fine strainer. Set aside until cool.

Step Two: Mousse

Mix 2 cups of the above coulis with ⅔ cup whipped cream (made from heavy cream), 2 tablespoons confectioners' sugar and 2 drops vanilla extract. Blend well. Do not beat. Serve well chilled.

NOTE: The coulis can be doubled or cut in half, remembering when you make the mousse to mix 3 parts coulis with 1 part whipped cream, 1 tablespoon confectioners' sugar, and 1 drop vanilla.

POUDINGS—Puddings

Bread and Butter Pudding   FOR 6

> 2 cups milk
> 1 cup heavy cream
> 4 egg yolks
> 2 eggs
> 1 cup sugar
> ½ teaspoon vanilla extract
>   Pinch salt
> ⅔ cup raisins, soaked in water ½ hour, then dried
> 6 tablespoons sweet butter
> 10 very thin slices white sandwich bread,
>   crusts removed, cut in half diagonally

Bring the milk and cream to a boil. Meanwhile, blend the egg yolks, eggs and sugar smoothly with a wire whisk. Stir in the vanilla and salt. Pour the boiling milk and cream over the egg mixture, a little at a time, stirring well to avoid lumping or scrambling. Strain through a fine wire strainer into a buttered pudding dish. Add the raisins. Melt the butter in a shallow pan and dredge the slices of bread in it. Place the slices on top of the mixture in the pudding dish, overlapping so that the top is covered entirely. Place the dish in a shallow pan with 1 inch of boiling water. Put in a preheated 275-degree oven 45 minutes or until the pudding is set and the bread well browned. If the top is not brown, place under the broiler. This dish should sit 2 hours before serving.

Pouding au Riz et Raisins Secs

[RICE AND RAISIN PUDDING] FOR 6

        1 quart water
        ½ cup rice
        2 cups milk
          Peel of one orange
        ½ cup sugar
          Pinch salt
          Drop vanilla extract
        ½ cup raisins, soaked ½ hour before using
        2 egg yolks
        1 cup heavy cream
        1 tablespoon confectioners' sugar

Bring the water to a boil; add rice and boil 5 minutes. Drain; rinse with cold water. Bring the milk to a boil, add the rice, orange peel, sugar, salt and vanilla extract. Blend. Simmer 30 minutes, stirring often to prevent lumping. Off heat, add the raisins and egg yolks, mixing quickly but well. Place in a deep ovenproof dish and cool 1 hour. Whip the cream stiff and mix into the rice slowly, working upward. Sprinkle the confectioners' sugar over the top and place under the broiler until well browned. Serve with a fruit sauce on the side.

Pouding aux Cerises Noires à la Meringue

[BLACK CHERRY PUDDING WITH MERINGUE] FOR 8

Step One: Pudding
        1 eight-ounce can black pitted cherries, drained

    1 quart milk
    ⅔ cup granulated sugar
    2 eggs
    4 egg yolks (reserve whites)
    2 tablespoons cherry liqueur
    1 tablespoon kirschwasser
      Pinch salt

Arrange the cherries in the bottom of a buttered pudding dish. Bring the milk to a boil. Meanwhile, blend the sugar with the eggs, egg yolks and liqueurs. Pour the hot milk over the mixture very slowly, stirring rapidly to avoid curdling. Add salt. Strain through a fine strainer onto the cherries. Place in a shallow pan with 1 inch of boiling water. Put in a preheated 275-degree oven 45 minutes or until set. Cool 1 hour.

Step Two: Meringue
    4 egg whites (saved from Step 1)
    ½ cup confectioners' sugar
    1 teaspoon lemon juice
      Drop vanilla extract

Beat the egg whites stiff. Add sugar, a little at a time, beating after each addition. Add lemon juice and vanilla. Beat in. Spread most of the meringue over the pudding. Place the remainder in a pastry bag with a fluted tube and decorate the top of the pudding. Put under the broiler 3 minutes. Brown lightly.

PÂTISSERIE—Pastry

Tarte aux Cerises Flambées

[FLAMING CHERRY TART]   FOR 6

Step One: Batter
    1 cup sifted white flour
    4 eggs
    1 teaspoon confectioners' sugar
      Pinch salt
    2 cups boiling milk

Blend the flour and eggs well. Add the sugar and salt and mix well with a wire whisk. Pour in the boiling milk, a small amount at a time, stirring quickly to avoid lumping.

Step Two: Preparing the tart
    4 tablespoons sweet butter
     Batter (already prepared)
    1 eight-ounce can pitted black cherries,
     drained and dried of liquid
    1 tablespoon confectioners' sugar
    ¼ cup Fine Champagne

Melt the butter in a 10-inch ovenproof skillet. When foaming, pour in the batter. Spread the cherries evenly on the batter. Cook over medium heat 2 minutes. Place in a preheated 400-degree oven 30 minutes or until set. Sprinkle with confectioners' sugar 2 minutes before removing the tart from the oven. Slide the tart onto a round serving platter. Pour the Fine Champagne over it and flambé at the table.

Tarte aux Pruneaux Charolaise

[PRUNE TART]   FOR 6

This is my Grandmother's recipe. The tart dough is like a bread dough without the leaven.

Step One: Tart dough
    2 cups sifted flour
    4 tablespoons sweet butter
     Pinch salt
    ½ teaspoon confectioners' sugar
    ½ cup cold water

Mix the flour and butter with your hands, kneading the two together well, but gently. When well mixed, add the salt and sugar, then the water, forming the dough which will be used for the tart. This dough should be made the day before.

Step Two: Cooking the tart dough
    ½ pound prunes, soaked 4 hours in cold water, then pitted
    2 tablespoons very fine sugar
    ½ cup Mirabelle liqueur

Roll the dough about ¼-inch thick to line a 10-inch tart plate or tart ring. Cut the edges so they will be even. Prick the bottom with a fork to give air to the tart. Fill the mold with the prunes and place in a preheated 400-degree oven 30 minutes or until pastry is brown. Sprinkle with sugar, pour on the Mirabelle and flambé.

Cheese Cake à la Walter

FOR 8

Step One: Filling

    1½ pounds cream cheese
    ½ cup sweet butter, melted
    1¼ cups confectioners' sugar
     1 tablespoon finely grated lemon rind
     1 tablespoon lemon juice
     1 teaspoon gelatin, dissolved in
      2 tablespoons lukewarm water
     1 cup whipped cream

With a wire whisk, thoroughly blend the cream cheese with the melted butter, sugar, lemon rind and lemon juice. Add the gelatin. When all the ingredients are blended, stir in the whipped cream. Mix well and set aside.

Step Two: Crust

    20 zwieback, grated into a mixing bowl
    ½ cup sweet butter, melted
    ½ teaspoon cinnamon
    ½ cup confectioners' sugar

Blend all ingredients well. Coat a round 1-quart pastry mold evenly with this mixture. Pour the cream cheese mixture into the coated mold. Place in the refrigerator overnight. When ready to serve, place the mold in a deep pan filled with hot water for a few seconds to unmold the cake more easily. Invert the contents of the mold on a serving dish. Sprinkle the cake with confectioners' sugar before serving. For an interesting variation, add ½ cup of shredded pineapple to the cheese mixture.

CRÊPES ET BEIGNETS—Pancakes and Fritters

Crêpes Flambées Crémaillère

[FLAMING PANCAKES]   FOR ABOUT 16 CRÊPES

Step One: Crêpes
> 1 cup sifted white flour
> 2 eggs
> 2 egg yolks
> 2 cups milk
>   Pinch salt
> 1 teaspoon granulated sugar
>   Rind of ½ lemon, chopped fine
> 2 tablespoons melted sweet butter
>   Salt pork rind

The batter should be made the day before, but, if necessary, it may be prepared 2 hours before using; do not refrigerate. Place the flour in a mixing bowl and add the whole eggs, stirring with a wooden spatula. Stir in the egg yolks, 2 tablespoons of the milk, salt and sugar. Blend with the spatula 3 minutes until very smooth. Add the rest of the milk, gradually, stirring well so the batter will not lump. Add the lemon rind. When ready to cook the crêpes, blend in the melted butter. Heat 2 or 3 crêpe pans 5 inches in diameter. Rub the pans with the fat side of the salt pork. Pour 2 tablespoons of the batter in each pan, moving the pan in a clockwise motion so as to spread the batter evenly. The finished crêpes should be very thin. Experience will teach you the exact amount of batter to use for a crêpe. Cook over medium heat 1 minute, flip the crêpe over and cook the other side 1 minute. This is approximate time. Each side should be a hazelnut color. Place on a round platter, each crêpe on top of the other to keep them moist until ready to use. The number of crêpes obtained depends upon your skill at making the desired thin crêpes.

Step Two: Sauce for 16 crêpes
> ½ cup orange juice
> 1 tablespoon finely grated orange rind
> 6 tablespoons sweet butter
> 2 tablespoons confectioners' sugar
> 1 tablespoon very fine sugar
> 2 tablespoons Green Chartreuse
> ¼ cup Grand Marnier

¼ cup Grand Fine Champagne or cognac
1 teaspoon lemon juice

Blend the orange juice with the orange rind in a flat chafing dish over an alcohol or canned-heat flame. Cook 2 minutes. Add the butter and confectioners' sugar. When simmering, place each crêpe in, one at a time, to cook for half a minute, turning it over. Fold each crêpe in a fan shape as finished and arrange around the side of the chafing dish until all have been cooked and well saturated with the sauce. Sprinkle very fine sugar over the crêpes. Pour the Chartreuse and the Grand Marnier in the chafing dish. Turn the crêpes several times in this liquor. Add the Grand Fine Champagne and flambé, basting the crêpes with the blazing sauce. Sprinkle the lemon juice on the crêpes and serve on hot plates.

Crêpes Soufflées Antoine

[SOUFLÉED PANCAKES]   FOR 16 CRÊPES

Step One
Make 16 crêpes from batter (page 380).

Step Two: Cream for stuffing the crêpes
      2 eggs, separated
      ½ cup sifted white flour
      ½ cup very fine sugar
      1 tablespoon Yellow Chartreuse
         Drop vanilla extract
         Pinch salt
      1 cup boiling milk
         Confectioners' sugar

Blend the egg yolks and flour with a wooden spatula, working well 2 minutes. Add the sugar, Chartreuse, vanilla and salt. Mix thoroughly. Pour the boiling milk over, a little at a time, stirring constantly with a wire whisk to avoid lumping. Cook over a medium fire for 2 minutes or until the mixture thickens a little. Remove to a mixing bowl; cool one half hour. When ready, beat the egg whites very stiff. Blend well with the egg yolk mixture. Spread a ½-inch-thick layer of stuffing on each crêpe; fold into pillow shape. Sprinkle with confectioners' sugar and place, uncovered, in a preheated 500-degree oven 5 minutes. Serve immediately.

Crêpes Flambées Confiture

[FLAMING PANCAKES WITH JAM]

Spread crêpes with jam of your choice, roll and arrange on an ovenproof platter. Sprinkle with confectioners' sugar and place under the broiler 2 minutes or until well browned. Pour Martinique rum over them and flambé. Serve immediately.

Beignets d'Acacia

[ACACIA BLOSSOM FRITTERS]   FOR 6

Acacia trees are any of various chiefly tropical trees of the genus *Acacia*, with compound leaves and very tight clusters of small white or yellow flowers. I found many of them around my home in Wilton, Connecticut, during late May and early June.

Step One
  12 acacia flowers
  2 tablespoons confectioners' sugar
  ¼ cup Grand Fine Champagne

Sprinkle the sugar over the flowers, then the Grand Fine Champagne, and marinate 1 hour before dipping in the following batter.

Step Two: Frying batter
  1 cup sifted white flour
  2 tablespoons melted sweet butter
  ¼ cup beer
  6 tablespoons lukewarm water
    Pinch salt
  2 tablespoons Fine Champagne
  1 teaspoon confectioners' sugar
  2 egg whites
    Cooking oil for deep frying

Blend the flour well with the butter, beer, water, salt, Fine Champagne and sugar. Let stand 1 hour in a warm place. When ready to serve, beat the egg whites stiff. Mix thoroughly into the batter. Dip the blossoms in the batter and deep fry at 365 degrees until brown and crisp. Serve with an apricot sauce made by mixing over a slow fire 1 cup abricotine (obtainable in jars), 2 tablespoons kirschwasser and ½ cup sliced almonds.

FRUITS—Fruits

Bananes Flambées Joséphine

[FLAMING BANANAS]   FOR 4

  6 tablespoons sweet butter
  4 bananas, peeled and cut in half, lengthwise
  2 tablespoons confectioners' sugar
  1 teaspoon lemon juice
   Drop vanilla extract
  6 tablespoons white Martinique rum

At the table, melt the butter in a chafing dish. When foaming, cook the banana halves 1 minute on each side. Add the sugar, lemon juice and vanilla extract. Bring to a boil, stirring. Pour the rum over and flambé, basting with a serving spoon. You should obtain a good syrup sauce from the rum and sugar. Serve on hot plates, spooning the hot sauce liberally over the bananas.

Pêches Fraîches au Champagne

[FRESH PEACHES IN CHAMPAGNE]

For each serving, dip a fresh, very ripe peach in hot water one half minute. Peel off the skin. Cut in two and remove pit. Sprinkle lemon juice over the peach to prevent discoloring and place the halves in a large stem champagne glass. Chill in the refrigerator. Sprinkle 1 teaspoon confectioners' sugar over the peach 1 hour before serving. When ready to serve, fill the peach glass with very cold, dry champagne.

14

A Word About Wine

Your taste in wine is as individual as your taste in beef: Some like their beef well done, some medium rare, some rare; some like it chopped raw and eaten à la tartare. And no matter what so-called good taste, fashion, or experts decree, your own preference should firmly dictate your choice. I know a renowned epicure, a great man with wines, who has the most peculiar taste in steak. He wants it overcooked, looking like shoe leather, with the bloom gone and the juice left in the pan. That's the way he likes it.

So it goes with wine. Be free to drink what you like, the way you like it. If a glass of red wine pleases you with chicken, or white wine with a sirloin, that's fine. It is your table and your palate. Here, I will give my idea of how to choose wines, based on my own taste and the knowledge I've gained over the years. Perhaps this advice will be of use to you. Or perhaps, you'll think I'm an old fusser and find nothing here that will help you. But it is an honest opinion, aimed at not insulting either the wine or the reader.

It is a special joy to a host to serve a fine wine and have it sincerely appreciated. It is a fine achievement when he weds the wine and the food happily.

There is, however, the risk of being "over-wined." By that, I mean there often is pomposity involved with the serving and drinking of wines. I find it boring to sit at a table and hear year, bouquet, body, limpidity, brilliance, etcetera discussed in endless detail while a beautiful woman sits ignored and the food grows cold. Mind you, I am not saying that I do not respect a knowledge of, and even a reverence for, wine. I have vast respect for wine and honor it above most of our benefits, except good health. I am merely saying that talking about it can be overdone, like saying "thank you" twenty times.

Ammerschwihr, Alsace

The Romans, who knew a good thing when they tasted it, dubbed wine the "milk of the good goddess." It is also truly said that wine is the intellectual aspect of a meal, and meats are the material part. When European civilization was wiped out by the invasion of the barbarians, wine, the mark of civilization, also vanished. I consider any meal without wine barbaric. After all, it is a simple matter to place an acceptable wine on the table. Not only is it an aid to digestion, conversation and décor, but in my estimation, a meal without wine is like a lovely woman without a smile. Before I go completely poetic let us get to hard facts.

If you want to know more about wines than I tell you here, I recommend three books by men I know. In my opinion, these are the best: *The Noble Grapes and the Great Wines of France* by André L. Simon, and *The Wines and Vineyards of France* and *Encyclopedia of Wines,* both by Frank Schoonmaker.

Now, briefly, let us take this over-mystified subject of wine in simple steps. First, classification:

Natural wines: To my taste, the best wines result from the natural fermentation of the juice of the grape. Also known as table wines and still wines, they have an alcohol content ranging from 9 per cent to 14 per cent. Among them are Burgundy, Bordeaux, Alsatian, Chianti, Moselle, Rhine.

Sparkling wines: These result from a complicated process by which a secondary fermentation is brought about in the corked bottle. Natural effervescence results; there are bubbles. The best known is champagne. It is also the best. Others, for my taste, are not truly classic. Although some people swear by sparkling Burgundy, for me it is a desecration of that king of wines.

Fortified wines: These are wines that have had brandy added, bringing the alcoholic content up as high as 21 per cent. They are both sweet and dry. Examples are sherry, Madeira, Malaga, port.

Carbonated wines: These I stay away from. They sparkle also, but the bubbles are artificial, not natural. The effervescence is created by injecting the wine with carbon dioxide during the bottling process.

Aromatized wines: Barks, herbs, flavors are added to fortified wines, producing a completely different character. Examples are May Wine, French and Italian Vermouths and most of the apéritif wines.

How to buy wines? A difficult question, almost impossible to answer simply and completely. Much depends upon you as a person, what you like. But the first thing you must acquire if you want to know and serve good wines is a knowledgeable wine merchant. Most, though by no means all, of those who are in this business try to educate themselves on the subject of their wines. They do so because they want their customers to return, and because most Americans are somewhat shy about buying wines, and usually ask for guidance in liquor stores as well as restaurants.

The man who sells you wine has sources he can turn to for information. His supplier, if not an expert, will always have an expert to whom he can turn to get answers to even the most difficult questions. Thus, when in doubt, ask the man from whom you buy your wine. You'll find out after a couple of visits and several questions whether or not he knows his business. If he blows hot and cold and double-talks, watch out; but if he says honestly that he doesn't know but that he will find out, you have a good man.

What questions should you ask? Well, that again is up to you. Most people ask about vintage, or what should be served with what. The first question is not easy, so I'll tackle it first. Vintage depends upon weather, soil, the producer—but especially weather. I'll list a few Very Good and Excellent years here, skipping the Good, Fair and Poor.

Burgundy, Red:	*Very Good*	1948, 1949, 1950, 1963, 1967
	Excellent	1945, 1947, 1952, 1955, 1957, 1959, 1961, 1964, 1966, 1967–1969
Burgundy, White:	*Very Good*	1948, 1950, 1953, 1955, 1957, 1963, 1967
	Excellent	1945, 1947, 1952, 1958, 1959, 1960, 1961, 1962, 1964, 1966, 1967–1969
Bordeaux, Red:	*Very Good*	1950, 1957, 1958, 1960, 1962, 1969
	Excellent	1945, 1947, 1952, 1953, 1955, 1959, 1961, 1964, 1966, 1967–1969
Bordeaux, White:	*Very Good*	1946, 1950, 1952, 1953, 1957, 1958, 1960, 1962, 1964, 1965, 1967–1969
	Excellent	1945, 1947, 1949, 1955, 1959, 1961, 1966, 1967–1969

For me, these are the important wines. And if you have the interest, there are complete charts available giving vintage years of all French wines. Quality may vary from wine to wine even though the years are good ones. Wines are not quite so variable as the vintners who bottle them, but there can be marked differences.

If you cannot buy the good French wines for your table, then I advise you to turn to your own wines, the American. These are good table wines and less expensive than even the poorest of the European wines. Out of snobbery a host will pour an inferior wine from France and sneer at the California or Finger Lakes labels. That, friends, is a table to which I never return.

True, most of the American wines are sweeter than their French counterparts. The Finger Lakes Country Reds and Whites are cases in point. But they have a delightful taste of the grape. The Almadén Mountain Red Burgundy and the Chablis are excellent; the Wente Brothers are doing grand work with Le Blanc de Blancs and others. So is Charles Fournier with Finger Lakes champagne; the Taylor people there are producing good table wines. The Johnson Estate in California's Livermore Valley is bottling very good wines, also the Novitiate of Los Gatos and Beau Rosé of Napa Valley. Unfortunately, I cannot list all the worthy vineyards, but I do suggest that you who are seriously interested in fine table wines at a reasonable price try your own American wines. A few tastings will enable you to find your own favorites.

It must be noted that most American wines cannot be put down: they cannot be aged. Frank Schoonmaker, however, reports that there are some very fine varietal wines in California that can be aged— vintage wines that can stand with the good ones of Europe. Two that may be aged successfully are Cabernet Sauvignon and Pinot Chardonnay, both rather expensive but worth the price.

But now, let me turn to the French wines, hoping that some names and descriptions will be helpful, and warning you to keep in mind that my feelings and preferences are at work here.

You probably by now are bored with the fact that I was born in Burgundy. But I am still going to quote what Charles Edward Montague said about the wine of my birthplace. He put it far better than I could. "Burgundy was the winiest wine, the central, essential, and typical wine, the soul and greatest common measure of all the kindly wines of the earth." There are those who will say that I am prejudiced, and they will be right. However, there has always been envy of the wines of Burgundy. Even at the end of the first century A.D., the Roman emperor Domitian had the vines of Burgundy torn out. Why? The Emperor was a lover of wine, and he did not want Burgundy to compete with Italy, which then had the leading vineyards. Of course, my own people (or former people—I am an American citizen) did their best to destroy the wines of Burgundy when in the name of liberty they confiscated the grand vineyards which had belonged to leading families and to the Church and sold them off in little plots. Ah well, despite them all the best still comes from my birthplace.

Wines of Burgundy

In Burgundy there are not many Château Bottled wines, but look for the Appellation Contrôlée, which means that a wine from one vineyard cannot be blended with another of different origin. This is to protect the consumer and also the honest growers. Each cork and label must be imprinted with the firm or propriétaire, and the specific appellation. Do not accept any wine that has not been so labeled. Burgundy offers a wide variety of white and red wines which are, if authentic, the best to serve with food. Most of the Burgundy whites are dry and will go well with fish, white meat, poultry, or even as an apéritif. The late Chanoine Kir named a very good apéritif, Vin Blanc Cassis: dry white wine mixed with a small amount of cassis (a syrup-liqueur made from cassis, a berry of the currant type). Most of the Burgundy reds, except for Beaujolais, should be aged for several years in your wine cellar.

Wines of Bordeaux

Bordeaux wines are of a different class than other Burgundy wines. The whites are rather sweet and cannot be served with some of my dishes. There is not a dry Sauterne or a really dry Grave. I may be prejudiced, but for my taste white Bordeaux wines are dessert, or maybe apéritif wines.

The château wines are at their best when vintage years are tops. The best Bordeaux reds are designated as Château Bottled, which means that the wine *has* to be of the specified château, property or vineyard. This designation also has to be printed on each cork.

The Bordeaux reds can be of great quality, and are called "claret" by the British, meaning light and pleasant, when of good origin.

Wines of the Loire River Valley

These are mostly white, except for an Anjou rosé and a Bourgueil red. They include some very interesting wines, both still and sparkling, which are delicate and go well with clams, oysters or other shell fish.

Saumur is a rather sweet wine that is good with dessert; Vouvray white wine will be acceptable as an apéritif; there is a Sparkling Vouvray, a natural bubbling wine, that can be served anytime before dinner.

Wines of Alsace

Alsace produces excellent white wine, which should be drunk young and should be served a bit cold, well iced. Alsace wines go well with fish with a white sauce, except for the Gewürztraminer, which is to me a bit flowery. Riesling, Muscat, Sylvaner, and Traminer are light and pleasant.

Wines of Jura

The Jura wines are in a class by themselves. There are white, rosé, and vin jaune (yellow wine). A very strong-bodied wine is Château Chalon, which should be served with a fish dish with a well-seasoned sauce; Rosé d'Arbois is a wine of great merit, dry and sharp. The yellow wine can be compared with sherry. The grapes are placed on layers of straw until ripe and then pressed, giving the juice a pale yellow color and also a taste of straw. This wine should be served as an apéritif, quite cold.

Wines of the Rhône Valley

The Rhône Valley produces some of the best white and red wines which are now being stocked in wine cellars. But aside from the good Hermitage, Côte Rôtie and, further south, Châteauneuf du Pape and Tavel, there is nothing special about these wines. The

Hermitage white is a wine with body; it goes well with a heavy white sauce dish. Of course, Châteauneuf du Pape has some of the best red light wines, and Tavel has some very good rosé wines, which lately have been surpassed by wines from Provence.

Wines of Provence

In southeast France, the French Riviera, wine growing and producing have been very successful during the past years. There are many new businessmen (négociants) who have become active in this industry. They have successfully put up some rosé wines and white wines which are acceptable but not great; these should not be bought for a wine-cellar collection. The best wines of Provence are made in the Alpes Maritimes section. The Var section claims a very much higher production. Their red wines are not recommended.

Wines of Champagne

As you know, champagne may be drunk any time and at any dinner, and no other wine need be served. It is good etiquette to serve champagne throughout a perfect dinner. And of course champagne is a very good apéritif. Champagne wines come in different categories: Brut, Extra Sec, Sec, Demi-Sec, Doux and Mousseux. Brut means that the wine has been made just from the grape juice without the addition of sugar or anything else. With Sec perhaps some sugar or other ingredients have been added. Demi-Sec has been sweetened. Doux and Mousseux are manufactured so artificially that they are not natural wines.

Now, let me get to specifics on my favorites:

Burgundy White

Chablis: A dry wine with a pale straw color. Goes well with shell fish and all other fish that have been prepared with a white wine sauce, or broiled, or sautéed; also with poultry or grilled or roasted veal. May be drunk as an apéritif, adding a little cassis. Can be aged a couple of years.

Pouilly and *Pouilly-Fuissé:* Dry white wines, a little lighter than Chablis, usually drunk young, will not age more than three or four years.

Beaujolais Blanc: Similar to the above wines, and can be served with the same dishes. There is very little made. It should be served young; at its best when one year old.

Beaune Blanc: Has more body than the above wines, with perhaps less bouquet. Can stand a dish cooked with a heavy sauce, goes very nicely with a well-seasoned dish like Homard à l'Américaine. Very little is produced. Can be kept a few years.

Musigny Blanc: Is a delicate wine, at its best with delicate sauces, or lake and river fish. Very little is produced. Will stand up to five years.

Meursault: A great white wine with the finest bouquet; has good body, is of a greenish color. There are not many wines to surpass this. Will be well appreciated with oysters, clams, all shell fish, poultry prepared with white sauce, meat and fish (grilled or boiled in a court bouillon). It is also a good apéritif. Do not

Poisson

serve too cold or you will break the bouquet. Will age to five years, but better when three years.

Montrachet: This wine is the greatest of all. Has flavor, bouquet and full body. Its color resembles that of Meursault. Will be very good with white, creamy sauces, or fish with a Sauce Hollandaise or a similar sauce. Should not be drunk until three or four years old. Will stand for eight to twelve years if well-stored.

Mâcon Blanc: A less important wine; inexpensive and will serve well as a table wine with ordinary meals.

Montagny: Another quite inexpensive white wine from southern Burgundy (Côte Chalonnaise). A very good everyday wine.

Corton Charlemagne: A great wine, with less bouquet but sometimes more body than the Montrachet. Can be served with fish or seafood, veal (grilled or with mushroom sauce), or with poultry prepared with white wine or sautéed. There is a very small production, so it is wise to store some of the best vintage years. At its best when at least five to six years old.

Burgundy Red

Pommard: A well-known wine, very fine bouquet, soft when at least five years old. Will go well with red meat (stewed), roasted duckling, game, venison or fowl or veal cooked with a brown sauce or red wine sauce. Deserves to be stored when young and not disturbed.

Volnay: A wine with a worthy velvet taste, soft, easy to drink when one has a fine vintage year. Will go well with delicately prepared meats or fowl, salmon cooked with red wine, abats prepared with brown sauce.

Nuits-St.-Georges: A wine that is comparable to Pommard, well-balanced, with a good body. Deserves to be stored for a few years before being served.

Beaune: A wine similar to Pommard and Nuits-St.-Georges. Should be served with similar foods.

Chambertin: A very great wine. The best from Gevrey-Chambertin is Clos de Bèze. It was the favorite wine of Napoleon. Will go well with a coq au vin or other dishes cooked with red wine. It is a wine of great durability, can stand many years.

Chambolle-Musigny: A much softer wine than the previous ones, lighter in body but much more refined. Has a little taste of blueberry. Will go well with light dishes cooked with red wine—lamb, fowl, sweetbreads, quail, and so forth. Do not serve it too young; three or four years will be necessary for its maturity. There is also a Musigny red which has the same characteristics as Chambolle-Musigny, since they both come from the same district.

Savigny: A red wine which is not too expensive but is dependable for an everyday wine, light and very agreeable.

Santenay: This wine has probably the most "gout de terroir," meaning a rather earthy taste. It contains a great deal of tannin, which causes a heavy deposit in the bottles. So do not shake the bottle when serving. Will be good with the same food as Pommard or Nuits-St.-Georges.

Clos de Vougeot: A famous name in Burgundy. The vineyards were planted by Cistercian monks around the twelfth century. The château is the headquarters of the Confrérie des Chevaliers du Tastevin, a world-famous wine organization of which I am a member. Its wine is of fine quality, can be compared with that of Chambolle, can be served with the same food. Will need to be aged at least five years before using.

Echézeaux: Rather light in color and body, pleasing to the palate. Can be served with light dishes. Will stand a couple of years.

Corton: This is one of the greatest wines of Burgundy, having class and elegance, a rather bright color, bouquet and body. Goes well with almost all meat, fowl or game birds cooked with red wine or red wine sauce. Very soft when aged for five or six years.

Richebourg, Vosne-Romanée, Romanée-Conti, Romanée-Saint-Vivant: These four red wines are the greatest in the world. There are only some thirty acres in production, including La Tâche and La Romanée. Therefore, if one is the lucky owner of a few bottles, one should nurse them as a very precious possession and only serve to connoisseurs. These wines will go very well with a roast venison, leg or saddle, cooked on the pink side, with chestnut purée and a poivrade sauce, into which a tiny bit of the wine will be poured before serving. They are also great wines for beef daube and canard aux pruneaux.

Beaujolais: Presently one of the most popular wines. Although from southern Burgundy, it is only in the last few years that it has been called a Burgundy. There are approximately nine or ten different appellations. It is an agreeable small wine, very good when drunk young. It is a fresh wine, meaning fragrant, and should be consumed quite cold but not, as certain experts claim, iced. Just bring it from a cool cellar or, if warm, place it in the refrigerator for an hour before serving. It is a fine wine for a picnic or just with a good chunk of salami, sausage or cheese. Of course, it is also very appropriate with a roast chicken, veal or boiled beef (pot au feu). If you can put up with the rising prices of this wine, please make it your everyday wine. Remember, it should be consumed young, one or two years old.

Moulin-à-Vent: Another pleasant wine from the south of Burgundy. It is one of the Beaujolais. Wines from Romanèche-Thorins are the same. These wines, like other Beaujolais, will go well with light dishes—for instance, with calf's liver or other abats, such as calf's brains or calf's head en tortue. Can age two or three years before serving.

Côte Chalonnaise and Mâcon: Include several very good everyday wines from southern Burgundy.

Mercurey: A red wine of distinction; although not too well known, it has merit. It is from the Côte Chalonnaise, has good body and bright color. Could compete with some of the Beaune wines. Can be served with beef, lamb, guinea hen or roast pork. A wine that should be better known.

What do you do with the wine after you obtain it? You store it properly, and then you drink it.

Ideally, you should have a cellar with little or no variation in temperature. It should be dark, and no more than 60 degrees; 50 is even better. Wine should be stored well away from the furnace and its ducts, placed on its side, horizontally, so that the wine in the bottle will be in constant contact with the cork. If you do not have a cellar, you can use a cupboard or a shelf, or a wine rack in a room, remembering that sharp variations in temperature are not good for the wine. Wine should rest in darkness, away from drafts, noise and vibrations.

White wines should be served cold, but not too cold or the bouquet will be spoiled. Fifty degrees is right. One hour in the refrigerator is enough. Keep the bottle in a bucket of ice near the table, and also have the glasses chilled.

When you go to the cellar for a bottle of red wine bring a wine basket. Slide the bottle horizontally in the basket, carefully so you do not disturb the wine. Carry it without shaking it. I like to bring a red wine from the cellar four hours before serving, and serve it at room temperature. About sixty-five to sixty-eight degrees is right for red wines.

When opening wine, cut the metal capsule well below the ring of the bottle-neck, not just flush with the cork. The lead capsule is treated with chemicals to protect the cork, and it smells bad; so the wine should never come into contact with the metal capsule. After you cut and remove the capsule, wipe the whole neck of the bottle carefully. Insert the corkscrew slowly through the exact center of the cork, and withdraw the cork with a straight, steady pull, without hurrying, but not hesitating either. After the cork is drawn, wipe the inside lip of the bottle with a clean cloth or paper towel. Smell the cork for bad odor, "corkiness." A cork can also become mushy and give a poor taste to the wine. If this has happened, or if the smell isn't right, purge the bottle immediately. Throw the two inches of wine from the neck into the sink. Often this will get rid of the corky taste. It is always a good idea, even if the cork smells right, to pour two ounces of any wine you are serving into your own glass first. "Dégorger" is the word for this. It is not an affectation. It is done so the host or the person ordering the wine at a restaurant will get the bad taste if there is any; also, so that the host can judge if the wine is up to his expectations.

I always decork red wine at least three hours before serving. This gives it a chance to breathe and results in a smoother wine with an added aroma or perfume. I also believe that clarets, port, and all Burgundies over six years old should be decanted. If you do not decant old wines there is the risk that some of your guests will get sediment in their wine. This is also the reason you should never shake a bottle of red wine—white either, but especially red.

Wine should be decanted in a clear crystal decanter by holding the bottle over a lighted candle in a darkened room, the flame just below the shoulder of the wine bottle (you may use a lamp or flashlight, but I find a candle best). The candle will highlight the sediment. Pour slowly, and stop decanting when the crust or sediment begins to come into the neck of the bottle.

If you are serving more than one wine, a light wine should come before the heavier; a dry wine before a richer wine. White wine is served before red; but red wine is poured before a sweet white wine.

Do not wrap a napkin around the bottle of wine you are serving. This was the mode at one time, but today guests wonder what you are hiding; and with the current interest in wines, if you are serving a good one, people will want to know what it is.

My rules for serving wines with food are simple. They may not be yours, but they please my sensitivities. Dry white wine with fish, white meats (veal), poultry and egg dishes. Red wine with red meat, game, any food that has been prepared and cooked with red wine. Sweet wine with desserts or with delicate foods such as mousses of ham or chicken.

Wine is essential to cooking, at least my kind of cooking—as necessary as herbs, spices, salt and pepper. Wine calls forth the subtle, natural flavors of most foods. While it seasons it also tenderizes. A simple rule of thumb on what wines to use in cooking: with chicken, fish and veal, use white wine; with lamb, game, beef and stews, use red wine. Also remember that the wine you will want to serve with the main course is the same wine you'll use in cooking it. Unless, of course, if it is an aged, rare Burgundy or Bordeaux. Do not buy so-called "cooking" wines. Use decent wines for cooking; do not risk spoiling elegant and expensive food by using inferior wine in its preparation.

In serving wine, do not fill the glass more than half full. And never use a colored glass. As André Simon says, "The first joy that a fine wine has to offer us is its clear, bright, cheerful and beautiful color, so the whiter the glass, the better it will be for the wine and for us." As for the shape of the glass, Frank Schoonmaker has done us a service by offering his own careful selection of wine glasses of simple, graceful crystal (they are available from the Seneca Glass Company, Morgantown, West Virginia). But remember—the wine is more important than your glassware.

To close, I will cite a respected quote to comment on the deplorable American habit of serving *cold water*(!) with meals. For this I turn to the Bible, First Epistle of Paul to the apostle Timothy: "Drink no longer water, but use a little wine for thy stomach's sake and thine often infirmities."

Schoonmaker's selection. Top row: 5-ounce Solera, for sherry, port, brandy, liqueurs; 7-ounce Château, white wine twin; 8-ounce Vin du Pays, all-purpose wine glass; 10-ounce Magnum, for great red Burgundies. Bottom row: 6-ounce Johannisberg, for Rhine, Moselle, Riesling wines; 9-ounce Cabernet, red wine twin; 8-ounce Champagne Tulip; 7-ounce V.S.O.P., snifter for fine cognac.

15

Equipment

It would be as unrealistic to try to instruct the readers of this book how to equip their kitchens as it would be for me to select their neckties or hats. You are individuals and only you know what the kitchen and cooking means to you personally.

If you have this book, then you are interested in cooking and have undoubtedly already gathered a number of excellent kitchen implements. I will not insult your intelligence by suggesting that you need a pepper mill, that a large refrigerator with a freezing section is a must, that you should have solid wooden unvarnished chopping boards or blocks, that a colander is necessary, a stove thermometer a good idea. A kitchen scale, a cheese grater, a funnel, a vegetable peeler, a ladle, a double boiler, measuring cups and a set of measuring spoons, soufflé dishes and glass baking dishes—all are probably already on your kitchen shelves or hanging from your peg board. You also probably have use for poultry shears, a food mill, a bulb baster, a drum sieve, a tamis (a sturdy drum-like sieve), a slotted spoon, wire whisks in various sizes, a rubber scraper, wooden spatulas, spoons and forks.

It is possible to accomplish much with few utensils. A skilled cook can produce excellent meals with less than basic equipment. I have had dinner prepared in the wilderness by a cook who used only a rusted wire rack, a smoke-blackened skillet and pot and a charcoal fire. The results would have made any first-class restaurant proud. At hunting camp I myself have made do with little else than a skillet (a can of black truffles and a little brandy helped). Cooking, however, should be a pleasure, not drudgery. And your equipment should serve that purpose.

It is both good fun and helpful to poke around in shops that specialize in kitchen equipment. One can learn much simply by walk-

Semur-en-Auxois, Burgundy

ing around, pointing at various objects and asking questions. Remember, too, when you throw up your hands at the price of a pot or a pan, that that particular tool probably costs less than what you are planning to serve for dinner. And the pot or pan will last for years.

The shops in New York City provide the most liberal education. Unquestionably the leader, and by far the most complete, is the Bridge Company, 212 East 52nd Street, N.Y.C. Fred Bridge, the owner, if you can get his ear, is virtually a professor of pots and pans, and has a remarkable knowledge of all cooking equipment. E. Dehillerin, 18 Rue Coquillère, Paris, probably has more copper than the Bridge Company, but unless you speak French you'll have trouble picking up information there. Bazaar de la Cuisine, 160 East 55th Street, N.Y.C., and the Bazar Français, 666 Sixth Avenue, N.Y.C., are also full-fledged academies of cooking accessories. If you are in or near New Haven, The Pottery Bazaar, 553 Whalley Avenue, is the shop with the most complete line of cooking equipment that I have seen outside of New York City. Mrs. Lee, or "Bert," will gladly answer questions. Time spent in shops such as these can really be of enormous help. Not as good, of course, as standing at the elbow of a first-class chef and watching him work, but few of us can do that.

I like a stove (preferably gas) where the heat can be instantly controlled, reliably bringing a sauce from a simmer to a boil with a simple twist of the control. If you do use electric heat, I hope you have the type of stove that promises exact timing and control. I understand it is quite satisfactory. Electric grills, broilers and rotisseries are excellent, as is an electric skillet. But you should shop carefully—ask questions, get a demonstration and do not buy cheap equipment. It will not hold up. An electric meat chopper, a blender and a mixer (the hand type is very good) are essential. Sometimes better results are obtained by hand-beating with a whisk than with an electric implement. Therefore, in some recipes I say to use the whisk. Whisks are especially good for mixing sauces, blending, beating eggs.

For your mixing bowls, glass and stainless steel are good, but you will find that the French solid copper bowl is the quickest for beating egg whites.

A rule with pots and pans, and even casseroles, is that they should be good conductors of heat and be heavy enough so they cannot be easily knocked over, making a mess of the stove and the dinner.

I like copper. It conducts heat evenly and fast. Copper pans should be heavy, covered with at least $\frac{1}{7}$ of an inch of copper

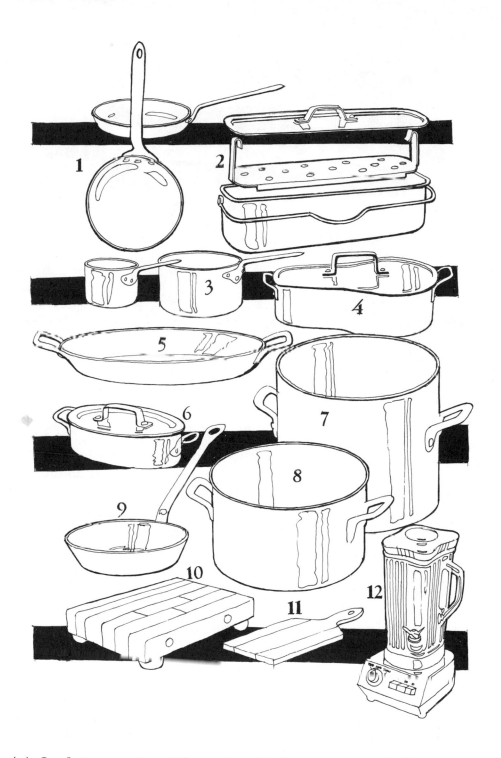

(1) *Omelette pans.* (2) *Fish poacher.* (3) *Saucepans.* (4) *Jambonnière (for ham, now rare).* (5) *Oval au gratin pan.* (6) *Oval casserole.* (7) *Stock pot.* (8) *Marmite pot.* (9) *Frying pan.* (10) *Chopping board.* (11) *Paddle board.* (12) *Blender.*

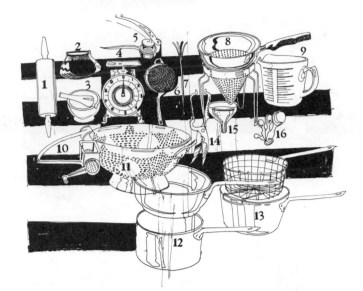

(1) Rolling pin. (2) Pastry blender. (3) Mortar and pestle. (4) Scale. (5) Garlic press. (6) Sieve. (7) Larding needle. (8) Food mill. (9) Measuring cup. (10) Mouli cheese grater. (11) Colander. (12) Double boiler. (13) Deep-fat fryer. (14) Shears. (15) Funnel. (16) Measuring spoons.

not these silly light, thin things that travelers are bringing back from Europe. Copper pots are usually lined with tin, but in time the lining must be replaced and this can be a problem. There is one brand of copper utensil, Legionware, invented by an Italian (an American citizen) that many professional chefs use. It is expensive, of exceptionally heavy copper and lined with stainless steel. It lasts forever and does an excellent job.

Cast iron, enameled, very heavy pots, made in France or Belgium or the Netherlands, are excellent utensils and bright additions to your kitchen. They are good heat conductors, will not color food, are easy to keep clean and are good for storing food in the refrigerator and serving from stove to table. In fact I prefer enameled cast iron to earthenware, ovenproof china, ovenproof glass and all other materials. It is always dependable.

Buy saucepans in several sizes, and stay with the metal handles. They are more versatile and can go from the top of the stove to the oven. They should range from heavy for slow simmering to light for fast heating.

Oval casseroles are best and can more easily accommodate everything from a hen turkey to a petite marmite. The 2-quart and 8-quart sizes should be enough. Buy baking dishes in both oval and round shapes. They can double for roasting and be used for the various dishes that require cream and cheese.

You will need a crêpe pan and an omelette pan—both black cast iron. Directions for caring for these pans will come with them. Follow carefully. Each pan should be used only for its express purpose and never washed.

You'll need a sautoir, a sauté pan with high straight sides. This has no equal for sautéing to perfection filets, chicken or whatever. And you'll want a long-handled poêle, sometimes called a chef's skillet. It has sloping sides and is unexcelled for browning small pieces of food. Moving the pan by the long handle prevents food burning and sometimes makes stirring unnecessary. These two pans should be copper.

All pans should have lids that fit tightly.

You should also have a fish poacher. No other pan does the job so well.

I won't quibble about knives. I recommend only carbon steel. It discolors, yes, but if you clean and dry the knives soon after using they won't discolor. And if they do, a bit of elbow grease and scouring soap or powder will make them shine again. Also, carbon steel has the best cutting edge and can easily be kept sharp by honing on a steel. Your basic collection should be a 10-inch cook's or chef's knife, which is designed for chopping but has many uses; an 8-inch chopping knife for smaller jobs, a 5-inch utility knife for paring and quick cutting and a 10-inch roast slicer. This should be enough to start. You will, however, find knives fascinating, even hypnotic, and may end up with quite a collection. Gleaming on a magnetic wall-holder, they give your kitchen a professional, efficient air. They run in size from a tiny fluting knife through the slender boning knife right up to the giant chef's knife that looks like a medieval weapon.

This should be enough equipment to get you started. As your interest grows, so will your collection. Keep stove, pots and pans clean, and knives sharp. A dull knife points to a dull cook.

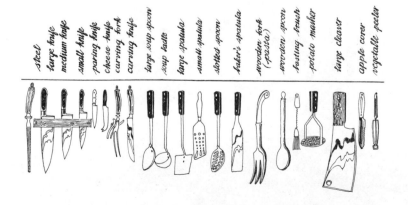

Chef's Reminders

Keep in mind that it is the presentation of food which will make the memory of a meal vivid for you and your guests. Arrange main courses attractively and individually on silver platters or handsome dishes. Dress up your dishes, simply but imaginatively, with watercress and parsley; make your own designs with tomatoes, lemons and radishes around birds or roasts you are serving. Purchase attelets (small stainless steel or silverplate spears topped with figures of a chicken, pig, steer, lamb, and so forth); run two spiced crab apples or cherry tomatoes through the attelet and spear it into the center of the roast before you present it. Not only will it add a spot of color, but the figure on the spear will immediately identify for guests what the main course is. Use care and imagination with flower arrangements. They bring your table alive. Mary Lou Scott, the wife of my co-author, uses one of the most effective approaches. She places fresh flower blossoms in a design right on the table, in the center. Express yourself both in decorating the main course dish and with flower arrangements. The pleasure will not only be that of your guests but yours.

Any chef worth his cap always has a clean white towel tucked in his belt, used to quickly wipe his fingers after tasting. For constant tasting is the hallmark of the skilled chef. And this brings us directly to the question of seasoning. It is the rule that all foods should be seasoned before cooking. But this procedure does require considerable experience and a knowledge of which foods need more or less salt and pepper and how much seasoning is right for a given quantity of food. Therefore, in all of the recipes in this book, I suggest that you go light on seasoning and taste as you cook, adding more if your taste so dictates. Food that is over-seasoned at the outset cannot be brought back, but you can, by seasoning carefully, bring any dish to the perfect point. Good cooks taste often; perhaps that is why most chefs I know are very thirsty men.

Use fresh herbs if you can. In the winter it may be difficult, but during spring, summer and fall, make the attempt to get fresh thyme and tarragon and the other herbs. It is simple to grow them in pots on your window sill. Most Europeans do this. Fresh herbs make a surprising difference in the flavor of foods. It would be unfair if I tried to give you a fast education in herbs in this book. Herbs are so important they deserve a book of their own. And they have an excellent one: *An Herb and Spice Cook Book* by Craig Claiborne. I do not think that it would be helpful to list here which herbs are to be used with which food. I have done that in each recipe where I think the herbs are necessary.

I suggest that you approach reading a recipe and following it the way most of us professionals do. I know few, if any, accomplished chefs who prepare dishes from recipes per se. They are so skilled and experienced that the recipes they employ are in their heads. But to lighten their tasks, they work ahead of their recipes, chopping ingredi-

ents, beating eggs, melting butter, grinding meat, dicing carrots, slicing onions, measuring wine. Like generals in battle, they consult the maps and get their troops in place. Study the recipe first. Then get your troops ready. You will note that I have listed the ingredients as they will be used. Study them. First do that chopping and grinding, slicing and dicing. Then go back and read the recipe over before beginning work again. Also, if the oven is to be used, preheat it to the suggested temperature. Do not heat the oven when you start the knife work, the chopping and the like. If you do, the kitchen may become too warm too fast and you may become uncomfortable while you are working. Preheat just eight minutes ahead. A chef, when he can, looks to his own comfort. For when he is at his best, so is his food.

There is nothing in this book that you cannot do easily. But slowly guide yourself in understanding the ways of successfully cooking and serving a dish by reading this book as you would a novel. You can do all the recipes perfectly after a few tries, perhaps even the first time, but I suggest that you go through the table of contents and first try dishes that appeal to you personally—perhaps dishes that you have already cooked, which you find done differently here. That also is the chef's way: he cooks his favorite dishes; then often, like a musician or a writer, he experiments to vary and improve these dishes. The creative chef finds this most enjoyable.

Plan your menu two or three days ahead, as we chefs do. Be economical. Use fruits, vegetables, meats in season. Don't plan to have a rack or crown of lamb in December when there are no spring lambs; the cost is high and the meat not at its best. Pork could be the buy then, and a crown roast of pork is as attractive and tasty as the lamb anyway.

If you have your butcher bone chicken breasts, a full chicken, a duck, or any meat, ask him to save the bones for you. They will make excellent stock.

Don't throw away certain vegetable peelings. Celery, mushrooms, carrots, tails of scallions and celery, bits and pieces of fresh tomato peelings, and other selected vegetables (not potato or onion peelings) are good for the stock pot, adding much natural flavor.

Menus: If you have fish as a main course, do not serve fish of any kind as an appetizer. If you have a white sauce with chicken or veal, do not have another white sauce on the menu. This rule also applies to brown sauces and red wine sauces. Tomato sauces, or tomato in any form, is never served twice at a well-planned meal. Nor are two fried items. Never two mayonnaise sauces. If you serve a rich dish like a quiche as first course, then make the rest of the dinner simple, broiled veal or chicken; something light should always follow something heavy. And never place a complicated meal with several courses before your guests and follow it with a very rich dessert. My favorite standby when I have an especially involved dinner is raspberry sherbet with white rum. After all, you want your guests to walk away from the table, not be wheeled.

Here are some unrelated thoughts that I long ago pasted to my memory. I unpaste them here and offer them with the thought that they may be helpful:

No man under forty can be called a gourmet.

The telephone cannot do your shopping for you. There is no substitute for your own eyes and fingers in shopping. No shopkeeper is going to tell you over the phone that his fruit isn't ripe or that the bloom is gone from his chickens.

It is the duty of every cook to bring his own intelligence to every recipe. Taste is the best tool. Recipes must be adapted to the quality and freshness of the food, the size of the vegetables, the kind of stove and heat, the acidity of the vinegar, the quality of the wine and the butter. When in doubt, taste the dish. One must cook by intellect and not depend completely on scales, measurements and thermometers. If you see the chicken is done and you are going by a table of weights which

states it has another 20 minutes to cook, remove the chicken. Your eye is the better judge, and the chicken is probably an especially tender one.

The pot or pan should not be much larger than the fowl or meat that is cooked in it. If it is, and you use butter, it will burn. Also, with pans that closely fit the object being cooked, juices are retained and final browning is easier.

When baking, be sure that you have a flat surface (a metal cookie sheet, or any other similar flat material that will conduct heat) to place your dish or pan on. I do not recommend wire racks. They do not give you an even heat.

Good bacon lean is red; the fat, white and firm.

Potatoes are much improved if peeled and placed in cold water overnight. It saves time in the morning and they are whiter and firmer. In steaming potatoes, place a cloth over them before putting on the lid. They will take less time to cook and be more mealy. Potatoes baked in their skins also will be more mealy if a small piece is cut off one end to allow steam to escape.

Aspic should not be put into the mold until on the point of setting. If this is done there will never be difficulty in turning it out.

For curry dishes, try baking a banana. If not too ripe, bake it in its skin in a 400-degree oven for 20 minutes.

Pour 1½ tablespoons dark port over each half of a prepared grapefruit 1½ hours before serving.

Fines herbes are five: tarragon, basil, chives, parsley, chervil.

Fresh herbs are less strong than dried ones. Double their amount in recipes.

To make vanilla sugar, place required amounts of very fine or granulated sugar in an airtight glass jar, add vanilla beans (about 1-inch of bean for quart jar), store until sugar takes on the vanilla flavor. Good with fruits poached in wine.

Fortified wines do not spoil after they are opened. All wines will last a few days in the refrigerator if promptly recorked after using.

To utilize unused mustard in cruets: Add vinegar, then fill with fresh grated horse-radish. This makes a good sauce for hot or cold roast beef.

To clarify fat: Dice pieces of cooked or uncooked fat, place in a pan with water to cover, boil two hours, strain. When cold, a solid layer of white fat will be formed, which can be used for plain cakes or pastry and is better than ordinary lard.

Never use a substitute for butter. If you do, you will bring a substitute flavor to the dish. I always use sweet butter. Salt butter may give passable results, but it is often past its prime. And sweet butter does a better job when stirred into a sauce at the last minute to give a better texture and flavor.

To soften eggs that have been boiled too long: Put in cold water for half a minute. This softens, improves flavor. Hard boiled eggs should be plunged instantly into cold water after they are cooked. This prevents discoloring of yolks. When poaching an egg, add a dash of vinegar to the water; it will help the white adhere to the yolk. Eggs should always be at room temperature before cooking. It not only prevents cracking but enables you to time cooking more precisely. A cracked egg can be boiled wrapped in a piece of greased paper.

When boiling peas, the addition of a teaspoonful of sugar will improve flavor.

Vegetables will retain their color if they are plunged into cold water after cooking. When reheated, the color still remains. Also vegetables such as asparagus will stay firm.

To be sure that fowl or meat will brown well, wipe completely dry before cooking.

All liver should be sautéed quickly, and be pink in the center. Otherwise color, texture and flavor are displeasing.

I do not use a meat thermometer, but rely upon the chef's method: Pierce the roast of meat to the center with a metal trussing needle. Let it remain for one minute. Remove, bring it gently to your lips. If the needle is cold, the meat is not done; if warm, the meat will be pink; if hot, the meat is well cooked.

Green vegetables should be cooked in boiling water without a lid. Dry vegetables should be cooked in cold water with a lid.

Heavy cream and raw egg yolks will thicken sauces more delicately than flour. But be careful that cream sauces thickened with egg yolks do not boil, or you will have an omelet, not a sauce. To quickly thicken sauce, sprinkle in a little, just a little, arrowroot, and blend well.

Tomato seeds add nothing to a sauce or a dish. To peel and seed a tomato, dip the ripe tomato into boiling water for 30 seconds, then peel. (Dead-ripe tomatoes do not need dipping.) Cut the tomato horizontally in half, hold a half in your hand and squeeze. The seeds pop out. With cherry and plum tomatoes just cut a bit from the top and squeeze.

Do not add water to any sauce. Wine, stock, broth, consommé (even if canned) are superior.

To keep food warm: If your stove doesn't have a warmer, use an asbestos pad over a burner, keep heat low, and place the plate of food on top. A chafing dish will keep food warm on the serving table, and there are many "food warmers" on the market. A very low oven can also be used, or a pot of simmering water with the plate of food on top.

Use warm plates for hot food, cold for cold foods. Nothing is more distressing than having an excellent hot dish served on a stone-cold plate. Warm the plates in the oven. But they should not be too hot for you or your guests to handle.

Never arrive more than fifteen minutes late when invited for dinner. Your host or hostess might be planning dishes that a late arrival will cause to fall flat or overcook.

When in doubt about a "different" vegetable, try braised endive.

Allow all fowl and meats to "rest" ten minutes after cooking. This retains the juices, and makes the carving task easier.

Never boil a stew; it should just shiver on the heat. The stew's flavor is improved if you cook it without a cover.

The flavor of all cutlets is improved if the bread crumbs for rolling are mixed with pepper, salt and chopped fresh herbs.

Wooden spoons should be used for stirring and beating sauces and food. They don't scratch utensils.

Do not serve a soup *and* an hors-d'oeuvre at dinner. It is classic to offer one or the other.

Do not serve wine when you are offering an hors-d'oeuvre with a vinegar base. The tastes clash.

If your cream soup curdles pour it into heavy cream.

If your white sauce seems too bland, stir in a pinch of cayenne pepper.

When you eat a chop or a piece of meat, cut only one slice at a time. Not only is it good manners but it helps retain the flavor and natural juices—for your benefit rather than the plate's.

Three white onions will give more flavor to a dish than all the canned and bottled sauces and condiments on the market.

When making pastry, melt the butter or lard and beat it to a cream before mixing with the flour. Only half the usual quantity is required if you use this method.

To remove odor from the hands after peeling onions: Rub dry mustard mixed with water on the hands and thoroughly rinse in clean, cold water.

When cooking cauliflower place a piece of stale bread crust in the saucepan. It will take away the unpleasant odor. Remove before serving.

Add solid ingredients to cold or frozen desserts after mixture begins to set. This way they will be suspended and not all sink to the bottom.

Never use cheap "cooking" wine or brandy. You want the flavor of good wine.

Sprinkle freshly cut fruit with lemon juice to prevent browning.

One cup of heavy cream, juice of one lemon and two binding egg yolks make a simple classic sauce for chicken that is difficult to better.

Lightly boil sausages 5 minutes before frying them. It helps seal in flavor and prevents the skins from breaking.

My grandmother would try an inferior wine, grunt, and say, "Nothing here, it's like kissing a cousin."

Few of us live longer on earth than six or seven decades. If we do not eat well while we are here, what is the reason for being here at all?

Index

Page numbers in italics indicate illustrations.